STATION
OMNIBUS EDITION
COUNTRY

Cover photographs

Front cover: The old Roaring Lion hut on Nokomai station, Otago
Back cover flap: Huntaways on Molesworth station, Malborough
Back cover: Stud Marino rams on Little Valley station, Central Otago

ISBN 1-86958-885-1

© 2001 Text and photography Philip Holden

This edition published in 2001 by Hodder Moa Beckett Publishers Ltd
[a member of Hodder Headline Group]
4 Whetu Place, Mairangi Bay
Auckland, New Zealand

Printed by Toppan Printing Co., Hong Kong

All rights reserved. No part of this publication may be reproduced or transmitted in any form or by any means, electronic or mechanical, including photocopying, recording, or any information storage and retrieval system, without permission in writing from the publisher.

STATION
OMNIBUS EDITION
COUNTRY

Text and photography by
PHILIP HOLDEN

Hodder Moa Beckett

CONTENTS

Preface — 1

SOUTH ISLAND: HIGH-COUNTRY RUNS

Men of the Matukituki Valley — 6
On Mendip Hills — 14
An Interlude on Molesworth Station:
    When They Built with Cob — 23
Up the Awatere Valley — 27
Battlers on Mason Hills — 39
No Easy Ride on St James Station — 46
They Called It Morven Hills — 57
The Legend in the Deep South — 72
Mackenzie Basin — 85
A Country United — 95

NORTH ISLAND: FROM COAST TO PLATEAU

Coastal Stations — 104
Pride of the Wairarapa — 119
The Smedley Challenge — 127
East Coast — 135
Far North — 150
Tapu on Nukuhakari — 158
Plains Country — 165
Inland Patea Country — 179

ON THE MAINLAND

Stations of the Lewis Pass — 194
The Mount White Tradition — 206
South of the Rakaia — 222
The Gibsons of Malvern Downs — 234
All on Morven Hills — 242
Return to Earnscleugh — 248
The Promised Land — 254
On Fiordland's Doorstep — 266
A Legend Came This Way — 274
Valley of the Wairau — 282

NORTH OF COOK STRAIGHT

The Mountain — 290
The Mighty Ihungia — 300
Once Were Tussocklands — 310
Guthrie-Smith's Wonderful Legacy — 320
In the Grand Style — 324
Meeting Place of the Gods — 330
A Trio of Stations — 340
Showpiece of the Southern Wairarapa — 350
Going Home — 355

References — 356

ACKNOWLEDGEMENTS

Brancepeth: Hugh Beetham and Barbara Beetham.
Cluden: the Purvis family.
Double Hill: Ben Hutchinson, Ben Ensor.
Earnscleugh: the Campbell family.
Erewhon: Vickie Bryan.
Glenary: George Pinckney, David Pinckney, Graham Allan, Jake Stark, Brian Sparrow, Andy Holden, Ray Christie, Oliver Dickson, Barney Milne and Gary Cruickshank.
Glenmore: Anne Murray, Jim Murray and Nick Ensor.
Glenfalloch: Tom and Prudence Todhunter, Dave McKenzie, Simon Maxwell.
Glenhope: Charlotte and Rod Milne, Roy Veronese, Phil McCabe, Chris Pudney, Richard Gestorough, Bob Peden (Irishman Creek).
Glen Rock: Donald France.
Godley Peaks: Bruce Scott, Liz Scott, Greg Hand, Nigel Robinson, Phil McCabe, Tony Prestage, Chris Pudney, John Thompson, Craig Fosbender and Greg Heath.
Gwavas: the Hudson family.
Ihungia: Tony and Gay Hansen, Neville Higgins, Will Banks, Dan James, Tim Rhodes, Bruce Connolly.
Lochinver: Eric Campbell, Colin Grey, Mark Dickson and Rodger Lewis.
Malvern Downs: William Gibson, Robert Gibson.
Mangatu Blocks: John Ruru, Albert Horsfall, James Carrol, Eric Tamanui, Robert Milner, Darryl Brown and Robin Barabarich.
Mason Hills: Andrew Barker and Liz Barker.
Matangi: Stella Sanders.
Mendip Hills: Deane Harper, Lynne Harper and Murray Cooper.
Molesworth: Des Whiting (DoC).
Morven Hills: Richard Snow and Anne Snow.
Mount Aspiring: John Aspinall and Sue Aspinall.
Mount Creighton: George Burdon, Bruce Douglas.
Mount White: Richard and Sheri Smith, Kelly Frame, Jackie Frame, Johnny Anderson, Robert Calder, Hamish Marshall.
The Muller: Steve Satterthwaite, Nicky Satterthwaite, Lyall Barriball, Craig King, Craig Kendall, Tony Watson, Rachel Smith and Mary-Anne Watson.

Ngamatea: Jack Roberts (Timahanga), Jenny Roberts, Margaret Apatu, Graham Lunt, John Roberts and Marty Crafer.
Nukuhakari: John Austin, Cheryl Austin, Brian Kurigr and Don Woodds
Ohinewairua: Richard Hayes, Mark Hayes, Chris Green, Andrew Fenemor, Dave Armistead.
Orongorongo: the late Earle Riddiford, Rosemary Riddiford.
Oruamotua: Valerie Cottrell.
Otangimoana: Eddie Hose, Dianne Campbell and Gordon Williams.
Otupae: Jane Dick, Gary Mead.
Paua: Neil Dempster, Bronwyn Dempster and Ben Caper.
The Poplars: John Shearer.
Poronui: Paddy Clark, Belle Clark and Shamus Howard.
Potae Estate: John Pardoe.
Puketiti: Des Williams, Ben Green, Dave Walsh, Noeline Awarau.
Puketoro: Rodger Lougher.
Redcliffs: Willy Ensor, Andrew McKay.
St James: Jim Stevenson, Andrew Riddle, Harvey Riddle, Dean A'Court, Michelle Arapere, Peter Mills and Graeme Lilley.
Smedley: Jery Jeromson, Di Jeromson and the rest of the staff and cadets.
Springvale: the Holden family.
Te Awaiti: John Gannon, Doreen Gannon, Geoff Gannon and Gus Ford.
Te Paki: Ian Bullen
Te Rangi: Max Dunn, Jack Abraham and Tim Hoey.
Tutira: the Reiri family.
Waiau Hereford Stud: the King family, James Lowe.
Waipaoa: David Clark, Ray Parsons, Margaret Parsons, John Berry, Dean Aitkens, Boyd Devereux, Alistair Wallace, Peter Crosson and Errol Koia.
Waiorongomai: Jack Matthews, Raymond Matthews.
Whangaimoana: Alastair Sutherland, Jacqui Sutherland.
Wharekauhau: the Shaw family, Joe Houghton.
White Rock: Tim Ritchie, Deborah Ritchie, Anne Quinn, Graeme Bolton and Desiree Bolton.

BY THE SAME AUTHOR

New Zealand Non-fiction
50 Great Farmstays in New Zealand
Pack and Rifle
Hunter by Profession
Backblocks
The Deer Hunters
Seasons of a Hunter
The Hunting Breed
On Target
The Wild Pig in New Zealand
The Golden Years of Hunting in New Zealand
The Golden Years of Fishing in New Zealand
New Zealand: Hunters' Paradise
Holden on Hunting
The Deerstalkers
A Guide to Hunting in New Zealand
The Hunting Experience
Hunt South
Wild Game
More Holden on Hunting
Fall Muster
On the Routeburn Track
In Search of the Wild Pig
Station Country
Always Another Hill
Wild Boar
Holden's New Zealand Venison Cookbook
Station Country II
Pack and Rifle (1995 edition)
Great Hunting Yarns
The Way of a Hunter
Station Country III
New Zealand Hunter
A Backcountry Journey
Walking the Routeburn Track
The Milford Track Adventure
Walking the Abel Tasman Coast Track

Young Adult Fiction
Fawn
Stag
White Patch
Razorback

Children's Fiction
Lucy's Bear

Children's Non-fiction
Sheep Station

Australian Non-fiction
Outdoors in Australia
Along the Dingo Fence
Crocodile
Wild Pig in Australia

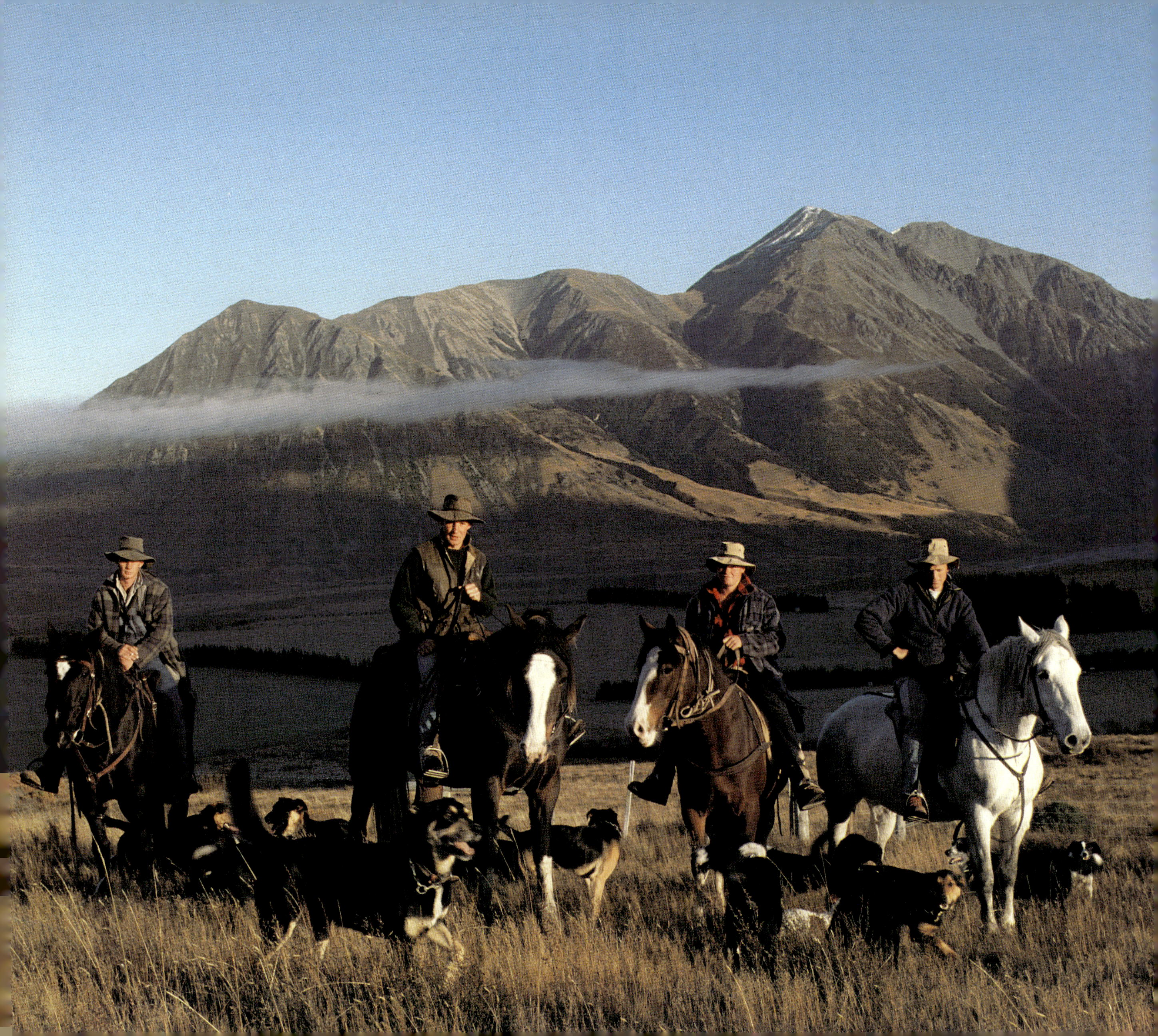

PREFACE

For me the word 'station' brings to mind colourful images of sprawling homesteads set amidst exotic trees planted many years ago, picturesque huts, horsemen and their wonderful dogs, hardy sheep amidst the tall tussock, and contented cattle grazing on lush river flats. Things like that…

April 1990 — I was in the valley of the north branch of the Von River, in the Thomson Mountains, on Mount Nicholas station, the largest run in the Southern Lakes District. The mustering team was out on the hill, so I saddled Nigger, a black gelding, and headed off across the tussock flats to take some scenic shots. Soon, Nigger and I were ranging high above the valley. I took a number of photographs, then put my camera away, and sat there in the lovely sunshine. I thought about the fall muster, now drawing to a close. What a magnificent experience it had been! From a purely photographic aspect alone it had been tremendous. How could I go wrong in that type of setting and with such subjects as genuine high-country musterers and their hard-case dogs and spirited horses?

It came to me then: why not write a book about the stations scattered around the country? The two *Station Country* books presented here in one volume are in effect a direct result of an idea that was given life on Mount Nicholas Station as a restless Nigger pulled at his reins, and pipits and skylarks also made the most of the first fine day in quite a while, and as the sun flooded the valley of the north branch of the Von River.

To set the record straight, a station was originally the actual place a runholder based himself to work the property. Eventually the word came to mean the entire kit and caboodle — buildings, land and stock. Normally a station was a large block of land, either government or Maori owned or both, but the name station still applied if and when the property became freehold. Today it is generally accepted that any property with the capacity to carry over 2000 sheep may be considered a station.

SOUTH ISLAND

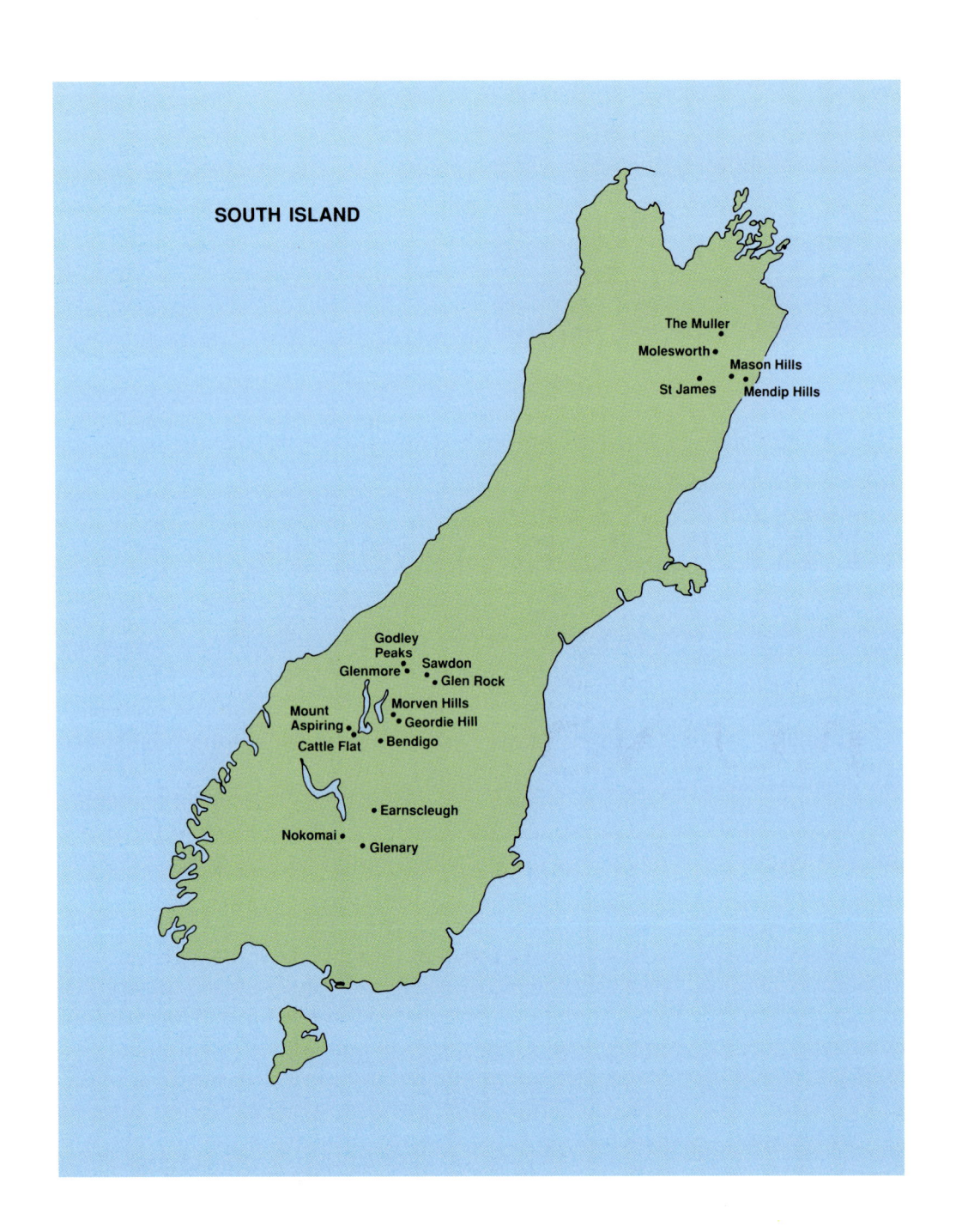

- The Muller
- Molesworth
- Mason Hills
- St James
- Mendip Hills
- Godley Peaks
- Sawdon
- Glenmore
- Glen Rock
- Mount Aspiring
- Morven Hills
- Geordie Hill
- Cattle Flat
- Bendigo
- Earnscleugh
- Nokomai
- Glenary

Pages 4–5 photograph:
Ray Christie admires the vista on Glenary station.

SOUTH ISLAND
HIGH-COUNTRY RUNS

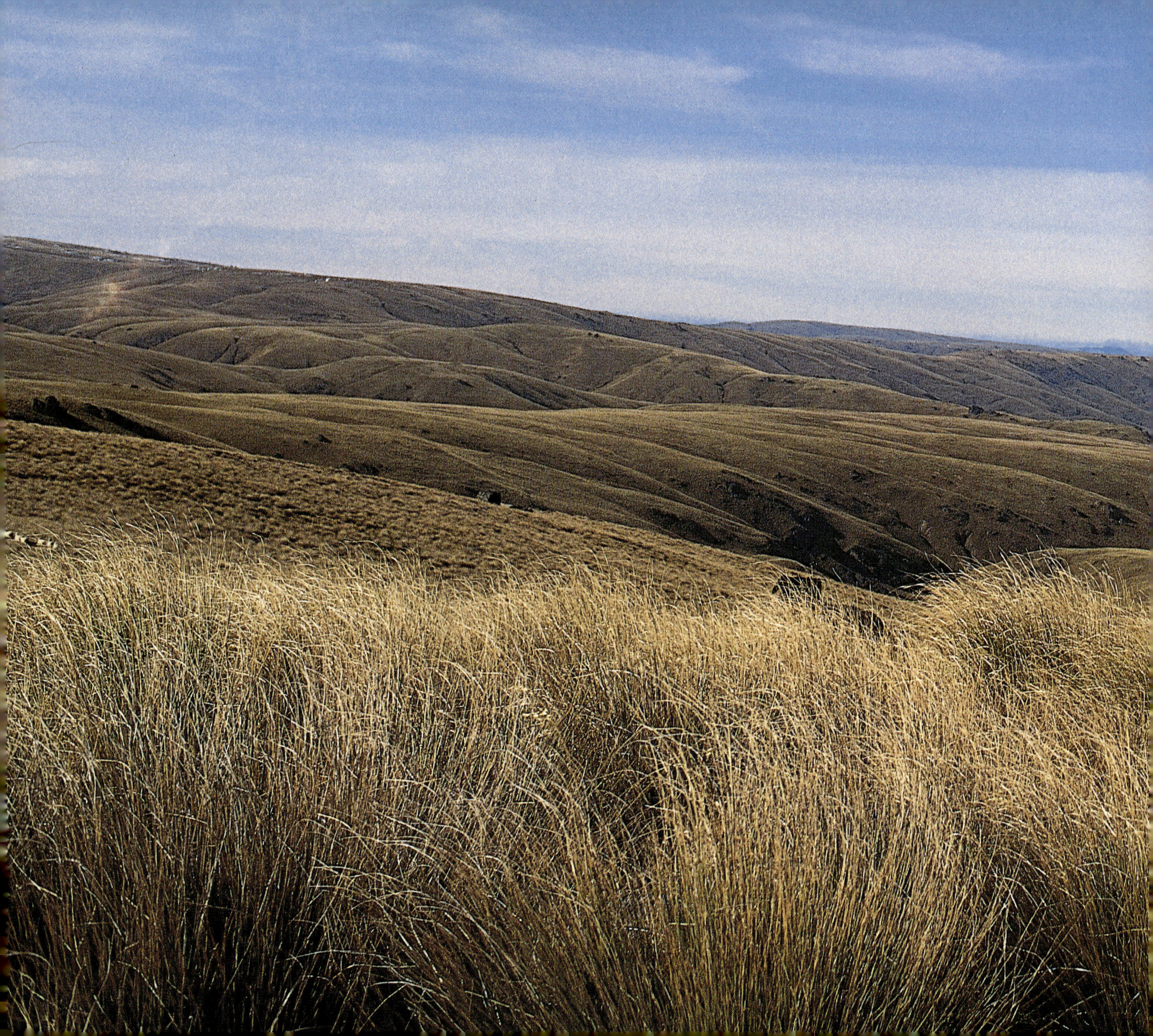

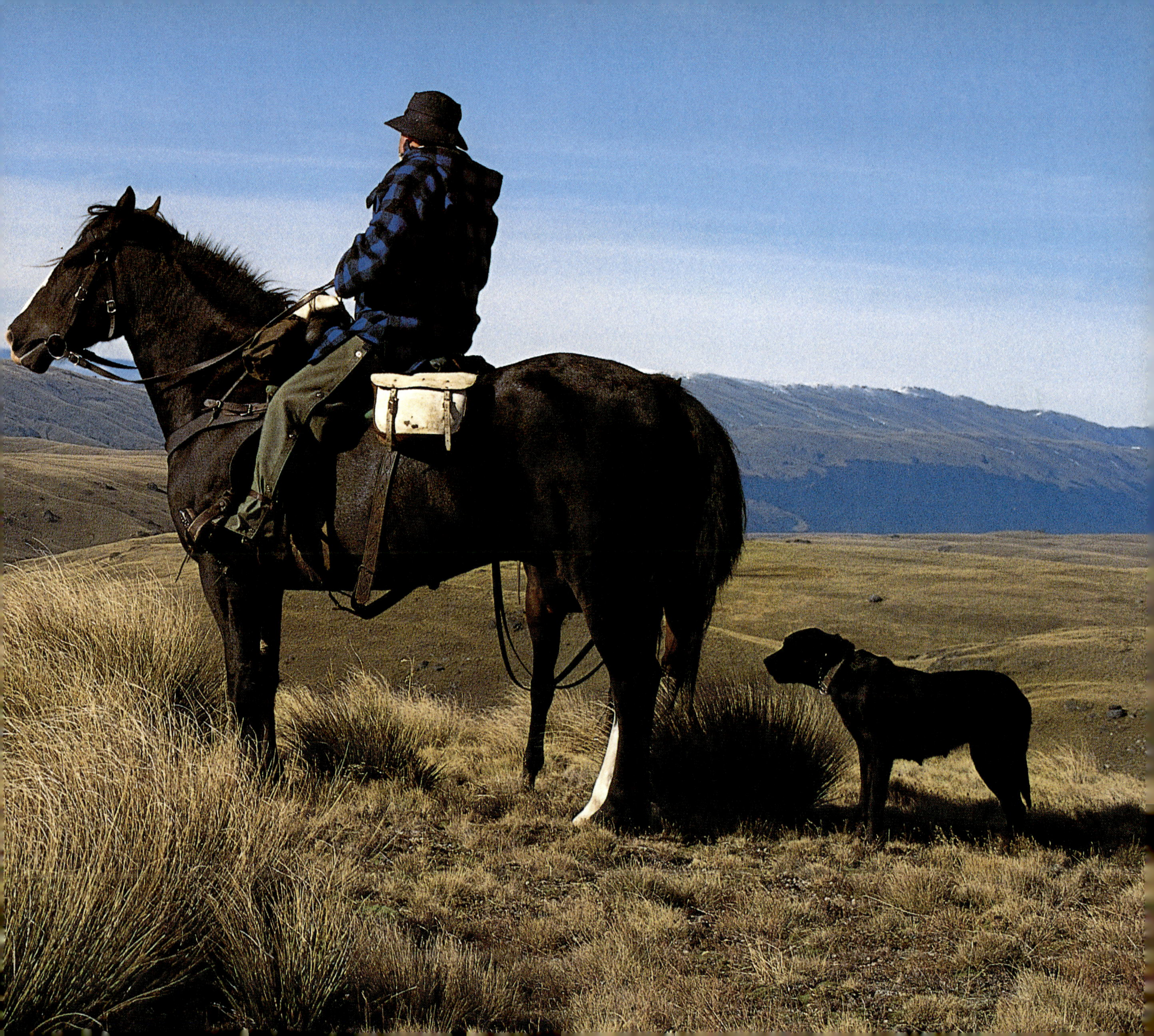

1

MEN OF THE MATUKITUKI VALLEY

John Aspinall tossed a hand in the direction of a steep mountain face directly behind the homestead on Mount Aspiring station, the last station up the Matukituki Valley, where the road finally peters out and all that's left is for you to put on your tramping boots, strap a pack on your back, and make the most of Mount Aspiring National Park.

'That whole face up to the snow-line was covered with heavy bracken once,' John said matter-of-factly. 'Wouldn't think so now, would you?'

I had to agree with him; virtually useless country was now highly productive. 'So just how did you do it?'

John smiled, pleased at my interest. 'We sprayed it with Roundup first off.'

'Fixed-wing?'

He shook his head. 'No, chopper.'

'Roundup, eh? Shows you just how effective it is,' I said, sounding like a rather stilted actor in a TV commercial.

John bobbed his head up and down. 'Yes, I've used several chemicals before, but Roundup's been by far the most effective.' He paused. 'It's by far the cheapest, too.'

They had used Roundup on the mountain face in May and August of 1989 and in the spring of that year they had had a burn-off. Later, grass seed was spread over the entire area in 45 very productive minutes by Alexandra-based helicopter pilot Brian Beck. Various grass seeds were used, 'a real witch's brew', as a smiling John put it. He rated the several types of red and white clover as the most important, because they activated the essential nitrogen process.

'Let's go inside,' John suggested, rubbing his hands briskly together. 'It's cold out here.'

He wasn't wrong. It was getting colder by the minute.

MEN OF THE MATUKITUKI VALLEY • 7

Mount Aspiring homestead.

8 • STATION COUNTRY

The Aspinall family.

It would be snowing on the tops, up there above the heavy mist.

'Besides,' he went on, 'I think Sue's made coffee for us.'

I followed John Aspinall gratefully into the warm kitchen cum dining room. There was a stunning, almost panoramic, view of the valley, the wide river flats, the forested slopes beyond and the tussock faces. I remarked on it while I sipped my coffee and Sue Aspinall smiled and said yes, it was a lovely view, and no, they never got tired of it.

The Aspinall family had been associated with the Matukituki Valley for over 70 years and three generations had farmed it. John, a youthful 40, knew no other life than that of a high-country runholder. The same thing, for that matter, could be said of his 70-year-old father, John Charlton ('Jerry') Aspinall, now retired in Wanaka.

Mount Aspiring station dated back to 1877, when Scotsman Ewen Cameron took up 8100 hectares in the west branch of the Matukituki and called his run Glenfinnan. Cameron was a hardy soul; he had to be. This was daunting country, and it was a long ride to town at Wanaka. Rainfall was heavy below the permanent snowfields of the Main Divide, anything up to 3700 millimetres a year, and winters could be brutal. With access to firewood essential, he had to build his home on the far side of the river, against the face of the forest. So the dreaded, snow-fed west branch of the Matukituki had to be crossed each time he went out for supplies. Cameron built his home and sheep yards but, apparently, not a woolshed. Rather, he chose to take his 7000 sheep (almost certainly Merinos) to the big woolshed on Wanaka station at Albert Town when shearing time came around.

No one knew exactly why Ewen Cameron sold out in 1885 or thereabouts, although one year he had lost 80 percent of his flock in a storm. Perhaps the isolation played a part in his decision, or maybe he was weary of

Hereford cattle in winter on Matukituki station.

having to play second fiddle to the river. Whatever the reasons, in 1886 he moved to Cattle Flat station, down-valley by a good stretch and much, much closer to Wanaka. The homestead was on the same side of the main branch of the river as the route to town. The Matukituki could still prove a handful when stock were trapped on the far side by floods, but the problems it presented were not nearly as bad as at Glenfinnan.

Hugh Macpherson was the new owner of Glenfinnan station. He and his wife built a more substantial home than Cameron's rather crude shack, with a picket fence around it — they were here, they thought, for the duration. But in 1899 the Matukituki River claimed Hugh's life. Distraught, his wife sold the station to Duncan Macpherson, possibly a relative. It may have been at this time the station was renamed Mount Aspiring.

The practice of taking sheep out to Wanaka station for shearing still persisted. Wanaka station, founded in 1860, was a huge run incorporating, among others, Glendhu, West Wanaka, Mount Burke and Minaret stations. They ran 56,000 sheep there in the early 1900s. So in 1903 the Macphersons again took their sheep to Wanaka station to be shorn. On the return trip, disaster struck. Many sheep perished in a snow storm. The gritty Macphersons were very nearly ruined.

In the early part of the new century, a young Englishman called Jack Aspinall arrived in New Zealand. Aspinall, a ship's cook, either signed off in Port Chalmers, Dunedin, or jumped ship — a common enough practice then. He turned up at Makarora station, where he found work as a cook-handyman. Later he went to Cattle Flat station, now owned by enterprising Wanaka businessman Theodore Russell. Jack Aspinall returned to his native country when the First World War broke out but, in his heart, he knew he had not seen the last of Otago. When the war was over, he returned to civilian life and spent some time in his home town of Liverpool, where he met his wife, Amy. They sailed for New Zealand soon after they were married.

Cattle Flat homestead dates to 1920.

Meantime, Duncan Macpherson had lost interest in his property. During the war his wife had drowned in the Matukituki when her gig overturned. He allowed the station to fall into decline before he decided to sell up.

The lease for Mount Aspiring station came up soon after Jack Aspinall found himself back in the Wanaka district, but he lacked the funds to purchase it. Not to worry — his previous employer at Cattle Flat came to the party. Theodore Russell had sufficient confidence in Jack Aspinall that he financed him into the property. The Aspinall connection with Mount Aspiring station had begun.

The property was much larger than it had been in Ewen Cameron's day, being all of 29,000 hectares, but it was without stock. Initially, then, the Aspinalls stocked the run with cattle, bringing a considerable mob over the Lindis Pass. After only three months they suffered a serious setback when the homestead burned down. It was August, the heart of winter, and snow covered the river flats. One wonders what impact that had on a lass from Liverpool, a very long way from home.

But the Aspinalls were made of stern stuff. They built a new home on the same side of the river, where the firewood was. There was always the river to contend with — three cursed crossings of it to the road end. You could never, ever, take it for granted. River crossings have a way of changing and the flow of the river — even in periods of very little rain — was always deceptive.

On 23 October 1921, John Charlton 'Jerry' Aspinall was born in Cromwell. Life up the Matukituki was tough for a small boy. The awesome nature of the land and the unpredictable weather was something you just had to live with. But it didn't end there, did it? There was an ever-spreading population of red deer, and untold numbers of rabbits out on the flats. Rabbits, of course, had long been troublesome closer to Wanaka but, until fairly recently, had not worked their way up the big river valleys. You could blame the early settlers for that. There was no one to blame for the kea, however. The only mountain parrot in the world was a native with, as it turned out, a liking for the kidney fat of sheep.

In an attractive little booklet he published in 1990, simply titled *Keas*, Jerry Aspinall recalled:

> My very first experience of the other side of the kea's habits occurred when I was around ten years old. It was late in the month of May and my father took me to the top of the bush-line in deep snow on the steep slopes behind the present Otago Boys High School camp in the west branch of the Matukituki valley, a kilometre beyond Hell's Gate. There we found a number of sheep snowed in and a small flock of keas feasting on the carcases of the animals that had died as a result of their unwelcome attentions. Some had plunged headlong off the ridge they had been on and got themselves bogged in deeper snow below. In those days keas were not protected. They were regarded as the High Country sheep farmers' menace.
>
> We had gone prepared. The .22 was the favoured weapon, for although it was not silenced, its report or 'bang' was much quieter and less frightening than a shotgun blast. It was effective if used with care and accuracy. This was most important, because at the sound of a wounded bird's warning cry of alarm the rest of the flock would fly off, perhaps for miles. In those far-off days a bounty of seven shillings a beak was paid — two shillings from Central Government, two shillings from the local County and three shillings from the runholder on whose property the bird was shot.

While red deer no longer concern runholders, keas and rabbits most certainly do.

They had deer, rabbits and keas to contend with on Mount Aspiring station: seemed like there was no way you could win that fight. Nor could a man overcome cancer; in January 1942 it finally cut Jack Aspinall down as effectively as a chainsaw cutting firewood. Jerry was 20, and managing a high-country run on his own. In 1950 he married Phyllis Manson of Wanaka. They would have four children, John being born in 1951 in Cromwell.

A major reduction in the station's size took place in 1957 when, during a review of the lease, Jerry readily agreed to hand over 22,500 hectares for the then provisional Mount Aspiring National Park. It was no great loss: the mostly alpine country, often deep under snow, was overrun with deer and chamois and untold numbers of keas.

By now, John was six years old and life was still very basic on the run. Phyllis recalled that isolation was the main problem; you seldom had visitors. It was a

25-kilometre ride to Cattle Flat to pick up the mail, and supplies came from Wanaka, three days away using horse and dray. The newspapers came in bundles of 25.

Now, years later, I was talking about those times with John. Not that long ago, really — less than 40 years. 'Dad still had his troubles with keas,' John said. 'He's estimated that his losses for every year he was on the run were between three hundred and four hundred sheep.'

Today, it is difficult to visualise a flock of keas, 50 strong, killing a complete mob of sheep. One winter, when they were especially bad, Jerry Aspinall shot 400. Yet the keas still posed problems in 1968, when Jerry purchased 580 hectares of land from Cattle Flat station. They built a homestead there, on the sunny side of the valley; a spot called the Glenfinnan Terraces. Although they were less than five kilometres from the old homestead, there was an amazing decrease in the rainfall — around 750 millimetres less each year — and there was considerably more sunshine over winter. And the river no longer ruled their lives. But the keas . . .

'We put hoggets up on the hill that first winter here,' John said, referring to the mountain face directly behind the homestead. 'Keas killed over thirty of them — they drove them over a couple of bluffs. Dad went up and shot them.'

The conversation turned to deer. Back in the late 1950s and early 1960s the Forest Service, rather than the Department of Internal Affairs, had the awesome responsibility of deer control. It was a time when deer had no commercial value whatsoever — they were merely pests.

John laughed softly, reflectively. 'Well, you'd see the deer every day when you were out working. They were a part of the everyday scene. You'd see, oh, thirty, forty, perhaps as many as seventy. It was common to see stags on our best winter blocks; they knew where the best, sweetest country was. I can recall seeing ninety once.

'Dad used to organise a drive every autumn, after we'd mustered out the sheep. He'd have perhaps fifteen shooters spread out in, say, a big basin, so that they'd cover all the main routes they'd use. They'd get two hundred, no trouble.'

'In a day?'

'Yes, in a day.' John shook his head. 'Never see deer numbers like that again here.'

Nor anywhere else in the country, I thought.

Ironically enough, by the time John decided to go into deer farming, the helicopter shooters had cleaned up just about every deer in the valley. The result was that he had to purchase the initial stock. Four young hinds had cost $2500 each. Ten grand the lot. Four years later, as the market slumped, those same deer would be worth $1100. Today? Well, John's expression turned even more melancholy at that question.

'Three hundred dollars for a good one.'

A little later we went outside again. It was a mite warmer now — maybe three degrees Celsius instead of two. Still, it was the right side of freezing.

Fourteen years had now passed since Jerry Aspinall had retired to Wanaka and I asked John how his father was keeping these days. A heavy frown crossed John's face.

'Dad has cancer now. It's probably terminal but he doesn't accept it.' He shook his head. 'He's going the same way as his father.'

Jerry Aspinall would die at his home in Wanaka in February 1992.

Presently, I continued up the valley of the Matukituki. The heavy cloud cover remained and there was no opportunity to observe Mount Aspiring's distinctive 3027-metre peak. Sheets of ice-laced rain fell at regular intervals. Cross-bred sheep and cattle grazed on the river flats; bird life was abundant, including oystercatchers, spur-wing plovers and gulls of various types. Soon I came to a signpost that read 'Cameron Flat'. The old homestead was across the river. The Matukituki was wide here, fast flowing, a little cloudy. There was no bridge. But then, hadn't that always been the problem for those who built their homes on the western side of the Matukituki?

2

ON MENDIP HILLS

There was grass on Mendip Hills, lush grass knee-deep to a tall horse in many places. Indeed, it was quite likely there hadn't ever been as much feed on this 6000-hectare North Canterbury run as there was in the mid-summer of 1992.

'Amazing, isn't it?' Deane Harper gestured expansively at the rolling green hills that stretched almost unbroken to the west. 'From the third week of August until late in October there wasn't a drop of rain here. Hell, you could've seen a mouse running just about anywhere on the place.' He shook his head, as if it had all been a nasty dream. 'The rains started in November. Since December' — he gestured again — 'the growth has gone crazy. Thing is, we've had so much heat, so much moisture.' He smiled, his blue eyes lighting up a tanned face. 'Don't think I'm complaining, though. It's a good way to be.'

'Bit different to Central, eh?'

Until quite recently, Deane had worked on Bendigo station in Central Otago.

'You're dead right there!' He laughed at the comparison while making a nifty gear change. The light-green ute jolted up a steep incline, a scrubby gully off to our left. 'What's it like there now?' he asked. It had been eight months since he had resigned his position as manager on Bendigo.

'Real dry, as usual.' I raised an eyebrow. 'What did you expect — something like this?'

Deane laughed softly. 'Hardly.' His expression turned wistful. 'Great country down there, though.'

'Miss it much?'

He shrugged. 'Sure. Who wouldn't, eh?'

I knew full well what he meant. There is something very special about the Central Otago landscape; there is nowhere else quite like it. Do you know Central Otago?

In the early days the Conway River provided Mendip Hills station with its only access to the coast.

16 • STATION COUNTRY

Have you seen the high, rock-strewn, almost barren ridges and the bone-dry, sheltered hollows under ragged outcrops of rock where hardy Merino sheep find shelter from the searing sun of February or the bone-numbing winds of July? Up there you'll find that needle-pointed Spaniard grass flourishes and that rabbits scratch with vigour at the wind-dried soil and increase their numbers at an astonishing rate.

'Reckon you'll ever go back?' I asked.

'To work there, you mean?' Deane Harper smiled an odd little smile. 'One day, I guess,' he finally said.

In his thirtieth year, Deane Harper was blond in the way that bronzed lifeguards are. By the standards of the time, he may be judged fairly tall. He might have seemed young to shoulder the responsibility of managing one of the most prestigious runs in the country, but age had very little to do with it. He had what counted: experience and savvy.

When Deane was born, his father, Tom, was working on Mount Nicholas station. Tom was head shepherd then, working for Phil and Judy Hunt. Later, Phil would go on record as saying that Tom had the best team of dogs he ever saw follow a man. Given that Phil Hunt was on Mount Nicholas for 28 years, Tom's dogs must have been extraordinary.

So what were Deane's earliest recollections of Mount Nicholas? He remembered the men killing mutton and recalled with remarkable clarity three huge red stags hanging in the killing house. They were gutted, blood dripping onto the concrete floor. That was in 1966 and Deane Harper was all of five years old. That year Tom Harper moved on, having been on the run for 22 years. Mount Nicholas wasn't just a job, it was home. But now it was time to leave.

Tom Harper found work on a 400-hectare farm near Becks, Central Otago, but that didn't last long. There was nothing wrong with his work; it was just that the owners

Stud Merino ram (inset) on Bendigo station.

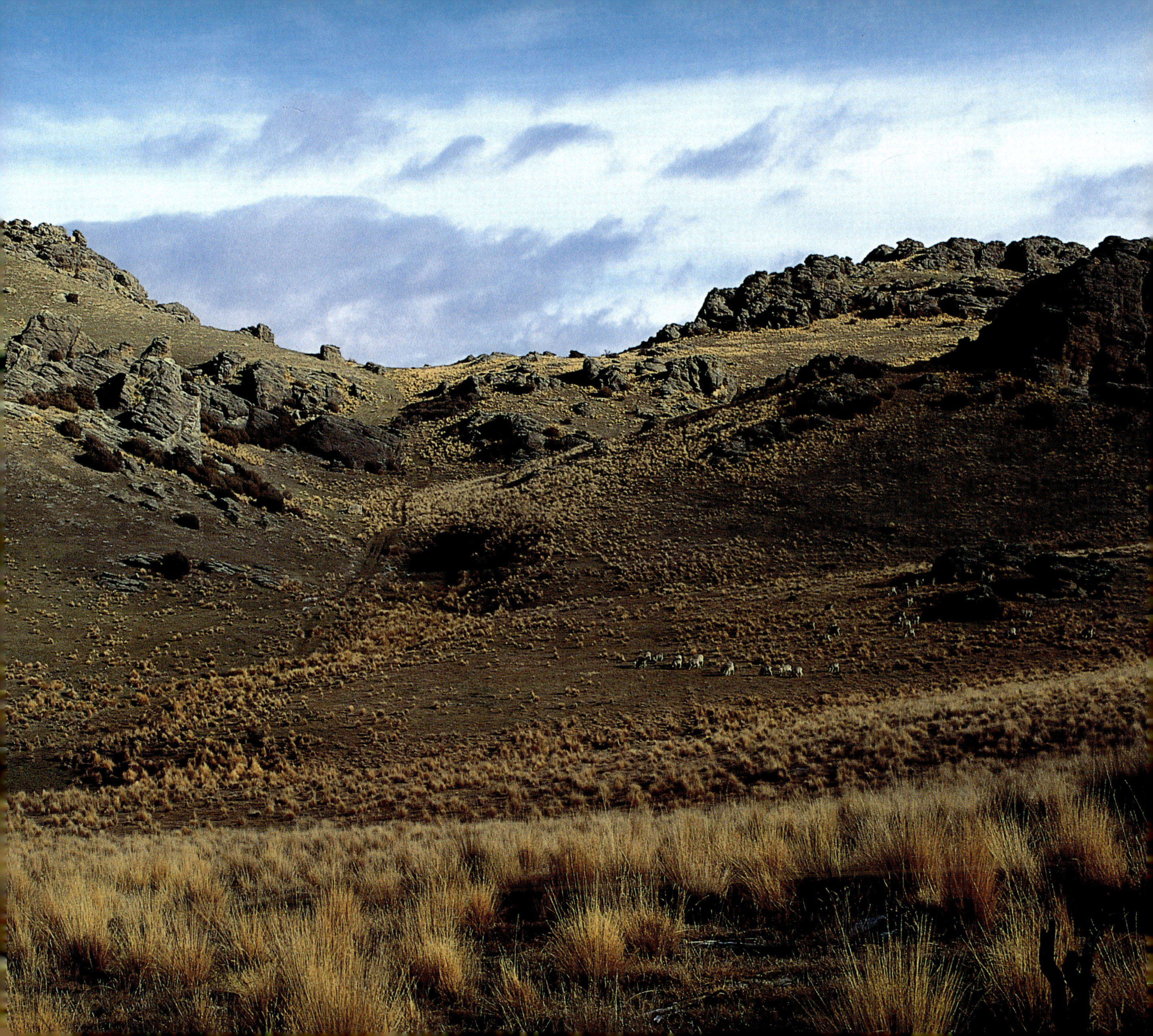

sold up. Tom was out of a job and his family was out of a home. You can't be too choosy in a situation like that and Tom took a shepherd's job on Bendigo station. It filled a gap, as it were, until a manager's position cropped up on Drybread station, over Omakau way.

When he was 15, Deane Harper attended Telford for a year. Telford was a boarding school in Balclutha where they taught everything there was to know about farm and station life. Well, almost everything — some things you just had to have for yourself. Common sense, for one thing; you couldn't hope to hold down a job on a station without that. After Telford, Deane put in two years as a farm cadet on a fair-sized property at Millers Flat, Southland. The boss dealt mostly in cattle — a quick turnover merchant buying lots of calves, fattening them up then selling them off.

In his late teens, Deane moved back to Central. The Southland weather, even at its best, was never that pleasant. For a time, he worked on Criffel station, near Wanaka, then he went to Cattle Flat station. Then he found casual work: tailing, this and that, anything to make a dollar. As long as it was on a station, that is.

In 1982 he found himself back on Bendigo station for three weeks' casual work, mostly tailing. The run was owned by John Perriam. It had been a long time since he had been there and yet Deane clearly remembered the craggy, weather-shaped rocks up behind the homestead profiled by the westering sun, the men shooting rabbits. They were always shooting rabbits on Bendigo.

By this time, Deane had met his wife-to-be, Lynne, in Wanaka. She was an Ollerenshaw from Balclutha. When John Perriam offered Deane a full-time position, he accepted. After they were married, Deane and Lynne lived in a dried-brick cottage consisting of a large kitchen, small living room, one large bedroom and two small bedrooms. It was the last dried-brick house on the run, and it was about 80 years old. The Harpers' two daughters, Jodie and Billie, were born while they lived on Bendigo station.

'Yeah, they were good years,' Deane recalled as we came to a halt on a grassy rise on Mendip Hills. He flicked off the ignition and went on. 'John was good to work for, no question about that. But I'd really gone as far there as I could.' A pause. 'So when this job was advertised, well, I talked it over with Lynne and she was all for me having a go.' He smiled in a genuinely self-effacing way. 'Real lucky to get it, I guess . . .'

More than 60 people had applied for the manager's job on Mendip Hills. Luck? No, I don't think it came down to the flip of a coin.

Deane Harper opened the door of the Toyota and stepped outside into the lovely sunshine. 'C'mon — I'll show you the pig trap.'

There had always been wild pigs on Mendip Hills; at one stage the place was overrun. It was so bad back in the 1920s and 1930s that the property probably supported more pigs than sheep. They had men on the place hunting pigs full time. They got two shillings for every token (snout and tail) handed in.

'There were pigs on Bendigo, too,' Deane said, striding

Right: *With the Inland Kaikoura Range in the background, Deane Harper pauses where pigs have been rooting on Mount Stewart's western slopes.* Below: *At the pig trap.*

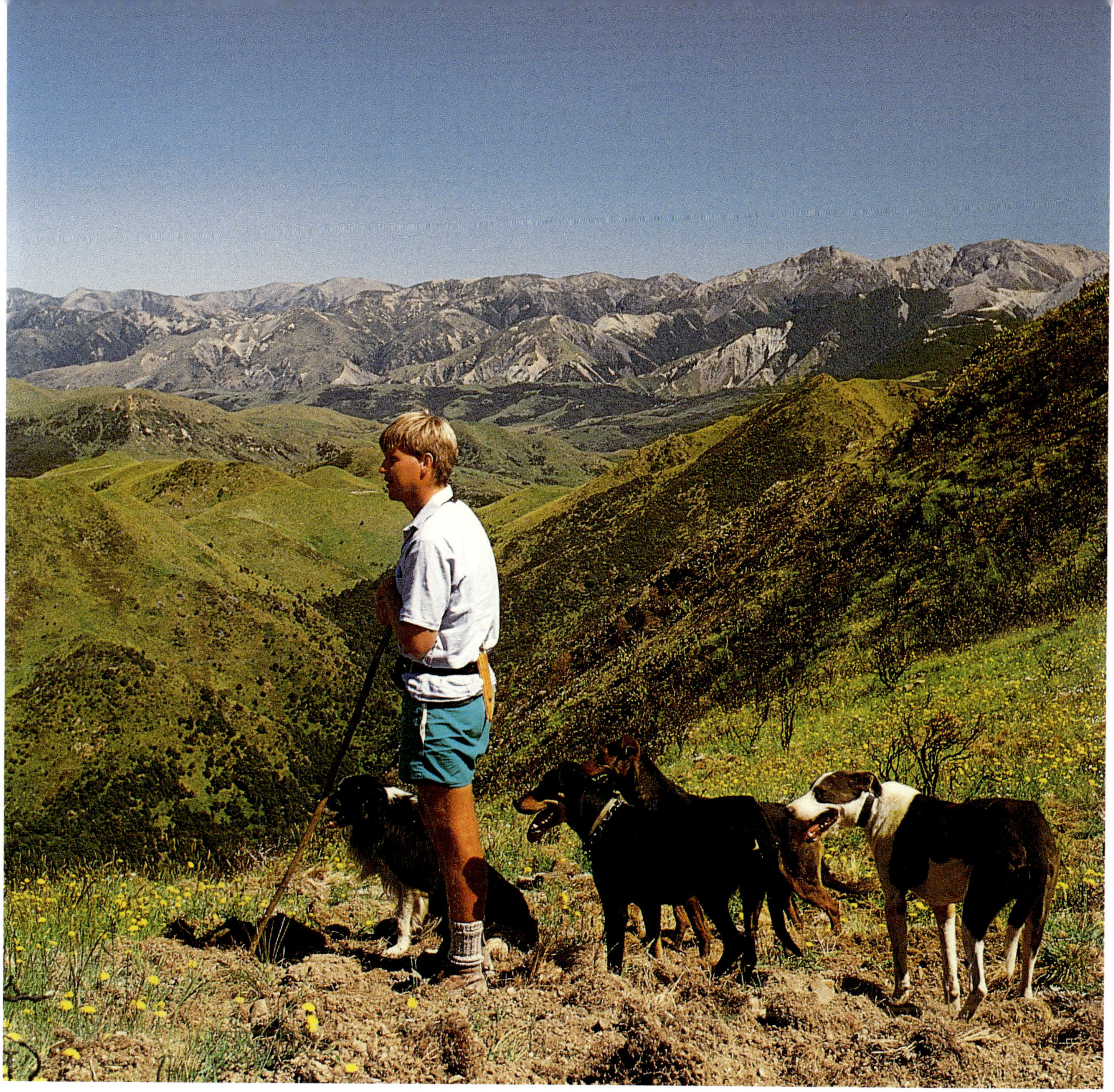

through dew-soaked grass. 'But you'd know that, right? You didn't see them all that much, though. They kept on the move. Different type of country, of course.'

He looked hard at the pig trap as we neared it. He accepted the fact there was no pig in it with a stationman's philosophical lift of his shoulders. The pig trap was empty — apart from the bait, a heap of yellowing bones and what was left of a stinking sheep's carcass even the blowflies had given up on.

'Works pretty well,' Deane said.

The roughly rectangular, box-like affair was constructed of extremely strong wire mesh, a little over a metre high and perhaps three times that in length. The hinged door was propped open with a gnarled manuka stick so that as a pig shouldered into it, the stick fell down and the door swung shut. More pigs, arriving later, could enter the trap by pushing against the door but, once inside, there was no way to escape.

'Not the place for an extended stay,' I said drily.

Deane smiled.

'Caught many in it?' I asked.

'At times.'

'Well?'

'We got a dozen in here once.'

'A dozen! What were they — all piglets?'

'Mostly. But there were three sows and a fair-sized boar in there, too.'

'Poor sods!'

'Bit cramped, all right.'

'What's a fair-sized boar, by the way?'

'Hundred and fifty pounds.'

When Deane Harper had arrived at Mendip Hills, in the late autumn of 1991, he had been quite shocked at just how many pigs there were and the damage they were doing. 'It was incredible, really,' he admitted. 'I just hadn't expected it.' Every time they went out they would see pigs. They were running in mobs 30 to 40 strong. As for damage, well, hundreds of hectares of cultivated land was churned over. So they declared war on the pigs, hunting in their spare time and encouraging private hunters.

One local identity who often hunted pigs on Mendip Hills was 36-year-old Murray Cooper. Murray stood a couple of metres tall; he was by far the tallest pighunter I have ever met. He farmed on the family property, Huyton, north of Cheviot. He first saw pigs on Mendip Hills when he and his brother were fencing there in the mid-1980s. Terry Beard was the manager then and, since he was a good mate, there was no problem about gaining access to the run.

In more recent times, Murray had hunted there with his mate from Christchurch, Peter Munro. Murray's top finder — a huntaway named Rug — teamed very well with Peter's crack team of pig-dogs. Murray reckoned there were more black pigs in that part of the country than any other colour. Smoky grey was common, too, and the biggest boar — 230 pounds dressed out — that Murray had taken on the run was smoky grey.

That wasn't the biggest boar taken on the station. A 245-pounder was killed late in 1991. It was bailed up on the northwestern side of the station, near the boundary with Neville Hyde's Ngaroma. Neville's son Tim, Jack Watson and Brendon McClintock were in on the demise of that big tusker.

Deane told me they had taken nearly 400 pigs off the run in just eight months. There were still plenty of pigs there, though; they were as resilient as rabbits. Deane turned away from the trap.

'You'll see another one later on — might be something in that.' He paused and then said over his shoulder, 'Might not, too.'

We drove on. Distantly, below Mount Stewart (939 metres), there were cattle on the grassy slopes. They were moving, heading down. Some of the men were working with them, Deane said. They ran Corriedale sheep and Hereford cattle on the station. The sheep numbered 19,000, but Deane saw cattle as the better proposition. For every dollar you made on a sheep you had to spend 80 cents; whereas, with cattle, which also required far

The imposing homestead dates to the time when the Rutherford family owned Mendip Hills station.

less work, you laid out 20 cents for each dollar gained.

The other pig trap was empty, too. Still, we were both expecting it, really. The trap was out in the open, and at this time of year pigs tended to stay in the shady gullies. Cool winter weather, from end of March onwards, say, made them far more adventurous.

In the afternoon of the same day, I had a chat with Lynne. A bright, vivacious person in her mid-thirties, she was missing her friends, but that was to be expected. Eight years on Bendigo was a long time — eight months on Mendip Hills was something else.

We were sitting in the large sitting room of the homestead. Rarely used, it smelled musty, like something from a distant era. We could, had we felt so inclined, have sat in the kitchen, in the drawing room, or in the games room. The homestead on Mendip Hills, with its seven bedrooms, was a mansion, really. It was built in a time when master craftsmen took immense pride in their work, when this country was still a colony and the sun was never going to set on the British Empire. In those times, the station employed a butler, servants and a gardener. Today, Lynne cooked for the single men and you made your own beds. No one bothered getting dressed for dinner any more, either.

While Lynne and I were talking, young Jodie, bright as a summer's day, came to see what was up. Who was this strange person talking with her mother? Jodie was a very down-to-earth child, a pretty typical country kid. Take the time when Deane's job for the day was to take some cattle from Bendigo to Lindis Peaks station. Lynne was off to get her hair done in Wanaka, but Jodie didn't want to go with her. Walking behind a mob of cattle suited a two-year-old much better. Deane protested to no avail. So off they set, father and daughter, and a bellowing herd of cattle strung out along the highway.

Five hours later, Lynne turned up at Lindis Peaks to pick up her husband and daughter. As it turned out, they were just arriving with the cattle. A proud Deane said Jodie hadn't dragged her feet once.

Now, back at Mendip Hills, Lynne said, 'Off you go!' to a grinning Jodie and turned back to me with a rueful smile that said 'Kids!'

'Bit of a hard case, eh?' I said.

'You're telling me!' Lynne exploded.

'Tell me that story you told me yesterday.'

'Which one?'

'About the rats.'

Lynne glanced at my tape recorder.

'Should I . . . ?' she said dubiously.

'Why not?'

She laughed. 'Okay.'

One evening on Mendip Hills, Lynne went to lock up the free-ranging hens for the night. As usual she gave them a few scoops of grain. For once, however, she forgot to put the lid back on the grain bin.

Next morning there were six hairless baby rats in it. Ugh! She clamped the lid on and walked away. She would tell Deane about it when he came in for lunch — he could deal with them. But for some reason she forgot all about the rats in the grain bin until the next morning. It was Sunday, a good day to lie in. Jodie, of course, had other ideas about that.

Deane, half asleep, groaned as their daughter pestered them about getting up.

'Jodie,' Lynne said, 'go and look in the grain bin.' Anything to get rid of the little pest, she thought.

'What for?'

'There's a surprise in it for you.' Cruel, Mother, cruel. Jodie leaped off the bed, darted from the room.

'What sort of surprise?' Deane asked. Lynne told him.

It was at least half an hour before Jodie returned.

'What have you been doing?' Lynne asked.

'Oh, those rats in the grain bin — they're all dead.'

Deane, now propped up on one elbow, said, 'They must've eaten too much, I guess.'

'Oh, no!' said Jodie, quite matter-of-fact about it. 'I hit them on the head with a rock.'

It turned out that Jodie had also failed to replace the lid of the grain bin. So that when mother and daughter set off to free the hens for the day, they found two big rats in there.

Lynne said to Jodie, 'Do you think you can kill them, too?'

Naturally, she thought that Jodie would be terrified of the idea. But no! Jodie hunted for — and soon found — a big stick. She headed towards the grain bin, watched by her mother and Teddy, a rather enterprising Jack Russell who enjoyed the good life on Mendip Hills. Now, raising the stick, Jodie went to hit one of the rats. When the stick came down the rats reacted, seizing the opportunity to escape by grasping the stick with sharp claws and running up it.

With a scream, Jodie dropped the stick and the rats leaped towards the ground. At which point Teddy got in on the act. With hair-trigger reflexes, he proved why his very special breed had long been used to kill rats. Teddy struck twice. Snap! Snap! Two dead rats, each bitten cleanly through the head, lay on the ground.

Reckon Telecom's lovable Spot couldn't have done it any better.

AN INTERLUDE ON MOLESWORTH STATION:
WHEN THEY BUILT WITH COB

It stood in the lower valley of the Acheron River on the Marlborough-Canterbury border, as it has done for 130 years. Today, it was known as the Old Acheron Accommodation House, a well-preserved link with the region's colourful history.

When it was built in 1863, however, its main function was as a resting place for foot-sore travellers and saddle-weary stockmen and drovers working the rugged inland route between Nelson and Canterbury. There were eight rooms, some with bunks, most small with low ceilings. For a fee, one could enjoy the comfort of a bed, partake of a cooked meal and knock back a stiff drink with mine host. The horses, of course, were stabled, although the stables no longer exist.

In later years, Acheron became an outstation of St Helens; when that run was taken over by the Crown and amalgamated with Molesworth-Tarndale in 1949, the building was still used as a stockman's and shooter's camp. During the 1960s it was used as a base camp for workers constructing the road and a transmission line through the station.

Now, on the same day that I put Mendip Hills behind me, the Old Acheron Accommodation House came into view across a valley bottom ablaze with summer wild flowers. In January and February every year the road through Molesworth station was open to the public. The station was still owned by the Government, and DoC administered this facet of it. It was definitely a case of user pays. DoC had two wardens on the job, camped for ten-day stretches in a caravan at each end of the station. This could be termed the southern end of Molesworth station, and the warden on duty was Des Whiting.

It turned out that Des had strong family connections with the station. His grandfather, George, had worked here as a 15-year-old. Over on Tarndale, Des thought, where he'd had something to do with wool wagons. Also his mother's brother, Bruce Hunter, a deer culler, had camped here at Acheron in the late 1940s and early 1950s, as had a cousin, Kevin Martin.

I asked Des about deer on the station.

'Pretty scattered today,' he replied, 'but they do seem to be building up again. Don reckons he's seeing more these days.' Don Reid was the manager of Molesworth.

'That's good to know.'

'Yeah, isn't it?' He smiled. 'Got a nice sort of chamois the other day over near Tarndale. Lots of them about.' Des's trophy measured ten and a half inches.

I left him to collect another fee and strolled over to the low-slung Acheron Guest House, in under the long verandah. It was pleasantly cool inside, but then, cob dwellings were known to be cool in the summer and warm in the winter; it was one of their great virtues. Cob was a primitive form of concrete, used mainly when the more common building materials — wood and rock — were not available. In the case of timber, that was often the direct result of the fires of the early Maori moa-hunters and, later, the extensive burn-offs of short-sighted European settlers.

Cob, then, was a wet mixture of earth and clay reinforced with animal dung and chopped straw or tussock. Mixed on site, it was worked over with a long-handled dung fork. Often a horse was used, harnessed to a bar attached to a revolving post; the trampling gradually worked the mixture to the correct building texture. The horses probably didn't think too much of that idea.

The walls, which tapered sightly as they climbed, were erected without a mould or framework, so it paid to have a good eye for a direct line. They were built on a solid foundation, usually stone or brick overlaid with dirt and clay, which served as a floor when the whole lot was rammed down good and hard. The floors, however,

Acheron Accommodation House.

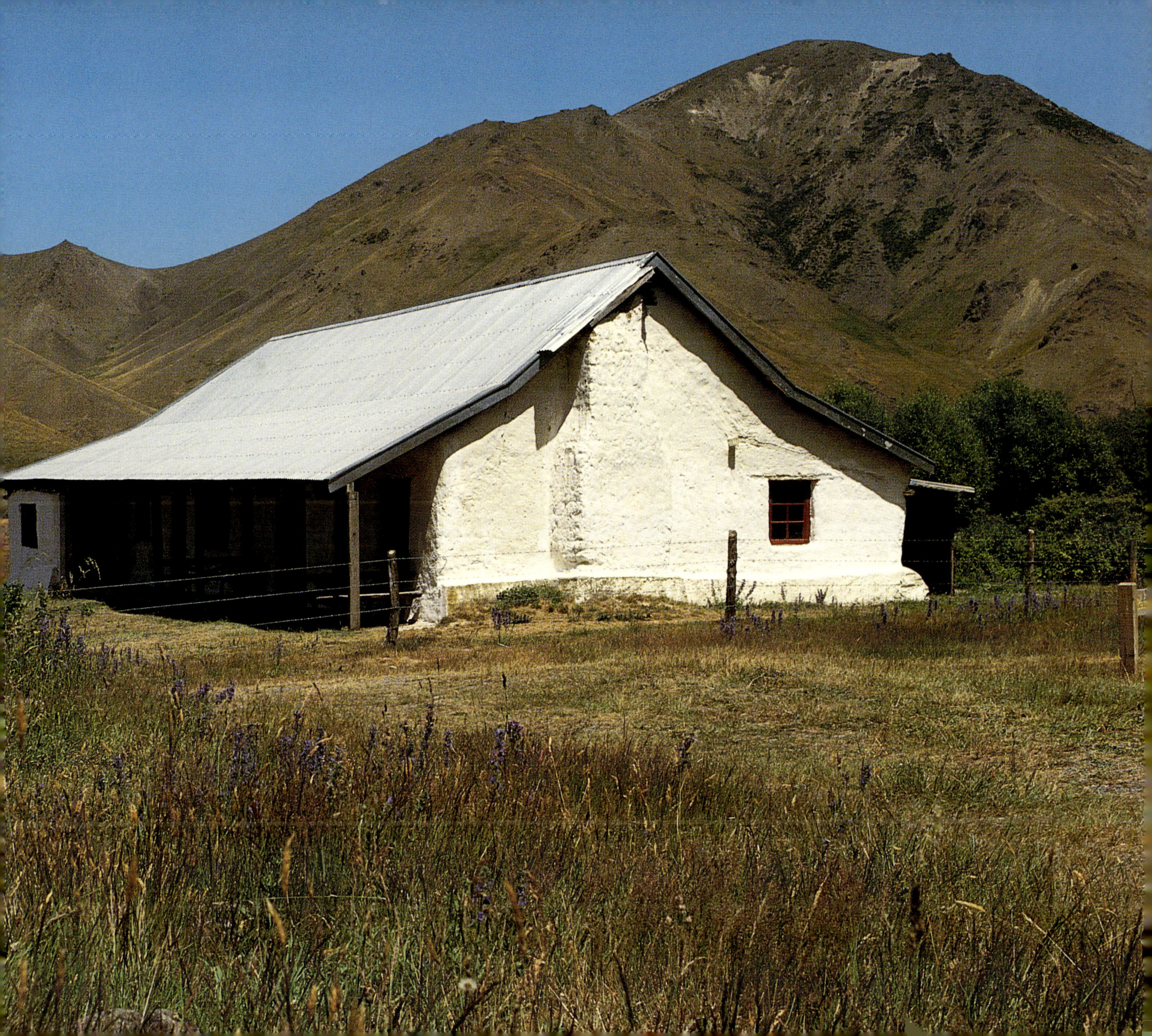

This cob oven, for making bread, may date to the period when the Muller was first established, in the early 1850s.

With more recent alterations, the cob homestead on the Muller dates to 1902.

tended to be rather uneven. The finished walls were a good 60 centimetres thick at the bottom, hence their fine insulating qualities.

To smooth over the walls a sharp spade or an iron cob parer (a form of trowel) may have been used. Since there was always a great risk that the cob would crack when dry, the corners tended to be rounded off. A mud plaster was often used to cover the walls to ensure better waterproofing. When the cob was fully dry it was time to cut out the doors and windows. This was not as difficult as it might sound because, as the walls were being built, lintel timber beams were fitted at the appropriate places. As far as the roof was concerned, the central beam was usually a solid log of beech. Roofing might be tussock thatch or, more likely, corrugated-iron sheeting.

While rarely seen in the North Island, cob buildings were comparatively common in various parts of the South Island, including Otago, Canterbury, Marlborough and Nelson. On Langley Dale in Marlborough, for example, the original homestead was built of cob. This was a single-storey affair with attic rooms. The stables had a cob base and timber lofts. This still stood today and in fine condition. Also in Marlborough, a cob homestead and men's quarters were built on Bluff station, then called Kekerengu, in 1858–60. In North Canterbury, a cob cottage was erected on the Glens of Tekoa station in 1857. It served as a homestead until the present brick one was built in 1865. The cob cottage was then put to use as a schoolroom. They went the whole hog on Moutere station in Central Otago, where the homestead, woolshed, barns and sheds were all of cob.

Returning to Molesworth, there is another historic cob building for the traveller to see on the largest station in the land. It is the original two-roomed homestead, built in 1865 by John Murphy. Look for it on the right-hand side of the road as you enter Molesworth from the northern end. The present-day homestead is near here but is not open to the public. And, of course, there is the Old Acheron Accommodation House at the other end to linger at. That was built by Ned James. He would have been delighted to know that 130 years later it was still standing; after all, it took him a whole year to build it.

4

UP THE AWATERE VALLEY

Among the many stations found in Marlborough's Awatere Valley is an amalgamation of three runs, called the Muller. The original block of 16,500 hectares was taken up by Dr Muller, the first resident magistrate of the province, in the early 1850s; Langridge, some 14,000 hectares, was first held by a resident of Nelson, Thomas Ward, in 1851; and Richmondale, about 15,500 hectares, was once part of Hillersden. The three runs became one in 1925. The next owner of the Muller was Thomas Cawthron, of Nelson; he in turn sold it to his nephew, John Shirtliff, in 1896. Shirtliff's association with the station would be a long one. The first dwellings on the Muller block were of cob; the homestead, however, could not have been very substantial because Shirtliff replaced it in 1902, and again cob was used.

In 1953 the entire property was handed over to the Shirtliffs' son-in-law and daughter, Mr and Mrs Ian G. van Asch. In 1965 the property was sold to a group of North Canterbury shareholders, mainly the Satterthwaite family. They called themselves Muller Station Ltd.

Today the Muller was 36,500 hectares, among the largest runs in the country. By any reckoning it was wonderful country. It was raw-boned and spare and intensely masculine, quite different from the gentler, more closely settled valley.

In the early hours of 16 January 1992 I awoke with a sudden start. Where was I and what was that noise? A second later it clicked: I was on the Muller and the sound that had woken me was that of iron-shod horses moving restlessly past the homestead.

A deliciously cool breeze infiltrated the guest bedroom through a half-open window. After the two very humid nights I had spent on Mendip Hills it was a lovely change.

Still, we were 790 metres up here at the homestead, and at that altitude humidity was rare. It was only when the thunderheads built up over the valley in early summer, say, that the humidity became uncomfortable, and even then it didn't last too long. So really they had a most agreeable climate on the Muller, not, some say, unlike that of Central Otago.

Close by, a horse neighed, a soft sound of communication. A distant whinny, carried on the night breezes, came from the direction of the stables. In the long row of kennels a dog barked loudly; I waited for others to join in but there was only one bark. The breeze ruffled the drawn curtains, a feather-like touch on my face. Again a horse neighed.

I swept back the blankets, slipped out of bed, and peered outside. It was a lovely night with heaps of moonlight. The horses were close, near the fence containing the homestead and its grounds. Motionless, they were big, darkly outlined shapes. Station hacks wearing waterproof covers. They moved on, slowly, hooves making ringing, metallic sounds on the driveway. I wondered why they had woken me; they were, after all, comforting sounds in the night, weren't they?

The previous day, with Molesworth behind me, I had followed the unsealed road that would eventually bring me back to State Highway 1, maybe 25 kilometres south of Blenheim. Before then, however, I faced a two-hour drive down through the valley of the Awatere River. The country was both big and spectacular. It was the kind of high, grassy place where you'd expect to see large herds of semi-wild horses and oilskin-clad stockmen moving cattle, and hear the rifle-like crack of a whip. The Inland Kaikoura Range, off to the east, was looking a real treat, with its many high ridges and razor-backed spurs highlighted by the westering sun, each one as sharply profiled as the gapped blade of an axe. Beyond a high

The Hereford-Angus cattle are yarded.

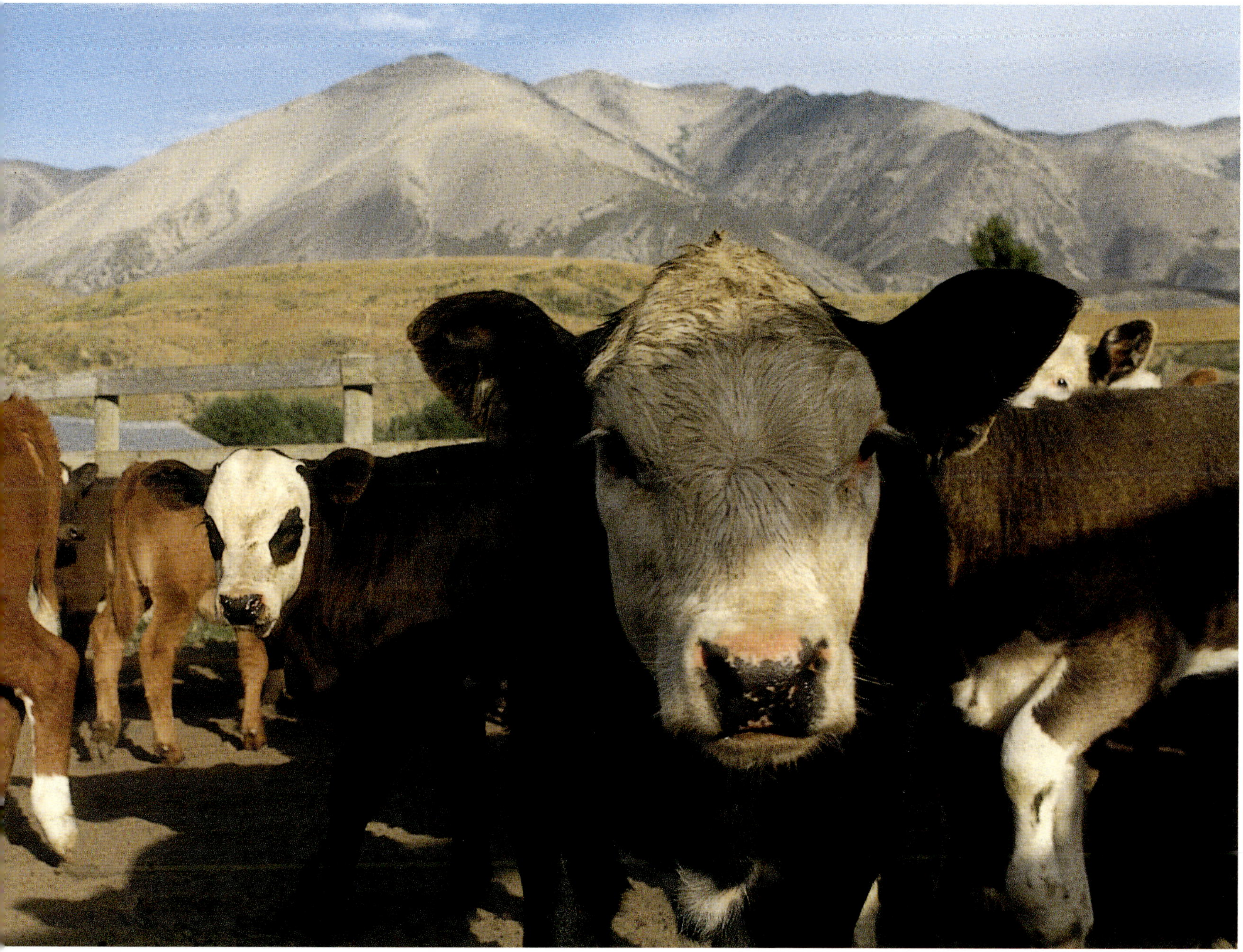

fence, I saw deer grazing on a hill face. They froze when they noticed the strange vehicle, then started to run. They were never really meant to be behind high wire.

A signpost on my left arrested my attention: MULLER STATION. I braked to a shuddering halt, near-new radial tyres skidding a little. Cattle, feeding near a creek, whipped up their heads: what was this? I got out and the air was warm and clear. Cattle bellowed. I got back into the car and took the road to Muller station. It climbed up to a low line of hills, from where I got a good view of the run.

The nerve-centre of Muller station was contained within the river valley and, because it lay on the far side of the Awatere, access was via a short wooden bridge hemmed in, on the far side, by large willow trees. I could see a fair number of buildings: sheep yards, a shearing shed, stables, plus some older-style dwellings — in real good nick — that had obviously been built well before the turn of the century. Beyond the main homestead, cows and calves were contained in a big paddock close to the cattle yards. Further out, on the near side of a pleasing stretch of the river, a small group of horses were feeding.

On the far side of the river the foothills, fold upon sun-dappled fold, all browns and golds in the lowering sun, climbed up to the brawny shoulders of the mountains. Always the mountains. It really was a lovely scene and I savoured it at some length, pleased that I was here in the summertime. A little bit of paradise, I knew, not seen by many.

There are times in almost every writer's working life, when he or she gets a gut feeling that there is something worth following up here, another link in the chain, that must be seized now, because tomorrow might be too late. Right now, looking down on Muller station, I heeded my instinct. I drove across that narrow wooden bridge, into the shade of the big willow trees. They had been planted well over a hundred years ago, in all probability. They were wonderful trees, providing shade along the river bank. I felt sure that whoever had planted them would have been delighted at what they had achieved.

At the Muller homestead, I met Steve and Nicky Satterthwaite and two of their daughters — Julia, aged nine, and Olivia, aged five. A third daughter, Kate, aged 11, was at boarding school and would, I was told, be home at the weekend. For a few minutes it seemed to me my timing was especially bad. Nicky, a slim blonde, was barbecuing a meal in the small, paved courtyard while Steve, wearing shorts and smelling of horses, had obviously put in a big day's work.

But then Nicky asked me to share their meal. The children smiled at me, at ease with themselves, not overawed by a stranger in their midst; I liked that. Steve offered me a beer. They were so genuine in their offer, seemed so pleased to have someone call in on them, that I warmed to them at once. The back-country traditions are alive and well on the Muller. So, while Nicky kept a watchful eye on the chops and sausages and Steve added some homegrown venison steaks to the hot plate, I chugged on a big, chilled bottle of beer and thought that Christmas had come real early this year.

Later, Steve and I sat at the kitchen table while Nicky and the kids watched a mini-series on television. The reception was lousy up the Awatere! I touched on the size of the station: 36,500 hectares. That's a whole heap of country, particularly when you consider the mountainous nature of most of it. Steve smiled; its very size, I suspected, was what appealed to him.

'Sure it's big,' he said, the smile gone, his manner matter-of-fact. 'Bloody big, in fact. But we manage okay.' He ashed his cigarette. 'The idea is to have good staff you can trust.' A thoughtful pause. 'I'm lucky with my staff. Top bunch. You'll get to meet them in the morning.'

I had accepted his offer to stay the night, saying that the shearers' quarters would be fine. But they wouldn't have any of that — it was the guest room for me.

Steve went on to tell me about the neighbouring runs. There was Molesworth, of course, and Glazebrook, which was owned by Landcorp. Then there was Waihope

Simmental bull.

Downs, in the head of the Spray River, and Upcot and Middlehurst, run together by Bill and Robbie Stevenson. All of these were large runs, Steve told me, but, the further you went down-valley, the better the country became and naturally the properties were much smaller.

'Up here,' Steve said, uncapping another bottle and giving me a direct look, 'we tend to stick pretty close together. In fact, you'd go a very long way before you'd find a more closely knit community. We've even formed our own association up here.'

The stations in the association were Glenlee, Mount Gladstone, Gladstone Downs, the Camden, Awapiri, Upcot/Middlehurst and, of course, the Muller. Warming to his subject, Steve went on to tell me that the association had built their own sale yards at Upcot, because it was centrally placed. They held a lamb sale there in the third week of February.

Lighting another cigarette, Steve filled me in about stock numbers on the Muller. They had a flock of 14,000 Merinos: 4500 ewes that went to the rams, 5500 wethers, and 4000 hoggets. The wethers, he added, were out in their summer range, beyond the Shingley Range, grazing over 14,500 hectares in the catchment of the Acheron River. I could see the Shingley Range from the Muller homestead — it appeared to be nothing but rock.

I had seen deer on the Muller, and Steve told me they had 500, running on 180 hectares. Interestingly enough, they were using an elk/red-deer stag cross-bred animal

Lyall Barriball.

over the red-deer hinds to produce bigger, heavier offspring. There were also a hundred or so red-deer stags, raised primarily for velvet. Much of this country was, of course, once a red-deer stronghold, but that had changed dramatically when the helicopter boys moved in. There were, however, still a few wild deer on the place; at the roaring time it wasn't unusual for several red stags to turn up hopefully at the deer pens.

They also had a herd of predominantly Hereford-Angus cross-bred cows, over which they used Simmental bulls. That day they had brought in the cattle I had seen near their southeastern border with Molesworth. It had taken four hours on horseback — a good trip. Steve, by the way, was still wearing his dirty shorts; he still smelled like a horse after it's been running. Of course, you can smell of much worse things than that.

'We'll be working with the cattle in the morning,' he said, and took another drag on his cigarette.

It occurred to me that with his rugged good looks, blue eyes, deep tan, dark hair and gunfighter moustache, he could have easily been mistaken for the Marlboro Man. *Come to where the flavor is.* Sure, that and the lung cancer, too. But the man sitting across the table from me, with a tendril of smoke drifting across his face, was no highly paid model wearing a sheepskin jacket, leather chaps and stetson, twirling a tightly coiled lariat over his head as he thundered across a sagebrush plain in make-believe cowboy country. No, this was the genuine article, wearing shorts instead of jeans. He did, however, wear a wide-brimmed hat — that went with the territory.

So what were they doing with the cattle in the morning? 'Usual stuff this time of the year,' Steve replied, suddenly running out of steam, bone weary. 'Y'know, earmarking, drenching, dehorning the bull calves; that type of stuff.'

He yawned behind a raised hand. The stockman needed his bedroll, like five minutes ago. He glanced at his wristwatch — after 11 o'clock. It had been a long day for each of us, although mine had started on Mendip Hills. Was it really the same day?

Steve pushed back his chair, stood up, stretched his shoulders. 'Time for bed, huh?'

'Right.'

'Got everything you want?'

I nodded; Nicky had made sure of that.

'Okay, then.' He smiled. 'Give you a call at five o'clock.'

Five o'clock? Sparrow's fart!

It was not yet sun-up on Muller station, but there was toast and tea for breakfast. Steve had already gone and the horses were saddled. There was movement at the station. It was still and cool when I went outside; had to be a good day, I thought. Nothing surer.

Already the cattle had been rounded up and driven into the yards: 240 cows, 217 calves and some bulls. The cows and calves were making a horrendous racket as they churned up the choking dust that lifted, smoke without fire, into the ever-lightening sky. To the west rose Shingley Range, massive and almost threatening.

Steve's staff were hard at it. They were: Lyall Barriball, head shepherd; Craig King, shepherd; Craig Kendall, cowboy; Tony Watson, handyman; and Rachel Smith, casual worker (she lived with Lyall in the head shepherd's old cottage). The only member of the staff not there was the cook, Mary-Anne Watson.

The cattle — cows and calves but not the few bulls — were driven into a narrow, chute-like race. Then they were separated — one this way, one that — into separate yards. Eventually, then, cows and calves were all separated. The calves bawled out, missing their mothers already. Fair enough. Calving started here on 5 October, making them on average three months old, just babies, really.

The calves were then driven into the same type of wooden-railed chute you'd see bucking horses contained in at a rodeo. All tightly packed, nose to tail, they were then prodded with a big stick so that, one by one, they arrived at the end of the chute, which was actually inside a shed.

Craig King.

Craig Kendall.

Here they were held securely in place by a wooden guillotine-like device that closed around the neck of each calf. A stock, if you like. Then they got the treatment: earmarked, drenched, and dehorned if necessary. It was safer to be a heifer calf, rather than a bull calf. The calves were castrated without fuss by Steve, using a bloody knife with surgical precision. The testicles were tossed — *plop!* — into a big bucket. As each calf was dealt with, Rachel made an entry in a notebook.

Set free, the calves, badly shaken, rushed to find their mothers, who had already been turned out. Upon making contact with their young, the mothers clearly showed great concern for their well-being. Meantime, another lot of cows and calves were going through the same process.

Also in the meantime, the Simmental bulls were taking full advantage of the situation. In fact, they were enjoying themselves immensely, leaping up on the cows on heat. At such a time the humour can be ribald.

'Mass rape,' was Craig Kendall's droll contribution.

Standing alongside him, the head shepherd grinned as though asked to say 'Cheese'. Some of the yet-to-be-separated calves also climbed, with considerably more difficulty, onto the backs of cows that, because they were so tightly lodged together, were unable to do much about it. According to Steve, they were merely trying to follow the bulls' example or, as he put it, 'just foolin' around'. Whatever they were up to, it had better be worth it — once Surgeon Steve had given them the chop-chop they wouldn't be up to it. They would be just like wethers, deprived of perhaps the most basic act of all.

At nine o'clock on the dot a flat-deck truck pulled up at the cattle yards. Morning tea had arrived, and Nicky was there to give Mary-Anne a hand. With the heat already building up, and the work exacting, they were all glad to stop for a short break. We helped ourselves to freshly made muffins and coffee and sat down against the wooden rails, in the shade.

Sipping my coffee, I watched calves wandering around and making sounds of distress; obviously they had been unable to find their mothers. There! Reunion. Mother licking her young one's face. Other calves were lying down, looking sick, or in shock. It was understandable: some shocking things had taken place here.

Empty cups were refilled. The pile of muffins gradually diminished. Smokes were lit.

'Finish by midday, Steve?'

'Yeah,' was the laconic reply.

Soon, Mary-Anne was asking, 'Everybody had enough?'

Everybody had. Empty cups were taken to the back of the truck and stacked away, and the truck drove off.

It was back to work on Muller station, up the Awatere.

At last, Rachel jotted down the last entry for today: 217. It was all done: 103 heifers, 114 bull calves. Steve, grimy and blood spattered, looked pleased it was all over, for now, anyway. Come daybreak next morning it would be all on again. More cows and calves to bring in.

'Time for a lolly scramble,' Steve said to me.

'Huh?'

All was graphically revealed as Steve went to the full bucket the blowflies had gathered about. He hurled its grisly contents onto the ground. There were no children waiting for them, of course, just station dogs. They got stuck in as if they hadn't been fed in a week, gobbling up the testicles with loud crunching sounds. Some bush wag, years ago, named these delicacies mountain oysters. Never fancied them myself, you know. It occurred to me that a sensitive soul might have turned green and thrown up. Well, those Muller dogs would have cleaned that up, too, no worries!

It was nearing noon and the day was hot. It was time to shift the cattle, so Steve gathered up the reins and mounted his fine chestnut. Steve looked good on a horse; so too did Craig and Mary-Anne, taking a break from more mundane chores such as washing up and making meals for ravenously hungry single men.

They worked the cattle out of the home paddock and drove them along the bank of the river. The grass was lush along there and the dogs took the opportunity for a quick dip in a meandering stream. Across the bridge they went, bellowing, most of the calves subdued.

'You don't take them too far,' Steve said. 'They need plenty of time to recover.'

'Particularly the bull calves,' I pointed out.

Steve nodded, straight-faced. 'Yeah, particularly those.'

Tony Watson.

They pushed the cattle to the crest of the hill and then let them wander down the far side, to the wide flats flanking the road.

Later, Steve told me they would be working with cattle until the end of the month, all going to plan. We were at our ease then, enjoying a beer before the evening meal, just as they did on so many properties around the country. Not quite a tradition, you understand, but heading fast in that direction.

I wondered aloud what they got up to after they had finished with the cows and calves. What, for instance, did their overall year entail?

'Well,' Steve said, 'I really think our year, as you put it, starts in September with shearing rather than now in January.'

'Start there, then,' I suggested.

'Okay,' he said, nodding. 'The last Monday in September is the designated date to begin shearing; we don't obviously always get going then but' — a lazy lift of his shoulders — 'that's when we plan to. We shear the ewes then, and they also get treated in case of possible fly strike. Then we —'

'Do they get flyblown much here?'

Steve shook his head. 'No, it's much too dry as a rule; not enough humidity, I guess. But it still happens now and then and you can't afford to get caught out. In a country this size a fly problem can be terribly insidious, and, by the time you realise you've got one, well, you can lose a few before you know it's there. So prevention's far better than cure.

'Anyway, once the ewes are done they go out to their lambing blocks. Next we muster the hoggets and wethers and shear them in November; the wethers then go back to their summer range in the Acheron — you'd like the Acheron, great country! Oh, the bulls go to the heifers on the first of December and to the cows nine days later.' There were 23 of those huge Simmental bulls on the run.

Steve raised his bottle to his lips and drank deeply. 'There's tailing and haymaking going on, too, in the pre-Christmas period. Always damn busy.' He tapped my empty bottle. 'Another?'

'In mid-February we take all the cattle — that includes the bulls as well — out to the head of the Acheron. They

Herding cattle across the Awatere are Steve Satterthwaite (foreground), Mary-Ann Watson and Craig King.

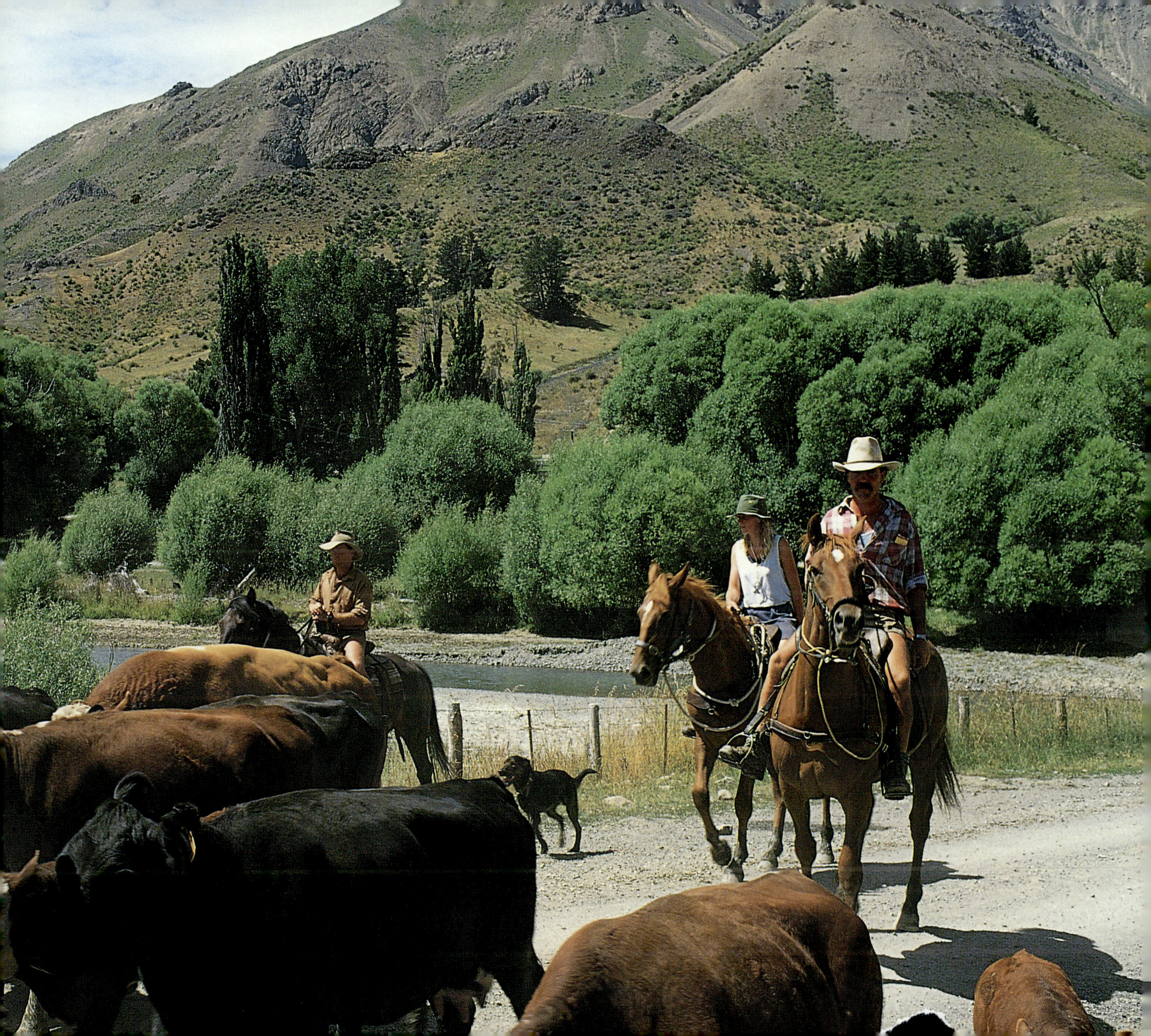

stay out there until the autumn muster. It takes three days to get there and we all enjoy it immensely.' The cattle, he added, were in real high country out there and the lowest level they would graze at was 1300 metres.

'Soon as we get back from there,' he went on, 'it's weaning time for the lambs; they get drenched too. The main thing is to have them done by the third week of February.'

'Your sale?'

'Right. Once that's over, the ewes get out in the summer country too. So really, the Awatere country is pretty much destocked.'

'A bit of a spell?'

'If you like.'

Another period of general stock work followed this, a time when Steve's thoughts, like those of so many high-country runholders, were turning more and more to the fall muster, arguably the most significant, interesting and fulfilling event in a station year.

'Well, we used to start the muster on the first of May, but because we got caught out with bad weather a few years running, we decided to bring the date forward by a whole month.' He smiled ruefully and ran his splayed fingers through his hair. 'However, that didn't make it any better. You were just as likely to get dirty weather then, too. Anyway, we don't have a set date to start now, we wait and see what the weather's up to before we begin.' He looked at me across the table. 'You have to be flexible, don't you?'

'No arguments there,' I said.

Steve smiled. 'So this year we'll just wait and see.'

The fall or autumn muster on Muller station took around 10 days; they did not use horses and the men, climbing to around 2100 metres, up where the highest-ranging Merinos foraged, had to be super-fit. All up they covered 14,500 hectares; it was country to test the mettle of any musterer and his dogs. Lower down, they also mustered the cattle. Then they took them home, sheep and cattle in one big mob.

'They get along okay?' I asked.

Steve nodded. 'Surprisingly so.'

Back at the station headquarters the shit, as Steve indelicately put it, really hit the fan, for this was a period of intense activity involving long hours. Firstly, the sheep and cattle were separated, and the sheep then given priority, while the cattle, out on the river flats, were largely ignored. The sheep were drenched and crutched, and the rams put with the ewes in the second and third weeks of May. Later, the ewes went to their lambing blocks, the wethers to their wintering blocks, and the weaned calves, all fully recovered now, ranged over 8000 hectares of the Awatere River country.

'The calves work up the side gullies,' Steve went on, 'but mostly they hang around the river flats. Basically we use them to clean up the country as' — he smiled faintly — 'vacuum cleaners.'

Steve had been on the Muller for more than half his life. He was 18 years old when his father, Clive, had become the principal shareholder of Muller Station Ltd. Even then, something had stirred deep inside him when he saw the wonderful country of the upper Awatere Valley; this, he had realised, was where his future lay.

On Muller station, Steve first worked as a 'cowboy'. In Australia the term is given to someone who milks cows, cleans vehicles, tends gardens, gets the winter wood in, fixes fences, and is on call for anything that the boss may wish of him. It is not a good position. But on the Muller it was different. The name was used to describe someone like fresh-faced Craig Kendall, who was learning all aspects of life on a high-country run.

Later, Steve advanced to head shepherd and in 1980 he took over the management of the station. Today the property was still owned by Muller Station Ltd and Steve, rather than his father, was the principal owner. It seemed to me after meeting Steve Satterthwaite and watching him at work with his happy staff that this sprawling 36,500-hectare run in the upper Awatere Valley was in the very best of hands.

5

BATTLERS ON MASON HILLS

On a Friday evening heavy rain began to fall on Mason Hills station, tucked away to the west of Mendip Hills. It was just one of a number of properties spread along the inland Kaikoura route, the mostly unsealed State Highway 70, linking Waiau and Kaikoura. A sudden chill came with the wet stuff.

Andrew Barker, tall and dark haired, reckoned it was time to call it a day, soon as they'd finished this pen. There were no arguments from his wife, Liz, who had been working with him in the sheep yards. It was a typical scene for this time of year: eartagging sheep and vaccinating them against footrot, all too common where northern Canterbury soon gives way to Marlborough. They had finished with two-thirds of their one-year-old Merino hoggets and the rest would keep until morning. The next day would be fine all over Canterbury, according to the weather forecast I'd picked up on the car radio. Fine and hot — 27 degrees Celsius in Christchurch. Yet the weather was always dicey around here, the country lodged between the Kaikoura Range, to the northwest, and the coast, not too far away in the east. The elements could hurl just about anything at you. The locals accepted that; they didn't have any say in the matter.

I took shelter under the sagging bough of a massive pine tree while the Barkers got on with it.

'Wag!' Andrew bawled.

A big, shaggy-coated beardie sheepdog bounded into sight. With an effortless leap that would have pleased the jockey of a top steeplechaser he cleared a high fence.

'Here, Wag!'

Wag was the top all-purpose dog on Mason Hills. He could work sheep or cattle, and just loved hunting pigs; he knew exactly what was required of him here.

When his tall master jerked open the stiff gate, he gave the stupid hoggets an urgent hurry-up, and they did the right thing by entering the shearing shed, where they would shelter overnight. Flapping her arms like a well-dressed scarecrow suddenly come to life, Liz moved up behind them, shouting, 'Hey! Hey! Hey!' Quickly, Wag backtracked, oblivious of the stinging rain. Again he performed his neat fence-leaping trick.

More sheep were brought up to join those in the shed. The rain hammered on the corrugated-iron roof. As the hoggets jostled together the air was filled with bone-dry dust and you could smell droppings and urine but, above all, wet woollen blankets. Soon the shed was full to near capacity, the last hogget tucked up for the night. I hoped they knew how to sleep standing up.

Looking well pleased, Andrew turned to me. 'Fancy a beer?' Wet, dirt-streaked face smiling.

'Absolutely!'

'Me, too.'

Wag, sitting on his rump, grinned up at me. It was nice to be made so very welcome on Mason Hills.

Over at the comfortable old homestead, we switched damp gear for dry gear and while Liz bustled around in the kitchen Andrew and I settled down in the sitting room and strenuously uncapped bottles of beer. The station, Andrew said, was once part of Highfield station and came into being about 1900, when that run was split up. It was taken on by Andrew's grandfather, Harold Atkinson, three years later. Unfortunately, Atkinson's only son was killed overseas on active duty during the Second World War and Andrew's father, David, who had married Harold Atkinson's daughter, ran it for his father-in-law. When Atkinson died, the run remained as part of his estate.

Andrew Barker became the manager on Mason Hills in 1975. Two years later, he met Elizabeth Oswald at the wedding of a mutual friend. Liz was back-country through and through, hailing from Duntroon station in the Awatere Valley. Eventually they married, Liz moving from one station to another. Today they had a nine-year-old son, Matthew.

The Barkers, Andrew went on, had run the place mostly on their own since 1987, because of the cost of farm labour. Working it on their own meant a saving of around $20,000 a year, a single shepherd's wage and accommodation. Naturally there was a much-increased workload for both of them. There had, however, been some compensations, and when Liz joined us she touched upon some of them:

'To justify having staff means they have to generate a lot of extra income over their wages. For one thing, there are a lot of hidden costs in their accommodation.' She paused and sipped her gin and tonic. 'Having staff means they are always with you — at work, at meal times — so, as you can imagine, there is very little real privacy. Without staff — as we are now — means you can go and come as you please; you don't have to make provisions for them.' Again she broke off, expression thoughtful. 'There's no getting away from the personal side of their lives, too.'

'Much better on your own,' said Andrew, staring into his glass.

'It's a lot less stressful,' Liz added in her well-modulated tones. No backblocks schoolhouse to finish off her education, I thought, something much better than that.

'Surely having to do it all by yourselves for most of the year is stressful too?' I pointed out.

'Course it is,' Liz shot back quickly. 'But we think we have the answer, don't we?'

Andrew bobbed his head and explained. The Barkers were in a period of transition on Mason Hills, designed to cut back on the workload. The plan was to have a flock of straight Merino wethers rather than the cross-bred Border Leicester/Merino ewes that had ranged the station's 2600 hectares for so long.

'Can you imagine how simple it would be with only wethers to look after?' Andrew said enthusiastically.

'No lambing! No tailing!' His brown eyes flashed excitedly

The Mason River.

with the enormous possibilities of it all and he slurped his beer with great gusto.

'The time involved with producing lambs is so great,' Liz said, catching my eye. 'And so many things work against a good lambing percentage.' The weather, for one.

They had already sold off a lot of the cross-bred ewes, Andrew explained, and they had some 3500 Merino wethers on the run now. They would increase this number to 5000, buying the additional 1500 wethers (lambs) at a forthcoming Merino sale in Tekapo. They had chosen Merinos over other breeds because of their suitability, their hardiness and, above all, because of their prime wool.

'In the meantime,' Andrew went on, 'we'll soon be bringing in the ewes and weaning their lambs — something else we won't have to do in the future.'

'I heard the market isn't bad for lambs this year.'

'Right,' Andrew agreed, 'it's picked up a bit. We've got two and a half thousand we're going to sell off soon.'

'Where?'

'Here — on the place. We should get a top price of around twenty dollars and, at the bottom end, fifteen dollars. Hmm . . . we'd be satisfied with that.'

'You have cattle here, too?'

'Yes. We might increase their numbers as well.' They had a herd of 350 Hereford cattle, which included eight bulls.

Liz said, 'It's all a bit of a gamble, really.'

'But a calculated one,' I said.

Liz nodded. 'It'll be very interesting to see just where we are two years down the track, won't it?'

Andrew laughed — all of life was a challenge, wasn't it? They had, after all, taken a huge risk when they had decided to purchase Mason Hills from the family trust. They had borrowed heavily from the Rural Bank to do so and had also taken with gratitude a no-interest loan from members of their family. Really, it had been touch and go in tough economic times, with the farming industry in a slump. But they had come through intact, paying back the last of the money owing just last year. So instead of Andrew being a manager on Mason Hills — as his father had been — he and his wife owned it. Actually owned it! For the Barkers that was a wonderful feeling; you really couldn't describe it.

The imported four-wheel-drive vehicle crunched across the gravelly bottom of the Mason River. It was Saturday, just after daybreak, and the river was running low; the water was clear. Many times, when it was in flood, it presented the Barkers with a real problem. Since all but 40 hectares of their run was on the western side of the river, crossing the Mason was an almost everyday event. Just one more reason, Andrew said, for going into wethers.

A pair of healthy-looking rabbits, plump as turkeys, watched our approach; Andrew was just on the point of stopping and reaching for a rifle when they scuttled off into a nearby belt of scrub. Andrew, working through the gears, eyed their departure. 'Rabbit Board boys were through here a night or two back. Reckoned they shot sixty-seven.'

'Not a bad night's work.'

'Hmpph!' went Andrew, shaking his head. 'Don't believe them.'

We started up a steep, corrugated track. Off to the right there was a lovely view of the river and the grassy flats. A pair of paradise ducks were on the flats among the grazing cattle. Beyond the river you could see the shearing shed and, as the view gradually extended, the station homestead. You couldn't see the hoggets, though. They were still inside the shed.

The weather was good, too. It would be hot later; the air had that certain feel. Hotter than in Christchurch, maybe 30 degrees. The Nissan, growling in low gear, made easy work of a steady climb.

'Good buy, this,' Andrew said, slapping the dashboard with one hand.

I was rather pleased the other one remained on the steering wheel. We were heading to a high and grassy block, the best part of the run, Andrew thought. Considering they still had a heap of sheep to attend to it was good of Andrew to offer me a look over their property. As we worked steadily uphill, he was telling me a rather unusual story about an encounter he had had with wild pigs.

In December of 1991 they had taken on a casual hand, Anna Maxwell, to help with the mustering. The build-up to shearing time — just before Christmas — was always a brutal period and they worked 15-hour days on the place then. The extra help made things a little easier, but only just. The Barkers favoured female casual hands, not because they worked better or were paid less, but because they didn't eat as much!

Liz and Andrew Barker in the sheep yards.

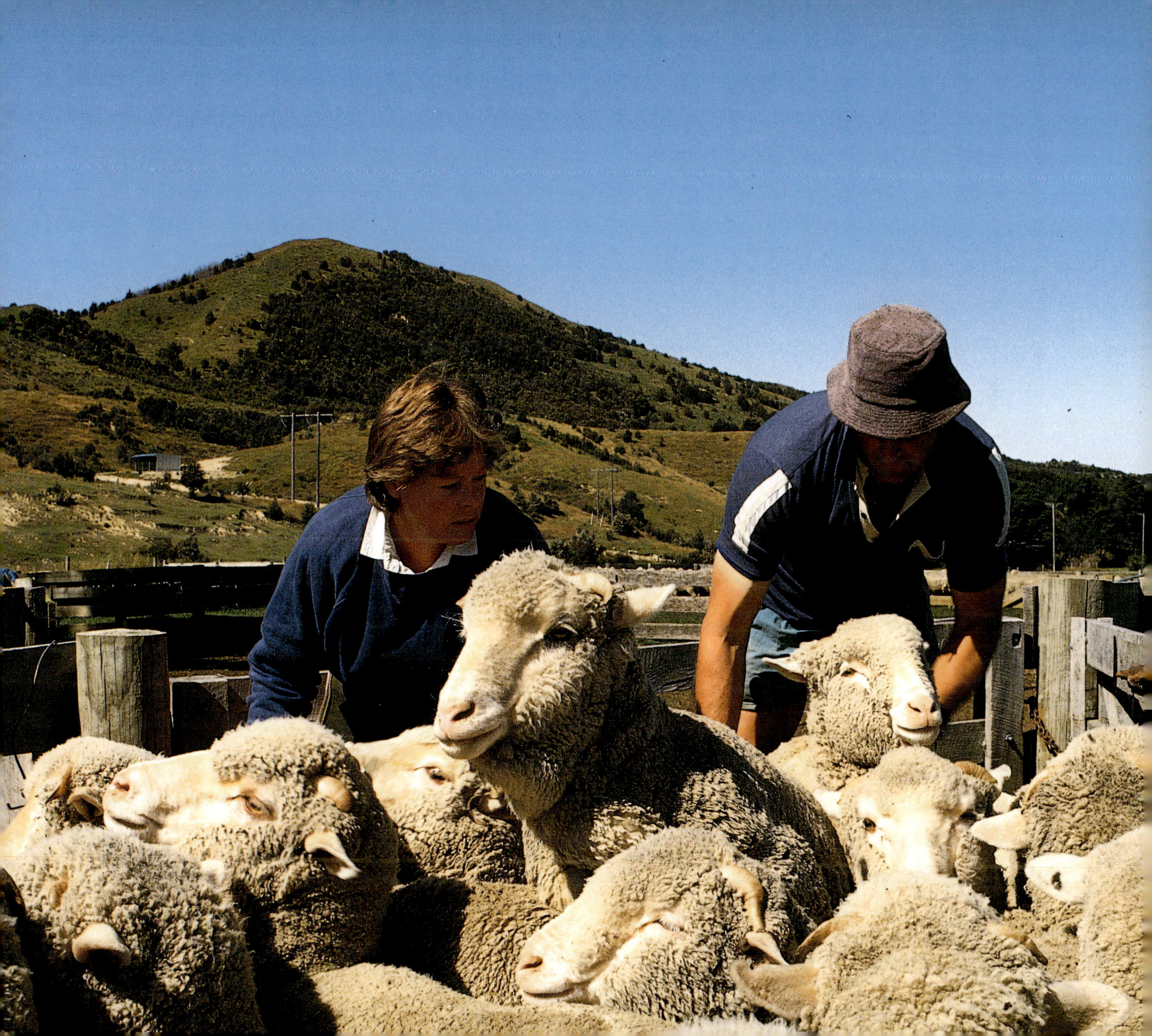

One less rabbit on Mason Hills.

On the day in question, Andrew, Anna and Andrew's young niece, Libby Weston-Webb from Auckland, were out mustering sheep. Checking his mare, Andrew put his heading dog, Skip, onto some ewes. In a gully bottom, however, Skip's attention was suddenly diverted. He barked loudly, insistently.

'Oh, shit!' Andrew groaned to himself. 'The bugger's onto a pig!'

There was nothing for it but to go and get it over with, because it was unlikely that Skip, his blood racing, could be called off. Dismounting, Andrew handed the reins of his horse to Anna and then started down-slope. Skip was holding a medium-sized black sow, the most common colour for pigs on the run. The sow was squealing. Fair enough, seeing Skip was latched onto one of her ears.

Andrew ducked in behind the sow and grabbed a back leg. He reached with his free hand for the sheath knife at his belt and his hand closed around the wooden grip. Then he felt a gentle nudge in the backside. Had to be one of the other dogs come for a look, maybe to help out. Stupid mutt! He half turned, lashing out with a booted foot. But his kick found only empty space and he saw that he was facing a rather large black boar.

Heart hammering, Andrew spun about and dived behind a handy tree. The boar would surely come after him. But no, it simply walked to where Skip was still holding the sow and without anger or fuss pushed the dog off. Immediately the sow bolted; not so the boar. He stood his ground, summing up the situation: a man behind a tree and two, no, three dogs unsure what to do. The boar swung his head, grunted several times, and then sauntered after the sow.

'I could,' Andrew said, 'have easily put the dogs onto it. But I didn't want to. You see, there was no malice at all in that boar — he hadn't tried to hurt me or Skip. All he wanted to do was protect his mate.'

We were nearing a good number of cows, a huge bull among them.

'I really admired his courage more than anything,' Andrew finished, shaking his head with a look of admiration stamped clearly on his face.

The highest parts of Mason Hills are not excessively high, reaching 900 metres. Up there, however, it is true South Island high country — a splendid sweep of tussock, a high plateau dotted with ragged outcrops of rock. Off to the east lay Mendip Hills. Sheep were scattered all over the broad expanse of grass and everything glowed as though burnished under the rising sun.

'Fantastic!' was my summing up.

Andrew smiled. 'Thought you'd like it.'

Incredibly, however, there was danger up here. How could there be on such a lovely summer morning? In winter, perhaps. Say a blizzard was raging, snow building up in the hollows, the chill in the wind great. But now? The danger had nothing at all to do with the elements. It was danger of an unexpected sort, the type you rarely come across. The whole high block, known as the Blowholes, was riddled with potholes.

Between them, Mason Hills and the adjoining run, Annandale, had 365 mapped holes, the result of a survey by the University of Canterbury. Some of the potholes were narrow, say, 30–40 centimetres across, others had an entrance big enough to swallow a full-grown cattle beast. Many of the holes weren't deep, but others plummeted straight down to untold depths. No one knew how far they penetrated the earth's surface. It was thought that potholes were still forming on both stations.

Over the years the potholes, with their smooth sides, had claimed many victims. Back when red deer ranged this land in large numbers a few of them had slipped into a pothole, to die a lingering death. Some of the Barkers' stock — sheep and cattle — ended up at the bottom of a hole, too. In some instances you could peer down into a pothole and see the bones down there.

For Liz, in particular, that high block was somewhere she would rather not go. In fact, she hated mustering up there. She didn't really know why. It was safe enough providing you stayed on well-defined stock trails and kept a sharp eye out for newly formed holes. A good stock horse could sense a pothole, so there was no real danger.

Liz was up there on her own on a day she will never forget. She was riding Becky, a dark bay mare, across the Blowholes block. Ahead of her the sheep milled. One of her heading dogs was swinging back towards her, high-stepping through grass that gleamed in the sun, lovely silver tussocks. What could possibly go wrong on such a wonderful day, as only a few puffy white clouds drifted over the tops of the Kaikoura Range?

For a moment, Liz looked away from the heading dog. In that instant the dog was gone. Like it had never been there. Gone without even a startled yelp. Reining in Becky, Liz dismounted and cautiously walked her mount to where she had last seen the dog. There was, she knew, only one possible explanation. There, mostly hidden in the grass, was a pothole. The almost sheer sides leading into its mouth were grassy, untouched by stock.

Liz crouched close to it. It was a narrow pothole; you couldn't see its bottom. She called the dog's name. No reply. Just the slight breeze shifting through the bending tussocks and the bawling of sheep. She called again, more loudly, half afraid to hear her own voice.

'It was,' Liz recalled, 'an uncanny feeling, the most awful feeling, really. One moment she was there, the next gone. Not a sound.'

6

NO EASY RIDE ON ST JAMES STATION

The first men to move into the St James country were Thomas Carter and Richard Timms, in 1859. They divided, either by mutual consent or perhaps the flip of a coin, the Clarence River valley (above the latter-day St James homestead); this stretch of country included the valleys of the Alma, Severn and Acheron. Carter found himself in possession of the lower part of the block and Timms the rest of it, extending to Lake Tennyson. Both men ran cattle.

In the early 1860s more settlers moved into the area. In 1862 George Edwards took up 6500 hectares in the Edwards River (named for him). Edwards did not run stock there and a year later transferred the block to George Willmer. In 1863 W. L. Fowler took up a block on the Stanley River, which he named Stanley Vale, and about this time a man called Travers acquired land on Lake Guyon, which included the Ada Valley.

The West Coast Gold Rush of 1865–66 opened up new and lucrative markets — beef on the hoof — for these early runholders. Even so, Willmer sold out to James Jones and J. L. Broadbent in 1865. This was a somewhat tenuous partnership: Broadbent terminated it in February 1867. Lacking sufficient funds of his own, Jones formed a partnership with two brothers, Edward and Thomas Pavitt. Many consider these men, and particularly Jones, were the real founders of the present-day St James station.

By 1866 Timms had apparently had enough of raising cattle up the Clarence and sold out to Carter. Next winter, during the 'Great Snow of Sixty-Seven', Carter perhaps wished he was elsewhere, too. His stock losses were substantial. Jones and his partners were hard hit as well; they did not recover fully from their losses and two years later they were declared bankrupt. The Pavitts blamed Jones for bad management, but the mortgagees had

On St James station, the red building is the old cookshop.

enough faith in Jones's ability to retain him as manager, a position he held until 1872, when the run was taken over by John McArthur. McArthur was a Scottish shepherd who, before coming to New Zealand, had worked on sheep stations in Australia. If any man could make St James into a paying proposition, well, it was generally considered that he could.

The Lake Guyon run was incorporated into St James station in 1879, as indeed were a number of much smaller, largely forgotten runs that were either abandoned by disgruntled settlers or sold by mortgagees. By the winter of 1895, St James station covered 57,500 hectares and carried 33,000 sheep. In June of that year yet another great snow caused havoc; 9240 sheep were lost.

After 30 years on St James, McArthur sold out to W. H. P. and A. L. Platt; they in turn sold out to C. H. Ensor in 1916. Ensor believed that Corriedales were the answer on St James; two years later heavy snows all but wiped them out. The fortunes of St James slumped but somehow Ensor clung on, grimly, until 1927 when the run changed hands yet again.

The new owner was James Stevenson, who had land at Flaxton and Fernside, north of Christchurch. Stevenson sold off the remaining Corriedales and went into Merinos in a big way. Soon they were carrying 13,000. When James Stevenson died in 1948, his eldest son, Jim, took charge of the huge run, and he still ran the place today.

By any reckoning St James station, sprawling over 81,000 hectares of truly wonderful country and taking in the watersheds of three rivers — the Clarence, the Waiau and the Boyle — rated among the South Island's great high-country runs. They presently carried around 2000 cattle: Herefords, Angus and Angus cross. Back around the turn of the century, when St James was owned by John McArthur, there were close to 40,000 sheep on the place. Today, there were only about 1000 Border

On a high point overlooking the valley of the Clarence River, wild horses watch for danger.

Leicester/Merino cross-bred sheep out in Edwards country. But it was neither cattle nor sheep that back-country types thought about when the name St James cropped up: it was horses.

There had been horses on St James for well over a hundred years, famous horses that carried the blood of thoroughbred and Clydesdale. Today, they ranged the Waiau River flats, living in a semi-feral state. The overall herd numbered around 150 and they were found in three different valleys, each mob of wild horses ruled over by a stallion. The St James horses had long been sought after. Back in the days when there were horse-drawn trams in Christchurch, for instance, they were often pulled by horses that were born on the station. St James horses turned up at many a horse sale in the upper half of the South Island; they were eagerly sought by shepherds and stockmen, types who could recognise a good, sturdy, high-country hack.

Today, Jim Stevenson was in his late seventies, and had been calling the tune on St James for over 45 years. After so long on the station, he seemed a part of it. When Jim Stevenson barked out a command, men jumped. How high? Well, that all depended; some could clear a pretty high fence. In appearance, Stevenson was deceptively slight. While the years had naturally taken a toll on his physique, he was still as tough as old saddle leather, stringy as a short bit of frayed rope. The fact that he was nudging 80 years of age and could still mount a horse in the predawn and spend the rest of the day in the leather spoke for itself. Jim Stevenson was never really talkative when a stranger was around. Not even that well-known back-country scribe Peter Newton could get much loose change out of Jim Stevenson when he was researching one of his books. Fair enough.

Every two years Jim Stevenson and a team of well-chosen musterers headed out for a week to round up some of the horses ranging the Waiau River bottom-lands. They were then driven some 40 kilometres to the station homestead, located at 820 metres in the southeastern section of the station, for the January horse sale.

It was mid-January when I contacted Jim Stevenson by telephone. I very much liked the idea of meeting him; after all, legendary horsemen are rather light on the ground nowadays. The idea of visiting the station held great appeal, too, and I considered the famed horse sale a must. Naturally I introduced myself and — 'What d'you want?' Stevenson's voice was reed thin and testy.

They said that Jim Stevenson had only two kinds of days: good days and bad days. Guess which this one was. Rather taken aback, I explained that I was writing a book about various stations in the country, how I would like to include a short piece on St James, and how very much I would like to meet him.

A heavy silence followed my well-chosen words.

'D'you know what time of year this is?'

'Pardon?'

'Don't you know this is one of the busiest times of the year on a station?'

'Well, I —'

'I'm up to my neck in all sorts of things right now. The horse muster for one thing.'

'We needn't have a long chat, Mr Stevenson. Ten, fifteen minutes ought to do it. You do live in Hanmer rather than out at the station, don't you? So any time you can fit me in will be —'

'No! I'm much too busy to see you now.'

'It is okay if I attend the horse sale . . . ?'

'Course it is! It's an open day on the station. Anyone can attend.'

His tone clearly suggested he was talking to the village idiot, which, for the record, one of my early school-teachers considered I was. While she may have been right about that, I like to think I've improved a little since then.

'Perhaps I could have a few words with you at the horse sale,' I persisted.

'Well,' said Jim Stevenson heavily, 'I might have the time to say g'day to you.'

And with that, he put down the telephone. Clunk!

I arrived in Hanmer Springs early on the eve of the St James horse sale. It was an indifferent evening, really: might rain, might not. As I sprawled out in my car, chewing thoughtfully on a rather plastic hamburger and sipping at a soft drink that might have been in the fridge 10 minutes, I mulled over the information I'd gleaned at the pub. It wasn't difficult to spot in a place the size of Hanmer Springs.

The horse muster had gone real well: they had 38 horses in a paddock near the sale yards. Jim Stevenson was in town right now, but before daybreak he would be heading out to the St James homestead, 14 kilometres away over a dirt road. Some of Stevenson's hands were camped at the homestead, among them Harvey Riddle. I knew he'd been working on the run on and off since 1940.

'Harvey's a good bloke,' I was told. 'He'll talk to you, no worries.'

That's what I wanted: no worries. But wouldn't it have been real nice to corner Jim Stevenson, I mused, to ask him about the trip down from the valley of the Waiau. But I'd been warned to stay well clear of Jim until after the horse sale was over, so I would have to seek out my information elsewhere. Unless, of course, Jim Stevenson opened up after it was all over. That was about as likely as the Clarence drying up! Yes . . . Harvey Riddle seemed a good place to start. No point in waiting until morning, either. Hell no! They'd all be flat out then, jumping to Jim Stevenson's tune.

All primed up, I left Hanmer Springs at about eight o'clock. In decidedly gloomy conditions I barrelled along the road to Molesworth and St James and made a hard left turn where the road forked to head straight to St James. In the fast-failing light I could just make out the blurred shapes of cattle on the scrubby flats by the Clarence River.

I'd been told I couldn't really miss the homestead — it wasn't far past the stock yards. Suddenly I saw wooden-railed yards to my left. The 38 horses, I thought, were close to here, bedded down for the night, most likely. I wondered if in the future they would think about their place of birth — those lovely sun-drenched valleys. None of them would miss the winters, though, the having to paw through ice-crushed snow to feed on frozen tussocks.

There! A long, low-slung building on a rise, with a fence between it and the road. There was a light in the window. As I pulled up the door opened and a tall man emerged. I got out: it was cold, woolshirt cold. Dogs howled behind the homestead somewhere. I felt like howling back at them and maybe I would've under a full moon.

'What d'you want?' the man demanded in a deep voice. It was starting to sound like a catch phrase around here.

I clambered awkwardly over a gate, walked over, said who I was.

'You the joker who writes the books?'

I admitted I was. He nodded. 'Read a couple of 'em.' He didn't say what he thought of them; perhaps that was just as well. 'Andrew Riddle.' He held out a big, hard hand. Harvey's son? I wondered.

A much smaller, older man appeared behind Andrew Riddle. He looked like he'd been up and down the creek a thousand times. He peered at me like a near-sighted morepork in broad daylight.

'Harvey Riddle,' Andrew said, introducing his father.

'Come on in,' Harvey said with a smile. 'It's cold out here. Cuppa tea?'

The homestead was a disappointment: it wasn't a homestead in the accepted sense, being only about 20 years old. The original homestead would, I believe, have been the real thing: large, gracious, possibly a show place. It was hard to tell now, though — all that remained of it after a fire in 1949 were the remnants of two brick chimneys. What stood here now was more of a cookhouse and musterers' quarters: kitchen cum living room, big wooden table, couple of bedrooms, and so on. It was all very basic, but plenty good enough for those that roll their own smokes, play endless games of 500 on snowbound days, or look longingly at centrefolds in dog-eared *Playboy* magazines.

On the run!

Bearded Andrew straddled a chair while his father, looking pleased to have company, fussed about making a brew. Andrew had been on the place since last September, doing general station work. I asked him if he liked it.

'Wouldn't be here if I didn't,' was his succinct reply.

Since it was clear I wouldn't get much loose change out of Andrew, I turned to his father. Harvey was 74 years old, and looked it, too. It's a hard life in these high hills.

Harvey was young and strong when he first came to St James in 1940. They carried around 12,000 Merino sheep on the place in those days and over winter the staff moved from the station headquarters (where I was now) to the Ada homestead, 40 kilometres away, up in the upper Waiau country. The winters were tough on St James, real tough, and even these hardy Merinos often fared badly. There were always substantial losses and the general opinion was that it was time to switch from sheep to cattle.

The winter of 1941, Harvey recalled, was particularly bad. Snow storms raged, one after another, and you couldn't ride anywhere — not when the white stuff was belly deep to a tall horse. Then in August it got even worse. Back at the St James homestead the snow piled up on the roof of the kitchen until the weight became too much and the roof simply caved in. Worse, out in the upper Waiau, sheep trapped in deep drifts, even buried alive, were dying. It was only when they mustered in the spring that they fully realised how severe that winter had been, how many sheep had died. Harvey reckoned it was 7000, about two-thirds of the flock. It was time to get out of sheep, all right. Eventually all that remained of the once large numbers of Merinos that ranged St James was a token force of half-breed sheep — raised for mutton — out in the Edwards country.

During those 'war' years, Harvey Riddle was one of a five-strong team that mustered on four stations from

October through to June. They were called a flying gang. Apart from St James, they worked on St Helens (which lost half of its flock in 1941), Woodbank and the Hossack. Each man was allowed a maximum of five dogs; they received a tucker allowance of one-quarter of a sheep every second day. The men visited each station three times, weaning, dipping, shearing and participating in the big fall musters. From June to October the flying gang sought other work and, since they didn't know anything except a life on the land, they turned to rabbiting or deer hunting. As rabbiters they were employed by the stations, but as deer hunters they were in it for themselves. In either case they worked on stations they knew; Harvey invariably turned up on St James, where he hunted mostly red deer.

Deer were incredibly thick on St James then, he said. Out on the Waiau flats, particularly in the spring and early summer, when new growth was a lure, it was nothing to see as many as 200 out feeding. Winter saw them up in the big basins, pawing through the snow, just like feral horses, to get at the coarse tussock. Mostly the deer ran in little mobs, usually close together, so that, if disturbed, they might group together and escape via a high pass.

You watched them for a while before making a move, to find which of the hinds was the leader, so you could nail her first. Wind right? Off you went, belly down, in the grass. Getting closer and still closer until you could see the individual hairs on their coats and smell the hinds, which often urinated down their back legs. Now you half raised yourself and lifted your open-sighted .303, then closed tight the bolt on a hardnosed bullet or, more likely, one that you had filed away until the soft under-lead at the end was exposed. It would expand on impact then, a do-it-yourself dumdum. Kiwis and Aussies were doing the same thing overseas at the time, only with human targets.

You sighted in on the dominant hind, fair in the guts. The sound of the shot was extremely loud. There was no tell-tale sound of a hit, there never is with a gut-shot animal. The hind lurched forward with the sudden impact of the shot but, as expected, she didn't go down. She stood there, back hunched, real sick. The rest of the deer naturally gathered about her. And so you fired again and again at mostly standing targets, the barrel getting hotter and hotter, until all but the hind were down and then you gave her another one and she, too, was out of her misery.

Maybe you rolled a smoke. Presently, you reached for your skinning knife, and touched up the curved blade with a steel. Then you went to work, ripping off steaming pelts. A good price was 10 shillings and 6 pence per pound; you could make decent wages hunting for deer skins on St James station in the early 1940s.

Now, so many years later, when the sight of a deer on St James rated a mention, Harvey Riddle, no longer that keen young hunter, put a cup of tea in front of me and gestured at a packet of biscuits. I thanked him and then asked how many deer he would have shot over a winter.

'Between five and six hundred as a rule,' he said, spooning sugar into his cup. 'Could've shot lots more, of course. Skinning slows you down.' So did packing them out, I knew. 'There was a government culler here one year — 1943, I think it was. That was in the winter too. Plenty of snow that year.' The shooter was Archie Clarke and he had shot 1200 deer.

'Eventually the flying gang broke up,' Harvey went on, munching on a biscuit, 'and Jim asked me if I'd like to stay on and keep an eye on things. I was the manager, I suppose.' He smiled rather wistfully. 'Been coming back to St James ever since.'

The bedroom door opened and a broad-shouldered, strongly built young man stood there. He was tall, too. He gave me a rather bleary-eyed look as introductions were made, and a handshake designed to separate the men from the boys. This was Dean A'Court and he'd been on the horse muster. They'd be rising well before daybreak out here and he'd hit the sack early; after all, a young bloke needs all the shut-eye he can grab.

Next day I cornered Dean. 'What were you doing before

Dean A'Court shoeing his horse.

you came out here?'

Dean was wearing his station uniform: moleskins, blue shirt, riding boots and broad-brimmed hat with brim pulled low. On him the gear looked good; it was, of course, practical clothing — those big hats, for instance, are not for show.

'Down in Wanaka shaggin' around,' Dean said at length. 'Went round the rodeo a bit — breakin' in horses.' A big lift of his shoulders. He was not too happy, I knew, talking about himself. Still, what 18-year-old would be?

'Where's home, Dean?'

'Okains Bay.'

'Where's that?'

'Where's that!' he echoed, a look of mock indignation on his tanned face. 'Okains Bay. Banks Peninsula. Akaroa way. Jesus!'

I felt like apologising for being such a dumb bastard. I wondered, then, what it would have been like out here last winter, looking after the place on his own, just as Harvey Riddle had done all those years ago for the same boss. How many 18-year-olds could have handled the isolation? Few could have handled the horsebacking that went with a job on St James. But maybe all that shaggin' around he'd done in Wanaka had put a few years on him, eh?

'The snow was deep all right,' Dean said, talking about last winter. 'Lasted too. Nine weeks of it.'

But he'd had plenty of firewood, tons of food, and it wasn't a case of sitting on his arse out here — hell no! There was work to be done. They wintered bulls near the old Ada homestead and close to the cookshop cum stockmen's quarters. The bulls were not fed hay; they had to make do. They were Herefords, able to survive and perform in a wide range of conditions. In winter the bulls tended to gather together in the snow-bound gullies and therein lay the problem. The food they required was up high, on the more exposed, snow tussock faces. Someone had to get them up there. Not on horseback, on foot. Someone, for instance, like Dean A'Court.

'You have to walk 'em real high,' Dean explained, ''cause that's where the tucker is, y'know. Snow? Shit, it was bloody deep! You'd end up fair stuffed.

'Jim'd come round now and then to see how I was. Usually he'd tell me to shift this mob there or that mob somewhere else. It's hard, y'know, 'cause he's got his way of doing things and I've got mine.' A pause. 'But you've gotta' — he shrugged those broad shoulders — 'do it his way, haven't you?'

Fair comment. One thing for sure, though. Young Dean A'Court wouldn't jump a fence for any man.

Meantime, I was back in the cookshop on Thursday night and Dean was telling me about the horse muster. He didn't attach too much significance to it; it was all in a day's work, really. Only the likes of you and I would have got excited about the idea of bringing 38 high-spirited, unbroken mares and geldings, aged between two and five years, down from the Ada country to where they were now held.

All up, nine people had participated in the 1992 horse muster: Jim Stevenson; Dean A'Court; Florence West, well-known Canterbury horsewoman; Judy Akers and her eight-year-old daughter, Anna (wouldn't she have a grand story to tell her class mates?); Lynny Morris; Harvey Riddle; Michelle Arapere; and Earle Lunn the head stockman. Earle, tough and grizzled as an old bear, had a long association with St James. He worked on the station most of his life, as did his father, uncles and grandfather. The family had a wonderful local tradition going back over a hundred years.

Breaking a long silence, Andrew Riddle reckoned that when Jim, his father (a sly, sideways glance at Harvey here) and Earle, in his early fifties, were all camped out here it was known as the old men's rest home. Harvey raised a tiny smile at that and young Dean, starting to really come awake, laughed like it was the best joke he'd heard in ages. You're never going to be 74 years old when you're just 18, right?

It was 10.30 by the time I parked my car a couple of hundred metres from the cookshop, down on the flats, within sound of the Clarence. The night was clear, with a strong wind whipping through the grasses. Using my car as a windbreak, I made camp. I rolled out my bed — groundsheet, two sheets, two blankets and an unzipped sleeping bag that could serve as a bedspread. It had been a fair while since I'd done this. Last time it was on a remote sheep station in South Australia. I didn't have to concern myself about snakes this time, not that I ever really did. Most Australians have never seen a snake; you can even go long periods in the outback and never see one. I'd seen my share, though. They were always more scared of me than I was of them.

It must've been in the early hours, around two o'clock, when I woke with a sudden start, senses on hair trigger. You're back with Mother Nature out here, a star-filled sky for a roof and grass for a mattress. A full moon was galloping across the night sky. It was bright enough to have picked up a bridle and gone looking for a horse in the night paddock on a station that still relied on them. That bright.

Over near the cookshop there were two buildings in clear view — the old stables and cookshop, the latter now serving as a workshop cum blacksmith's shop. Down-valley, immense steel pylons, carrying high-tension cables, might have been mechanical giants marching steadily across the valley bottom.

Suddenly my attention was arrested by movement. There. Two, three metres away, a rabbit reared up on strong hind legs, the better to see, and to scent. I smiled and turned over to face my vehicle, the wind swirling mostly at my back. Up the Clarence River, on St James station, at the Tussock Motel.

I woke again a little after dawn. The overnight mist was lifting from the flats, but it was still cold enough to warrant a down-filled ski jacket and a woollen hat. Grabbing a towel and soap, I tramped to a nearby stream.

For breakfast I had fruit, and as I sipped my tea I noticed there was movement at the station. Outside the blacksmith's shop several horses were already hitched to a wooden rail. A vehicle was arriving; headlights were no longer required.

According to Andrew Riddle and his father (a gentle soul, really), it would be possible for me to photograph the horses as they were being driven on the last leg of their journey — a couple of kilometres — across the valley bottom to the sale yards. The best position, they thought, was up on a hill directly behind the cookhouse. They reassured me I would be out of everyone's way up there, but the problem was that neither Andrew nor his long-serving father carried any real weight around here. I finished my drink and set out to get Jim Stevenson's permission to photograph the horses.

The sun was coming up now and would soon cast a golden hue over the valley. Cattle were grazing down-valley and a few skylarks rose from the tussock, greeting a brand-new day with happy song. I felt that way, too. More vehicles were arriving; the sound of greetings came from over near the cookshop. The horses were still hitched outside the blacksmith's shop but, since I'd last looked over there, they had been saddled. As I cut through the

Peter Mills and Jim Stevenson.

dew-soaked grass, I could see several riders, mounted on fidgety horses, bunched together on a rise near the cookshop. Clearly profiled, they might have been extras awaiting their cue on the set of *The Man From Snowy River*. All but one wheeled away as I approached.

While I had never seen Jim Stevenson before, I had a fair idea I was looking at him now. He sat on a big gelding that stood a full 17 hands; he looked good on his horse, moulded to the leather, the legendary horseman himself. He was talking with a young man who'd just arrived. The bloke wore a collar and tie: a stock agent, for sure.

At that point Jim Stevenson spotted me. He all but stood up in the iron stirrups. I could have been anybody: a fisherman heading up-valley and wanting a few directions, an Australian grazier on holiday, curious about the horse sale, even Jim Bolger in disguise.

'Get off the place!' roared Jim Stevenson. Another bad day, obviously.

'Mr Stevenson —'

'Off the place!' He waved a hand in the air. 'No one's allowed here until the sale starts.' So much for the 'open day' on St James.

I stood there, unsure, feeling a damn fool. I didn't like to be put in that position. I'd jumped a few high fences myself when I'd first worked on sheep and cattle stations in Australia, but I soon gave that up. My foot always caught the top rail and I'd fall flat on my face.

'Peter!' Jim Stevenson bawled at the collar and tie. 'You tell him, right!' With that he spun his horse about and rode off, stiff-backed.

Peter Mills was a stock agent for Wrightsons, based in Culverden. It had been his responsibility to organise the horse sale.

'So what,' I asked him with a grin, 'did Jim Stevenson want you to tell me?'

Peter smiled sheepishly and explained that on sale day Jim was all fired up. You did nothing to annoy him, and he and the other stock agents (some of whom were arriving now) walked a very delicate line.

'Wouldn't go anywhere near the sale yards until they've finished marking the horses,' Peter advised. 'We keep right out of the way until then, too.'

I asked him what he thought about sale day.

'I really enjoy coming out here,' he replied. 'It's traditional; it's always been done. I believe they held horse sales here a hundred and twenty years ago. There's nothing like it in the South Island to the best of my knowledge.'

Nor up north, I thought.

It was a lovely morning now, and the heat was starting to build. I had been told it was usually hot on sale day. I was taking photographs of some of the old buildings when Dean A'Court rode by on a good-looking chestnut hack. He called out that his horse had cast a shoe so he was about to replace it. I ambled over to the blacksmith's shop to watch.

Soon after, several feral horses were spotted from the cookshop, which had a commanding view of the Clarence River valley. Riders went off to bring them down, Earle Lunn among them. I didn't get to talk with him and, seeing me there with a telephoto camera, he flashed me the sort of scowling look stockmen reserve for townies invading their particular patch. It turned out to be no easy

It's all happening at the St James horse sale.

task bringing those feral nags down to the flats. They were as spooky as deer, as flighty as chamois. But the riders knew what they were about and presently the horses were galloping past the old, 15-stand woolshed, tails streaming behind them, a drumming of hoofbeats. It was a grand sight.

By 11.30 a large crowd had already gathered at the sale yards, and more vehicles were arriving. The horses were contained in a number of individual yards, and each horse was numbered on its rump. Jim Stevenson and Peter Mills were in one of the yards. Peter had a pad in his hand, and was noting the merits of each horse, what a likely price would be. Station folk and holiday makers were also viewing the horses. It was a big event, all right.

At noon the temperature was in the high twenties, a dry heat. A carnival-like atmosphere prevailed. At one point I all but bumped into Jim Stevenson and we made brief eye contact; clearly he didn't recognise me as the person he'd bawled out a few hours before.

'Good horses,' I said. They were, too: the combination of thoroughbred and Clydesdale was a good one. You ended up with the right stuff, an animal that was well adapted to high country and never knew when to quit.

Jim Stevenson nodded, looked pleased. 'Yes, they are.' He raised an inquisitive eyebrow. 'You buying?'

I shook my head. 'Uh-uh. Just looking, Mr Stevenson.' He glanced at my camera bag, nodded again, and moved on with Peter Mills in tow.

At one o'clock sharp the horse sale started. The crowd had swelled to around a thousand people and more were arriving. The seven-strong Wrightson team swung into their highly polished act. One by one the horses were auctioned off. The average price worked out at $525.

Later, I managed to get a few words with Jim Stevenson over at the cookshop, and he was much more relaxed about things. He was still pretty much a closed book, though; whatever the reasons were they went way, way back. Main thing was, he was delighted with how the sale had gone.

7

THEY CALLED IT MORVEN HILLS

In the autumn of 1858 a 40-year-old Scot called John McLean checked his horse in a natural 1000-metre pass and gazed to the west, down into what we know as the valley of the Lindis River.

McLean — known more colourfully as 'Big Jock McLean' — hailed from the tiny island of Coll, off the west coast of Scotland. When his father died in 1836 John was 18 and, being the eldest of three sons, he took over the family farm. There were also two daughters in the family. Times were incredibly tough on Coll. Crops failed and disease was rife. The islanders at times had to resort to eating seaweed, and draining the blood of their cattle to form a kind of pudding. Many islanders left Coll, among them the McLeans. They emigrated to the goldfields of Australia. The three brothers, of whom John was always the driving force, opened a carrying business, which prospered, and they purchased a sheep station that, because of drought, did not.

Presently they heard that grazing land was available in New Zealand. Enough of the heat and the flies and months, even years, without so much as a drop of rain! In 1852 they arrived at Lyttelton. At first they purchased a 4000-hectare property — Ashfield — near Christchurch; two years later they acquired a 12,200-hectare block near Ashburton, which they named Lagmhor, after their home on Coll.

They say it was a wandering Maori chief named Huruhuru who first told John McLean of the vast grasslands of the Otago hinterland. To McLean, in the prime of his life, it sounded like ideal sheep country. Big Jock acted quickly on a once-in-a-lifetime opportunity.

With Huruhuru as his guide, he set off to locate this Eldorado of grass, beyond the mountains that turned gold as the sun dipped towards the west. They soon arrived in what today is called the Lindis Pass; the surrounding mountains, more like huge hills, were indeed lovely. McLean and Huruhuru went on, the Maori telling the big Pakeha that they were getting close now — a day or two's ride at the very most.

It was from a high point called Grandview Mountain that John McLean looked over a stupendous region of mostly open country. Here — by God! — was an empire of grass. This was enough for any man, and it was his for the taking. In a state of heady excitement, McLean returned home. He could not wait to tell his family what he had seen, to discuss its enormous possibilities with, in particular, his mother Mary, whose advice he had always heeded.

Given the laws of the day it was, of course, impossible for John McLean to gain sole title to such an area of land. So instead of John's making a sole application to the inappropriately titled Waste Land Board, three other members of his family (two brothers and a sister) also applied for the area. On 5 September 1858 they were duly granted a licence to lease the entire area, separated into four runs, for 14 years. Collectively this covered 143,500 hectares. Run 235 (33,200 hectares) was granted to John; Run 236 (48,600 hectares) went to Alexandrina; Allan got Run 237 (26,700 hectares); and Run 238 (35,000 hectares) went to Robertson. The four runs were bounded to a large extent by the Dunstan Mountains and by the Clutha River and, with Lake Hawea more or less forming its western boundary, the combined property extended from east of the Lindis Pass almost to Clyde, a distance of over 80 kilometres. They called it Morven Hills, after an ancestor, the Baronet of Morven. The McLeans had come a very long way from the tiny, storm-battered Isle of Coll.

It was left to John and Allan to make the four runs a going concern, a task of almost Herculean proportions. The two brothers, however, were undaunted. They had,

Through this valley, Big Jock McLean and his Maori guide, Huruhuru, came to the Lindis Pass.

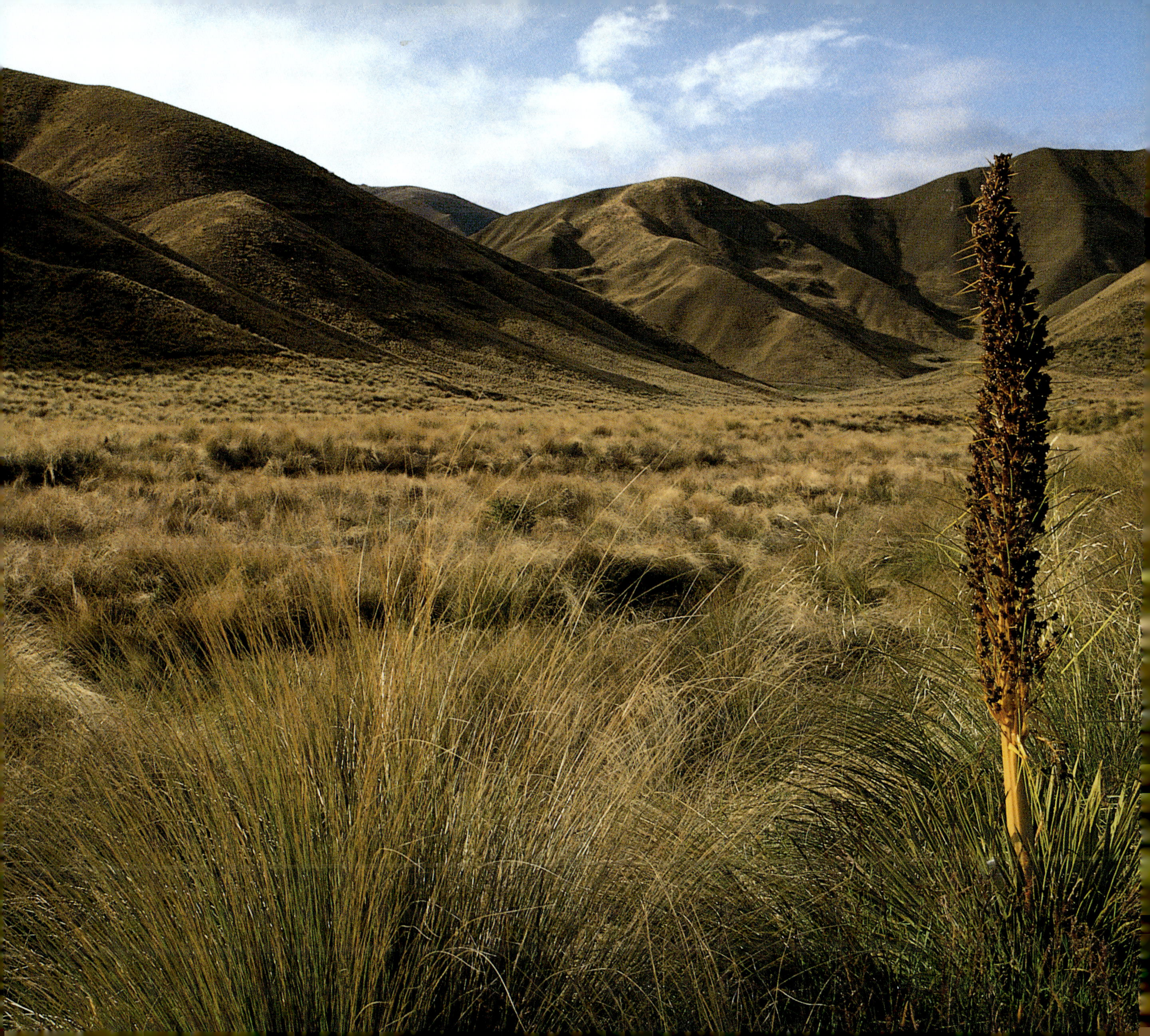

after all, seen the other side of the coin. By the mid-1860s, Morven Hills was a going concern: a homestead, stables, cookshop and workshop had been built on the Lindis River about 12 kilometres west of the pass of the same name. The huge, 34-stand woolshed was built later, in about 1876. The present-day Morven Hills headquarters were located here. When I visited, the old buildings still stood, strong and weathered.

They ran about 20,000 sheep here; mustering them over such an extensive area was a lengthy affair. Typically, most of the shepherds came from the highlands of Scotland. At one stage they had as many as 16 shepherds who could not speak English, conversing instead in their native Gaelic. One other thing: Big Jock would not hire a man who didn't smoke.

Morven Hills continued to prosper. In the early 1870s the flock had increased to 110,000. Convoys of up to five wagons, each pulled by a team of 12 or 14 bullocks, were used to transport the mighty wool clip up to and through the Lindis Pass to the port of Oamaru. The return trip, in excess of 330 kilometres, could take three weeks. It was at this time that rabbits, having crossed the Clutha from Earnscleugh station, gradually established themselves on Morven Hills. Soon they were everywhere. John McLean, far sighted as usual, could see no way of checking them; he knew the situation could only get worse. Some sources say the reason he put Morven Hills on the market in 1874 was the rabbits. The asking price, lock, stock and barrel, for the four runs was £128,000. This included 30,000 to 40,000 sheep, 200 head of cattle, 40 bullocks and 50 horses. It was purchased by Colonel Whitmore of Hawke's Bay.

By 1910, Morven Hills had had a succession of owners, and had been subdivided into a number of blocks. They ranged in size from 390 to 11,300 hectares but were all classified as small grazing runs. Many of the present-day runs in this area were once a part of the McLeans' empire, among them Bargour, Deep Creek, Ardgour, Lindis Peaks, Bendigo, Northburn, Cluden, Timburn and Hawea. The homestead block, including Forest Range station, was divided into six blocks in 1924.

Now, well over a hundred years after John McLean recognised the warning signs, there was still a rabbit problem in Central Otago. As many as 60 stations, including Morven Hills, were, in 1991, judged to be in a 'critical' state. Today's Morven Hills was 14,500 hectares in size; the whole run was contained within the boundaries of what was once Run 235. The Snow family had owned Morven Hills for 40 years, and Richard Snow, son of Max, was now the runholder.

Think of Big Jock McLean and his Maori guide, Huruhuru, the next time you drive through the Lindis Pass. Think about how McLean must have felt when he first saw the magnificent grazing country that lay beyond the mountains that turn gold in the evening sun. Think of a grand adventure.

On a brilliantly fine January morning, Merino sheep, strung out like lines of well-disciplined troops, gradually began to merge together into one big mob. They were climbing steadily towards the top end of a large block lying to the immediate east of the homestead on Morven Hills station. Above the sun-baked landscape, a 12-year-old Hughes 300C helicopter cast its darkly sinister shadow on the ground.

The pilot, Richard Snow, flashed me a reassuring smile and a split-second later we went into a long sideways sweep, losing altitude, the ground rushing to meet us. A few wethers sprinted out of a saucer-shaped hollow. We levelled out behind them at 70 knots, bucking the wind. The leading sheep suddenly stopped; its head whipped around and it spotted some other sheep. It was better to join up with them, to be a part of a mob, just one woolly backed animal standing shoulder to reassuring shoulder with others.

According to Richard, there were about 1600 sheep on this block, a high, mostly eroded place. Even from here — 100 metres above them — it was possible to not only sense

Top Merino rams on Morven Hills.

their apprehension but also to somehow feel it. We swooped in behind them fast. *Whump-whump-whump!* They jostled forward.

The sun, contained behind the lofty peaks of the northern end of the St Bathans Range, would soon top those rounded, grassy mountains. But at the moment the terrain was drab, lacking colour and definition, and it was difficult to pick out the sheep. It was that strange, indecisive period when dawn has passed but the day hasn't really started.

At this altitude it was, of course, cool and the sheep weren't reluctant to move. In the early morning they were up high on the rolling tops, making them easy to locate from the air. Later in the day they would have moved down to find cover from the heat. Like a dirty grey carpet the sheep rubbed shoulders. They began to converge at a gate Richard had opened earlier. There were no dogs to urge them on with shrill barking or, when master wasn't looking, a quick nipping of heels. There was no need: the helicopter had really stirred them up and it was like they knew what was expected of them. So when one sheep lunged through the gateway the rest followed without hesitation.

'Piece of cake,' was Richard's comment.

I wondered what an old-time musterer would have made of it all.

Some of the sheep leaped high off the ground once through the gateway. They might have been playful lambs. In fact they were wethers, raised for wool, mostly. On Morven Hills they could expect a useful lifespan of around seven years, then it was time for the chop. They would be flogged off as mutton or perhaps inadvertently labelled as 'New Zealand lamb' on the other side of the world.

Once they were all through the gateway, we went down. The landing skids settled on the ground with a sagging motion; they might have been air-cushioned,

Heli-mustering on Morven Hills.

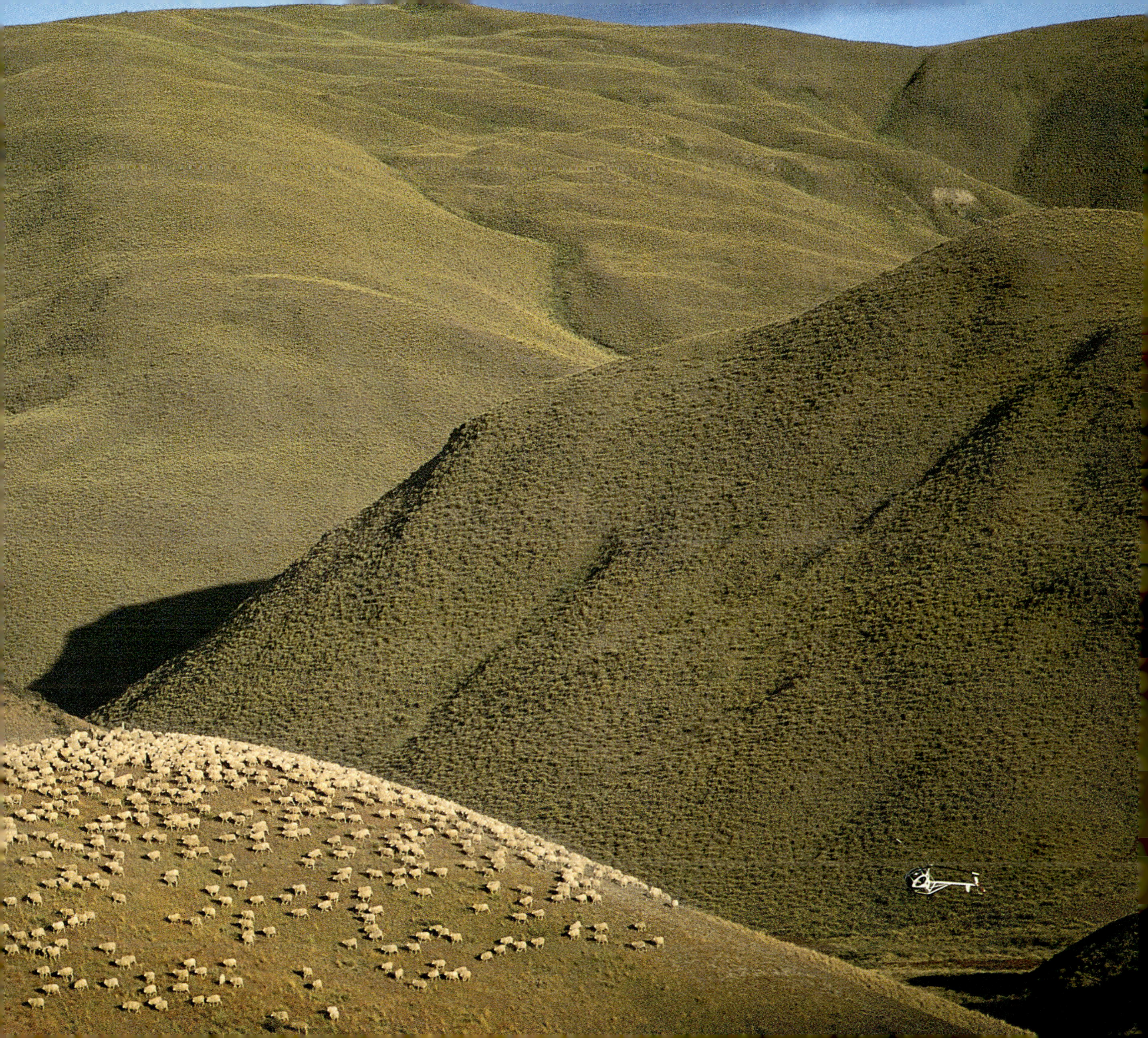

I thought.

Richard said, 'Back in a mo.'

Gate shut, he came back at the double.

It was 6.30 a.m. and it had, I realised, taken him just 15 minutes to muster the block. How long, I wondered, would it have taken them in the old days? Richard and I had lifted from the landing pad outside the hangar no more than 30 minutes ago. In that time a mustering team, using horses, would perhaps have only now reached the bottom gateway, the work still to be done. Perhaps they would have rolled a smoke, yarned a little, the head shepherd making sure that each man had his beat worked out. Then they would have split up: men, horses, dogs. Only their ghosts remained on Morven Hills.

Richard Snow looked pretty much at ease with himself. Why not? He was able to manage virtually all of the stock work on his own, and still have time to spend with his family. He could even help his handyman attend to numerous chores: fixing fences damaged by snow drifts or stock, gathering in the wood supply, attending to this and that in the big old woolshed on a rainy day. There was always something to do on a station.

Away to the west the sun suddenly hit the highest peaks, bathing them in a rosy flush. The Hughes reacted impressively to Richard's deft touch, the engine hammering away, a steady beat, rotor blades whipping through the air faster than sound. The helicopter is the most versatile airborne machine yet devised by man. Only rarely does it crash through engine malfunction: most accidents are caused by young, inexperienced pilots or by those, perhaps hunting deer, simply asking too much of the machines.

In this sprawling land of hills and mountains, a helicopter was worth a dozen top men, mounted on fine hacks, and any number of dogs. It was the sole reason Richard Snow could carry out so much work himself. Within a period of seven years it had become a vital part of life on Morven Hills.

We flashed over a low ridge and a big hare burst out of a clump of snow tussock. Now, with a short gesture, Richard indicated a hill face looming above us. The sun had just capped it; there were sheep up there, in the sun. Others, lower down, were already moving up to seek the warmth.

'Do that next,' Richard said.

Earlier, he had told me there were around 2000 on this particular block, and that, as with the block already mustered today, it was simply a case of shifting them to an adjacent block where there was more feed.

'Still not enough light for you yet, Phil?' He indicated the camera bag lodged securely between my feet.

I shook my head. 'Uh-uh, Richard. Give it, oh, thirty minutes or so. Should be perfect then.'

He nodded. 'Right-o.'

With that we touched down on a lonely knoll like an ungainly dragonfly. Richard killed the engine and slowly the rotor blades began to lose momentum. Silence gradually invaded the perspex canopy. A glance at the instrument panel told me we were at 2400 feet (730 metres), roughly 520 metres higher than the homestead but still considerably lower than the 2000-metre peaks dominating the eastern skyline. Below, a stream meandered through a narrow valley; higher it was a bottleneck. Some Hereford cattle were grazing near the stream, belly deep in tussock. A pair of harrier hawks were hunting, spread out but every so often merging together. Feathered mates of the open skies, with no natural enemies. It was a good life hunting rabbits or high-country mice on Morven Hills.

My mind returned to the first block Richard had mustered and I asked him how long it would have taken without a helicopter.

'Oh, about two hours, I guess.'

'And this one?' I gestured above us.

He looked up and dragged the back of his hand across his unshaven jaw.

'Bit longer, I'd say.' He paused. 'That's just to muster it, of course. You still had to get out here and back, remember that. I suppose it would have taken a full day in Dad's time to muster off both blocks.' He chuckled and tapped the instrument panel. 'This is the way to do it, you know. We'll be back home for breakfast.'

I turned my attention to the cattle: brown and white on a backdrop of faded tan. It was a real high-country scene. I wondered aloud how many cattle Richard ran.

'Around three hundred at the present time.'

'Sheep?'

'Hmm . . . let's say eighteen thousand Merinos and three hundred cross-bred sheep.'

'Cross-bred?'

'Border Leicester-Romney.'

'Those lambs with black faces . . . ?' I had observed them earlier.

'Right. We used a Suffolk ram over some of the ewes,' Richard explained; the black face is typical of the Suffolk breed. With a broad gesture, he went on. 'But this is really Merino country. They do incredibly well here.'

I followed the line taken by his hand and saw splendid, uncluttered country.

'And none better,' I said, meaning it.

Richard nodded, half turned in his seat, and smiled like a proud parent watching his child excel at sport.

'Yeah,' he said at some length. 'I think so, too.'

I couldn't help but wonder if he took his station for granted; he had, after all, been here all of his life.

An easy silence settled between us. Now, in the golden summertime, with the snow tussocks gleaming like ripe fields of wheat, the sky a cornflower blue, the sun moving ever so slowly down the hill face, it was nearly impossible to imagine winter out here. In 1991 they had the hardest winter in years in Central Otago and the Mackenzie Country. Not even the real old-timers could recall a winter like it.

'It was tough, all right. Creeks frozen up for months — one hoar frost after another. Lots of snow; it would've been several feet deep out here.' Richard smiled reflectively. 'We might not see another one quite like it,

Richard Snow.

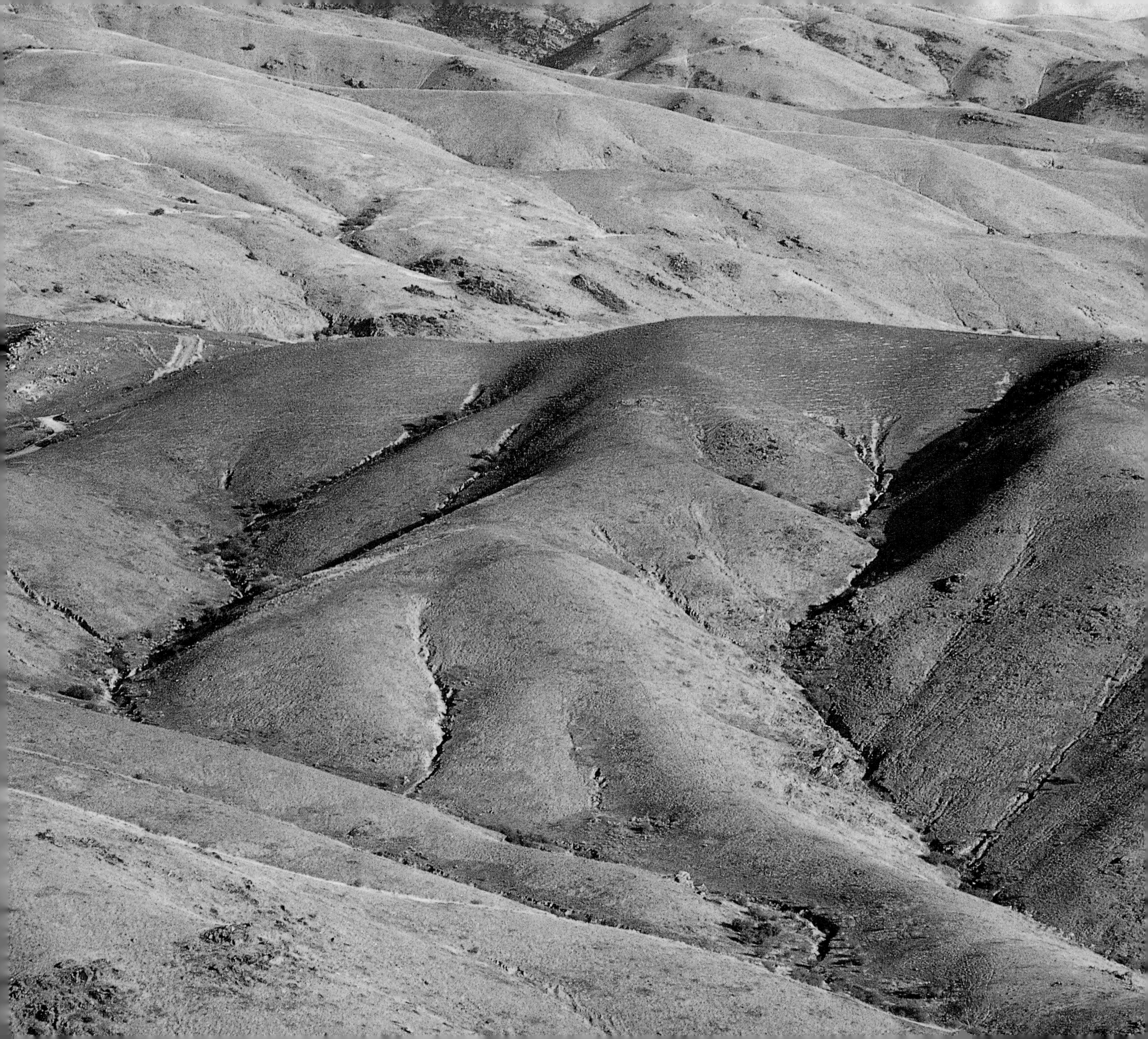

I guess.'

'You feed out, right?'

To my surprise, he shook his head.

'No, we don't. We spell five big blocks from September through to May and that sees them through. That block over there' — he stabbed a finger towards the lower slopes of the St Bathans Range, across the stream — 'runs right to the skyline.'

I thought of it all under snow. 'They make out okay?'

'Sure they do. It's surprising what Merinos can find to eat, you know; that's one of the main reasons they do so well here. Another thing, by the time the winter blocks are pretty much chewed out, well, there's growth poking through in the blocks we're grazing now. You spend a lot of time just shifting stock around in the winter. Have to. That's when a helicopter comes in so handy; you can really keep an eye on things.'

Not feeding out meant that Richard didn't have to concern himself with the hassles of haymaking and the upkeep of machinery — a considerable saving in both time and expense.

I changed the subject. 'You didn't say how many rabbits you were running out here as I recall.' All said with a perfectly straight face.

At the mention of the word 'rabbits' Richard's face altered dramatically, that good-natured expression departing as fast as rats quitting a rapidly sinking ship. One or two rabbits are okay; in fact, they are incredibly cute. They wouldn't hurt a fly, playing tag in the sun on a frosty morning. But when they number in their thousands it's something else entirely. Then they are enough to break a strong man's heart, to make him openly weep as they systematically destroy his livelihood.

'You should've seen it around here a year ago,' Richard said. 'These hill-faces were just moving. Hard to believe now.'

'What did you do?'

The ravages of rabbits are only too evident on Cluden.

'The Rabbit Board boys got really stuck in with 1080, mostly using fixed-wing aircraft. They dumped heaps of the stuff out here. That knocked them back all right. Since then, we've carried out regular follow-up operations with helicopters. Still rabbits here, of course, but you could say they're under control now.'

A short time ago who would have ever imagined rabbits being hounded from the skies? It was even more improbable than shooting deer from a helicopter would have seemed in the early 1960s.

'So what sort of numbers of rabbits have they taken off here?'

Richard knew I meant the helicopter hunters. 'Never taken count,' he admitted. He smiled wryly. 'Probably far too many to count if the truth were known. I believe they took about twenty-six thousand off Russell's place.'

Richard was referring to Forest Range, owned by Russell Emerson, the run more or less adjacent to Morven Hills. The two homesteads were situated very close together — by back-country standards. We had seen Russell Emerson heading east in his own helicopter earlier in the day, off to get his regular 50-hour check-up in Christchurch.

'Twenty-six thousand,' I mused. 'That's a helluva lot of shotgun cartridges, isn't it?' The master of the obvious, that's me.

Richard smiled coldly, a tight parting of the lips and nothing more. 'Lots of dead rabbits, too,' he said flatly.

'No real end to it, is there?'

He pulled a face. 'Not yet anyway.' He shook his head as though to rid it of particularly nasty thoughts.

Up on the hill face the sun had moved much lower; all the sheep appeared to be in the sun. Meantime, the Hereford cattle were still feeding, but the pair of hawks had moved elsewhere. I don't think they would approve of 1080 poison, do you?

'Ready?' Richard said.

I grinned and made a thumbs-up sign.

The lovely silence was suddenly no more and we lifted

off the ground, nosing forward, then started to climb. Up into a clear blue sky ruled by harrier hawks.

An hour or so later the hill block had been mustered as effectively as the one done earlier. Richard had made it all seem so easy, as though anyone who could fly a helicopter could be an airborne musterer. Not so. Apart from the required flying skills, you had to understand sheep, to know how they react. To give the job to just anyone with a licence to fly was courting disaster — an accident, as they say, just waiting to happen. One wrong approach and sheep would scatter hell west and crooked. In the truly dangerous terrain that high-ranging Merinos often inhabit, that same wrong approach could have fatal results. Sheep might plunge in their panic over steep cliffs.

I had taken enough photographs — the light had been excellent — and Richard picked me up from a vantage point.

'How would you like to see some rabbits?' he asked.

'Love to!'

'Show you a place where they are still pretty thick.'

I smiled. 'What's "pretty thick" by Morven Hills standards?'

'Thick.'

Should be interesting, I thought.

Rocky Hill block suited its name admirably. Much of it faced the sun and as we swooped across it there didn't appear to be too much to eat down there. It was your typical Central Otago landscape where rabbits have long been in charge: not quite barren, but getting too close for the comfort of runholders. Rainfall was about 850 millimetres a year, not enough to cause rabbits real problems, such as having the young drowned in the burrows. It looked like the type of place someone had in mind when they coined the phrase 'between a rock and a hard place'.

Like a raised hand momentarily blocking the sun the Hughes 300C cast a dark shadow across the hard, sub-blasted terrain. A giant winged predator was on the hunt. Look out! Suddenly I was seeing rabbits. There! There! And there! More rabbits than you could shake a stick at. More than you could count in a sweeping glance, ten times more. Maybe a hundred in sight at any one moment. They were all toey; they knew choppers meant death. They knew that to survive meant to run for cover as fast as possible, into burrows, under rocky ledges and even into patches of sweet briar.

We banked so that earth and sky merged. As we levelled out again — thank the Lord! — I saw continuous movement, a veritable plague of rabbits. There was something else down there, too. A feral cat, dark coated, unkempt, lean and hard muscled. The master predator was out hunting in ideal conditions, for here the larder was almost always full to capacity, the menu unchanging. Pound for pound the feral cat is arguably the most deadly killer of birds and small mammals we have in the back country. They take out hares with ease, the poor devils often dying of shock once a cat strikes. I loathe few animals, but I have no time for feral cats. Sensibly, the cat did not wait to be properly introduced.

'See it?' I hollered, gesturing furiously.

'Yeah,' replied Richard, low key.

Later, Richard told me that feral cats were common on Morven Hills, especially when there were ample rabbits. The helicopter shooters often saw them when they were after rabbits; only rarely did they see none at all. The helicopter shooters had no love of feral cats either and they went out of their way to nail them good and hard.

Until quite recently, feral pigs had also been common on Morven Hills. They had first appeared there about 15 years earlier. They had drifted in from the south, spreading gradually onto stations such as Bendigo, Timburn and Cluden, which, until then, had never had a wild pig problem. The last link in the chain had been Morven Hills, the most northerly extent of their newly found range. Unlike some runholders, Richard Snow did not panic when pigs moved onto his run and decided to become permanent residents. He was circumspect: it wasn't as though they were going to root up vast areas of

A helicopter view of mustering on Morven Hills.

grazing land. They preferred the brilliant red berries of sweet briar, with their high vitamin C content. They also grubbed up snow tussocks and Spaniard grass, feeding on the starchy roots, but that was no great loss, for sheep weren't equipped to do the same thing. Not with their rather tender noses, anyway. Of course the pigs dug up the odd rabbit burrow, cleaned up carcases, and took their opportunities where they found them. In fact, they were a handy source of fresh meat; getting a pig for a barbecue was a simple task.

Apparently there were a number of good seasons for breeding on Morven Hills, because the pigs started to multiply at a surprising rate — or so Richard thought. He was no longer seeing tight little mobs of four or five as he went about his daily business — now they were running to double figures. There was, he realised, only one answer: to control them before they exploded tenfold. Fortunately, controlling wild pigs on Morven Hills would never pose the problems it did in other parts of the province; on stations to the west, on the Pisa Range, for example, there was ample cover, large tracts of manuka scrub and dense areas of sweet briar.

So they started shooting pigs in earnest on Morven Hills: steady, systematic shooting that brought excellent results. The open country resembled a large fairground booth, the targets pigs, the rifles hard-hitting calibres. All up they may have taken 200 pigs off Morven Hills by the autumn of 1989. Maybe that many remained. At any rate, the carcases were not left to rot on the hills. They were air-lifted out to the homestead and later transported by road to a game recovery plant at Mossburn.

All went well until autumn changed to winter and another 30-odd pigs were shot on the station. When they arrived at Mossburn they tested positive for tuberculosis. The news rocked Richard Snow and runholders all over Central Otago, whether they farmed sheep, cattle or deer.

Open season was declared on pigs on Morven Hills; eventually they shot around 400 pigs on the run.

Now, in January 1991, as Richard Snow turned away from the Rocky Hill block, he was convinced that there wasn't a single pig anywhere on the run. Tomorrow and next week things might be different for, as Richard well knew, they would move in again. It was inevitable.

There is an interesting footnote to this short tale of wild pigs on Morven Hills. During the previous winter Richard had started to feel out of sorts, far from his usual energetic self. He became aware of a large, rather tender lump under one of his arms. The feeling persisted, and the lump grew in size. A doctor in Wanaka — although openly sceptical at first — confirmed Richard's worst fears. He had somehow contracted TB, possibly through a cut on his hand that had not healed.

It was, Richard learnt, only the third case of TB recorded in that part of the country. The other two instances were judged to be possum related, the men, of course, being trappers. Richard was put on a course of drugs; he could expect to feel very tired. He was unable to pass the regular medical checkup that all pilots are subjected to; unless he responded favourably to the treatment, there was a strong possibility he would lose his licence for a whole year. That would leave him in deep, deep trouble.

Initially his pilot's licence was revoked for a month, to give his body time to get used to the drugs. At the end of the month his case would be looked at again. If he did not pass then, Richard Snow would be looking for additional help on Morven Hills. However, he did respond very well to medical treatment and, after four nerve-wracking weeks, he was judged fit to fly.

Today, Richard was fit and tanned; he looked good. Apart from feeling tired at times, he believed he had the TB licked. I asked him whether he thought the pigs had caused it.

He chewed that question over. 'Yes, in a way I do blame pigs. I mean, wherever you find them you'll find the worst cases of TB, right?'

I nodded in agreement. 'That could apply to possums, too.'

'Sure it can,' he agreed. 'There's also TB in deer, cats, ferrets, and God only knows what else.' He lifted his shoulders in a resigned gesture. 'But really I don't know . . .'

'Neither do MAF,' I pointed out.

Amidst all the confusion, one thing was certain: it concerned Richard Snow. Should feral pigs ever infiltrate Morven Hills again — and they were present on adjoining runs — there was no way they would be given an opportunity to establish themselves.

Well away from Rocky Hill block, Richard Snow again touched the chopper down. We came to rest in a lonely spot where a single stone cottage stood.

'Thought you'd like to see this,' Richard said.

I nodded. 'Polsons hut.'

Richard looked surprised. 'How did you know it was called that?'

I grinned at him as we moved towards it.

Located southeast of the homestead on Morven Hills, and close to the boundary with Geordie Hill station, Polsons hut was in remarkably fine condition. It was a one-roomed dwelling with a corrugated-iron roof, built in the 1860s as a shepherd's or boundary rider's accommodation. In 1869 the hut was home to John Polson, his wife and their young son. Polson's job was a typical one on the big runs of the era: to keep a watch on both sheep and fences. For a fit young Scot it was not a demanding life and most likely he revelled in his lonely occupation.

It was an entirely different proposition for Mrs Polson. Her husband was often away from dawn till dark. Visitors were few at the stone hut, and only rarely did she see other women. Mrs Polson did the cooking on a wood- and coal-burning stove. As autumn gave way to winter it was essential to keep the fire going all night; the hut, lacking the insulation of a ceiling, was brutally cold otherwise.

THEY CALLED IT MORVEN HILLS • 71

The winter of 1869 was a hard one on Morven Hills. Mrs Polson was pregnant and the stone hut — several slow hours by wagon from the homestead — was no place for a woman soon to give birth. But the Polsons were of hardy stock; they thought they could cope. Events, however, would prove otherwise, a story best retold by the Rev. Ian Polson, their grandson:

Polson's hut was still in remarkably good condition. The walls were still straight and the timber, in the dry atmosphere of around 600 metres, was near perfect. The grave was still there, too, near a big willow that had every reason to weep.

> Some weeks before my grandmother was due to give birth she was chased by a drunken man and given a terrible fright. In running away from him, she brought on labour prematurely and her twins were born not only without the last-minute preparations but also in the midst of a severe winter with a heavy fall of snow round the hut. No doctor, nurse or neighbour could be called and Grandfather Polson took the two babes on his knees and kept them warm by the fire, while Grandma attended to herself as best she could. But the cold and the prematurity of the birth plus the spartan conditions were too much for the twins and first one died and then the other.
>
> The snow was too deep for the police to come from Cromwell to examine them and indeed it was scarcely possible to bury them for the ground was frozen hard and deep. After their death, their little bodies froze in the hut. They were eventually buried a quarter of a mile from the hut and a willow, either planted to commemorate the spot or there already, still grows robustly over the barely legible tombstone.

Polsons hut: a lonely place for a shepherd and his young wife.

8

THE LEGEND IN THE DEEP SOUTH

It appears that Glenaray's first owner was David Hood — the run, stated as being 'between Clutha and Nokomai', was licensed to him for 14 years from 1860. Little is known about Hood; his connection with the property was brief. In 1861 John Gow purchased the run and it became known as Gows. He stocked it with cattle, which did well, topping the Dunedin sales on a number of occasions.

When Gow died in 1873, the lease had all but expired. His trustees obtained a new lease for 10 years, but the run was sold the following year to David McKellar who relinquished his rights to it to a cousin, also named David McKellar. Almost certainly it was the new owner who named the run 'Glenaray'.

In 1875 a combination of rabbits, swarming like locusts over the land, and a devastating winter, during which most of his stock was lost, eventually forced McKellar off the land. Following his departure, Glenaray's story was one of a succession of owners, either banks or private individuals, the latter more than likely land speculators out for fast profit.

In 1898 things changed dramatically on Glenaray. The run was purchased by George Pinckney and his brothers-in-law, Bernard and Jack Tripp, for £12,000. At this time Glenaray consisted of 1200 hectares of freehold land, about 24,500 hectares of leasehold land, and roughly 16,000 hectares of wild native bush, along with 13,000 cross-bred sheep. The Pinckney family's 95-year association with Southland's largest run had started.

George Pinckney was born in Wiltshire, England, and in 1885, at the age of 22, he arrived in New Zealand. Young George's ambition was clear: he wanted to become a successful sheep farmer. In 1893 he married Edith Tripp, of Orari Gorge station, in South Canterbury; later, they purchased a farm at Geraldine.

Now, with 35-year-old George Pinckney the driving force in the partnership, Glenaray prospered as never before. It also increased dramatically in size: it was George's policy, whenever possible, to buy small farms lower in the valley and so increase his safe winter country for stock. Eventually, then, Glenaray had swelled to around 53,500 hectares.

In 1921, a cousin of George's, H. W. (Bill) Pinckney, came out from England to learn all about high-country farming. What better place than Glenaray? Bill was just 23 years old and he had no intention of remaining for long in the colony. The trouble was, he met and fell in love with Kathleen, one of George and Edith's 11 children. So much for returning home then!

When both George and Edith Pinckney died in 1948, Bill, now owning a 10 per cent share in the station, took control of Glenaray. By this time his two sons, Peter and George, were strapping six-footers with a zest for life. In the aftermath of the deaths of George Pinckney and J. M. H. Tripp, the Pinckney family acquired total ownership of Glenaray. The run then carried 30,932 sheep, 980 cattle and 80 horses.

Bill Pinckney died following a short illness in 1973. By that time he had, of course, handed over responsibility of Glenaray to his two sons. Peter handled the day-to-day running of the station and George looked after the business side of things. They were a good team. While Peter would get married (to Ann Lowry), George remained a single man. Peter and Ann would have three children: David, Thomas and Anna.

On 14 May 1982, Peter and Ann set off for Queenstown in the station's newest acquisition, a Bell Jet Ranger helicopter; the machine was piloted by a neighbour, Scotty Williamson. Some say they went to Queenstown to service the machine, others that they had some work to attend to on a holiday home they owned there. Possibly it was a combination of both. On the return trip they ran into bad weather and were unable to land at the station. They tried to put down at Riverside but, in the attempt,

Above Waikaia Falls on Glenaray station. This land is used for only three or four months of the year because of heavy snow.

crashed. There were no survivors.

Recalling that time, George Pinckney told me that, having known Peter and Ann's teenage children for so long, he felt responsible for them. He moved into their home and lived with them.

'We just took it from there,' George said. A long, reflective pause followed those words and, with the deeply ingrained hurt rising to the surface, he added with a heavy sigh, 'That's the way life goes, I suppose.'

When he finally retired to Queenstown in 1991, George, in his early sixties, had spent almost all of his life on Glenaray.

Through fissure-like gaps in the early morning mist I could see a blanketed horse standing motionless as a statue on the river flats. Then, suddenly, the horse had vanished, gobbled up by the mist, and there were deer in view. The deer appeared toy-like; the Hughes 500C was always climbing. Below, to the left, a dozen or so paradise ducks, strung out in single file, marked the course of the Waikaia as it snaked across cultivated land, then, suddenly, was lost from view where it broke free of the beech forest.

Gradually the blanket of mist lifted, revealing the clear-cut path of the river as it continued its journey to link up with the Mataura River, some five kilometres northeast of Riversdale. Still we climbed, the land starting to change form as the beech forest gradually gave way to open country. This was the start of an immense plateau. To the west were the craggy, snow-topped peaks of the Garvie Mountains, to the east, the more rounded tops of the Umbrella Mountains, while directly ahead, on the sun-flecked skyline that marked the end of the plateau and the run's northernmost boundary, was the Old Man Range.

The Hughes 500C headed north into a gusty wind. In a state of constant wonder, I saw grass as far as the eye could see. Amidst it were tarns, a wide expanse of tundra-like ground called Boggy Spur. There were outcrops of rock, some quite spectacular, deep gullies with names such as Welshmans Creek, Gorge Creek and Burns Creek, each feeding the turbulent Waikaia River. All the land I could see belonged to one station: Glenaray, the legend in the deep south.

My headphone suddenly crackled with a burst of static and then a voice said, 'They used all this for summer grazing only — three, maybe four months of the year. Can't do anything else with it the rest of the year. Far too much snow.' The matter-of-fact words came from the middle-aged, greying pilot Graham Allan.

Again the river was below us: the west branch of the Waikaia. It was contained in a narrow valley. Graham reduced speed and the helicopter went into a gradual descent. Ahead, on the true left of the river, smoke gushed from the chimney of Jack Mack's hut. The sun was playing on the high peaks at the head of the valley as Graham prepared to land. Out from the hut, on the flats, horses were feeding on a big bale of hay; some wore night covers, some did not. Either way they took no interest in the helicopter's approach; Glenaray horses know all about helicopters. Horsemen and dogs were angling up the steep, tussock-clad slope directly behind the hut. We went into a long sweep, banked, and came in over the massive rock next to the hut. A dead horse, chilled by an overnight frost and missing a few choice chunks, was in residence on top of it. We landed with scarcely a bump about a hundred metres from the hut.

I unhooked my safety belt, took off the headphones, and clambered out of the machine. A couple of horses — big, husky animals — broke off their feeding to give me a studied appraisal. Finding the subject matter of no interest whatsoever, they sensibly resumed scoffing.

'Pick you up in, say, forty minutes,' Graham said. 'Okay?'

'No worries.'

'Go on up to the hut — Jake'll fix you a brew, no doubt.'

At this point a clean-cut, able-looking type joined us,

Fall muster on Glenaray station.

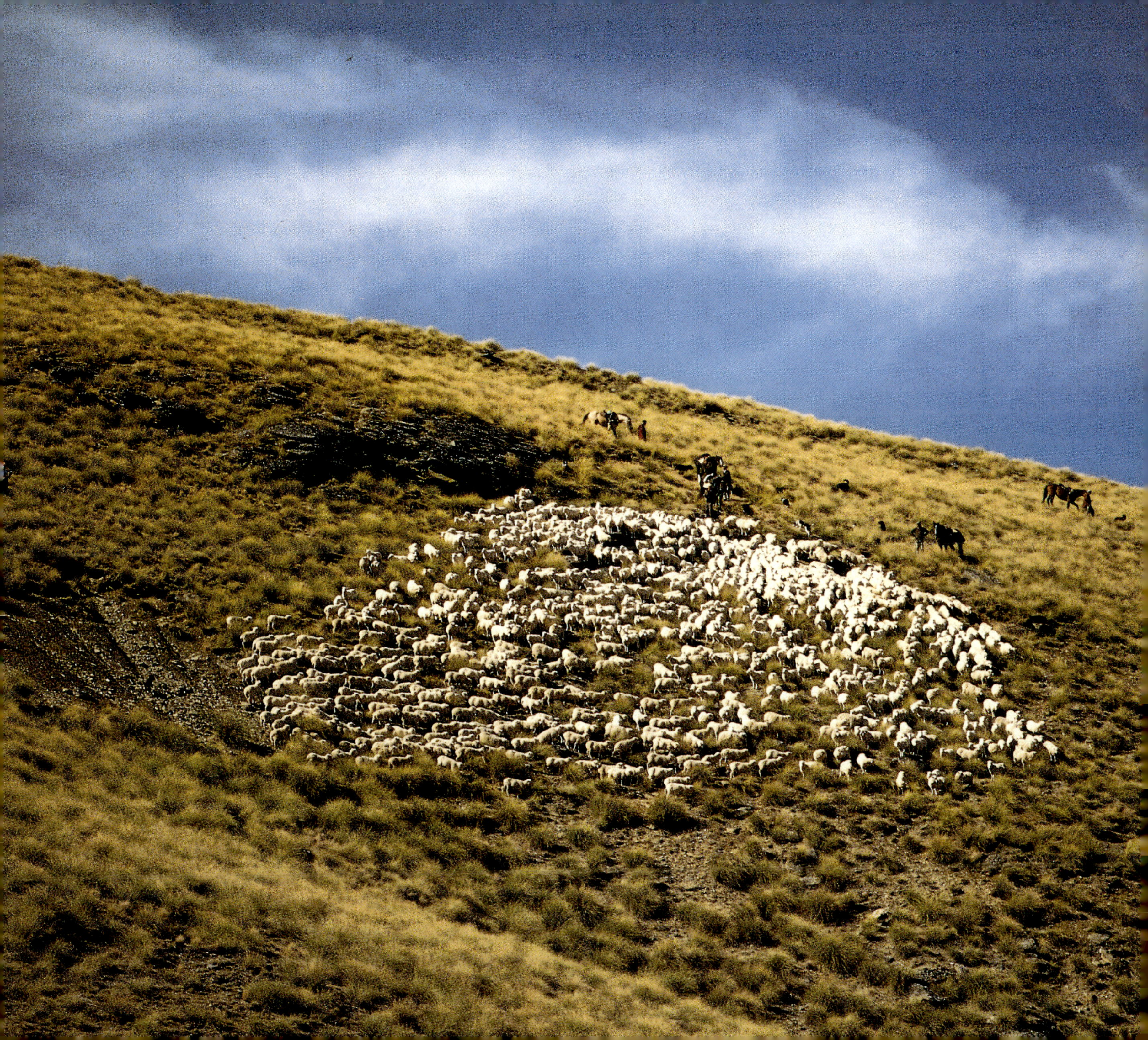

dressed for a day on the hill in rugged outdoor gear, no frills. This was Mike O'Donohue, head shepherd, a position he had held for a year. The fall muster was into its third day and the plan was that Graham would drop Mike off close to his beat. Mike was obviously doing it the hard way today — on shanks's pony.

I tramped to the hut. Crates of beer were stacked outside it; some were empty, some not. Given time every single bottle would be a dead injun. Naturally, the rum supply would be kept inside. One thing for sure: the boys would go on strike if they didn't have that for a potent shot or three of an evening. Inside the hut a short, stocky type was busy at work: the breakfast dishes were washed up and put away, a roast was sizzling in the oven and Jake Stark was making everything ship-shape. It was good to see; there's nothing worse than slackness in a high-country camp.

'Up to a brew?'

'Great!'

A big tin mug, suitable for any backblocks lad, was thrust into my hand.

'Sugar and milk's over there. Help yourself.'

'Thanks.'

It turned out this was Jake's nineteenth fall muster in a row on Glenaray. Sometimes he worked as a musterer, but usually he had the vital job of packer/cook.

Mug in hand, I looked out through the window, across the flats, watching the horses either feeding or mooching about. They were not being used today; their time would undoubtedly come.

'Fantastic country!' I enthused.

'Yeah, isn't it,' Jake agreed. He sighed heavily. 'Doesn't last long enough . . .' He meant the fall muster.

There were dog kennels out there, too. They were in sets of six, so that each shepherd kept his dogs separate from the others'; all up there was room for 42 dogs. Jake told me one of the shepherds kept his dogs out back, under Dead Horse Rock, the rock I'd seen on the way in. They fed the dogs on horsemeat out here — they simply

brought in an old nag and killed it. The poor horse was probably looking forward to the muster, too. There was one black dog, barking in frustration at being left behind. It'd be a proper bastard, I mused, if they all barked like that at once.

Leaving Jake to his chores, I went outside. The horses were still working away at the hay and the sunlight was gradually working its way down the mountain face across the valley. Right then, with the day before me, I wouldn't have changed places with anyone in the world.

Directly behind the hut were the remnants of a much older dwelling: a one-roomed affair, typically low slung, made of rock. This was probably the original Jack Mack's hut. It seemed Jack Mack was a shepherd here way back. At any rate, this was a boundary keeper's or boundary rider's camp, not needed after 1923. The more modern Jack Mack's hut went back a fair way, too. An extra room had been added a few years back, so that it was now L-shaped. Before then it would have been terribly cramped on a fall muster.

A sudden *whump-whump-whump!* indicated that

A little after sunrise at Jack Macks hut.

Graham was returning to pick me up. During the course of the day he would drop me off at three different locations, the better to see precisely what was going on. Once aloft, we followed Jack Mack's Creek to its source. Up in its basin-like heads two horsemen and their dogs were angling across a snow and tussock face. It was a compelling scene, the type of thing that would remain in my memory, as sharply etched as the peaks of the Garvie Mountains.

We swept past assistant stock manager Oliver Dickson and shepherd Brian Sparrow at 60 knots, low, whipping up the snow, and came to rest above Waikaia Falls, on the east branch. According to Graham, this was the Falls block.

'The boys'll be here soon,' Graham said. 'Won't be long.'

With that, he was off once more, lifting into the sky as effortlessly as an eagle. I figured he was about to check over the ground that the two boys would muster, so that he could tell them where the wethers were. It would save them heaps of time.

Only a short time after Oliver and Brian had joined me, Graham was back. They wasted very little time in conversation before Graham turned to me, saying, 'Leave you here for a while, okay?' It wasn't really a question.

So there I was, on my lonesome up above Waikaia Falls, in a high, magnificent, windswept place where they only ran stock three to four months of the year. I let my eyes wander, feeling a little awed, and certainly insignificant. It was easy to believe that unseen gods resided here in isolated splendour.

It was still only the third week of March, I mused; the snow had come early this year. Fortunately it wasn't deep enough to cause stock losses, being largely confined to the higher places. Only a little south of here, still in the plateau country, it petered out altogether. Snow, of course, was always a problem on the fall muster. Back in the days when the muster started later and lasted a full month, often extending into May, well, anything was

Time for the wethers to ford the river.

78 • STATION COUNTRY

likely to happen. The muster used to take so long because they had run ewes as well as wethers, so there were more sheep to muster. Also, they took the sheep right into the station headquarters, whereas now they were left about half way in, behind fences, in lower country. About a month later they were picked up and the final leg was undertaken. The fact that they now used a helicopter had also speeded things up greatly. The romance of the fall muster, however, of men and horses and brave-hearted dogs, was still there.

The fall muster of 1933 on Glenaray station had more than its share of problems. The mustering team found themselves at Blue Lake hut, isolated because of snow — 10 days of it at arguably the most miserable location on the entire run. The head shepherd, Alf Stivens, reckoned the men just about wore the face off the pack of cards. Jack Sinclair was one of the musterers in 1933. His wife later wrote:

> In 1933 the musterers started the fall muster from Jack Macks on 8 April and landed the 18,000, the first mob, on the station on 18 April. They then went out to Blue Lake. Snow started when they were on the top of the Titans and by the time they reached the hut it was very heavy, and snowed on and off for seven days, and was four feet deep around the hut. There were another 17,000 to be mustered but not a sheep to be seen, no mutton, no bread and no flour. The men had to make for home.
>
> The snow was too deep to go by the Titans so Alf Stivens decided that they would go by Bush Hut and Christies. After two days at the station Alf took most of the musterers to the Junction hut, Jack Barr, Bill and Jack Sinclair going to the Titan. The first day they made a track in the snow, taking turns in going in the lead with all the dogs behind them. They reached Patersons Spur and collected 600 sheep in the bush. It took six hours to get them back to Titan hut, usually a two-hour walk.
>
> On the third day they left Jack Barr to cook a meal. Bill Pinckney and Jack Sinclair headed over Misery for Gows Lake Falls. Nothing to be seen but snow, the two men slid under the falls, crossed Gows Creek and on to Mount Cameron. They thought they would meet Alf and the other men. It started to blow a howling nor'wester and with no sign of the other men they realised they would have to go for their lives to get over Gows Creek, which was rising quickly when they reached it. They followed downstream to where it divided into three. They took a running jump and got over the first two streams but the third was too wide, so they took off their clothes and threw them over to the far side. Jack Sinclair lay down with his walking stick, which Bill held on to for support against the current and reached the other side and then held the stick out to Jack, who thought it was best to jump, but landed in the current and bashed his hip on a sharp rock. Bill caught him and pulled him out.

Oliver Dickson and Brian Sparrow draw rein on the plateau above Waikaia Falls.

Now, so many years later, I started to think about the red deer that were out here once in force. Oh, to have seen it then. Had I covered the same ground in the early 1970s as I had today — lifting off from the station headquarters and being dropped off in the east branch of the Waikaia — I would have seen hundreds of deer. Today we hadn't seen a single one. Graham had said that he normally saw a few, but that was back towards the homestead, where there was ample cover.

The Waikaia red-deer herd was established in the early part of the century; the original stock most likely drifted into the Waikaia catchment from the Pomahaka River country, in the southern reaches of the Old Man Range. The Otago Acclimatisation Society had made two liberations of red deer in the Pomahaka, in 1901 and 1903. Another liberation was made on Argyle station around 1920. Largely undisturbed in the back country, the deer multiplied accordingly.

I talked with George Pinckney about deer on Glenaray and he told me that, while the Waikaia deer were not known for trophy heads, they were of good body weight.

'They used to come down on the swede crops in the winter and we'd go out with the men and shoot them with spotlights. I can recall large numbers of deer in the days when I was mustering; every day we'd see deer. In February, when we were mustering cattle on the tops, we'd see large mobs of stags in hard velvet. It wasn't out of the ordinary to see sixty in a single mob. Yes, Glenaray was one of the great places in the South Island for seeing red deer in those days.'

Barney Milne had worked on Glenaray for many a year and done his share of fall musters, too. Barney was out there in 1974, all right, and so were the deer. At the end of the muster they had seen over a thousand deer, spread over an area of 32,500 hectares. And that would have been only a small percentage of the deer that ranged Glenaray at the time. Barney went along on the next muster too; the party counted just 28 deer, but they saw eight helicopters, all there illegally.

The Pinckneys realised that at this rate there would soon be no deer left on the run. For some time they had been toying around with the idea of deer farming — just about every other runholder was doing it. They formed a working relationship with Wanaka-based Tim Wallace of Alpine Helicopters: Wallace's men captured the deer, some of which were taken to a four-hectare block on the station and the rest (Wallace's share) retained by his men. Today, more than 2000 red deer were behind high wire on Glenaray.

My pleasant reverie of deer was rudely shattered by the awful clatter of the fast-approaching helicopter.

High above Waikaia Falls — one of those magical spots almost no one knows about — there was a spectacular view to the northwest.

'There's Mount Aspiring,' Graham said. 'See it?' I raised a thumb. 'And there's Mount Cook, right on the skyline.'

Sure enough, the tallest mountain in the country was clear cut on the distant skyline.

We headed more or less south, staying on the true left of the west branch. This was the Weaner block. There! A horseman jogging through deep tussock, leading a saddled horse. It was Ray Christie, looking after Phil Flanagan's horse as his mate worked a steep hillside on foot. Ahead of Ray and his dogs, in sight one moment, lost the next, was a mob of spooky sheep. They'd been out here for a couple of months, undisturbed.

'Put you with Ray for a short time,' Graham said. 'He's a good mate of mine.'

We landed. Graham made the introductions and said he'd pick me up at a nearby outcrop of rock pretty soon. Ray and I yarned for a few minutes, then he was off after the wethers, which were getting away from him. I watched him ride away, his gelding striding with purpose through deep snow tussock. Ray Christie was a big, solid man and it would be no easy task carrying the likes of him all day.

They ran 20 brood mares, 25 hacks/packhorses, eight or 10 two-year-olds, and one draught stallion on Glenaray.

The idea was to produce an animal heavy enough to stand up to the rigorous nature of the country, and to achieve that they crossed a draught with a thoroughbred. The draught horse side was obviously here for size, power and bigness of bone, and the thoroughbred side for agility and endurance.

Glenaray horses were eagerly sought after. The young animals were broken in on the station when they were three years old, and the men did the job. Nothing was left to chance, however; they called on Gore-based Murray Jones to see that it was done right. Jones, a farrier by trade, was Master of the Eastern Southland Hunt and an expert in his field.

Until Graham picked me up, I stood on a ragged outcrop of rock and watched Ray working the sheep across a rather eroded hill face. His raised voice drifted back at times, as did the shrill barking of dogs. He and Phil Flanagan (wherever he was) were naturally part of a larger pattern: the other musterers, either alone or in pairs, were all pushing whatever sheep they had found in the same general direction. Later, they would all meet at a prearranged spot on the true left of the west branch.

By early afternoon I was ready for my lunch. I was sitting on a grassy bench on the true right of the west branch of the Waikaia River. It was lovely there in the sun, warm enough to doze off. Across the river I could see the tail end of the Weaner Block, where the team had arranged to meet. Munching on a cheese-and-Marmite sandwich, I gazed across the river to the tussock hill face dotted with clumps of Spaniard grass in full flower. Above the ridge the sky was azure, like a tropical sea. I savoured the utter, breathless silence of it all.

As I sipped my tea I heard a distant bark. I scanned for movement, but there was nothing. Then the unmistakable sound of the helicopter. It passed overhead, low, and it was gone. Silence. They didn't just use a helicopter for the fall muster. Graham Allan, in fact, worked full time for Glenaray and Argyle stations. He had been flying the same helicopter without mishap for 10 years; it was owned

George Pinckney.

jointly by both stations. Flying time over a year came to around 300 hours, with roughly 80 per cent spent on Glenaray.

Take a good look around Jack Mack's and it becomes apparent there isn't a single tree in sight. So how on earth did Jack Mack heat his lonely stone hut? He did it in the same way as the early goldminers on Glenaray, with peat. At Jack Mack's hut the peat was cut in November and left to dry. The man who had been given this rather tedious task would then saddle up and ride over to Blue Lake hut, where he would repeat the process. In the new year a party would ride out from base and stack the dried peat under cover, ready for the fall muster. The advent of the helicopter meant that peat as a means of heating and cooking became a thing of the past. Coal ranges were installed in the huts and fuel flown in. In time, hay for the horses came in that way, too.

The helicopter proved invaluable once in the late 1980s when, nearing winter, a mob of 70 heifers somehow escaped their block and, in a mood to wander, eventually gained the top of the 1500-metre Old Man Range, almost directly above Roxburgh. Head shepherd Skip Johnston was told about it, but it was too late. It snowed and the heifers were trapped. There was no way horsemen and dogs could even get up there, let alone drive the cattle to safety.

Skip was never short of a good idea. He decided to drive the cattle to a flat alongside a creek, some 200 metres below their present location. They could feed them in the meantime using the chopper. So Graham flew Skip, with his dogs on the back seat, out to the cattle.

With difficulty, for it is awkward and incredibly tiring working in deep snow, Skip forced the cattle to move. Often they fell, stumbled or rolled, but at last they reached clear ground. Weakened by their ordeal, they drank greedily at the creek and dealt with a big bale of hay in no time. For the next three weeks, every third day, Graham flew hay out to the cattle.

Then there was a real break in the weather; the snow-line retreated, but for how long? Something had to be done about the cattle: they couldn't remain there all winter long. Shaun Gibson and Kevin Reid, driving a bulldozer, managed to reach the ridge above the flat, and then, using a small blade, cut a narrow track down to the flat. The bulldozer started its return trip, uphill, to the ridge. Skip's dogs went to work, but it required very little prompting to get the cattle moving. The young ladies, in fine fettle, trotted eagerly in the wake of the bulldozer and eventually were returned to lower grazing country.

The vision is splendid: Ray Christie on his beat.

THE LEGEND IN THE DEEP SOUTH • 83

Fall Muster

It is the Autumn muster
The weather's reasonably fair,
The breeze is soft and gentle
But the sky is not too clear.

Seven men rode out this morning
Dressed in all their gear
With horses, dogs, and whistles
Sounding in the morning air.

One more followed later
With the pack-team all in tow;
Another took the dog tucker;
All heading towards the snow.

For twenty days they've gone —
Seventeen if fine —
Leaving only three young men
And gardener Norm behind.

So all is quiet on the station front
And slowly pass the days
Till homeward bound the musterers come
With all their noisy ways.

Back to the Landrovers, utes and Rodeos,
Loud voices, boots and noise.
The station will hum with life again
When back home come the boys.

They'll talk of all the miles they've walked,
Of all the things they've seen,
Of icy creeks and snow-topped peaks
And where they haven't been.

They'll talk of other musters
When the camera team came out,
Of people, dogs and horses.
That's what it's all about.

Early starts, hard work and cold,
Comradeship and fun,
But soon it will be over,
The Autumn muster done.

Glenda Wills
Station cook, Glenaray, 1984-92

Suddenly there was movement on the ridge across the river. Voices carried clearly on the wind. Sheep spilled over the skyline, breaking like an incoming tide. They were as flighty as spooked deer. Gradually the men, on foot, headed them down towards the river. At this point the west branch was narrow and rock bound, falling quickly, more of a good-sized creek than a river.

'Get behind!'

'Ho! Ho! Ho!'

The piercing sound of a shepherd's whistle. Dogs barking. Sheep bawling.

'By the Jesus I'll fix you smartly!'

Before long the wethers arrived at the water's edge. They didn't want to cross it, that was obvious. Wet wool weighs heavily and is slow to dry. But they had no option; the dogs, snapping at their heels, saw to that.

This was a great back-country scene: sheep crossing the river, some, with admirable agility, leaping from rock to rock; dogs pausing to drink; men mixing together, some squatting down on their haunches, reins looped around tanned forearms. Time enough to roll a smoke if you indulged, to chew on a blade of grass if you didn't.

At last the wethers were across the river and up on a wide bench, where the grass was deep and the footing soft and springy. The men left the sheep there. Tomorrow's muster would begin at this point, and these sheep, plus whatever else was ranging this side of the river, would be pushed southwards. Off through the deep tussock went the mustering team in single file, horses very nearly nose to tail. The big, lovely horses, bred for the country, were heading home to a rub-down, a good feed and a night blanket. No wonder there was a spring in their steps.

The musterers topped a spur above me, paused, and then went on. Home was maybe an hour's ride away. They were joined by a late arrival, Andy Holden mounted on Jim, his gelding. Slowly Andy worked his small mob down towards the river. They reckoned Andy was a hard case, an East Coast boy a long way from home.

Presently, Graham did the right thing and proved he

David Pinckney.

hadn't forgotten about me. Later, we picked up head shepherd Mike and transported him back to Jack Mack's. It was mid-afternoon now, with just a hint of coolness in the air. There would be a frost overnight. All of the men were back at the hut. Some were attending to their horses or dogs, others were relaxing with a brew in the hut — Jake's roast mutton would go down well after a rum or two. It was nice to knock off early. Still, they'd put in a big one yesterday, not arriving back until after dark, about 7.30 p.m. Tomorrow would be another early start, up before the pipits left their tussock beds.

9

MACKENZIE BASIN

There are few places in this country that grip me as easily as the Mackenzie Basin. It is a high, harsh land, a huge and treeless basin hemmed in by brutally formed mountains that for most of the year are capped with snow. I never tire of driving through the Mackenzie Basin; I expect I never shall. All told, there are 42 properties classified as high-country runs in the Mackenzie Basin. One of them is Sawdon, between Tekapo and Burke Pass.

It was a fine morning in late autumn as I drove across the Mackenzie Basin towards Tekapo. The sky appeared limitless; it was as clear as a mountain stream spilling over smooth rocks. The country reminded me of the heart of Australia in a terribly dry time.

There were still rabbits on Sawdon, however, living on memories of past feeds. About one-third of this run, owned by Rob and Anne Allen, had been devastated by rabbits to the extent that they could not run stock there anymore. Throughout the Mackenzie Basin, large tracts of heavily damaged land were now considered valueless; it was believed the worst affected stations would, during 1992, see a reduction in value of up to 60 per cent, a marked contrast to increases of up to 50 per cent in farmland east of Burke Pass.

At Tekapo, I took a short coffee break and checked my road atlas. Yes, the way to Glenmore and Godley Peaks was just out of town. I put State Highway 8 behind me and followed an unsealed road that more or less followed Lake Tekapo's western side. The country was marginally better than what Sawdon had to offer, but it was still brown and rocky, the grasslands rolling away to distant mountains, with hardy Merinos making do. There were badly sagging rabbit-proof fences along here; some of them had been there since the 1930s. I pressed on, radial tyres not too happy in the loose metal.

Hereford cattle on Glen Rock station, Burke Pass.

I suddenly caught sight of a large fenced area to my left. It was on Mount St John station, which the Army used; cowboys and Indians in the Mackenzie high country. A sign told me this was DSIR land. One of the research boys was standing out in the tussock, taking a reading of some sort, while gazing away to the west like a Swanndri-clad Moses looking for the promised land.

Above the tawny landscape a sun-blurred harrier hawk moved in leisurely flight. Perhaps it was simply taking advantage of the thermal currents; perhaps it was scavenging. Most likely it was ready for whatever turned up, alive or dead. The Mackenzie Basin was ideal country for small predators: cats, ferrets, stoats and weasels.

In 1990 two MAF scientists, John Robertshaw and Don Robson, studied cats and ferrets as possible weapons against rabbits, at 20 sites in the Mackenzie Basin and Central Otago. They ran an extensive programme of trapping and eartagging cats and ferrets. They concluded that there was one predator — cat or ferret — for every 20 hectares of ground. Each predator killed, at most, two rabbits per week; over the course of a year, then, each accounted for 100 or so rabbits. MAF believed that this made a significant impact on rabbit numbers when populations were low, following an extensive poison drop, say, or during a particularly severe winter. On the other hand, such a kill-figure had very little impact when rabbit numbers were high.

The road dipped, and there, off to my right, was Lake Tekapo, a lovely stretch of water. I had never seen it so low, though the same could be said of all the hydro lakes in the district. It was a real shame that almost all of the rain was being dumped up north. A signpost arrested my attention: GLENMORE.

I stopped the car and got out. Glenmore country didn't look any different: the ground was rock hard. Over a fence, a dozen or so big fat rams eyed me warily. One of them stamped a hoof hard on the ground. They moved away from the hay they'd been feeding on, some of them looking back over their hunched shoulders with a rather haughty look. Glenmore was a noted Merino stud: I suppose they had every right to think they were a cut or two above the rest.

I had timed my arrival at the modern homestead on Glenmore just about perfectly — Anne Murray had just made a fresh batch of muffins. While I enjoyed a rather late morning tea, Anne's husband, Jim, and their single shepherd, Nick Ensor, were hard at it over at the sheep

Jim Murray and Nick Ensor working with Merino ewes.

yards. Usually they employed a married shepherd, too.

Glenmore, Anne Murray informed me in well-modulated tones, had been in Jim's family for three generations and, since their son was keen on the land, that long association seemed set to continue for a good many years yet. William was at Lincoln University and their two daughters, Kate and Pippa, were at Otago University.

The homestead, Anne continued, was at 730 metres, and the station, sweeping back towards the main divide, climbed to around 2300 metres. They ran 9500 sheep, all Merinos, and some 200 to 300 head of cattle, mostly Angus, and had 300 red deer penned.

'How about wildlife?' I asked hopefully.

Anne Murray's eyebrows shot up with mock

indignation. 'What?'

'You know — deer, chamois, thar . . .'

She laughed. 'I'm not telling you that!'

Winters were hard here — often brutal — and so supplementary feeding was essential. This year they had made 2500 big round bales of hay to see them through the winter.

When I asked Anne about the rabbits she pulled a face.

'We had a very good poison last year. At the moment their numbers are well down but it's a problem that's here forever.' Her voice turned even more emphatic. 'You're never going to get the very last rabbit.'

I sipped my coffee and mulled that over while Anne checked on lunch. By poison, Anne Murray had meant 1080-impregnated carrots. In 1990, between April and August, 6000 tonnes of carrots (150 truck and trailer loads), plus 500 tonnes of oats, were spread over 130,000 hectares of the Mackenzie Basin and upper Waitaki Valley. A third of these carrots were poisoned with 2000 litres of 1080; the rest were used as bait. An even bigger operation, in which nearly twice as many carrots were used, took place a year later.

'Can all the damage be put down to rabbits?' I asked.

'You mean here in the Mackenzie Basin?' She shook her head. 'No, it can't, really. What you're seeing here is a combination of damage by rabbits and, also, hieracium; you can't separate one from the other.'

I had been hearing about the dreaded hieracium from one end of the South Island to the other. I asked Anne to elaborate.

'Hieracium is a hawkweed, of which there are several kinds. It's a low-growing, broad-leaved plant which, once the ground cover is removed by rabbits or erosion, simply takes over and forms a tight-knit, mat-like carpet. It chokes out the tussock.'

Lines of concern formed on her forehead, and I had a

A light autumn snow dusts the mountains above Woodburn station, between Fairlie and Burke Pass.

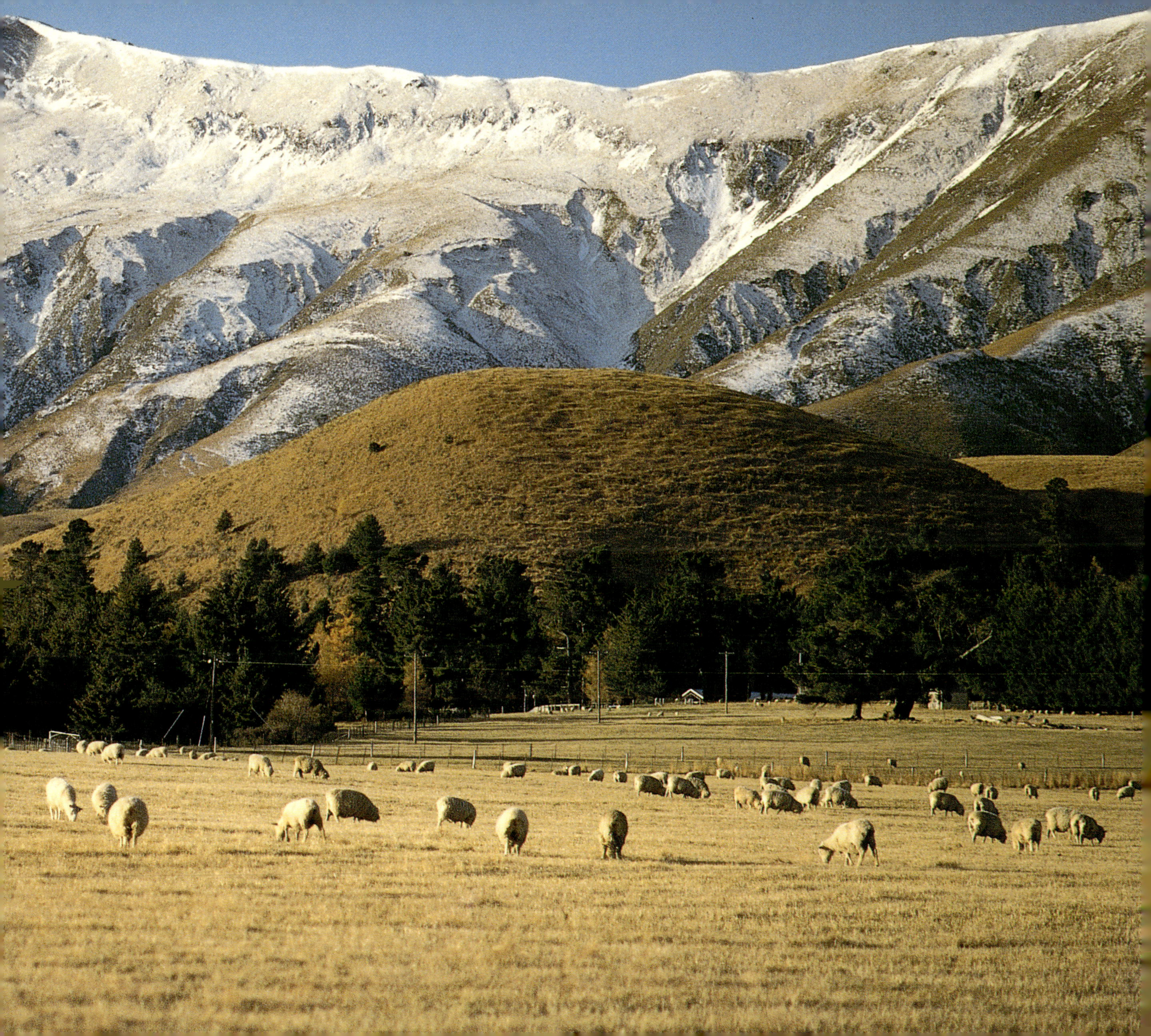

powerful hunch that hieracium was an all-too-common topic of conversation in this particular homestead.

'Sheep don't like it, I hear.'

Anne Murray nodded. 'Yes, it's totally unpalatable where they are concerned. If you look around here, you'll see it on the hills: it has a sort of grey look to it. In the spring it's a solid mass of waving yellow seeds.' She paused. 'Did you happen to notice the DSIR plot on your way in?'

'Uh-huh.'

'Well, Dr David Scott has been working there for many years — at least twelve — on hieracium. So far he hasn't come up with a solution to it. Nothing that's viable or practical, anyway.'

Meanwhile, an old Jack Russell had mooched into the kitchen. He flopped down on the floor near me and, ignoring my matey overtures, closed his eyes and started to doze. Jack's day of chasing rabbits were, I thought, all in the past.

'Another muffin?'

Following Anne Murray's succinct directions, I arrived in due course at the sheep yards. In the background were the shearers' quarters, with low hills beyond, a tell-tale blue-grey smudge on some of their faces and tops.

Jim Murray was tall, and rangy with it, a man for the Mackenzie Basin and no mistake. He and Nick were in the process of selecting ewes to go to a particular ram type. These ewes were among 800 — the pick of the flock — that had been chosen for a very important duty here on Glenmore: to breed top rams. In a separate yard were five such rams, Glenmore's best. I bet those handsome woolly studs, casting speculative glances at the milling ewes, couldn't wait for the action to start.

For a while, I kept Ruffy company. Ruffy was a big, hairy, doe-eyed beardie sheepdog with a friendly disposition. Ruffy, I quickly discovered, liked to have his ears fondled and be told he was a good boy. Then it was time for me to press on to Godley Peaks.

Ruffy, the beardie sheepdog.

'Right,' Jim said with a smile, 'we'll see you later then.'

'Far to Godley Peaks?'

He shook his head. 'No — just a few miles down the road, that's all.'

'Thanks for sparing the time.'

'No problem. Have a look around the place later on if you've got enough time.'

Nice offer, I thought. 'Thanks again.'

The Cass River, rising from glaciers high on the southeastern slopes of the Liebig Range, forms a natural boundary between Glenmore and Godley Peaks stations. Godley Peaks was first taken up by Tom Hall in 1858. Legend has it that he made his original selection from a map, a common enough occurrence then. He set off to take up his land on the western side of Lake Tekapo, but, for some unknown reason, didn't take up the land that he had leased; rather, he crossed what is today Glenmore — his choice — and started his station using the Cass River as his southern instead of northern boundary. We may presume that map reading was rather low on Hall's list of skills.

No matter. Tom Hall had his block of around 6500 hectares and he set to with admirable gusto. He soon had a dwelling built, sheep on his range, and a woolshed on the way: all within a period of just over a year. It was about then that Tom Hall's error was discovered. He was somehow able to retain the block, but it became known as Halls Mistake or The Mistake.

Hall remained up the Godley for 10 years. Various runholders followed, among them the Rutherfords: John, Edmond and Robert. They learned all about hard winters; in 1895, for example, they lost about half of their flock, some 7000 sheep. In 1921 the station came into the hands of Jim Murray, a relative of the present-day owners of Glenmore. He renamed it Godley Peaks, which is odd, as there are no 'Godley Peaks' on the run. Murray held the station until 1937, when John Scott took over. Today, the son of John Scott was the runholder on Godley Peaks.

The 23,500-hectare station was some 50 kilometres in length and about 8 kilometres wide. The elevation was 760 metres at the homestead, rising to nearly 2500 metres out back. They ran 11,000 Merinos and 150 head of Hereford cattle. Bruce Scott had a manager and a single shepherd to assist him, and much of the running of the station was left to the manager, Greg Hand. Bruce Scott wore two broad-brimmed hats; he was also Mayor of the Mackenzie Basin, a position he had held for six years. It was an exacting

Bruce Scott.

one, demanding that he be away from home three and sometimes four days a week.

Born on the station in 1938, Bruce Scott had hardly been away from it in his 54 years. Like his father, he was spare of build, whittled down over the years by the demanding environment. There was much activity going on around us as we chatted by the woolshed: sheep

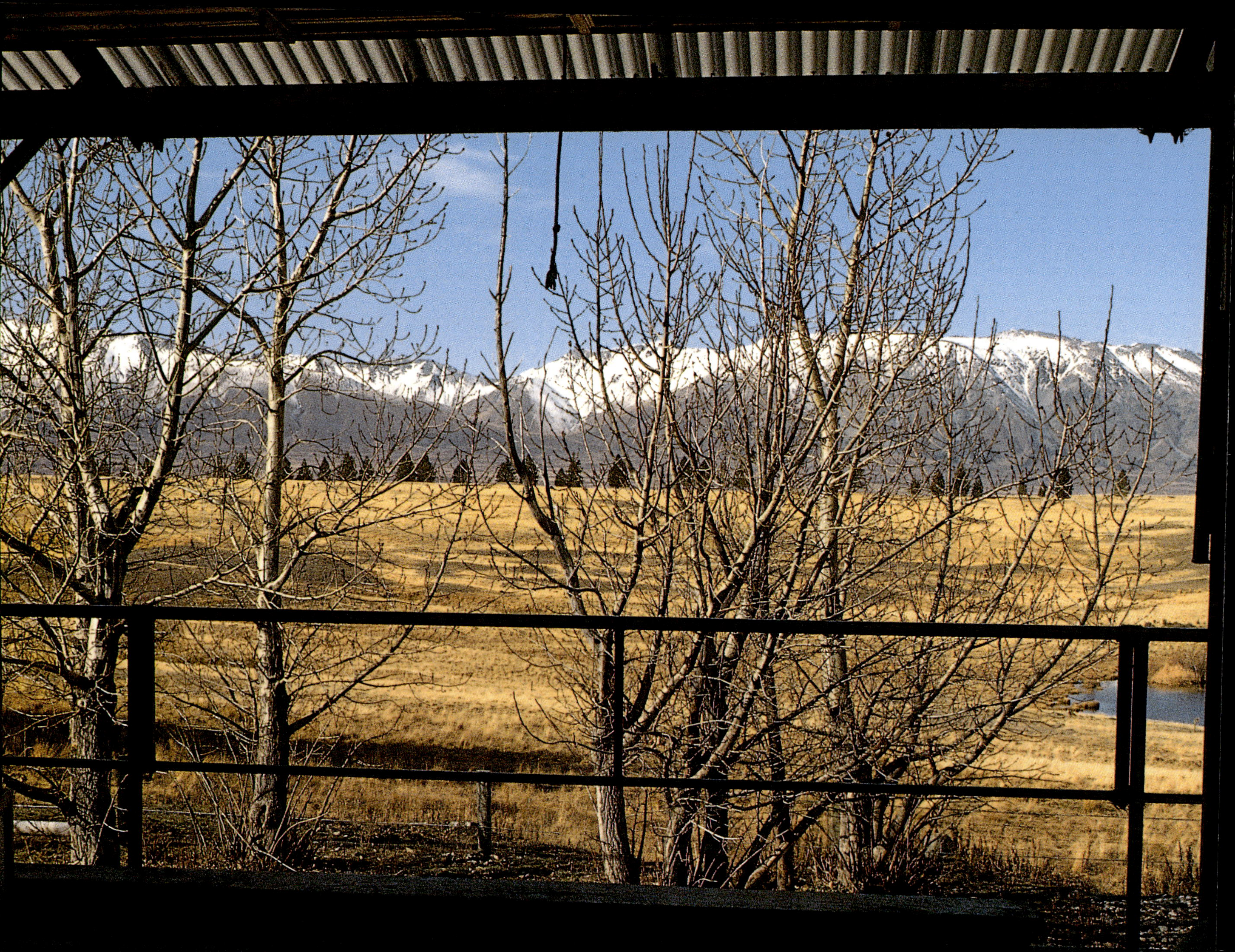

bawling, dogs barking, the raised voice of 18-year-old Nigel 'Ned' Robinson. Like Greg Hand, Ned was a Fairlie boy. Here on Godley Peaks he was a trainee shepherd. Ned was turning a milling mob of ewes into a yard directly behind the woolshed; in the woolshed, acting as a link between Ned and a six-strong shearing team, was Greg Hand.

'Come and see what's going on,' Bruce suggested.

We started up a long ramp leading to the main floor of the woolshed. 'Good looking shed,' I remarked.

Bruce grinned from ear to ear. 'Yes, isn't it!'

The woolshed was a mere six years old. The one it had replaced — then over 100 years old and still good for many more years' service — had taken the full brunt of a gale-force wind that had whipped up the valley. It was around 6.30 a.m. when Bruce had found the damage: the roof was gone and most of the sides had caved in. The wethers inside were unhurt, but were standing, totally dejected, in the pouring rain. The shearing that year had been down the road at Glenmore. A lot of thought had gone into the design of the new woolshed, with a great deal of input from shearers. The finished job — clean lines and highly functional — had delighted Bruce Scott.

At the top of the ramp, before following Bruce inside, I paused and took in the lovely view across the lake to the Richmond Range. That was station country, too: Mount Hay, near Tekapo, then Richmond, facing Godley Peaks, then Mount Gerald, more in the shadow of the Two Thumb Range, and, finally, Lilybank. Inside the woolshed Bruce Scott was gathering up a big armful of wool and the shearers were heads down and bums up. The shed hands were keeping the floor clean and, out of sight, Greg Hand and his dogs were keeping the pens, adjacent to where the shearers worked, full of jostling greybacks.

Somehow, I managed to corner one of the shed hands, Craig Fosbender, and he explained that they were doing a

Looking out to Richmond Range from the woolshed on Godley Peaks station.

full belly crutch: all the belly wool was removed and any stains or dags were removed, too.

I caught up with Greg Hand, who gave me a bone-crunching handshake. Greg had been the manager here for a year, but had put in 14 years on the place before that. Bruce reckoned he was a top bloke. He wasn't tall, but he was a real bundle of muscle. Like many rugby-playing station blokes, he had a crew-cut.

'Good station to work on?' I asked.

'The best, mate!' Greg said emphatically. 'Bruce is a great bloke to work for.'

Greg was giving one of his dogs, a huntaway, a hard time — or maybe it was the other way round — as I turned away and strolled back to where young Ned was at work.

Ned Robinson was a clean-cut sort. He told me that he and his father, Ken, who had been a shearer for 23 years, loved the high country. For Ned, being here on Godley Peaks was the ultimate. He had good accommodation, too; he cooked his own breakfast, but had lunch with Greg and his wife, Nikki, and his evening meal with Bruce and Liz Scott.

'You're doin' okay,' I told him.

He grinned, showing good teeth. 'Shit, yeah!' Then, 'Hey, Rock!'

Rock the big huntaway did his thing with a few reluctant-to-move sheep.

To Ned the best part of the job was undoubtedly the autumn muster, a classic event on Godley Peaks. The men camped at four huts and took 18 days to do the entire muster on foot, ranging up to almost 2400 metres — making it the longest foot muster in the country. A good sort of general physical fitness is not enough to cope with the demands inflicted on one's body during a muster. What is required is the stamina of a pedigree bull!

This year was a very special one for Bruce Scott: it marked his thirty-eighth autumn muster on Godley Peaks. At long last he had shaded his father's record. John Scott had mustered on more than Godley Peaks, of course; on

John Thompson and Tony Prestage belly-crutching ewes.

Mount Cook and Mount Hay, to name just two. John Scott was a living legend in the Mackenzie Country; his peers, the best judges of all, called him the Iron Man. He was still mustering on the hill at the age of 70. It seems to me that his son, Bruce, might be up there too, when he gets to that age. He'll be up there with the brooding gods, wearing hobnailed boots and a battered Swanndri, hillstick in hand, working the dogs, bringing the flighty sheep to lower ground.

It is worth noting that the station's accountant, Christchurch-based Graham Mars, had taken part in 21 musters on the run; that, according to Bruce Scott, was 'quite unique!' Another regular was Rick Mains, the younger brother of the All Black coach. A schoolteacher in Dunedin, Rick had notched up 14 musters.

There was an honesty about Bruce Scott that was endearing, a quality that must have been apparent to those who kept him in the mayoral office for six years. That honesty was there, naked as a flame, when he talked about the reasons why his 25-year-old son would not be taking on the station when Bruce retired.

'Paul was always very mechanically minded, you know,' Bruce said. 'He rode a push-bike the very first time he got on one.' A reflective smile. 'But he just doesn't see the sense of high-country mustering; he just doesn't love animals.

'He went to Australia a few years ago and drove big tractors in the west; later, he drove trucks interstate. His sister, Helen, went over to see just what her big brother was getting up to. Know what she's doing now? Driving a dump truck at a gold mine somewhere in Western Australia!'

'Is she coming back?'

'You tell me!' Bruce shook his head, but it was a good-natured gesture. 'People sometimes ask me if I'm disappointed that Paul doesn't want to be a runholder. My answer is no, I'm not. He's been strictly honest with me and I respect that. He did come back a few years ago to give it another go. He did a season of haymaking and when it was over, he said, "No, Dad, I can't pretend. You see, if it's got four big rubber tyres and a big motor, yes! But if it's got four legs and shits, no!"'

I laughed and, while he'd no doubt told that one before, so, too, did Bruce Scott. It takes a very special kind of man to respect and understand why his only son cannot find fulfilment in the same way that he has.

10

A COUNTRY UNITED

On Glen Rock station, runholder Donald France switched off the noisy engine of his tractor and, after clambering down from the enclosed cabin, cast a thoughtful eye over some of his sheep as they rushed eagerly to feed on the hay he was depositing at regular intervals across the snow-locked paddock.

It was 10 days since the big snows had come to this part of the country. Even now, in the Burke Pass region, one of the hardest-hit areas, it was still brushing the topmost wires of the fences on many stations. Here on Glen Rock, a 14,000-hectare property carrying over 7000 Merinos, it was the biggest snowfall that Donald and his brother Alistair had seen since the family took on the place in 1958. Those who could recall earlier times reckoned it was the biggest dumping of snow since 1945.

The summer of 1991–92 had been a difficult one for many runholders in the South Island; conditions were very, very dry. Worse, the autumn that followed was the driest on record. Feed for stock was scarce. Not wanting to make inroads into the precious winter feed, many runholders took a calculated risk by leaving most of their stock up in the high country for much longer than normal. Naturally, they listened intently to every weather forecast that might warn of imminent snow.

With very little notice, the snow started to fall during the early hours of 8 July. It fell almost continuously for 36 hours over a broad band of country: Marlborough; North, South and Mid-Canterbury; and North Otago. The snow was a metre deep around most of the homesteads in this huge area and was considerably deeper at higher altitudes, where most of the stock was.

The depth of the snow, while causing hardships of a type all too common, was not a disaster in itself. The real problem was that this was not wind-driven snow, blown

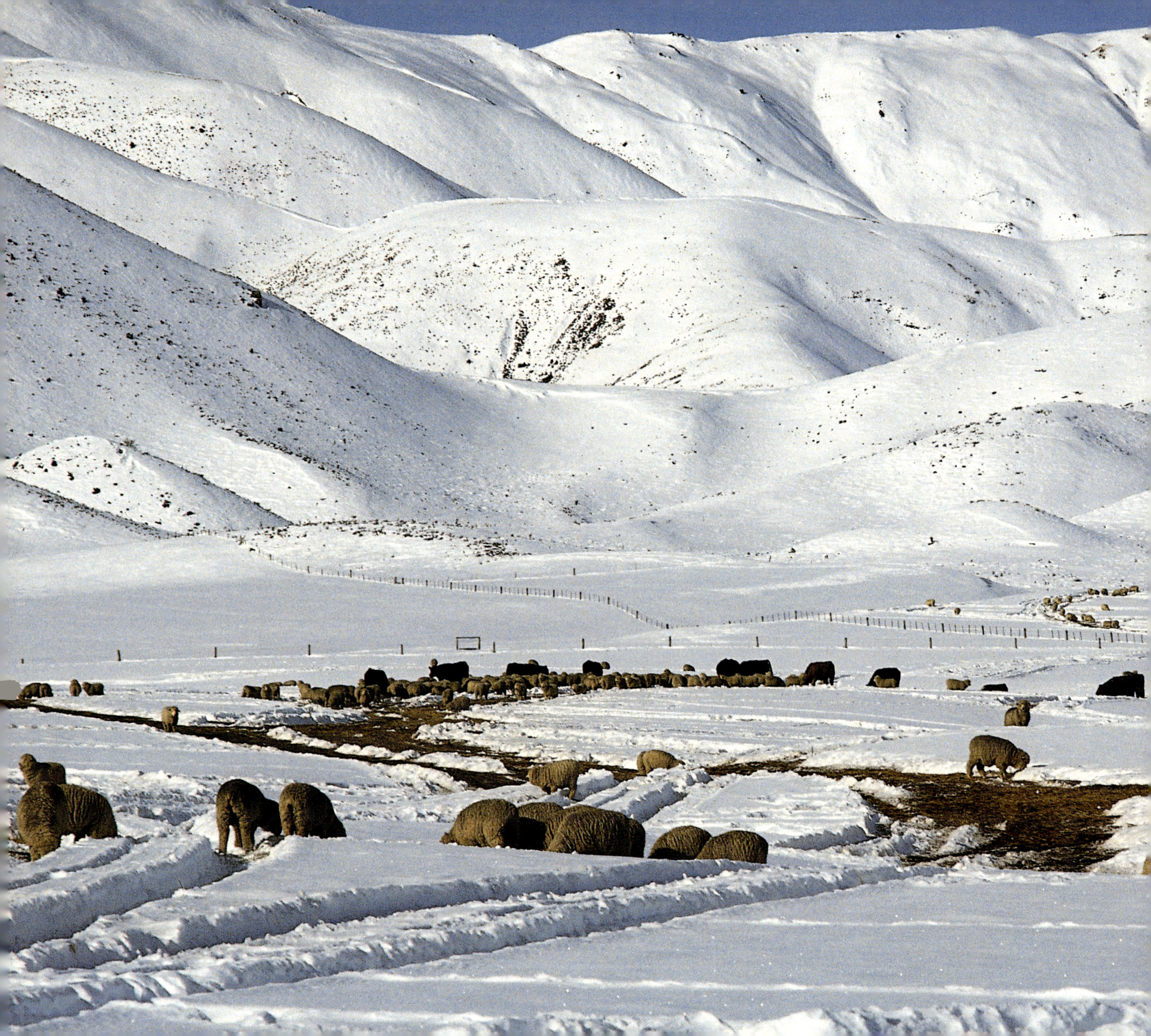

Left: *July 1992, near Burke Pass.*

Donald France has trouble feeding out in deep snow.

off exposed ridges and mountain faces and dumped in sheltered spots. When that happens there are areas left clear of snow, which stock depend on to survive until the snow melts or stationhands arrive (usually by helicopter) to rescue them by digging trails in the snow. This is called snow-raking and is by far the most detested occupation on any high-country run, since it involves working at high altitudes with exhausted or stubborn sheep.

It was estimated that around 500 properties were badly affected by this even blanket of snow. Stock at risk was thought to number around a million sheep, 100,000 breeding cows and untold numbers of fenced deer. Some runholders fared better than others, for their stock was at low-to-medium levels and could be reached by bulldozer or tractor. This was the case, I discovered when I caught up with Donald France, on Glen Rock station. It had taken them five full days to create a network of trails in the 1.5-metre-deep snow to allow the sheep to move down

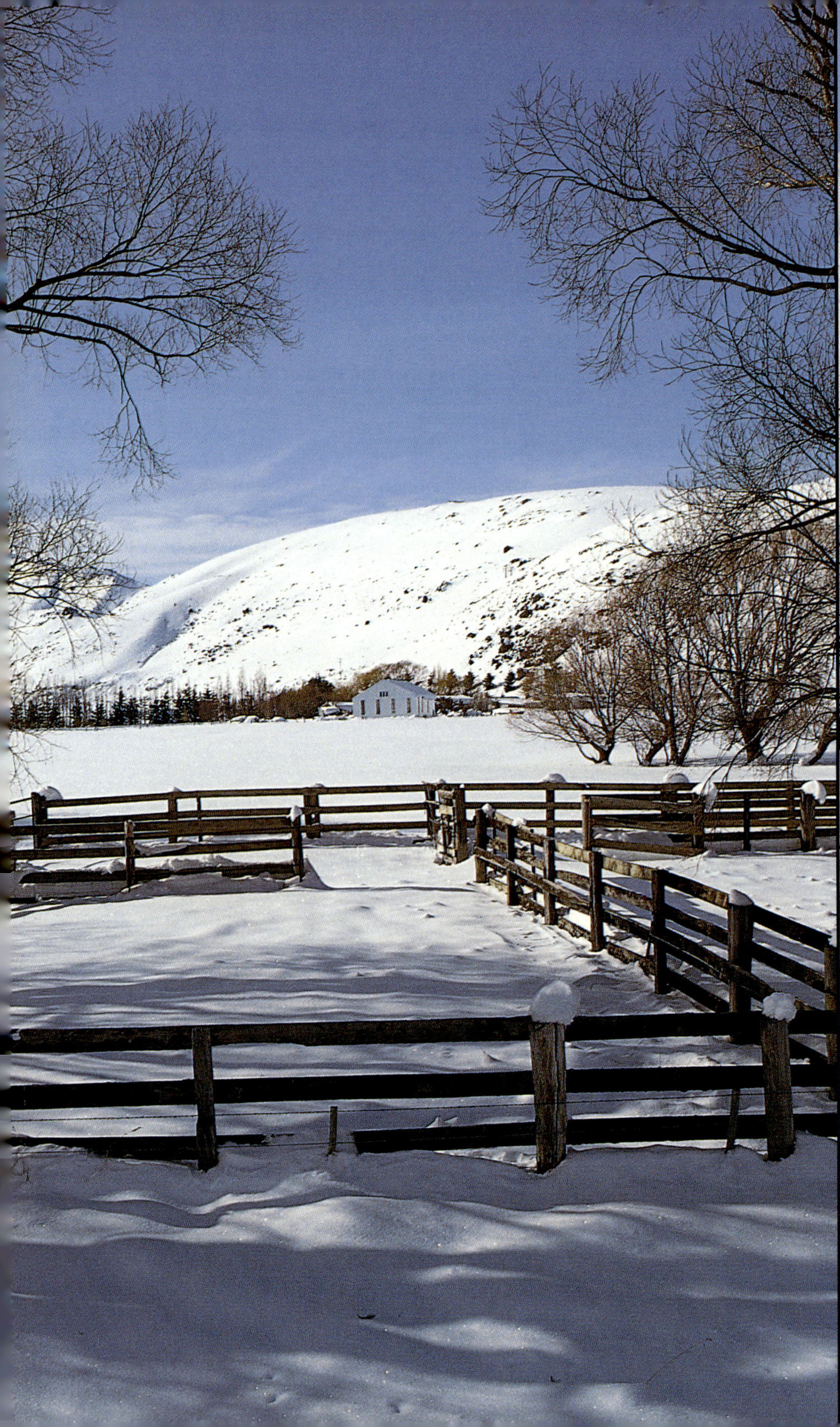

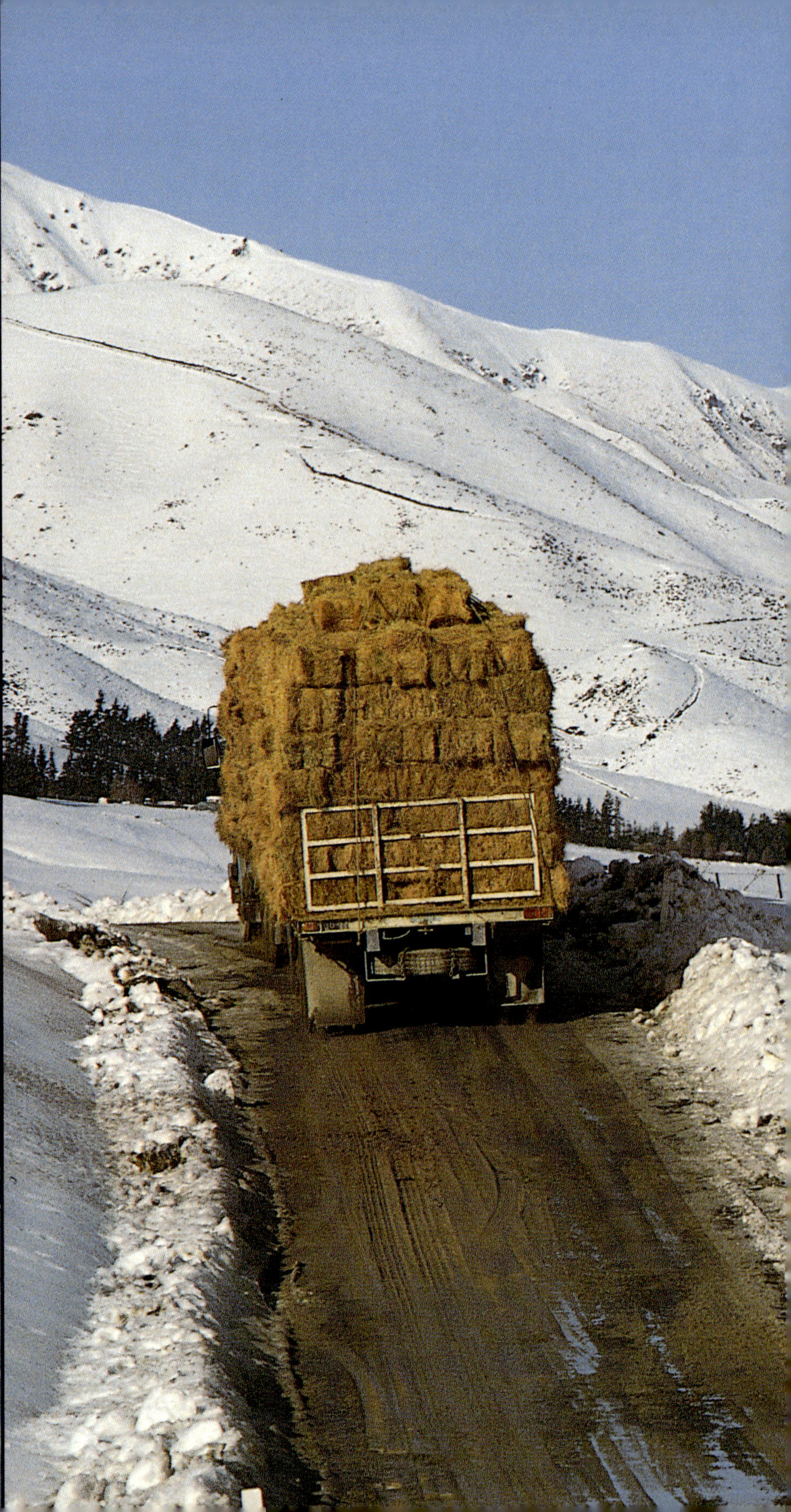

to where Donald was feeding out.

Other runholders were not so lucky: their stock was too high up for a bulldozer to reach them. They were in desperate need of help. What followed was a massive volunteer stock-rescue operation of a type not seen before in this country. Television viewers from one end of the country to the other watched enthralled as the saga unfolded before their eyes. They saw incredible scenes of a snow-blanketed land, woebegone sheep trapped on high ridges, resolute men and women making trails in belly-deep snow and carrying weakened sheep on their aching shoulders and they saw helicopters taking hay to starving animals. And it was all played out in the awesome majesty of the South Island under deep snow.

Just who were these people that had volunteered their help? Well, they included army and air-force personnel, staff of the BNZ and Westpac banks, prison inmates and Lincoln University students.

On Mason Hills station, which I had visited earlier in the year, Andrew Barker said, 'It almost brings tears to my eyes, the help we've had.'

On Mount Possession station in Mid-Canterbury, runholder John Whyte really spelled it out. 'We get it pushed down our throats that this is an indifferent and uncaring society, but it's not. We've had assistance from complete strangers up here — the way people have rallied around has been wonderful.'

Later, hay donated by North Island farmers began to arrive in the South Island. Grateful runholders in the worst-affected areas choked at the generosity of their North Island counterparts. Overall stock losses would, of course, not be known until the spring musters but, in the meantime, one thing was clear: without that outside help many South Island runholders would, in the winter of 1992, have faced almost certain financial ruin.

Far left: *Sawdon station, near Tekapo, under snow.*
A truckload of North Island hay bound for a South Canterbury station.

NORTH ISLAND

- Te Paki
- Paua
- Te Rangi
- Limestone Downs
- Nukuhakari
- Mangatu Blocks
- Waipaoa
- Otangimoana
- Lochinver
- Poronui
- Ngamatea
- Timahanga
- Smedley
- Brancepeth
- Te Awaiti
- White Rock

Pages 102–103 photograph:
On Nukuhakari station.

NORTH ISLAND
FROM COAST TO PLATEAU

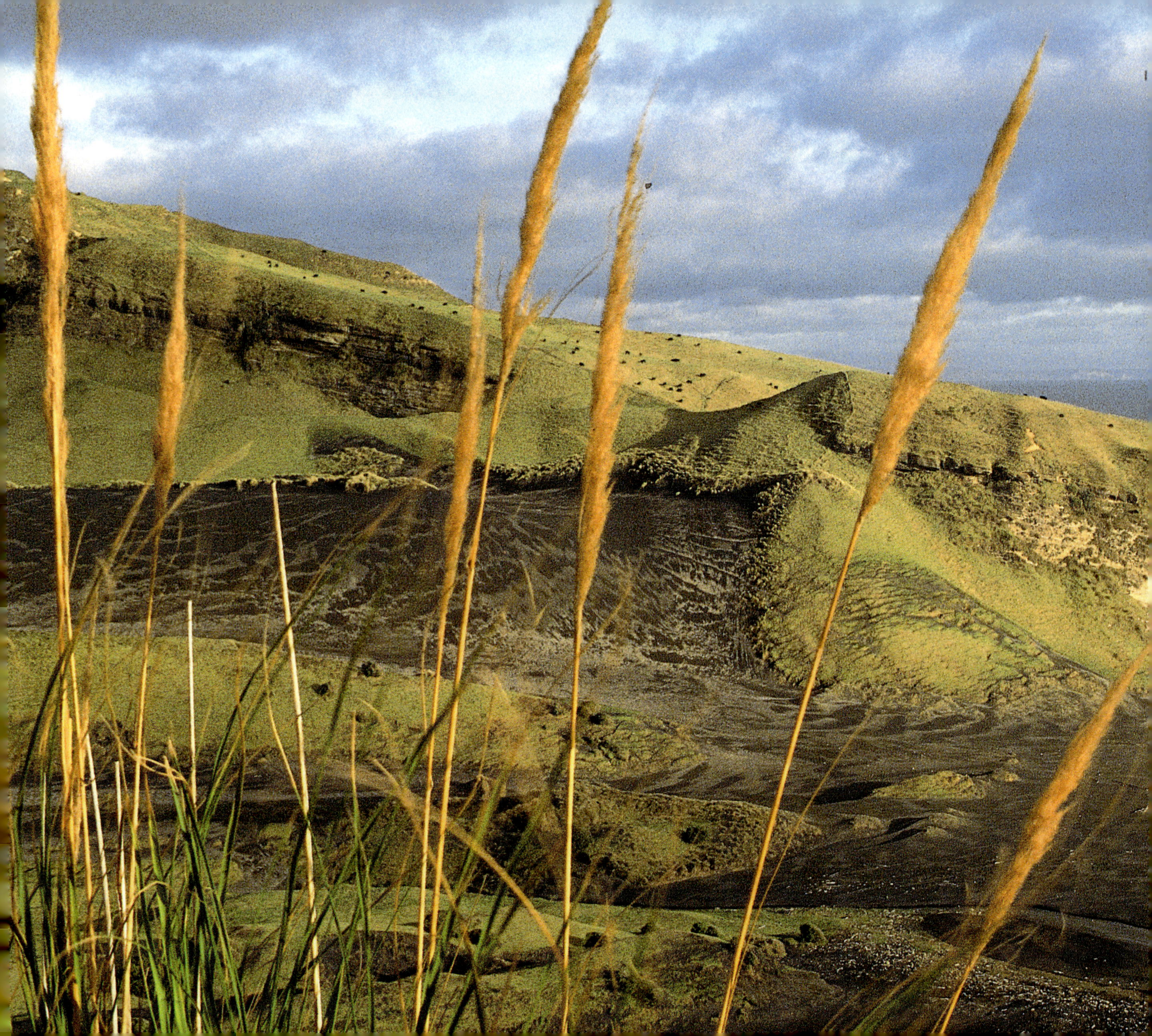

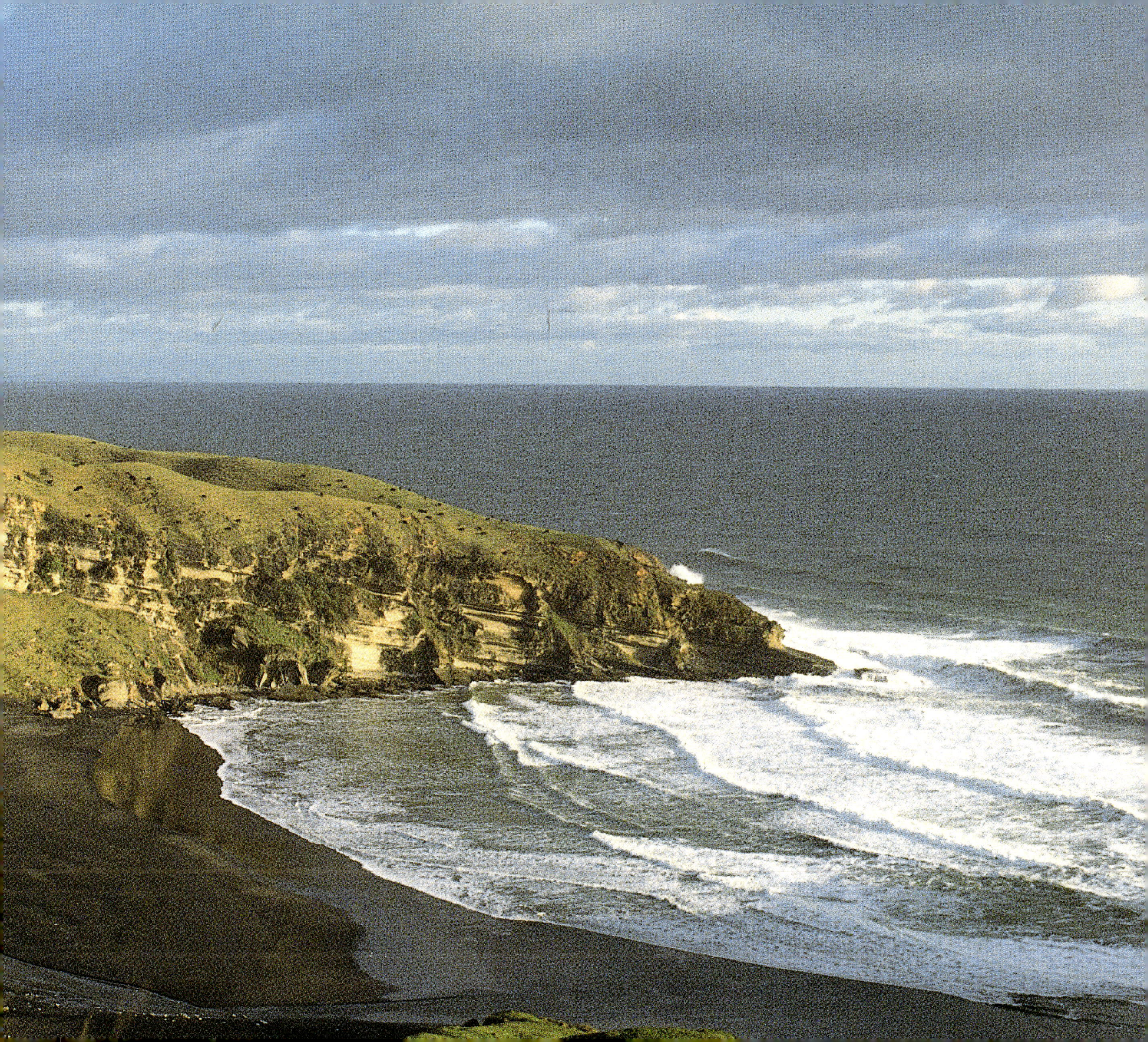

11

COASTAL STATIONS

Te Awaiti
On a superb Thursday afternoon in late April, I drove with great anticipation through the pleasant little town of Martinborough out towards the Wairarapa coastline. I was about to start the North Island leg of this project in earnest. It was mostly station country out beyond Martinborough, one property merging with another, stations that were once a part of much bigger holdings.

Presently a large woolshed perched on a hilltop caught my roving eye; the main station complex would be up there, too. It was Lagoon Hills, once an outstation of the property I was heading to, Te Awaiti. A small settlement — Tuturumuri — loomed up. A local hall, primary school for station kids, a few station buildings, no traffic lights, no pub, and not a local in sight. A few fat-gutted sheep were cleaning up the roadside, a couple of perky magpies perched on a sagging fenceline, and a weary old nag stood in the middle of a paddock with his head down. It was all happening at Tuturumuri.

There was a fork in the road at Tuturumuri. One route meandered off in a more southerly direction, down towards the lofty Aorangi Mountains; the other went to my destination. The road, rather like a country lane, weaved between low, attractive hills that were now starting to flatten out as suddenly the coast came into view. I pulled off to the side of the road and got out as a smoke-belching school bus jolted past. A smiling kid waved at me and with a grin I returned the gesture.

I walked out onto the beach. On it there were piles of driftwood. The small sand hills were coated with tussock, the tussock itself coated with sea spray. Out to sea white-maned horses were galloping towards me, stretching out as the race to shore continued. I realised how little of the sea I had seen over the last couple of years. Behind me,

Te Awaiti station.

sheep were grazing at ease on the gently sloping hills. All this, even the beach, was station country in the southern Wairarapa. I pressed on.

On a fine afternoon in autumn, when the air is clear, one's first view of Te Awaiti station is simply stunning. From a headland, where the unsealed road suddenly cuts back to skirt a tidal lagoon, you look directly across the sea at your destination. You see, first, the sea, white-capped waves rolling in towards the beach in an endless procession; beyond the beach, where horses mooch around, the station buildings stand below high, protective hills, hemmed in by the land on three sides; in the foreground there is a low-slung homestead dating to 1894.

Quite awed by it all, I thought of the time, not that long ago, when stout-hearted Europeans of British descent came up this coastline from Wellington, bringing sheep and cattle with them. Men like Daniel Riddiford, Richard Barton and Robert Cameron had all come this way in the

Perendales on Te Awaiti's rugged coastline.

COASTAL STATIONS • 107

mid to late 1840s; legend has it they acquired their blocks by ballot or the flip of a coin. Richard Barton settled the most southerly block of land, which he named White Rock, Daniel Riddiford took up the Tora and Te Awaiti blocks, and Robert Cameron pushed on further to the north, taking up what became known as Pahaoa and Glendhu.

The shrill blast of a shepherd's whistle rang out as the manager of Te Awaiti station — John Gannon, still powerfully built in his mid-fifties — strode with purpose behind a 2000-strong mob of sheep. They were heading south along a narrow, coastal shelf north of the homestead. Again John blew hard on his whistle; heading dogs and huntaways responded with enthusiasm. Even when there wasn't any work for them John gave his dogs a run every day: to him they were as important as people on an operation such as this.

John was assisted by his 30-year-old son, Geoff, and a married shepherd, Gus Ford. Geoff had once worked the rodeo circuit in New South Wales; six years ago he had returned home with his Australian wife, Carolyn, to work alongside his father on Te Awaiti. Gus had been a casual hand until quite recently, but now he was on the permanent staff. That suited a man with two children; it had been one of his young ones that had waved to me from the school bus the day before.

Geoff was mounted on a trailbike, while the others, unusually, were on foot. They mostly relied on horses when carrying out stock work on Te Awaiti's nearly 6900 hectares. All up, there were 38 horses on the station, including 18 brood mares. The station's stallion was called Royal Fencer. In May, John and Geoff broke in the three-year-olds.

It was another lovely morning; in fact, I'd had nothing but good weather since I'd left Queenstown three days ago. There was a warm wind coming off the sea. The sea was a deep, deep blue just offshore, turning to a hazy, washed-out blue in the distance. Sheep weaved between outcrops of rock or clambered over them with the sure-footed agility of their Perendale breeding. Inland, beyond the fertile flats, the green hills reared up suddenly to around the 500-metre mark.

For the Maori the temperate Wairarapa coastline had much to offer. The rocky foreshores still contained many types of shellfish, and the sea was bountiful. They had come here long before the first Europeans, such as William Colenso, had trekked south from Hawke's Bay along this comparatively easy route. They had cleared the ground of flax and toetoe and had made gardens, where they planted kumara. The weather was kind here — frosts were almost unknown and crops grew all year round. The Maori added to their diet with berries, such as the fruit of the karaka.

My eyes tracked over the large hillside and the many karaka that flourished in narrow gullies or huddled together in groves on sunny terraces where, in all probability, there had been well-tended gardens in times long past. I clambered down off my rocky knoll and angled across the flats to link up with John Gannon. He was leaning in a relaxed manner on a stout hillstick. There was an amiable look about him and I was happy about that. You see, John Gannon was a tall man with the muscle-packed shoulders of an axeman and hands like well-matured hams; he weighed in excess of 100 kilograms. When he told me he had never been beaten at arm wrestling, I was sensible enough not to roll up my sleeve and suggest we get on with it.

John Gannon was born in Wanganui in 1938. He lost both parents at a very early age, and had been raised by a great bear of a man called Rankin, who came from Northern Ireland. They lived next door to a farm, where John spent much of his time: he liked the sense of space, the animals, the whole way of life. It seemed entirely natural that when he left school at 15 he should seek a job on the land, and that the land would welcome him and never relinquish its hold on him. His first job was working as a cowboy for Leyton Elliott, who owned a considerable amount of land — farms and stations — in that part of the country.

Later, Elliot sent him up country, to his 2000-hectare station called Opaku, in Patea County, South Taranaki. Much of Opaku had yet to be broken in, so John found himself with a hard-bitten team of manuka cutters, men who knew all about burning the candle at both ends. It was winter: always wet, often bitterly cold. No place to be living under canvas, but that was the way of it. The work was back breaking, first light until last, hardly stopping for a smoke or a brew. The work put hard, ropy muscle on John's lean frame and made him realise that there were far more interesting ways of making money.

Two years down the track John Gannon was on Dunard station, near Mangamahu. This, too, was around the 2000-hectare mark. A man called Hec Wallace worked on a nearby station. Hec was getting on then; he had worked in the district for most of his life, employed by just two families. Hec was very highly thought of, a good, loyal servant. While John Gannon toiled away on Dunard, Hec Wallace at last called it quits.

The trouble was, Hec had never given too much thought to tomorrow. He hadn't put any money away or bought a house. It turned out there was no place on the station for Hec, not even a draughty room in the shearers' quarters. Hec ended his days working as a live-in caretaker at the Margaret Watt Home For Girls in Wanganui. A lousy way for a stationman to finish up.

Hec's misfortune worked to the advantage of John Gannon. It was an even more telling lesson than the sight of a bunch of sore-headed track-cutters returning to the job stony broke after a riotous few days in town. It made John aware of the future. He would have to provide for himself in later years; it was no use expecting someone else to do it all for you. Later, when John became a station manager, he always tried to encourage the young men who worked for him to save some of their wages. Mostly he had succeeded, too.

Meantime, up on the hill, Geoff's big black huntaway,

Big John Gannon.

four-year-old Black, was doing what he did best: chasing sheep out of a karaka-choked gully. Below, Geoff was hollering out instructions. They were an excellent team.

When I joined him, John Gannon was still propped up on his hillstick.

'Enjoying yourself?' he asked.

'Too true.'

He nodded. 'Good.'

'Great dog your son's got.'

'Yes, it is.'

I gestured at the sheep. 'Why are they taking them in to the yards?'

'These are two-tooths and we're about to do a second shear,' John explained, keeping a watchful eye on what was taking place. 'Thing is, Phil, we don't put our two-tooths to the rams like they do on some places because I don't feel they are strong enough yet. They did that here, too, until I stamped it out.'

'So these sheep are around — what?'

'Fifteen months old,' John answered. 'We'll put them to

the rams when they're four-tooths.'

'They're two years old then, right?'

John confirmed it with a nod.

'Another question.'

John smiled good naturedly.

'Why Perendales?'

'Good question.' He smiled. 'Well, I guess I like Perendales for their mobility, their ability to fossick. As you can see' — he waved his hillstick as though it were a scythe — 'we have some real steep country here. Even steeper further back. Perendales are comfortable there, no problems.' There was a lengthy pause. 'Course, there's a wee bit of Romney in them, too.'

'Why?'

'That increases the wool weight considerably.'

With that he moved across to his left, closer to the sea, where the coastline narrowed and underfoot there was nothing but sharp, cutting rock.

Left to my own devices, I decided to press on ahead of the sheep — to find a spot from which to photograph them — in the four-wheel-drive John had kindly put at my disposal. Before reaching the vehicle, however, I found myself staring at a deep spoor and, kneeling, I recognised it as the fresh hoof mark of a fair-sized red stag. It was consistent with what John had told me the previous evening: that during April and May, in particular, red deer were in the habit of coming down from the hills to feed on the kelp washed up on the beach. Quite often, in fact, they could be spotted on these same flats but, more likely, up on the hill faces, soaking up the early morning sun.

Apart from the fact that Te Awaiti is a coastal station, its main attraction where I was concerned was its long and colourful association with red deer. For the record, red deer were first liberated in the Wairarapa in 1862. The animals — one stag, two hinds — were turned out on a property near Carterton. Red deer did remarkably well in the Wairarapa and nowhere was that more apparent than on Te Awaiti.

T. E. Donne, whose excellent writings provide an illuminating picture of deer stalking in the early days, wrote about Te Awaiti in his book *Red Deer Stalking in New Zealand*:

> I think I am correct in stating that formerly the best stalking in the North Island was obtainable on that great expanse of country known as Te Awaiti station on the eastern coast, which in my day was owned by the late E. J. Riddiford.

Edward Riddiford took over the station after the death of his father, Daniel. Edward, a man of great drive, became known as 'King' Riddiford.

It was, of course, 'big heads' that drew the likes of Donne to Te Awaiti. The Windsor Park herd, from which the three original deer came, had been replenished from English, Scottish, German and probably Danish stock. The result of this, wrote Thomson in 1921, was:

> . . . in the Wairarapa herd stags that are remarkable for their massive antlers, some of which are of the German type, and others again more resembling the Scottish form. The antlers do not grow to great length, but some are very wide in spread, and there is a great proportion of 'Imperials', the most number of points recorded being twenty-two. The stags mature their antlers early. A number of heads have been shot on Te Awaiti showing the abnormal development of the back tines, such as is seen to be the case in the great Warnham Park stags in England.

Donne was first lured to the Wairarapa in the 1890s. On Te Awaiti he was guided by Roderick M'Gillivray, then employed by Edward Riddiford. According to Donne, M'Gillivray was well over six feet, could walk all day and every day, could shoot well from either shoulder, and

A red stag on Te Awaiti station.

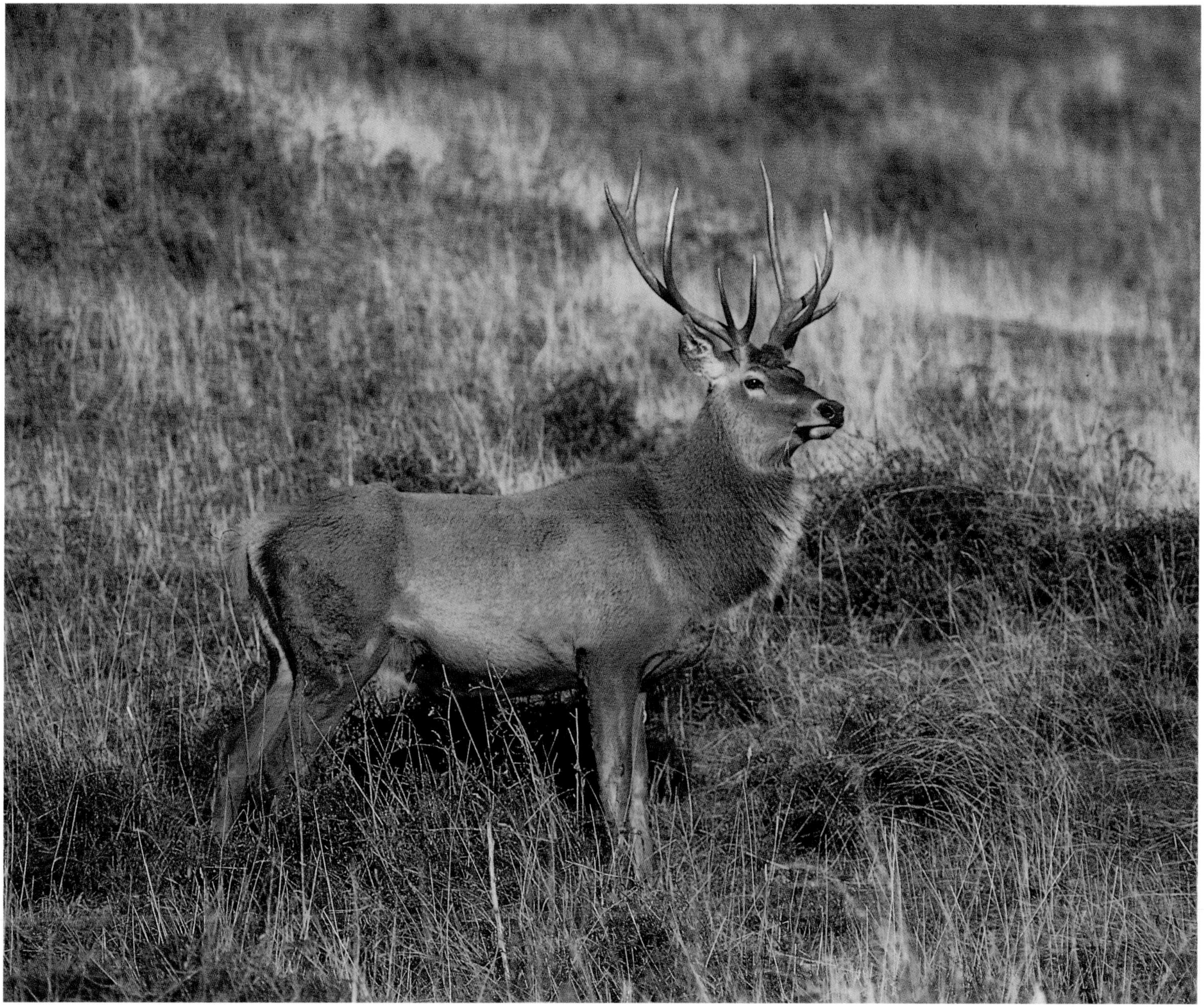

knew all the ways of the wild deer. It is worth noting that, while Edward Riddiford was not a keen hunter, he was

> . . . kind in giving visitors to New Zealand permission to stalk stags on his property and in generously providing accommodation and all other requisites, including the use of horses.

Certainly Edward Riddiford was proud of his red stags and was delighted when his guests, such as Donne, obtained a fine trophy.

In 1905 a hunting trip was planned on Te Awaiti station by two of Edward Riddiford's sons — Lieutenant D. H. S. Riddiford and his brother, Vivian — and Oliver and Willie Bunny. Oliver at that time was the manager of the property which, under Edward's rule, had increased to around 32,500 hectares. They intended to try out a distant part of the run, where several stags were reputed to carry fine heads. This was a vast area of manuka scrub that covered perhaps 2800 hectares. Well inland from the coast, it had in all probability been fired by the Maori in pre-European times.

On the day before this grand expedition was due to begin, Willie had the bad luck to badly sprain his ankle. By the following morning it was so painful that he decided not to go, and, cursing his rotten luck, he watched the hunting party ride off. They were well provisioned for a lengthy stay and, in keeping with the times and the fact the Riddifords were among the privileged, they took a cook with them.

Six days later the hunting party returned. As Willie hobbled towards them, smiling a greeting, he could tell things hadn't gone to plan. Despite nearly five full days of hunting — up early and out until dusk — they had accounted for only one stag, a fair sort of 12-pointer. They had seen few deer, which was very unusual on Te Awaiti. Willie listened sympathetically and then, to the amazement of his disgruntled friends, he showed them what he had shot in their absence: two 13-pointers and a 17-pointer that took their breath away.

On his own and finding time dragging, Willie Bunny had saddled a horse early one morning and set off to check some sheep on a far part of the station. One was likely to see deer almost anywhere on the run, so he'd taken a rifle with him. Following the bush edge, he had spotted a movement in the trees. Checking his mount, he saw for an instant a large stag. He had dismounted and peered intently into the forest, but to no avail. The stag was gone on silent hoofs. Willie, trembling slightly, had been sure the stag was carrying a wonderful head.

Sensing that the stag could return, Willie had tied up his horse and sat down on a commanding spot. An hour had passed, then another. Still he had kept up his patient vigil. As the day neared noon, he had again observed a deer in the forest — yes, it was the same stag.

He had slowly raised his rifle and, taking a deep breath, waited until the stag paused. Then he had fired and the stag dropped in a leg-thrashing heap. It was a 17-pointer with an antler length of $38^{1}/_{2}$ inches and a spread of 36 inches. Willie's two other trophies were obtained when he spotted them from horseback, and then dismounted to shoot, in the Ram Paddock Creek.

It is said that the brothers Riddiford and Oliver Bunny had extensive, as well as highly colourful, vocabularies. As they looked at Willie's three trophies, in particular the 17-pointer, and then glanced dismally at what they had achieved, it is more than likely that they expressed themselves fully.

By the following year it was reported that the 'Wairarapa Forest is probably the best-stocked red-deer ground on the globe. On Te Awaiti the deer may now be seen in bunches of up to one hundred strong.' Interestingly enough, in the previous year it had been estimated that a staggering 10,000 head of red deer roamed that particular country.

Over the years, deer increased tenfold on Te Awaiti. In the 1920s men were hired to hunt them during winter. During a period of three years two men, paid two shillings and six pence per tail, accounted for over 3000 deer; this was remarkable considering they spent just nine months actually hunting.

The huge scrub block hunted by the Riddifords and Bunny could still be found on Te Awaiti, and on adjacent Lagoon Hills, too. Geoff Gannon, a keen hunter, told me that some of the manuka was exceptionally tall — six metres perhaps. There were also some magnificent stands of timber in there, beech, mostly. There were plenty of red deer; it was nothing to see a mob of 30-odd in the spring. Only a few weeks before my visit a 14-pointer, measuring 42 inches in length, had been taken. In fact, the stags were so good that the station had gone into the trophy-hunting business. There were also wild cattle and big boars ranging the scrub block. All the action you could want.

When you combine the hunting with Te Awaiti's other attractions — a lovely climate and wonderful fishing (crayfish galore), it seems to me that a young musterer who lives for such things on his off-duty days couldn't do better than to work under big John Gannon on Te Awaiti station.

White Rock
It is not the eight-stand woolshed nor the other interesting buildings you first notice about the place; it is the great, jagged-edged slab of marble-white limestone thrusting out of the white-capped breakers almost directly in front of the main station complex.

It was logical for Richard Barton to name his station after this particular landmark. In *Reading the Rocks*, a guide to the geology of the Wairarapa coast, the rock is described as being 'rather like the bones of an old whale'. Basically, the rock is the skeleton or remnants of an immense sheet of limestone that geologists believe covered southeastern Wairarapa about 50–60 million years ago.

The historic White Rock station was still owned by direct descendants of the original settler, Richard Barton. When he died in 1866, his third son, William, took over the station, and ran it very well. William died in 1938, leaving the property to his five daughters. Of these

White Rock.

daughters, three would marry. From those marriages, interest in the 7300-hectare station would gradually spread out so that by the end of the 1980s at least 30 people were directly involved. The shareholders had different objectives; some wanted their money out, while others wanted to pour more money into the station. The station, through bad management, was not in good shape: much of the once-cleared country was fast reverting to scrub and fences were down or in poor condition.

Crunch time came in 1990. The outcome was that three of Richard Barton's direct descendants — Tim Ritchie, Anne Quinn and Ben Lutyens — cared enough about White Rock to buy out the other shareholders and subdivide the place between them. Interestingly enough, both Anne Quinn and Ben Lutyens were born in England. The northern half of the original White Rock became known as Riverside and went to the Lutyens family; the coastal half, retaining the name White Rock, went to Tim Ritchie and Anne Quinn.

I was being put in the picture, on a fine Saturday afternoon, by Tim Ritchie. We were standing next to a simple stone cairn erected by the daughters of William Barton in loving memory of their father. Catching the sun, the cairn stood on a bare hillock. From there we could see the station buildings and that great white rock. By turning around and facing the mountains — the way the cairn was actually facing — we could observe the Aorangi Mountains, including Mount Barton, named after William.

'Your great-great-grandfather, Tim?' I said, indicating the cairn.

'Yes . . .' he replied quietly.

Earlier, I had been taken on a whistle-stop tour of the station by Tim and his manager, Graeme Bolton. They were an interesting contrast. Tim was 41, of average height and good build, with a clipped accent. He was a switched-on type, very likeable, in blue sweater and trendy jeans. Tim was someone in the city: general manager of Corporate Affairs, the New Zealand Meat Producers Board to be precise. He had been in the meat industry for over 10 years, mostly on the commercial side. Graeme Bolton was 34 years old, tall and slim. Born in Waipukurau, he'd spent a lot of time on stations, including Te Awaiti. Graeme had reckoned you wouldn't get a better boss than big John Gannon. For his part, John

Tim Ritchie stands alongside the cairn erected in memory of his great-great-grandfather.

COASTAL STATIONS • 115

Gannon had said that Graeme was a top stockman and that he'd been sorry to lose him when he had got the manager's job on White Rock.

Anne Quinn told me that Graeme had a wonderful affinity with animals, but put him in downtown Wellington in peak-hour traffic and he'd be as much out of place as Tim would be mounted on a horse with a big mob of sheep to control. The main thing was, Tim and Graeme respected each other. They shared a common goal: the improvement of White Rock station. Graeme was assisted by a single shepherd, Roddy Cameron. They intended to put another full-time shepherd on the payroll, which would eliminate the need for casual labour at, say, shearing time.

I asked Tim Ritchie what his plans for the station were.

'One of my objectives is to improve the property — not necessarily back to its former glory but at least to leave the place in a better position than when we bought it for future generations and hope that one of my children will be able to carry on, whether full time or in a position like myself — that is, having the best of both worlds.'

Tim Ritchie did have the best of it: a lucrative and fulfilling career, and a station a mere two and a half hours' drive away to escape to at weekends and holidays. Tim and his wife Deborah had three children: Anna (12), Lucy (10) and Timothy (6). I hadn't met any of them the previous evening — they had been tucked up for the night when I had arrived at the cottage. My first meeting with the youngest had been early this morning. In fact, we met at the door to the toilet; the six-year-old was coming out, I was going in. He was half asleep, in pyjamas and dressing gown. I said, 'How are you?' He looked up gravely and, most assured, replied, 'I'm very well, thank you.' A young version of his father, I thought. What would he make of his magnificent heritage — White Rock station — if it became his responsibility?

That, of course, was a very long way in the future. Today was what counted to Tim Ritchie. They ran 14,000 stock units (peak time) on the station, comprising Romney sheep and 550 Angus-Hereford cattle. There were 20 horses: mares, foals, hacks, and a stallion. Like John and Geoff Gannon, Graeme Bolton was into horse power. You couldn't watch out for stock or dogs or things of general interest when you were mounted on a trailbike — you were too busy watching out for hidden stumps or holes.

In May of 1991, Graeme and a single shepherd, Wayne Jipson, had been mustering the Turnpike block. Across the Opouawe River, it was nice, easy country, a sensible place to run two-tooths before a second shear. Graeme, riding a chestnut gelding called Banded, had the higher beat, while Wayne worked lower down, pretty much in the creek, pushing the sheep down-gully to the river flats.

Down on the flats, the two shepherds rode towards each other, the sheep moving before them. Graeme could see that something had deeply upset Wayne who tersely explained that he'd come across three dead sheep, killed and half eaten by a pig. Leaving the sheep, the two men went upstream to the three kills, which they examined at some length; they did not make a pretty sight. All of them, the men decided, had been killed over the last couple of nights. While the two-tooths were not fully grown, they were nonetheless a fair size — quite chunky, in fact. It would take a powerful and determined animal to bring them down, one that struck under the cover of darkness.

The two shepherds on White Rock considered that a pregnant sow, or one with young, could have been responsible, for a sow's craving for calcium is powerful at such a time, and that, of course, could be found in the bones. But it was more likely to be a boar. An ardent hunter of deer and pigs, Graeme felt sure that the pig had only recently wandered onto the station. There was good pig country close by: the Aorangi Mountains and, of course, the big scrub block on Te Awaiti and Lagoons Hills. Where it had come from didn't really matter; what did count was putting an end to its horrendous activities. Unless checked, the animal would kill again, night after night.

A deeply pensive station manager returned later to the homestead he shared with his wife, Desiree. The two had met while Graeme was a shepherd on Moeangiangi station, near Tutira, Hawke's Bay, where Desiree had been the cook. They had married while Geoff worked under John Gannon at Te Awaiti; the place would always be precious to them.

Over an early dinner, Graeme deliberated about the pig. They could try for it at daybreak, hoping it would return to one of its kills overnight, and would still be there, gorging itself, when the sky turned grey. Better still, they could go there tonight. Wayne wasn't too happy about a night-time foray in search of a potentially dangerous boar, so Graeme turned to Nigel Gooding, who was currently bringing some of the fences on the place up to scratch.

Torchlight played weakly on the ground as the two men headed up the creek. Only Nigel was armed, a scoped .270-calibre rifle. Graeme's two pig-dogs trotted eagerly alongside their master: Rowdy, a black huntaway finder, and Jake, a yellowish bull mastiff holder. They were a well-seasoned team, more often successful than not.

They were close to one of the kills when Rowdy suddenly paused. Up went his head; he scented deeply. Something was tainting the wind's chilly breath, something that smelled warm and alive. Rowdy vanished.

Typically, Jake held back. He would wait until his mate barked in a way that told him a pig was bailed and it was up to him to get there fast and hold it good and tight until their master arrived and despatched it with blade or bullet. Then, no real distance away, Rowdy barked. A heavy silence. Still Jake had not run off. The holder and his master knew that the pig had broken.

Again Rowdy barked; this time Jake rushed into action. The men — elated, excited — ran hard, too. The pig Rowdy had bailed up was a boar. He stood under the manuka tree where he had, until rudely disturbed by this canine idiot, been feeding on the remains of one of the dead sheep.

The boar was as black as the night, as black as the

The men's quarters date to the 1930s.

bottom of a closed-in mine shaft. He was armed with tusks — formidable weapons brought to needle-like sharpness by constant honing. Moreover, he was big, more than 300 pounds. He was the kind of boar no holder should ever attempt to contain.

Unseen by the men, who were still perhaps 40 metres away, Jake went in on the boar and went in fast. It was the usual holder stuff: grab an ear, maybe a fold of loose skin behind the shoulder, maybe one of the testicles. The boar struck once; it was all that was required. Jake, lurching, collapsed a few metres away as the men ran up.

'Watch it!' cried Graeme, waving his torch about.

Bug-eyed, Nigel saw the partly illuminated boar as Graeme found it.

'Shit! It's a whopper!' Nigel yelled. 'Quick! Get up a tree!'

'You can't!' Graeme shouted back. 'It's standing under the only one there is!'

Taking a deep breath, Graeme yelled at Rowdy to get the hell out of there. The black finder responded to the command, backing out of harm's way as Nigel fired. The .270 belched flame and the boar reared up suddenly, climbing to stand near upright on its hind legs, then toppled backwards, legs thrashing. Nigel shot it again and there was no movement whatsoever.

Too choked to speak, Graeme crouched beside Jake, his wounded holder. He ran his fingers through Jake's rough coat. Afraid to move him, Graeme wrapped Jake up in his Swanndri. The night was cold, turning colder by the minute: that would, he felt sure, cause the flow of blood to stop. He would return in the morning and see what the situation was then.

Desiree, who had a soft spot for all of her husband's dogs, was shocked by the latest calamity to hit their thin ranks. She insisted on returning with Graeme in the morning. Fearing the worst, Graeme tossed a long-handled shovel in the back of the four-wheel-drive before they left.

Amazingly, Jake wasn't dead; he was actually standing up, a bit wobbly on his legs but upright all the same. Using the Swanndri as a sling, they carried Jake out to the four-wheel-drive. Later, Desiree took him to a vet in Martinborough. Following a blood transfusion and a course of antibiotics, Jake healed quickly. Within a month he was back on the hill chasing pigs.

A stone's throw from the woolshed on White Rock station stood a long line of buildings: men's quarters, cookshop, and so on. They could date back to the early 1930s; no one was quite sure of their exact age. The very end building on the northwestern side was far more substantial than the single rooms the shearers and shepherds stayed in; it was, in fact, the dwelling used by the family over the years. Today, Anne Quinn was staying there.

Having accepted Anne's kind invitation to join her for Saturday dinner, I found myself after dark in her comfortable sitting cum dining room. There was, I thought, a lovely lived-in atmosphere there. There was also a lovely atmosphere in the pit of my whisky-warmed stomach. The heat of an open fire on my back felt pretty good, and Anne provided stimulating company.

Anne Quinn had lived in many of the world's most glamorous cities. She had had a varied career, including a stint as Shirley Bassey's secretary. The mesmerising Welsh singer was just about to tour New Zealand for the first time in 25 years, and Anne suggested I come to her concert in Wellington and — wait for it — be introduced to her. I digested that with another sip of whisky. Introduced to Shirley Bassey? What a thrill that would be. But I shook my head with an ironic smile and explained that my itinerary was too tight to allow me to be in Wellington that night; and I wouldn't be anywhere near Auckland when she strutted her stuff there, either. It was a real pity: Shirley Bassey was one of the world's great entertainers.

Presently we were joined by Graeme and Desiree, and, a little later, Tim and his wife. Good company, lovely meal, excellent wine. It was a top way to spend a Saturday evening.

Early on Sunday morning I said my goodbyes to the Ritchie family and drove on down to the seafront. The sun speared across the sea, playing on the rock. Ever since I had arrived I had found myself drawn to White Rock. It was as though it held a secret, something I really ought to know. When I had mentioned this to Tim and Anne they, too, admitted that it had a compelling fascination for them. They had no idea what it was. It made me wonder if Richard Barton had felt the same way about it, too.

At any rate, my visit to two of the Wairarapa's coastal stations was over as I headed inland to Brancepeth station, near Masterton, where I was expected for lunch. For a moment I reflected on what Graeme Bolton had told me about what working on such famous old stations as Te Awaiti and White Rock meant to him.

'You know that the traditions are here. You know that a lot of people are looking at you because these stations are so well known. You're proud to work on them. It gives you the incentive to carry on.'

Tim Ritchie, Anne Quinn, Graeme Bolton. Things aren't too bad 150 years down the line, are they, Richard Barton?

12

PRIDE OF THE WAIRARAPA

Now in his seventy-third year, Hugh Beetham had been associated with Brancepeth station over a period of enormous change. The property, founded by his family in 1857, became among the most notable in the entire country; it was the pride of the Wairarapa. Today, Brancepeth, gradually reduced over the years to its present 1500 hectares, was but a shadow of the mighty station it once was.

It was late Sunday morning as I arrived at Brancepeth, an easy run from White Rock. I stood outside the magnificent, baronial dwelling that was home to Hugh and Barbara Beetham. Work on the first homestead had started in 1857; additions were made 20 years later. Then, in 1905, it was largely dismantled and the present two storey structure built. Facing the homestead there was a well-manicured lawn the size of a small park. Exotic trees, from England, were scattered about the lawn, casting their golden-coloured leaves on the ground.

I turned to Hugh Beetham and said, 'It's quite lovely.'

He nodded in agreement; he had heard it all a thousand times and more. 'Would you like to see the first whare they built on the place?'

'Love to,' I replied.

With that, we walked briskly towards a reddish-brown whare or hut. Pit-sawn weatherboard planks had been used, the roof was hand-cut totara shingle, and the windows were small, fitted without the aid of putty. The whare had stood here for 147 years, and looked like it would still be here in that time again.

'Built to last,' I said.

'That was the way of it then,' Hugh Beetham agreed.

So this, I thought with no little awe, was where the Beethams had decided to make their first home in the wilderness. They had leased a block of some 4100 hectares

120 • STATION COUNTRY

approximately 25 kilometres east of Masterton. The block consisted of open grassy valleys, deep gorges and rolling hills; much of it covered with a dense forest of totara, rimu, beech and kahikatea.

Hugh Beetham tapped me on the shoulder. 'They lived under a tent-fly while they built it. Lived off the land, too. Wild pork, native birds, whatever they could find. They ran out of gunpowder nine days after they got here. Know what they did? They walked back down the coast to Wellington to get some more and then came all the way back again.' He shook his head. 'Can you imagine that?'

The Beethams — like many pioneering families — were a family of great fortitude and courage. They came from far-off Yorkshire and took up huge blocks of unbroken land; they accepted the hardships that invariably went with such a daunting undertaking. They had arrived in Wellington on 1 December 1855. William (44) and Mary (41) had seven sons and three daughters. William, in partnership with a man called Hutton (who soon pulled out of the arrangement) had obtained the lease to the block in late 1856 or early 1857. It had been taken up for William and Mary's sons; William himself had taken on a small farm at Naenae in the Hutt Valley. It was left to Richmond (21), William (20), George (17) and Hugh (16) to break in the new block. The boys tackled the job with enthusiasm and confidence. They faced great difficulties when they first introduced sheep because the whole area was overrun with wild pigs and dogs.

The story of how Brancepeth got its name is particularly appealing.

It was hot that day in 1857. Out on their block, two of the Beetham boys — most likely William and George — were building the whare I was now standing beside. They had erected the framework and were putting up the rafters. One of them suddenly noticed a big wild boar; it had just appeared at the edge of the forest. Keen to see just what the boar got up to, he nudged the other and held a finger to his lips. They watched in silence as the boar, continually sniffing the ground, moved closer and closer. Presently it reached the framework of the whare. Curious, it moved slowly through the frame so that, for a moment or two, it passed directly below the two brothers. Suddenly recognising the significance, one of the brothers said softly, 'Braun's path'. In old English dialect this meant 'the path of the pig'. They were both aware that Brancepeth Castle, in the north of England, had risen on what had been a track used by wild boar for many centuries. The Beetham boys had a name for their block: Brancepeth.

Perhaps the most notable event in the saga of Brancepeth happened in the Hutt Valley on 20 October 1858. The occasion was the marriage of Thomas Coldham Williams — the fourth son of a prominent North Auckland family — to Anne Palmer Beetham, eldest daughter of William and Mary.

Known far and wide as TC, the 33-year-old was tall and handsome. He was exactly what the Beetham boys, struggling through lack of capital to get ahead on their pig-ridden block, might have hoped for in their sister's choice of husband. TC was wealthy; he had made a considerable amount of money selling beef to the British forces stationed in Auckland during the Land Wars. He was keen to invest some of his money in the land, and he got on famously with his new brothers-in-law. They talked it all out and decided to form a partnership: the Beethams would work the block and Williams would provide the finance.

The Williams-Beetham partnership would last until 1905. With money no longer a problem, the station was on its way. New roads were built, creeks were bridged. Huge gangs of men were hired to clear the forested land. They were known as bushwhackers and, using cross-cut saw and Kelly axe, they indeed whacked down the forest. From the forest came timber to construct more buildings. The mighty totara provided wood for post-and-rail fences

Brancepeth, in all its grace and splendour.

The store was the second building to be erected on the station.

The men's quarters.

that will last forever.

Whenever possible, the partnership purchased more land; by 1870 it had doubled in area. When the original 1860 woolshed became too small, a new, 24-stand shed was built at Te Parae, an outstation. In 1883 they purchased a 6300-hectare bush block north of Tinui. They called it Annedale, after Anne Williams.

By the end of the 1880s Brancepeth was undoubtedly *the* station in that part of the country. It was easily the biggest and by far the most valuable station in the Wairarapa. While the Williams-Beetham partnership was legally dissolved in 1903, it wasn't until two years later that the station was subdivided among 15 members of both families. By this time, Hugh was the most dominant of the Beethams and he retained the homestead area and surrounding country, in excess of 5300 hectares. Annedale, at 6300 hectares, including Te Parae, was taken over by Williams and later divided among his 13 children.

The grandson of Hugh Beetham, bearing the same name, turned away from the old whare, explaining that the building adjacent to it was the original coachhouse, dating to the early 1870s. The old coachhouse was also kept locked; Hugh Beetham produced a key and the heavy door creaked open. I peered inside as a shaft of cool sunlight speared over my shoulder and spread over the solid wooden floor. Particles of dust hung in the still, slightly stale air.

The past was still alive in the coachhouse. A fully mounted buggy, gleaming in near-mint condition bore the name Thos Wagg and Co. Hanging on the walls was all

The family stables, with Hugh Beetham's saddle in the foreground.

sorts of paraphernalia from the coaching days. There were six individual horse stalls, not for station hacks but for the family's own mounts. There was a saddle that Hugh Beetham had ridden in for most of his working life. There was no name on it. Just a New Zealand stock saddle, Hugh Beetham said. Up there on a high cross-beam hung an American roping saddle that belonged to Hugh Beetham's son, Ralph. He had worked for a time on a cattle ranch in Hawaii and had bought the saddle there.

'The coachman slept in here,' Hugh Beetham said, indicating a small room.

Incredibly, his livery gear, including top hat, still hung in a cramped wardrobe. I could suddenly see in my mind's eye the coachman, cheeks freshly shaven, quite splendid in his ornate finery. So, too, could I imagine the horses in their stalls, a groom tending to them.

Back around the turn of the century, when the station had as many as 400 workers on its payroll, there were in excess of 100 horses, including two stallions. Brancepeth, in fact, was famous for its horses and horse sales were held regularly. Many of the men also had their own horses. Sometimes, then, you might have seen 200 or 300 horses in the horse paddock. What a great sight that would have made!

We walked out of the coachhouse and into the sun, which cast a pale light on the fallen leaves of the season. Hugh Beetham indicated another building. It was small, tucked in behind the homestead, and was the second building on the place. This was the store, where station staff and their families could purchase at cost a wide range of goods, from aspirins to a three-piece suit. In the early days all the stores came into the station from the coast; Castlepoint was the only real access. When the Williams-Beetham partnership was formed and work had gone ahead in leaps and bounds, as many as six bullock teams were in almost continual use.

Near the store was the station library, which Beetham had founded in 1884 for the use of everyone on the place. The station clerk, who also looked after the store, was in charge of the 4000-book library. When required, books, papers and magazines were taken by packhorse to outlying stations. Station staff paid two shillings a month for access to the library, which was considered superior to the one in Masterton at the time. Today there were no books in the library: Hugh Beetham had donated them all to Victoria University in 1966.

I also saw the cookhouse, where bread was made for outstations and camps, and the singlemen's quarters which, Hugh Beetham said, would probably never be used again. Lane Cottage, a neat little house hiding behind a fence, sheltered the schoolmaster during the 25 years there was a school on the station.

Brancepeth wasn't a run-of-the-mill property. It covered, at its peak, pretty much the entire Wainuioru district. The station was a way of life not only for the Beethams but also for everyone who worked there and regarded it as home. And they, of course, worked in a variety of occupations, as can be seen from this 1907 scale of wages.

Head shepherd	£125 a year, plus bonus
First-class shepherd	30 shillings a week
Second-class shepherd	25 shillings a week
Head fencer	40 shillings a week
Fencer's mate	30 shillings a week
Fence repairer	25 shillings a week
Rabbiter	25 shillings a week
Head stockman	35 shillings a week
Stockman's mate	25 shillings a week
Head ploughman	35 shillings a week
Ploughman	22 shillings 6 pence a week
Station cook and baker	30 shillings a week
Cook's mate	22 shillings 6 pence a week
Outstation cook	20 shillings a week
Fairly permanent stationhands	25 shillings a week
Ganger (in charge above)	35 shillings a week
Cowboy	25 shillings a week
Casual hands	20 shillings a week

It is worth noting that wages were 'all found' (board included) and that the men almost always worked in pairs, with senior men having the right to choose their own mate.

Presently, Hugh Beetham and I started back to the homestead. It was cool and overcast; winter wasn't very far away. How, I asked myself, could you call such an impressive building a homestead? The showpiece had stood there largely unchanged since 1905: it had 32 rooms, and some 148,000 super feet of timber, all cut on the place, went into its construction. The floor area was 4100 square metres. It was more a mansion than a homestead, built in far grander times, when the links with the Old Country were rock solid.

'Come inside,' Hugh Beetham said, ushering me into a small entrance hall.

Relics of the past were here, too, as well as trophies of the hunt: red deer heads, pig tusks. Red deer had been introduced onto the station in the 1870s. They had been carefully protected until they established themselves into

Hugh Beetham taking advantage of the autumn sunshine.

three main herds. Then trophy hunting, taking only the very best heads, began. Deer had never become a problem on Brancepeth. The pigs had 'bred like blazes', Hugh Beetham reckoned. The situation had got so bad by the late 1870s and early 1880s that the station had placed a bounty on them, which reached as much as 10 shillings per snout. While that had certainly done much to curtail their numbers, there was another reason for the eventual extermination of pigs on the station.

Rabbits had been introduced into the Wairarapa in the mid-1870s by a man named Carter. A decade later they had a stranglehold on much of the region. It was so bad on Brancepeth that, unless something drastic was done, they would simply take over. The first Hugh Beetham came up with the idea of fencing in the entire station. At that time the run covered some 23,000 hectares, so it was an enormous task. Hugh Beetham was not overawed and the work went ahead. These were not normal rabbit-proof fences; they were much stronger — 40-centimetre gauge wire buried a full 25 centimetres in the ground. Some of the fences still existed today. Once the station was fully fenced, the run was split into four and each block fenced in the same way.

Then the eradication of rabbits started in earnest. Of course, they did not wipe out the rabbits, but they brought them under control. The fencing, however, proved fatal for the pigs. They were trapped! Gradually, their numbers were whittled down; there were no more pigs coming onto the place from the nearby heavily bushed country. By the late 1880s and early 1900s there were no more wild pigs on Brancepeth, although the rabbit problem would resurface again and again.

In the gracious smoking room, with its high stud, book-lined walls and gun rack containing firearms of a distant era, Barbara Beetham served coffee and biscuits. She and Hugh had been married for nearly 50 years. From what I could gather, they had lived here together since the end of the war. Barbara's family name was Barton — she was a direct link with the founder of White Rock station. The trend of our conversation was nostalgic. Brancepeth was not of the future or the present; it was the past that counted here.

While Barbara Beetham prepared a late lunch, I flipped casually through the pages of *They Came To Wydrop*, David Yerex's fine account of the Beetham and Williams families on Brancepeth and Te Parae. My attention was arrested by a full-page photograph, with the caption: 'Hugh Beetham on Sally with his sheep dog Mick in 1956'. Hugh Beetham looked just the story on his stock horse and I said as much.

Hugh smiled reflectively. 'You know,' he said as the smile died, 'there aren't any horses here today.'

'How do you feel about that?'

'Feel? Well, if you must know I find it extraordinarily sad; it's incredible when you think about it. Really, I can't get used to the fact that there isn't a single horse on Brancepeth any more.'

Barbara Beetham entered the room then, a slim lady of immense style; I wondered how many visitors she and her husband had entertained over the years in this room alone. There was also an illustration of Barbara Beetham in the book, a photograph of a painting done by Sir William Dargie in 1958. She appears quite lovely; Barbara Barton must have been considered quite a catch in 1942.

Hugh Beetham looked at his wife as she sat down on a sofa. 'I was just telling Philip that we haven't got any horses here any more.' He was getting more upset by the minute.

Barbara Beetham nodded. 'Nor deer, either!'

At the mention of deer, Hugh Beetham's face came to resemble storm clouds brewing over the nearby Tararua Range. 'All my life we've had deer on Brancepeth and now, like Barbara says, they've all gone, too!'

By early 1982 there were only a few deer remaining on the station: a herd of perhaps 12 animals that resided in a bush gully of about 12 hectares. The Beethams put out the word that these deer were not to be shot. Later that same year they were uplifted by helicopter and no doubt ended up on a deer farm somewhere.

I thought about Brancepeth in earlier days and I couldn't resist saying, 'No pigs! No deer! No horses!'

Hugh Beetham laughed a hollow laugh. 'No wild dogs, either! Occasionally someone's pet'll take off and kill thirty or forty ewes and that's quite impressive — particularly my temper!'

Barbara Beetham added, 'We're really suburbia now . . .'

The words seemed to hang in the air for a long time. I reflected on Barbara Beetham's words as I put Brancepeth behind me later that afternoon. Until I reached the Masterton–Castlepoint Road I was travelling across what was once all Brancepeth land. Today the station was split up into about 45 farms. How marvellous it must have been for those people who farmed here to dwell on the past, back to a time when Brancepeth was truly the pride of the Wairarapa.

13

THE SMEDLEY CHALLENGE

Bellowing, several hundred head of cattle ambled rather haphazardly across a green hill face tinged with brown. Moments later, two horsemen edged left to right into the postcard-like scene, jogging after the cattle. There were clumps of trees scattered about: massive totara, multi-leaved beech and kahikatea, the tallest of all forest dwellers in this country. In the dewy grass there were small, winding trails, the tell-tale marks of possums foraging overnight. A bellbird announced its presence; its song was as pure as snow. The early morning sun was lurking surreptitiously behind low clouds; perhaps, later, it would be coaxed out of hiding. Away to the west clouds banked hard against the unseen shoulders of the Ruahine Range.

The place was Smedley station, in southern Hawke's Bay, and it had been a cadet training farm for 61 years. The manager of the station, 39-year-old Jerry Jeromson, was medium-tall and well built with it. During the course of my guided tour of the 3250-hectare station we had driven to this commanding spot, from where it was possible to observe two cadets carrying out their duties.

'It's a lovely spot, Jerry.'

Jerry nodded, pleased at my reaction. 'Hmmm . . . it is,' he agreed, fishing into the deep pocket of his blue wool shirt.

'Bit like a park, really.'

He nodded a second time. 'A lot of Smedley is like that.' He paused to pop a filter-tipped cigarette into his mouth. 'It's like the trees were deliberately thinned out and left standing in that fashion.' He finally got around to lighting his smoke.

I jerked a hand in the general direction of the horsemen. 'Who're the boys?'

With satisfaction, Jerry blew out a cloud of smoke.

Cadets Lincoln Harris and Jason Hammond.

'Jason Hammond and Lincoln Harris.'

I grinned. 'I'm not that much wiser, y'know.'

'Jason's on the broken-coloured horse, Jesse, and Lincoln's on the chestnut, Di. Any clearer?'

'Much. What's the huntaway called?' I asked referring to a big black-and-tan job moving between the horsemen.

Jerry's face was without expression as he replied. 'Buggered if I know. He belongs to Lincoln. You'll have to ask him.'

The big huntaway was racing uphill in huge, leaping bounds; no effort at all. His master's shouted commands carried clearly to us on the breeze. A few cows, until then intent on breaking away from the main bunch, suddenly thought better of it and, snorting, wheeled about and bolted back down-slope. Up above them the huntaway perched his solid rump on a ridge and watched them carefully: just you dare!

Jerry explained that they were shifting the cattle to a

different block as part of a rotation system that, as he put it, 'helped to clean up the paddocks this time of the year'. All up there were 209 cattle on paddock-cleaning duties here, out of a total herd of around 500. We watched the cattle, and then the horsemen, fall out of sight over the low skyline. Jason and Lincoln had appeared so much at ease on the horses as they shifted the cattle that it would have been easier to believe they were hard-bitten drovers, nearing the end of a long trip, rather than mere cadets. Jason, from Napier, was in his second year here; Lincoln, also a second-year cadet, had the advantage of coming from a station background: Tangiwai, near Waiouru.

Jerry had also been a cadet here, in 1970–71. Later, he had put in 18 months on Smedley as a single shepherd. Other station jobs had followed that, Twin Rivers in the King Country for one example. He had also found time to get married, to Di, 17 years ago; they had two children, a boy and a girl, now both teenagers. Jerry had been farm manager on Te Whanga, an Angus stud near Masterton, when this job had come up a year ago.

Jerry, Jason and Lincoln would never regret the time they spent on Smedley. What they learned here was invaluable; moreover, the friends they made became friends for life. Very special bonds, forged by living and working together in a rural environment, have long been an accepted thing where the air is good to breathe and the weather is of the utmost importance.

Precise details about Smedley's beginnings are unclear. It was taken up in the mid to late 1850s. The size of the original section is unknown, but the first runholder was certainly Josiah Howard. Born in Lancashire in the 1830s, Howard came from a family of silk millers, who, it would seem, were well-to-do rather than, say, working class. Josiah Howard was probably in his mid-twenties when he married; it would be a short-lived affair. Tragically, his wife and child both died on their first wedding anniversary. Howard was distraught at this double blow. His hurt was so intense, so very personal, that he vowed

Jerry Jeromson.

that he would never marry again; and he was true to his word. Restless and unhappy, Howard decided to leave his homeland. He reached New Zealand via a short stint on the Australian goldfields. He went to Central Otago first, but did not stay long. Presently, he arrived in the North Island and made his way to Napier.

Although Howard knew absolutely nothing about farming, he arrived at the Government Land Office with a view to taking up a section or block of land. He studied a map of Hawke's Bay; land not yet taken up was shaded accordingly. Hmm . . . that looked promising. Howard was looking at a block some 30 kilometres northwest of Waipawa. Yes, he would settle for that one.

Josiah Howard, a registered landowner, albeit with a much lighter bank balance, provisioned himself and then started out to locate his block. He was alone — a self-reliant and adventurous man. Howard found his block after travelling up the Waipawa River; he called it after his home town in Lancashire.

Later, Howard was joined on Smedley by his brother, James, and later still by his nephew, Robert Hilton, the son of his sister, Elizabeth, a widow. Given time, Elizabeth would marry again, to Thomas Baker, whom she met in Queensland. They, too, came to Smedley and went into partnership with Josiah Howard. Smedley, with the acquisition of other sections adjoining it, grew to about 3100 hectares. They ran sheep, of course: by 1872 the flock stood at 1200; eight years later, it swelled to 5000.

During the 1880s Robert Hilton and his mother and stepfather pulled out of Smedley and went to Australia; James went his own way too. Smedley is said to have reached its peak stock numbers in the mid-1890s, when the flock stood at 17,000. Howard would have been in his mid-sixties, not a robust young man. Nevertheless, he continued to run the station. Some said he was a difficult man; perhaps his failing health had something to do with that. Things started to slide on Smedley as Howard's health grew worse. The flock, largely uncared for, decreased in numbers and fences and gates fell into a sad state.

Eventually, Josiah Howard became too ill to get around his station. He would have known, of course, of the state it was in, and perhaps there was by now a financial angle that made changing anything well-nigh impossible. When Howard died in 1919, he left his beloved Smedley to the Crown, an act suggesting there had been serious family disagreements that had not been resolved.

Josiah Howard's will stated that Smedley was to be carried on as a farming venture, and as a place where young people of Hawke's Bay could be trained in all aspects of farming and station life. If Josiah Howard had never before openly professed his love of his adopted country and, in particular, his adopted province on the east coast of the North Island, then he did so now.

It would, however, be a full 10 years before his wishes came to fruition. In January 1931, five cadets arrived, the first to dare take up the Smedley challenge.

With the nine o'clock sun slanting through a tight canopy of beech trees crowding a narrow track, Jerry Jersomson made a slick gearshift and kept up an informed running commentary about Smedley.

I observed sheep on a hill face. 'Romney?'

Since 46 percent of all sheep in this country are that breed, it was about as good as an educated guess.

Jerry bobbed his head up and down. 'Yeah.' His voice was flat, matter-of-fact.

I decided to take an even deeper plunge, something like a stock agent wanting to impress the hell out of a prospective client. 'Two-tooths, I suppose?'

'Uh-huh.'

'They look in good condition.'

'That they are.'

All up, they ran 10,900 Romney sheep and there were about 2900 of them on the hill face we had put behind us.

'Thing is,' Jerry said without prompting, 'Smedley is a working station that must be run commercially. An annual profit is required to cover the cost of each cadet.'

'They don't pay to come here, do they?'

'No,' Jerry replied with a positive shake of his head. Ash from his dying smoke fell onto his shirtfront.

For the record, the cost of the cadet scheme, which naturally varied from year to year, came to $148,255 in 1990; the cost per cadet worked out at $8205.

Fancy the idea of attending Smedley for two years, do you? Well, preference is given to applicants whose parents live in Hawke's Bay, and you'll need to be between 15 and 20 years old. The scheme runs for two years, with 10 cadets in each year. Accommodation is provided and cadets are paid a weekly allowance; there is even a cash bonus for completing the cadetship. The training programme is extensive and includes much more than a normal working shepherd is ever likely to be asked to perform. It is a scheme more for future station or farm managers and is second to none in this country. It was now June, and this month the cadets were studying everything: from breaking in horses and shearing, to external and internal parasites and putting together a CV.

Smedley station complex.

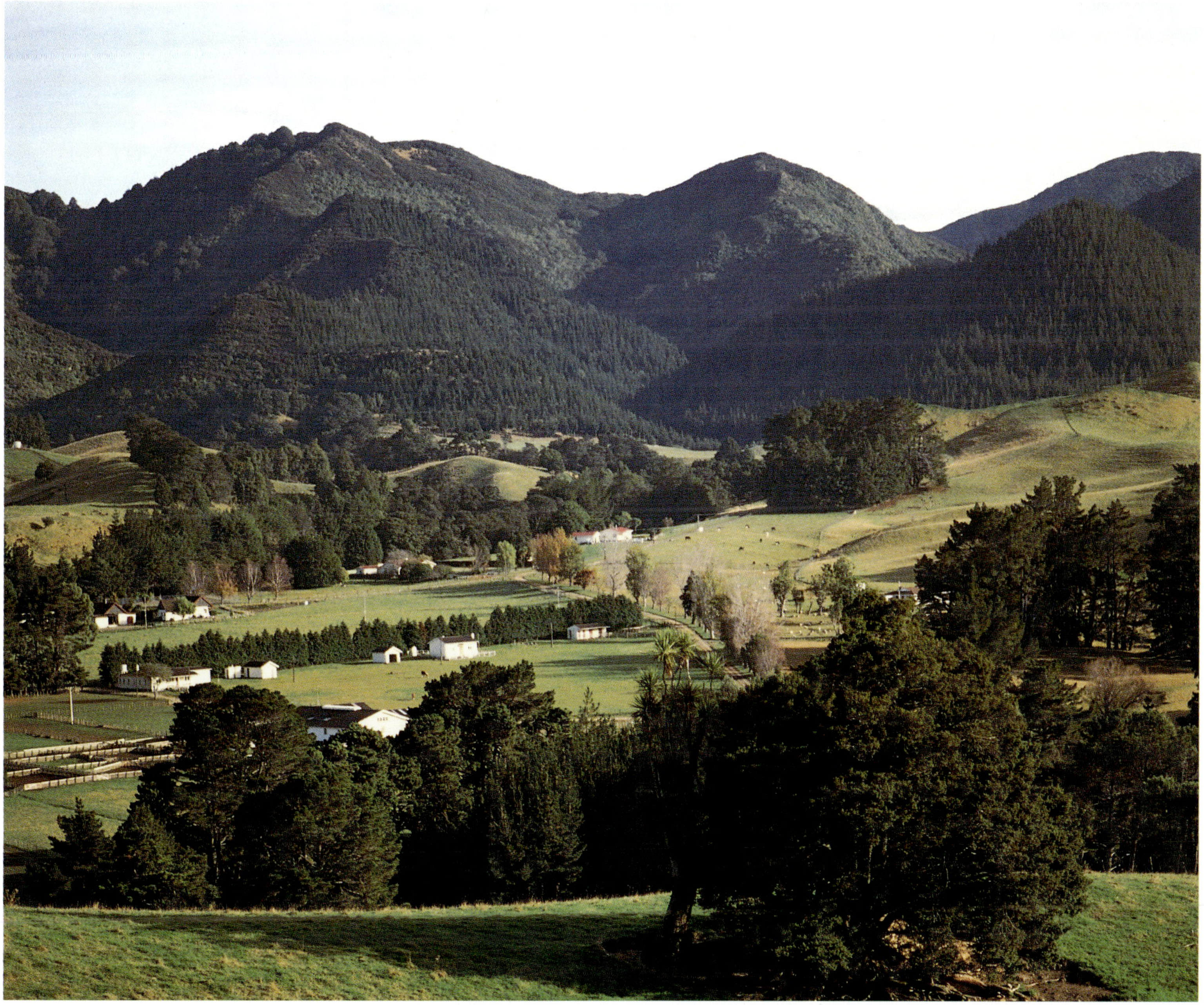

Soon we arrived at a deer pen. It was a lovely morning by this time, and it struck a deep chord in me, long hidden. I recalled with fleeting nostalgia the other early winter days I'd savoured in Hawke's Bay, deer culling in the Kaweka and Ruahine Ranges, or out on the Rabbit Board beyond Rissington.

With a big yank, I opened the gate to the deer pen; a few hinds trotted away to link up with a larger bunch. Jerry drove through and I closed the gate. The hinds, I thought, did not appear too happy with their lot. That was understandable: they had recently been deprived of their fawns, aged about seven or eight months. The fawns were the reason Jerry had called in here; he wanted a word with stock manager Steve Caswell, who, with two cadets, was waiting at the yards where the fawns were held.

While Jerry cornered Steve, I had a brief and humorous exchange with the two cadets, both locals. Second-year cadet Steven Kingston hailed from Clareinch station, at Waipawa; Simon Ewen, in his first year, came from Waipukurau. They were pretty typical of the cadets I spoke to, both relaxed and happy natured. And here, like anywhere else, that started right at the top — with Jerry Jeromson. There is no way you would see smiling, contented cadets if they had a miserable sour-faced boss.

Jerry swung his compact frame easily into the driver's seat and, as he started up the engine, he said, 'The boys enjoy working with deer. So do I for that matter.'

We pulled away and left the deer pen behind.

'They get a big charge out of hunting deer, too,' Jerry said suddenly.

'Aha! So there's a few on the place, eh?'

Jerry nodded. 'More than a few. Plenty!' He stabbed a hand through the open window. 'The heaviest concentrations are over there.'

I followed the line of his finger to Smedley's northwestern boundary, at the southern end of the isolated Wakarara Range.

'Deer all over the place at times,' Jerry continued. 'The boys usually see something when they're out mustering.'

He paused. 'Course, rifle safety is taught here. Most of the boys have got rifles; they store them at my place. There's a rifle shoot each November, too.'

At a high point near Smedley's back boundary we stopped for morning tea. We had seen pigs rooting in a block called Little Baldy; apparently that wasn't too common on Smedley these days, and Jerry had reckoned some of the boys would like to hear about that. We also saw some of the 800 goats employed on the place to control weeds and gorse. They were out in a big, rough block that looked good for pigs to hide out in. It was difficult to tell if the goats were really earning their keep out there or if they were simply mucking around.

Sipping my tea, I looked across the valley, way beyond the Makaroro to the Ruahines. I wondered what the numbers of deer were like there now that the backside had fallen out of the venison and live-game capture market. Most likely they'd be making a good recovery.

My mind slipped back in time. I was looking at the North-Eastern Ruahine block, where in 1963 I'd put in a hard winter. I smiled as I turned to look at the nearby Wakarara Range. Barry Hunt and I, in an attempt to boost our poor monthly tally, had decided to cross the valley of the Makaroro and spend a few days up on the Wakararas, where, Barry had reckoned with sublime confidence, there were plenty of deer. No doubt there were — in the spring! We trudged with heavy packs to the crest of the range, about 900 metres. By then the weather had really packed in, but we had a broken-down whare to camp in. In the morning we packed up and shot through, and arrived back at our lovely hut with nothing to show for our efforts but wet arses.

Jerry's voice broke into my contemplation. 'Did you know there's a wapiti hanging around here?'

'You're kidding me, surely?'

'No way!'

I could see he was serious. 'On Smedley, you mean?'

'At times.' He indicated the Wakarara Range. 'Probably hangs about there more, though.'

Red deer hinds.

Jerry, at my urging, went on to explain that the wapiti, a bull, had apparently escaped from a deer farm south of here about two or three years ago. It had been seen on Smedley by several of the cadets.

'You sure they knew what they were looking at?' I asked.

'Absolutely!' Jerry paused and then played his trump card. 'The point is, I saw it too!'

On that particular day, about a year earlier, Jerry had been out in a block called Donovans checking a flood gate. Suddenly, the bull had appeared before him in a small grassy valley. Perhaps aware that there was no threat here, the bull had trotted, rather than bolted, away, giving Jerry a real good look at him. It had been early in the year then and the bull had been growing his antlers, rather than displaying a full head. Pity. Jerry reckoned he was as big as! Wapiti and red deer breed freely; they are, after all, closely related. With a big bull ranging this country, that had to eventually reveal itself in the way of trophy potential. I said as much to Jerry, who looked somewhat glum.

'Trouble is, we've got an endemic TB area here now.'

'Possums?'

'Right! There's a huge population here. It's so bad you can see them feeding out in the paddocks in the daytime; that's a sure sign of over-population. There's TB right through them, of course.'

'So what's the answer?'

'MAF reckons it's a poison drop. And real soon, too.' He shrugged. 'So just what that's gonna do to the deer, well, I dunno.'

'That'll wipe out heaps! No matter what they say, Jerry, 1080 does not take any prisoners.'

'Yeah, I know,' Jerry said heavily. 'So what with the deer and the danger to our dogs . . .' He shook his head. 'It's a real worry, all right.' He reached for his smokes.

Breakfast time for twenty hungry cadets.

'It'd really break up any of the boys if they lost a dog.'

It was not difficult to understand Jerry's concern about the dogs and how it would hurt a cadet to lose one to poisoned bait or, more realistically, to something that had fallen victim to it. Because of the way the system worked on Smedley, the dogs had even more significance than your usual shepherd's team. A first-year cadet was not allowed a dog of his own, even though he might come from a station. At the start of a cadet's second year the wonderful moment arrived: a dog of his very own! Only one type of dog was allowed — a huntaway. Once the cadet could handle his dog to the manager's satisfaction, he could then have a second dog, a heading dog.

Jerry explained. 'I think it's an excellent way to start them off. By the time they can have a dog of their own, they really appreciate it. Because they haven't got a surplus of dogs to call on, they must learn to use what they have to best advantage. The dog must count!'

To avoid the possibility of any of Smedley's more than 50 dogs getting killed by poison, Jerry had just ordered 50 dog muzzles. The problem is, sometimes even that isn't an effective method of stopping the worst from happening.

Down from the higher country, on Smedley's eastern flank, we came to a grassy bench above the Makaroro Stream. There was a camp here known as Middle Whare; it dated to the mid-1950s. Close by was a small yard that, at a pinch, could handle 2500 sheep. A haybarn stood near a stand of trees, as did a hitching rail and dog kennels. The whare had, I think, two rooms. It was heated by a stove linked to an efficient hot-water system. No need to worry about power cuts at Middle Whare!

As we moved out of the whare and into a pool of sun, Jerry told me that the whare was an important part of a cadet's life here. Over winter they came out here, three at a time, and stayed for a week. They rode horses, of course, and sometimes brought a packhorse in with them, too. They did a lambing beat, maybe cut some scrub, and made sure there was ample firewood, not only for their use but also for the next bunch of cadets.

'Could have handled that when I was their age,' I said. Just imagine me and my mates from New South Wales out here. We'd have packed in a rifle apiece, too.

14

EAST COAST

Mangatu Blocks

The sun was up and smiling on a steep East Coast hill face northwest of Gisborne, where 1000-plus Romney ewes were being worked to lower ground by a Maori shepherd and his dogs. It was, I thought, a scene synonymous with this sun-blessed part of the North Island.

The station was called Wairere. It was just one of the properties belonging to the proprietors of Mangatu Blocks, a Maori farming enterprise on a grand scale. The stations ranged over 34,000 hectares of the overall 45,000 hectares that the incorporation handled. Basically, the land was contained in the south by the Urukokomuka Stream, in the east by the Waipaoa River and in the west by the headwaters of the Motu River. Most of the country they owned that was not farmed was found within the Raukumara Range.

I was standing ankle-deep in chopped-up mud in the sheep yards on Wairere. Alongside me was the manager of the station, 57-year-old Eric Tamanui. He had a long association with the property and with the region, and at one time he had worked on Te Apiti, one of the bigger stations owned by the group. As a matter of fact, Eric had got married while working on Te Apiti, but that was six kids ago, now.

The state of the sheep yards was the reason they hadn't started shearing yesterday but now, with the sun, things should dry up quickly and they'd get cracking first thing in the morning. The yards were waterlogged partly because of recent rain, and partly because a nearby creek, which Eric indicated with his gnarled hillstick, often flooded and the waters went right through the yards.

'Has that been a problem here for long?' I wondered.

'Yeah — years,' Eric replied.

'Maybe they should've built them somewhere else,'

I pointed out brightly.

Eric shook his head. 'Where else would you build 'em around here, eh?'

Good point. On Wairere — like so many East Coast hill-country stations — you're flat out finding any level ground at all.

By this time, the Romneys were much lower, beyond a little creek and on the far side of a narrow grove of trees. Eric turned his head in that direction so that I was looking directly at his profile. His was a strong-featured face; it was also a face full of kindness and compassion and I knew instinctively that Eric Tamanui would have the deep respect of his large family.

With the sheep almost on level ground, I glanced across at the shepherd, Bo Milner, and wondered why he was on foot — after all, East Coasters dearly love their horses. Along with the pig, horses were perhaps the only useful thing the Pakeha ever provided from their point of view.

'Oh, we do use horses here,' Eric said. 'Almost all of the time, too. The reason Bo's on foot is that he wants to get real fit.' Maybe I was looking a wee bit blank, because Eric hastened to add, 'The football season's started, you know.'

Bo Milner played for the Whatatutu team.

Eric tossed a hand in Bo's general direction. 'Have a yarn with him if you like.'

So, with a smile of thanks, I left Eric and trudged through the clinging mud to Bo.

'G'day!'

'Nice day for it,' he replied.

Bo was tall and well built, a handsome man. A slow smile built on his face as he eyed my weighty camera bag and the large tripod. The smile grew bigger, then became a fully charged grin, so that his teeth showed white and his eyes danced with laughter.

'Oh,' he said, 'I suppose you're from the *National*

Robin Barabarich and Darryl Brown working sheep on Te Hua station.

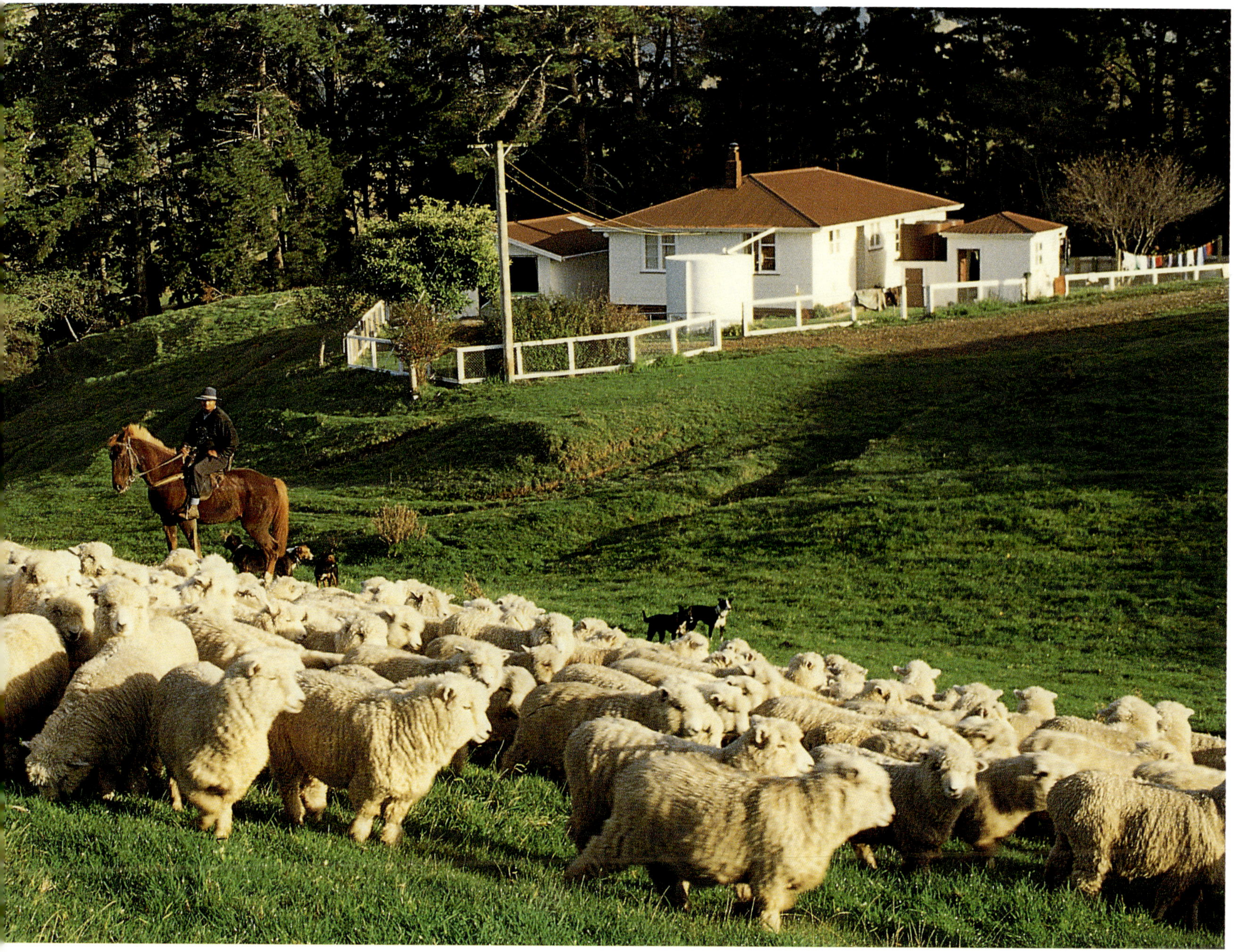

Geographic, eh?'

Presently, it was time to leave Wairere to the men that so ably ran it. I drove away from the boggy sheep yards and the milling Romneys, which were being driven into the big woolshed where, prior to shearing, they would spend the night. At least it wouldn't be wet underhoof.

Soon I came to Te Hua station, where I caught up with head shepherd Darryl Brown and shepherd Robin Barabarich. Darryl told me that his boss, Kaioha Cairns, was away. It was the same story here as on Wairere: Darryl, mounted, and Robin, on foot, were also bringing a mob of sheep into the main station complex.

With his long hair and warrior-like looks, Robin, who told me he was a dead-keen pig hunter, looked to me as though he might, in a time long past, have just come down from the misty ranges with a troop of the inept Pakeha constabulary hot on his trail. Reckon Robin would have given them the slip, no worries.

The proprietors of Mangatu Blocks, interestingly enough, actually numbered as many as 3000, all belonging to the Te Aitanga-a-Mahaki tribe. Mangatu Blocks came into being with the Mangatu No. 1 Empowering Act 1883. The Act meant the land ended up where it should, in Maori hands. The new owners leased their land out to European farmers, so it was the Pakeha who first broke the land and brought in stock. Eventually there were 16 stations, each run separately, in Waikohu County, 55 kilometres northwest of Gisborne.

As the leases ran out they were not renewed by the East Coast Commission, formed in 1917. The Commission hired its own managers and looked after things for the owners, not always to their full satisfaction. This situation remained until 1947, when a committee of management was formed to administer the land of Te Aitanga-a-Mahaki.

Stock figures on the Mangatu Blocks for the year ending June 1991 reveal there were 126,767 sheep and 15,069 cattle on the stations. This made the incorporation by far

Eric Tamanui.

the largest single contributor to meat processed at Weddle Kaiti freezing works. In the same period, they sold 500,544 kilograms of wool for a gross profit of nearly $1.5 million; but for a world-wide depression in the wool market this figure would have been much higher.

As I parked my car opposite the Mangatu Blocks headquarters in Gisborne, I knew already that they had

Robert 'Bo' Milner.

an office staff of eight, including farm supervisor Albert Horsfall, secretary George B. Ria, and accountant James D. Carrol. Out on the stations they employed around a hundred permanent staff: managers, shepherds, drivers, carpenters and general hands. Seasonal staff, including fencing and shearing contractors, brought the total staff to about twice that number. Some 70 per cent of the workforce were Maori. The organisation's commitment to its people was at the very core of its success.

A particularly nice aspect of the set-up was that young Maori from rural areas were given an opportunity to learn basic farming skills through a cadet training scheme. Out on the various stations they were taught crutching, dagging, fencing, scrub cutting, docking and shearing. There was also plenty of scope for those who were mechanically minded.

In recent years, Mangatu had been looking to diversification and to investment related to the produce of the land. It was the major shareholder of Cedenco Foods Ltd, a natural resource farming company, processor and marketer, that supplied a variety of processed products, most notably tomato paste, direct to major food companies in this country and around the world. Cedenco, based in Gisborne, won the Prime Minister's Award in 1991 for 'outstanding export innovation'. Haumi Traders, another Mangatu subsidiary, was a merchandising company with sales exceeding $1 million a year, trading mainly in farm commodities.

On the horticultural side, Mangatu produced consistently high-quality grapes and kiwifruit. The grape production exceeded 400 tonnes a year, while annual kiwifruit production was between 20,000 and 30,000 trays. The incorporation had a separate division to administer the planting and tending of forest assets. Mangatu had been taking the opportunities provided by the East Coast Conservation Forestry Scheme to plant erosion-prone areas (a constant source of concern in the region). This would safeguard the land while opening the way to future diversification in commercial forestry.

It would be extremely difficult not to be impressed with the nerve-centre of the Mangatu Blocks: its office buildings covered 770 square metres. The foyer was dominated by a tall pou whakairo (carved pole). The intricate carvings on it incorporated the four basic patterns of surface decorations in Maori wood carvings: pakati (chevrons), unaunahi (fish scales), tara-tara-o-kai (fish pieces) and

A section of the pou whakairo at Mangatu Blocks headquarters in Gisborne.

puwerewere (spider's web). There were also carvings on the pole that represented ancestors of the tribe.

Two plaques in the foyer also caught my attention. One marked the dedication of the building; the other read:

> Ko ia nei te tihi o Maungahaumi. Na nga kai-hautu o Mangatu i timata, i arahi. Kua tutuki i tenei ra nga wawata, nga tumanako.
>
> This is the summit of Maungahaumi. The leaders of Mangatu pointed the way and provided the inspiration. This day, their hopes have been fulfilled.

Mount Maungahaumi is the dominant feature of the Mangatu landscape. It stands 1213 metres high. Legend states that the mountain, known as Munga, was named when repairs to the forward section (haumi) of the Horouta canoe, severely damaged at Ohiwa, were made with timber taken from the mountain. Paoa was captain of *Horouta*, and his name is perpetuated in the name of the Waipaoa River, the source of which he is reported to have discovered.

Beyond the foyer was the large committee room, which was the main feature of the complex. The room was fully carved, the work supervised by Hone Taiapa of the Maori Arts and Crafts Institute in Rotorua, and local expert Ngata Ruru. The latticework panels featured traditional designs; this work was undertaken by a group of local women under the guidance of Mrs P. Kaua. No less impressive were the rafters, decorated superbly with kowhaiwhai patterns by Mr J. Kingi.

Here in the committee room it was quiet and, as I stood there, a Pakeha in a Maori setting, I experienced that same sort of indefinable feeling as when I'd first looked closely at the carved pole. It made me want to walk quietly, not to be intrusive in any way. It could, I suppose, be likened to the sensation you might experience in a centuries-old church or cathedral in Europe. Whatever it was, it demanded the utmost respect.

Horses grazing on Waipaoa station.

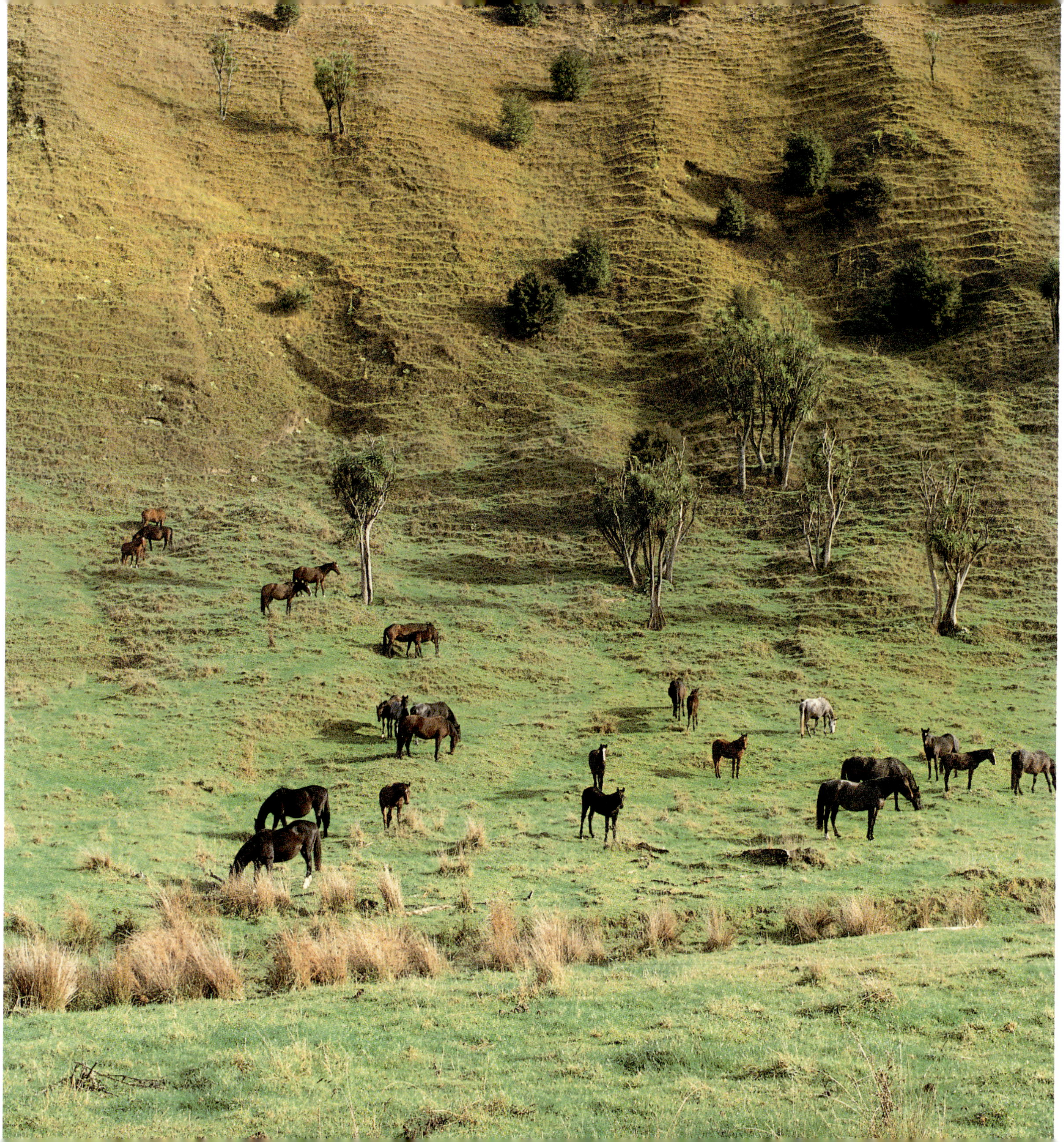

Waipaoa station

Under a hot sun, Ray Parsons and I climbed through tight-knit, wind-stunted growth. There were toetoe, flax, mountain hebes and pittosporums, and various kinds of growth I couldn't put a name to. They were tenacious enough to survive all that the elements could hurl at them at 1000 metres. Eventually we stood on Areoma's plateau-like summit. The mountain (see photograph, page 135) was the dominant landmark on Waipaoa station, one of the most notable properties in the North Island.

Wiping a shirt sleeve across his damp forehead, Ray smiled as we sat down together. The view was incredible, far reaching. I could see right out to the coast, to Young Nicks Head, that sharp-pointed, white-cliffed headland at the southern end of Poverty Bay. There was a station there too, bearing the same name. I could also see, to the southwest, the moutain known as Maungahaumi and, beyond that, the land of Te Aitanga-a-Mahaki.

'That's Moonlight over there,' Ray said, referring to Waipaoa's outstation.

I followed the line of his finger to a smudge of buildings on a hill top.

'Worth the effort?' Ray asked with an engaging smile.

'Been here before. Never a waste of time. Not with a view like this, anyway.'

A companionable silence settled between us; I was thankful for that. Not that Ray was overly talkative, you understand. It's just that too much yakking is about as welcome as another landslip on the East Coast. Yes, I thought, the climb had been well worth the effort. The bird's-eye view of the station was enough in itself, but as I sat there I also thought back to a time when the European had yet to arrive here, back to a time when a battle had taken place right here on Areoma. A long-standing feud between the Ngariki and Whakatohea tribes had finally ignited into open warfare, and the Ngariki, to whom Areoma was sacred, had retreated to the mountain top.

They had chosen well. Areoma was a natural fortress, with its rocky sides resembling the starkly formed battlements of a mediaeval castle. There was just one point of access, a narrow ridge perhaps two axe handles wide at its widest point. In a time when men fought hand-to-hand and weapons were, at best, basic, a token force of warriors could defend Areoma. It was here, then, with a fearsome drop on either side, most of the fighting took place.

The battle to take Areoma turned into a lengthy affair for the determined warriors of Whakatohea, but, despite losing many men, they refused to call it off. Unbeknown to them, however, the defenders of the mountain were in bad trouble: they had run out of water.

In later years, the elders of Ngariki would speak in awe of the daring feat of one of the warriors, Rawiri Tamanui. Somehow, under cover of darkness, Tamanui climbed down the face of the mountain and returned with water. It enabled his tribe to fight on and ultimately defeat Whakatohea. Indeed, Whakatohea paid a terrible price: only one of their warriors remained alive to tell his tribe's story.

Suddenly, my mind snapped back to the present, to the country that unfolded before me: Waipaoa station. There was a total 'farmed' area here of 8500 hectares, plus 3500 hectares leased to the Crown, of which 1900 hectares was planted in pine. The station was 65 kilometres from Gisborne; the Mangatu Forest and Mangatu Blocks formed two of the main boundaries with the station. The bulk of the country was of medium contours, with some steep gullies running through it. Rainfall was rather heavy, between 1000 and 1500 millimetres. Most of the rain fell in the winter months but, because the station was close to the mountains and forest, it received its share of useful summer northwest rain. The station was a private company known as Clark Farming Group, with its base in Gisborne.

In 1876 a 23-year-old Scot, John Clark, arrived in New Zealand. He wasted little time in reaching the East Coast, where he knew the climate was generally agreeable and there was land in abundance. Clark was hungry for land

The Birches high country from Areoma.

and had access to sufficient funds to make his dreams a reality. Before a year was up, Clark was a landowner of some substance, having gained title to 16,000 hectares at Okahauatiu. The land was a mixture of scrub and forest and clearing it was a task of mammoth proportions. Clark and his workforce tackled the block with enthusiasm and cleared 400 hectares a year.

By the turn of the century, the ambitious Clark had cast his net further, acquiring three more stations: Papatu, Opau and Paparatu. Yet the Scotsman's voracious appetite for land was still not satisfied. When Waipaoa station came on the market, it was owned by the company of Lockie, Muir and Others. It covered 13,700 hectares, of which just under a third was cleared and grassed. There were 30,000 sheep and 14,000 cattle on the station. The unbroken country was again scrub and forest — lots of forest comprising mainly tawa, a tall tree, the wood of which is white and soft and straight. Maori used tawa to make their long bird spears. Within the forested areas wild cattle, pigs and dogs were rampant. Clark did not have enough capital to pay the asking price, but he did have assets. It is thought that when he became the owner of Waipaoa station, John Clark had the biggest overdraft in the country!

Today, David Clark, the great-grandson of John, controlled Waipaoa station.

Retracing our steps, Ray Parsons and I crossed the highest point of Areoma and approached the spine-like ridge leading to its summit. Across a deep valley to the north the high escarpment-like country, at about the same altitude as Areoma, was known as the Birches. In the early days they ran hardy wethers out there, summer and winter. Wild dogs were still bad out there then and they played havoc with the sheep.

Nodding in that direction, Ray said that his older brother Dick, a farrier by trade, had got two pigs a couple of weeks back in a big, scooped-out basin below the escarpment. It looked top pig country.

'Many about?'

'Not as many as you'd think,' Ray replied. 'The boys give 'em a hard time. Back in the hills' — he gestured towards the tail-end of the range — 'it's a different story. Lots of pigs there. Deer, too.'

Being manager of such a prominent station as Waipaoa carried a fair share of responsibility. Ray Parsons had first worked on the land here on the East Coast, his home region, but that had been on a farm of around 400 hectares and you couldn't get too worked up about that, could you? Next, he went up to Tokomaru Bay to work on Waiau station. This was more like it: 5300 hectares. Other mustering jobs followed that; it was good for a young man who loved horses to get around and see what the rest of the East Coast had to offer.

Ray first came to Waipaoa station in 1977, as a shepherd. The manager was Chris Spence and the head shepherd was Tom Fleming. There had been Spences and Flemings — related or not — on Waipaoa station since 1902. Steve Satterthwaite turned up on Waipaoa too, at the same time. Steve was, as he put it, 'getting a bit of North Island experience' before he headed back to the Muller. Ray and Steve found they had a lot in common and they quickly became good mates. On leaving, Steve invited Ray and Tom to come south and see what real mustering was all about. They took up his offer and did a fall muster there, something neither man would ever forget.

Ray's next job was on 2800-hectare Te Apiti, as manager. Ray reckoned it was a good place to work, if a little isolated. You had to consider isolation when you were a family man. Ray had met his wife, Margaret, on nearby Arawhana station, where she was working as the relieving cook. Margaret was also from the East Coast and it wasn't long before they were married.

In 1984, Ray and Margaret shifted to another Mangatu Block station: Komihana. That too, was a fine place to work on, so, when the manager's job on Waipaoa station came up in late 1991, Ray was understandably reluctant to move. But there were good reasons why he should: the station school would take his four young children, for example. Waipaoa added up to a real challenge, something a man could get stuck into. Interestingly enough, the man Ray replaced was Ollie Dickson who, at the time of my visit to Glenary, was out there at Jack Mack's hut and loving every minute of it.

A heavy mist enveloped the land as Ray Parsons and I left the spacious homestead, where I had spent a pleasant night, for Moonlight. As we climbed around a steep hill face, the mist grew denser. Suddenly everything seemed a little unreal and distorted. Then the sun began to burn off the mist, spreading shafts of light across a large grassy basin through which meandered a lovely little stream. There were many well-spaced trees there; I recognised willows and poplars. They had been planted for a reason: to check erosion.

The more common tree on the station, however, was *Pinus radiata*. Between 1985 and 1989 they planted a total of 700 hectares in pine. In 1992 they would, over winter, plant a further 500 hectares and, in 1993, the same area of ground again. The first trees would mature in 2010. As David Clark said to me in Gisborne, 'While it's a

Senior shepherd John Berry, on Cyclone.

diversification, we have a huge, ongoing commitment to forestry. Pines will play a big part in the future of Waipaoa station.'

There were sheep grazing among the exotic trees, grey lumps lacking real form. Then, almost magically, the mist lifted and the sheep were revealed for exactly what they were, and the trees were all golds and browns and altogether lovely.

'Best time of the year, autumn,' Ray said.

The sheep were Romneys. Now, over winter, they would carry 17,500 breeding ewes and 6000 ewe hoggets. I had no idea where the hoggets were — maybe they'd all been cleaned up by wild dogs on the Birches! Lambing percentage here was, on average, 100 per cent; it was as high as 110 per cent in 1991. As many lambs as possible were fattened on the station and during the forthcoming year they were expecting to fatten 13,000.

By the time we reached Moonlight, the mist had taken firm control again and, as we pulled to a halt near the woolshed, there were gobs of rain glued to the mud-streaked windscreen. Moonlight was more than 100 metres higher than the homestead, which stood at 250 metres. The air was noticeably cooler; I imagined there were far nicer places to spend your winter on the East Coast than at Moonlight.

This outstation dates to 1909; it was John Clark's idea

Head shepherd Alistair Wallace.

to make the real base of operation more centralised. The name is not short on romance, and it came into being when the land here was being cleared and the men on contract, in order to fulfil their obligations on time, had no option but to take advantage of a moonlit night to put in extra hours. At Moonlight, which was linked to the main homestead by 10 kilometres of all-weather roading, they built men's quarters, a head shepherd's dwelling, a cookhouse, a big 16-stand station and everything else to make the place fully operational.

There was movement at the outstation as we clambered out of the ute. Three shepherds, leading big, sturdy hacks, approached us through the mist. They were capable-looking types wearing high-country clothing.

'Nice day for it,' remarked senior shepherd John Berry.

His horse, Cyclone, rubbed a velvet-soft muzzle against its master's oilskinned back. The senior shepherd ignored it with practised detachment.

'Yeah,' agreed Dean Aitkens. 'A nice day for it.'

Young Boyd Devereux merely smiled and said, 'G'day.'

'Much mist below, Ray?' John asked.

'Clearing by now, I expect. It will here, too.'

John bobbed his head seriously. 'Right. We should be ready to go after lunch.'

They were working cattle today. All up, 1000 head were to be drenched and given a copper injection — there was a serious deficiency of the vital element here. There were a fair number of cattle yards spread over the 158 paddocks on the station and two of them would be in use today; one here at Moonlight and another south of the homestead.

'Okay,' Ray said, 'we'll see you then.'

'Gonna see Pete?' John said, referring to Peter Crossan, a married man with two children. Peter lived with his family in a cottage at the main homestead complex.

'Yeah. He's only got Errol to help him, so I'll need to lend a hand for a while.'

Errol Koia was also married with two children and he was a general hand. At this very moment, Peter and Errol were mustering their share of the cattle.

'See you later then,' John said, starting off.

They went on, horses carrying big stock saddles, dogs running every which way.

'Come on,' Ray said, 'I'll introduce you to Alistair.' Head shepherd Alistair Wallace was a South Islander. He was mucking about with a four-wheel-drive vehicle, with its bonnet up.

'Nice day for it,' Alistair said, looking up.

Manager Ray Parsons.

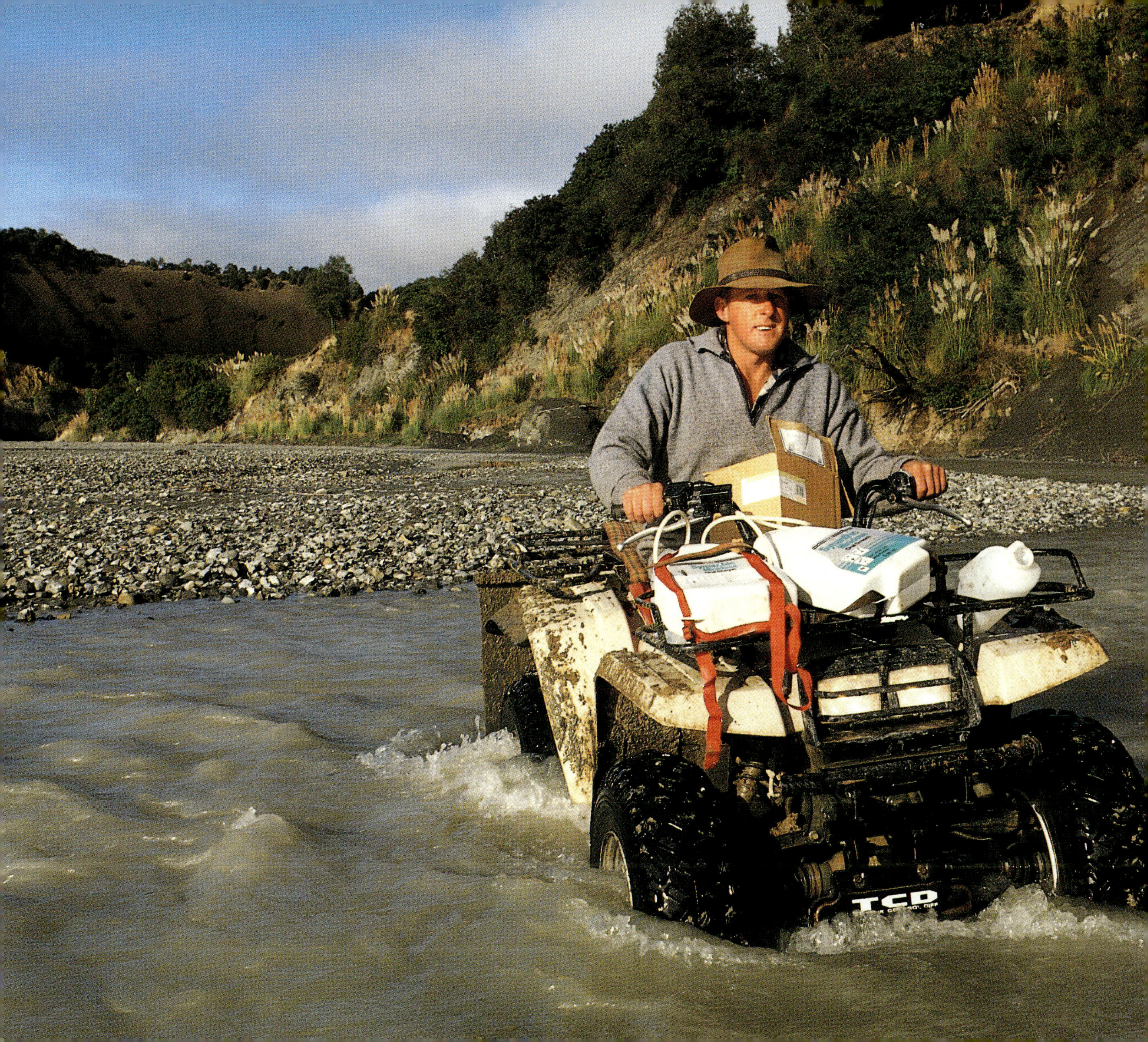
TCD

'Phil Holden,' Ray said.

A hard handshake. 'Heard you were coming,' Alistair said, looking about as excited as a gelding staring at a mare's trim rump.

They began to talk about the day's activities. Thousand head of cattle, was it? Right. How many were Peter and Errol handling? Two-thirty. Okay. Losing interest, I looked across at the mist-shrouded cattle yards. They ran 2250 Hereford-Angus cows and they, of course, went to Hereford or Angus bulls. However, a small number of Simmental bulls were put to the aged cows as a terminal sire. About half of the steer calves were sold as weaners at the Gisborne weaner sales, and, as a rule, 250 to 500 were retained.

Still the manager and head shepherd were deep in conversation as, slowly, the mist started to lift and the sun flashed on the wooden rails of the cattle yards, which, in a few short hours, would be crammed with bawling animals.

A hand tapped me on the shoulder.

'Ready?' Ray asked.

In low gear, and with yours truly perched on the back like a particularly bad afterthought, the farm bike crossed the last ford in the river near the old cattle yards at the southern end of the station. Our timing was well-nigh perfect. The shepherds were only just in front of us, to judge by the tracks and steaming heaps of dung at the water's edge.

Peter Crossan had dismounted by the time we joined up with them. He was holding his chestnut gelding, Chum, on a short rein and yelling out pithy commands at his dogs as they herded the cattle into the yards. When the last one had plunged through, Errol dashed up and locked the gate.

With a big grin, about as wide and genuine as you could get, Peter spun about as Ray and I ghosted up behind him.

'Pete,' Ray said.

A particularly lovely roan mare and her offspring.

'Nice day for it, eh?' Peter said.

There were horses grazing nearby, lovely looking horses. After yarning with the boys as they worked, I strolled over to take a closer look. It turned out they were much quieter than I expected, more approachable, but not so tame you could walk up and make a great big fuss of them. Without their offspring, the mares, of course, might have reacted differently, but for now they were protective mothers. A particularly lovely chestnut or roan mare and her young one allowed me to get within a few metres. Both had pure white blazes running down the front of their faces, but the young one lacked its mother's four neat white ankle socks and thick, flowing gold-coloured mane.

Horses were of the utmost importance on Waipaoa station. That had been evident from the early days; John Clark started a horse-breeding programme for replacement hacks. Over the last three years, however, there had been dramatic changes in the story of Waipaoa horses. In partnership with Jackie and John Cottle of Clevedon Park, near Auckland, Waipaoa station had, with the introduction of two top stallions, been breeding sport horses for the lucrative Asian market.

There was a family connection here; Jackie Cottle and David Clark were cousins. John Cottle, the famous

All-purpose stock dogs at rest at the old cattle yards. The red woolshed is perhaps 100 years old.

equestrian, had been selling sport horses to the Japanese for over 10 years. Also deeply involved with the exciting venture were Heather and David McKenzie, who managed the horse stud, called Wheturau, and David Clark's wife, Libby, who grew up in the heart of English racing, Epsom; her stepfather was a top horse trainer.

There were about 170 horses on the station; the special breeding programme was carried out from a base mob of 45 mares. Already 80 progeny had been born on the station, some of these were now ranging up to three-year-olds. Some of them carried the blood of Abbas Lad, the son of that most fashionable New Zealand sport horse stallion, Aberlou, who in turn was the sire of the world-champion eventer Messiah.

It was vitally important, David Clark said, that the distinctive roan colour of Waipaoa horses was not undermined in any way; it must keep shining through. It was also essential that a satisfactory balance be maintained between sport horses and station hacks. Waipaoa, after all, was first and foremost a working sheep and cattle station.

Turning away from the horses, I started back to the cattle yards. The sun was shining and there wasn't a single cloud in sight. Up on a hill, under cover, a pheasant made a rasping noise; within the cattle yards the horses, girth straps loosened, cropped at the low growth and the dogs, secured to a fence, dozed in the warmth of the sun. The men had perhaps half of the cattle done and they were laughing about something or other. It was indeed 'a nice day for it'.

15

FAR NORTH

Whichever way you looked at it, this wasn't a particularly good time to visit the northernmost station in the country. It could have been marginally worse: in a few weeks' time, for instance, the station would be devoid of all stock and the DoC-owned property would be up for lease.

On a rather gloomy May afternoon 25-year-old Ian Bullen, the caretaker manager of Te Paki station, was showing me over some of the property. In the main it was easy, rolling pastureland with large areas of scrub to the northeast and sand dunes off to the west. All very typical of the Aupouri Peninsula.

'Got rid of most of the horses already,' Ian sighed to himself.

They had always set great store by their horses on Te Paki; the largely Maori workforce had revelled in working with them. Not that long ago they had bred horses here, not just to supply Te Paki shepherds but also for all of the other government-owned blocks as far south as Whangarei. Horses weren't just a part of the job, they were a way of life. You felt good if you worked on a different block from Te Paki but rode a horse from there.

'Sheep and cattle next.' Ian's voice was plaintive.

The best part of 16,000 stock units, Perendale sheep and Angus cattle, would be moved to other Landcorp blocks around the country.

The four-wheel-drive angled across a sloping hill face. Presently, Ian stopped.

'This is the Lake block we're in now.'

There was a fair-sized pond nearby. It was fringed with reeds and a few mallards were filling in time out on the water — not a sensible thing to do in the duck-hunting season. There were cattle dotted about: 235 heifers, which, Ian explained, were on a rotational grazing system, four days here, four days somewhere else.

We clambered out of the vehicle as a wind came in from the coast, which lay, unseen, beyond the low sand hills. I tossed a hand in the general direction of the cattle; they were now eyeing us with much interest. 'Seems strange with no stock here at all,' I pointed out.

Ian raised his eyes to the sky as though he were a pagan seeking the immediate assistance of the only god he knew.

'Strange?' he questioned.

'Well . . .'

'More like bloody weird if you ask me!'

Te Paki had carried stock for at least a century. Now there would be nothing but the land, the woolshed and the homestead.

'So where will you fit into the new scheme of things?' I asked him.

Ian's face clouded over and he shook his head. He was not happy.

'Dunno, really . . . Guess we'll have to wait and see, eh? A lot will depend on who the new owners are . . .' His voice trailed away.

'But you'd like to work here when that happens?'

'Course! It's great country up here, you know. There's heaps to do when you're not working: pig hunting, fishing.'

I looked towards the scrublands. DoC reckoned this part of Northland carried medium-to-high numbers of pigs. Ian, however, reckoned there weren't too many, but I rather doubted if that were the case. You couldn't blame Ian for playing it down; they had enough pig hunters tramping about the station — legal or otherwise — without more troops and their canine mates invading the scene.

Ian shuffled his feet. 'Thing is, even if I wasn't offered the manager's position here, well, I'd like to stay on as a shepherd, you know.' He stopped looking away and gave me a direct look. 'Not many jobs out there, right?'

I nodded soberly. The Far North, like the East Coast, had been hit particularly hard by unemployment. I could see that the uncertainty of Ian's situation, the not knowing precisely what the future held, was eating away at him like a cancerous sore.

'Things'll work out,' I said.

'Maybe . . .'

Beyond the low sand hills the Tasman Sea broke on the rugged coastline between Scott Point and Cape Maria Van Diemen, just as it had when the peninsula was one vast kauri forest. It was in 1875 that the first European landowners came to the Far North. They were Samuel Yates, a young English lawyer, and Auckland businessman Stannus Jones; so little is recorded of the latter that we must presume he was a silent partner.

They purchased a vast area of freehold land north of Parengarenga Harbour, said to have included everything from North Cape to Cape Maria Van Diemen. Yates married a local Maori princess of, presumably, the Aupouri tribe. It is generally believed that during the eighteenth century the Aupouri, because of intertribal warfare, sought sanctuary on the narrow-necked strip of land that later bore their name. Despite this, warriors of the Rarawa and Ngapuhi tribes continued to harass the Aupouri and many a savage encounter took place on what is now Te Paki station. The fighting continued into the next century. By the 1830s the Aupouri had had enough and moved out of the region. But by now they were strangers on the mainland, with no country of their own. Within a decade they had shifted back to the Far North, occupying their old settlements and territories.

Soon Samuel Yates had acquired even more land. It adjoined his property in the south, some 32,500 hectares. When this was added to the land he already owned, it came to over 60,000 hectares. In turn, the enterprising Yates became a farmer, a storekeeper and, later, when hordes of almost fanatical fortune hunters stormed the Far North in search of fabulous treasure, a gum trader. The gumdiggers were particularly active where Te Paki station is found today. They were seeking the fossilised resin of the mighty kauri tree, a vital ingredient in varnish.

Such was the impact of Samuel Yates in the region that

he eventually became known as the King of the North. When he died in the early 1900s, his widow remained on the property. She moved from their first homestead, built at Tapotupotu Bay, to a new one. This was later replaced by the Te Paki homestead, still standing today.

In 1930 Richard Keene, a Wellington businessman, purchased Te Paki station. As in Samuel Yates's time, the only access was down Ninety Mile Beach on foot or horseback, or by boat. All station goods were brought in by boat; the station had a bullock team to transport goods to and from the deep-water jetty. Te Paki remained in the Keene family for 36 years. At the time they sold out to the Government in 1930, they ran 8000 sheep and 1400 cattle.

It was the Government's aim to make this part of the Far North into a major tourist attraction, the jewel in the crown being the lighthouse at Cape Reinga. The Lands and Survey Department reduced the station area to 2900 hectares and allowed the remainder to revert to native vegetation.

In 1986, Te Paki station was summed up as follows in a Lands and Survey information booklet:

> Part of Te Paki station can be seen from the road to Cape Reinga. The area is a mixture of clay and gumland soils suitable for breeding and fattening of cattle and sheep. At present, the farm has a stock-carrying capacity of 31,000 stock units and supports 16,000 Perendale sheep and 3500 Angus-Hereford cross cattle. Six Santa Gertrudis bulls were bought recently for cross breeding aimed at producing a yield of lean meat. Cattle are fattened in early summer so stock numbers are reduced during the normal summer drought. Because of the characteristics of weather in the north, the growing time for grasses continues through the warm winter and slows down in summer which is dry and often drought prone.
>
> In the spring 12,000 bales of hay and a 65-hectare crop of fine chopped silage are grown to supplement the shortage of summer and winter feed. There are 8–10 full time shepherds on Te Paki, including a farm manager. They use horses for mustering and lambing beats, and each man has five working dogs at his command.
>
> There are two public access tracks across the farm and visitors are welcome to walk on farmland provided consideration for animals and farm work is observed.

It is worth noting that the Te Paki Farm complex, situated on the route to Cape Reinga, attracts over 100,000 visitors each year. No other station in the country had to cope with this amount of through traffic.

I'd first passed through Te Paki station on a humid summer's day in the mid-1980s. Just off the road several Maori shepherds, wearing cowboy hats, had been working cattle. Most were mounted on broken-coloured horses, although one was riding a pacy white mare. They rode with the natural ease of Aboriginal stockmen on a vast station in the Northern Territory. There was good-natured banter and laughter among them. I'd called out a greeting and they had waved back at just one more tourist.

On this visit to New Zealand's northernmost station the sun didn't shine and there wasn't any laughter to be heard. The station seemed to be in a curious state of limbo, waiting for the great days to return.

South of Te Paki station there were two sizeable Maori-owned properties: Paua and Te Rangi. They were owned by the Te Kao-based Parengarenga Trust. The trust took its name from the many-fingered inlet on the northeastern side of the peninsula. Apparently Parengarenga can mean 'leggings made of flax' or 'the place where the rock lily grows'.

Around the inlet there were bridle tracks leading to the north. Most likely they were originally walking tracks developed by the Maori, later used for horse

Typical country on Paua station. The lake is the station's water supply.

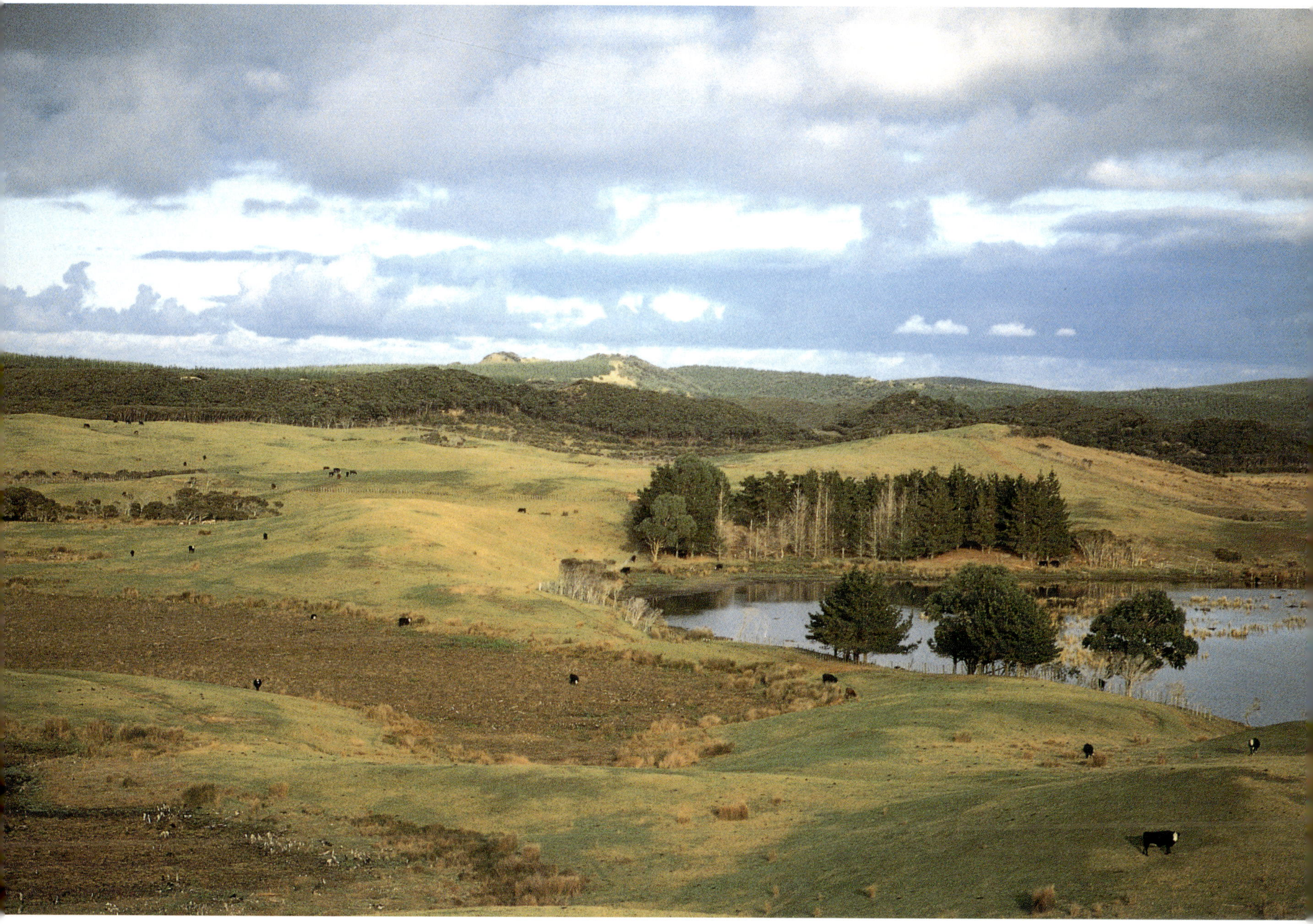

On Paua station: Ben Caper, Neil and Bronwyn Dempster and, on her pony, Nadine.

transportation. The harbour, found on Paua station, is one of a number of departure points for the annual migration in early March of the eastern bar-tailed godwit (kauka) to its breeding grounds in the tundra of Alaska and Siberia. The almost pure silica sand of the south side of the harbour is shipped to Auckland and Whangarei for use in glassmaking.

The land, as we already know, belonged to the Aupouri people. In 1958, when this area was a riot of scrub and fern, it was taken over for development by the Maori Affairs Department. Locals say it was alive with wild pigs. Two years later the Lands and Survey Department stepped in and they, on behalf of the Aupouri, turned the seeming wasteland into highly productive country. Tonnes and tonnes of superphosphate and lime, vital for this part of the country stripped raw of vital ingredients, were shipped by barge from Whangarei to the Parengarenga Harbour.

Neil Dempster's association with Paua station had spanned a decade now. Northland born, 51-year-old Neil had worked previously on Cape View station (south of Te Kao) and on Limestone Downs, a 3200-hectare property just south of Port Waikato. He had been the manager on all three. When Neil returned to the Far North in 1982, Paua was still handled by the Lands and Survey Department. In 1984 the Maori Affairs Department returned to the scene, but their tenure was short-lived, for in 1988 the Parengarenga Trust took full control of the land — including, of course, Te Rangi station.

Unlike yesterday on Te Paki station, when the cloud cover had refused to lift, this morning on Paua station the sun was shining and there was no wind to speak of. Neil

They are rightly proud of Paua station in the Far North.

Dempster was telling me that winter was his favourite season up here: the sky was usually clear, humidity was low and the days were warm. Here, as on Te Paki and Te Rangi, they carried their lowest numbers of stock in the summer. The lack of rain posed a real problem over the hottest months and the wind, which was rarely absent, burned off what little grass there was.

Neil waved towards a big lake that contained the entire water supply for the stock, about 1400 million litres. They were carrying some 8000 Romney/Perendales and 1500 Angus breeding cows. Earlier, I had noticed some men feeding out hay to cattle; it seemed rather early to be doing that, so I questioned Neil about it.

'Well, I tend to feed out prior to calving rather than during it; that saves autumn feed and we can then put the calves straight onto it.'

At this point, a large mob of cattle appeared in a nearby paddock. Moments later, a big black hat showed above a low rise and a shepherd jogged into view.

'Who's the cowboy?' I asked, poker faced.

Neil smiled. 'That's my head shepherd, Ben Caper.'

Neil went on to tell me that while Ben was over 60, he was still a top man. I didn't doubt that: Ben looked slim and agile and he carried his long hillstick as though it were a lance.

Later, I went out with Neil, Ben, and Neil's wife, Bronwyn, and their daughter, Nadine, as they mustered the base herd of 400 cows. It was more like a family gathering than anything else and it was obvious that the Dempsters thought the world of old Ben, who seemed to do everything in a gracious manner and who mounted his brown horse like a man 20 years younger. Clearly, living in the Far North hadn't done Ben Caper a scrap of harm.

On Te Rangi station, I caught up with manager Max Dunn near the woolshed; he was waiting for two of his shepherds to arrive. Max told me that he'd done all of his shepherding in Hawke's Bay before shifting north. He, too, spoke strongly about the lack of rain over the

On Te Rangi station.

summer, and of the burning effects of the searing, salt-laced winds that at times whipped across the narrow peninsula with unbridled fury.

'Drives you up the bloody wall, then.'

So reliant were they on stored water that a member of staff — called a waterman — spent three days a week over summer checking pumps, troughs and dams. Here on Te Rangi Pari 'Paddy' Etana had that job. The head shepherd, Max told me, was Lassie Nathan.

'Lassie?' I queried.

'Yeah, Lassie.' He started to smile.

'Like the dog, y'mean?'

'Uh-huh. Like the dog.'

Max laughed; so did I.

Perendales spilled into view like the incoming tide; a shepherd appeared, too.

Max nodded in his direction. 'That's Jack Abraham.'

'Is he related to the Abrahams on Te Paki and Paua?'

Tim Hoey.

Max Dunn.

'They all are one way or another,' Max said drily.

Another mounted shepherd turned up with his share of sheep: Tim 'Pudi' Hoey. Tim wore a big, big hat and, while he was not a tall man, his feet nevertheless very nearly touched the ground.

'For Pete's sake don't you dare photograph his horse!' Max exclaimed. 'The stupid-looking thing is only a kid's pony. Hell, we'd never live it down if a picture of that appeared in a book.'

Tim reined in for a few minutes and smiled goodnaturedly when Max had a dig at the animal he rode. Tim went off with a chuckle.

When he was out of earshot, heading towards the woolshed with his docile charges, Max said, 'Don't really know why he insists on riding it, you know.' He shook his head as though perplexed and then, suddenly, he started to laugh. That, I thought, was a damn sight better than how it had been up the road at Te Paki station.

16

TAPU ON NUKUHAKARI

The waves crashed on the gritty black sand and the chilly air of May was laced with salt. Then the waves retreated out to sea, only to reform and gather strength and then stampede towards the shore. A steady drizzle was falling as the 45-year-old manager of Nukuhakari station, John Austin, and I stood shoulder to shoulder at the high-water mark. Here, on the west coast of the North Island, the rampaging sea was a bewitching thing.

There were wild goats of many colours in plain sight; they favoured the steep, seaward-facing hills. The scuffed tracks of cattle marked the beach; they, John said with a smile, liked to play around on the beach. Gazing out to sea, eyes narrowed, he explained in his laconic manner — a sort of King Country Barry Crump — that Nukuhakari Bay was once a vital part of the station: this was where the surfboats brought in stores and where, just as importantly, the woolclip went out. So, like Te Awaiti and White Rock, Nukuhakari in its early days relied on sea transport for its survival.

Even today, Nukuhakari station, located at the end of a no-exit, unsealed road that wound through a low mountain range, seemed isolated, almost a forgotten place. Through traffic was non-existent.

To reach the station I had travelled through the valley of the Waikawau River, a particularly lovely watershed. In pre-European times this region was used by Maori as a major coastal route between Kawhia and Mokau. The trail, whenever possible, followed the line of the clifftops. Maori also found the climate and soil suitable for growing their staple vegetables, and wild pigs were well established here, too, before the first Pakeha moved in.

The great fighting chief of Ngati Toa, Te Rauparaha, came this way in about 1820. Te Rauparaha, on his way south, intended to gain control of the northern shores of

To provide access from the road-end to the main Waikawau Beach, this tunnel was dug out of the rock and sandstone hill-face in 1913.

Cook Strait and, of course, he eventually did. Maori legend says that Te Rauparaha and his warriors had a hideout somewhere along this coastline; many consider it was near Tirua Point, a distinct headland at the southern end of Nukuhakari Bay.

The first European settlers moved into the valley in 1909. For some it proved an ill-fated venture: the surveyed blocks were too small, they claimed, and the country too rugged. Perhaps they were just not cut out for the life. Those that stayed on, however, did not regret it. They discovered this was good country with a more than generous amount of rain.

Nukuhakari station, taken up by Newton King, came into being in about 1909. In 1910 the first wool was shipped out of the valley. The ships picked it up at Waikawau Beach (linked in 1913 to the road end by a tunnel through a rock-and-sandstone hill) and at the most northerly bay on Nukuhakari station.

Still the waves broke up on the black sand of Nukuhakari station, just as it had when Te Rauparaha and

160 • STATION COUNTRY

his people came this way 170 years ago. Perhaps an hour earlier, as we had driven out here, John had paused and pointed down to an attractive, sheltered valley. That, he said, was where they had built the first station complex. All that remained were broken-down cattle yards and a red-painted hut, the singlemen's quarters.

The complex had been built at the northern end of the run to be close to the beach. There were few places along this steep-cliffed coastline where it was possible to load surfboats. They used a bullock-drawn wagon to bring the wool down to the beach, but, because of the soft sand, they had to manhandle the bales of wool out into the surf; it was an arduous task, requiring four men per bale of wool. The station relied on casual labour to a large extent, mostly Maori, glad of the work.

The coastal steamer always anchored well offshore, with good reason. Every captain knew there were dangerous reefs and that in 1907 the steamer *Kia Ora*, a vessel of 312 tonnes, had encountered particularly heavy mist along this coast and was wrecked on Piritoki Reef, just off Tirua Point. Three men were lost; the remaining 18 crew members came ashore on the gritty sands fronting Nukuhakari Bay.

The weather was a force to reckon with on this coastline and the stationmen did not look forward to getting the woolclip out. The year of 1931 was a good example of that. When the *Progress* arrived off Nukuhakari Bay to collect the woolclip (272 bales that year), the weather turned nasty. It took four days to load the clip.

It was with marked relief, then, that in 1935 a road linking the station with the outside world was completed and shipping became a thing of the past. The King family moved the station complex south to avoid the expense of constructing several kilometres of roading. A new homestead, woolshed and cookshop were built in a pleasant little valley that ran down to the sea.

Presently, John and I turned away from the boisterous

John Austin stands outside the tunnel.

sea, and, sinking to our ankles in the giving sand, backtracked to where the station vehicle was parked. I was aware that there were even more goats on the hills sweeping down to the sea. In one mob there must have been at least 30, more goats than I had seen in a very long time. I pointed them out to John, who paused and gave them a withering look.

'Dog tucker!' he grunted.

'Hey, they're not that bad,' I fired back.

'The hell they're not!' Somehow, John managed that with a good-natured smile.

Goats were particularly thick all through this country; of course, there wasn't a market for them anymore. It wasn't that long ago that goats were the panacea for the country's farming woes — the new wonder animal, even replacing deer. They would produce quality fibre and, of vital importance on so many hill-country runs, clean up noxious weeds. How many animals enjoyed eating gorse? Since then wild goats had multiplied amazingly. Forget deer, this species had to rank first on any environmentalist's hit list.

'We often muster them in with sheep,' John said. He waved a hand in the direction of the highest point on the station, Mount Whareorino (650 metres). 'Heaps up there along the bushline.' He fingered his bristly jaw. 'Reckon we could muster as many as two thousand if we were really trying to.'

I gave him a hard look; he looked serious enough. 'Two thousand,' I echoed, like doubting Thomas.

'That's on a bad day!'

John Austin was one of a long line of managers that the King family had employed. Some didn't stay too long; others lasted years. Among those who did stay was John Grey, from Canterbury.

In the late 1970s, John Grey and his wife had been on the station for 16 years. They both loved the place. The isolation wasn't a problem, it was a blessing! So Grey, getting on in years but still highly capable, had no intention of moving this side of retirement. But fate can be fickle; it had something else in store for John Grey.

For a man who loved fishing, the station had the bonus of its coastline. The fishing was excellent, mostly snapper and kahawai. Like most fishermen, Grey was a creature of habit: he had his favourite spot on the coast, a narrow point near Middle Bay. In bad weather huge waves rolled in and obliterated it, so you had to pick your time with care.

On the day that John Grey decided to go rock fishing it was exactly two years since a head shepherd and his son had been swept off the same rocks and drowned. John Grey, however, was not a superstitious man, and the weather was calm, the waves small. But John Grey failed to come home that day. He, too, was slammed off the rocks by a wave he badly underestimated or simply didn't see until it was too late. As far as his family were concerned, he had vanished off the face of the earth, never to be seen again. The sea, however, usually tires of its victims and gives them up; nine weeks later John Grey's body came ashore well to the north.

There was much speculation in the district about Grey's death. Three deaths in less than two years? The local Maori were perturbed enough to do something about it: they placed a tapu on the station. The rules that govern tapu are those of negation and prohibition, so in placing a tapu on the station they made it a forbidden place. Only when the tapu was lifted would the station become a safe place again.

When the manager's job on Nukuhakari station was advertised, John Austin, a married man with two school-age children, was managing an Angus stud at Te Anga. John very much liked the idea of running a 4000-hectare coastal station. His wife, Cheryl, was all for giving it a go, too. Once the Austins arrived on the station, they very quickly became aware of the tapu. While John, your basic down-to-earth Kiwi bloke, attached no importance to the tapu, Cheryl wasn't so sure. Right from the day they arrived, even before they were told of the tapu, she had thought there was something rather unsettling about the place, something elusive, like a half-recalled dream fading until it might not have happened at all.

When she told her husband of her feelings, John, not unkindly, gave a rather cynical laugh. John Grey and the others had just been out of luck; their numbers were up. Weren't fishermen — in the sea, river or lake — always getting themselves killed? Forget the tapu — that was just a fairy story.

A few weeks went by and still Cheryl was ill at ease. Then the local Maori came to the place where John Grey had been swept off the rocks on Nukuhakari station. They lifted the tapu on the place; in effect, the station had been purged of all that was evil. Incredible as it seemed to her, Cheryl immediately felt a deep sense of well-being about being there. It felt safe, like stepping out of a dark room into brilliant sunlight.

Years later, sitting in rain-sodden clothing near the back bay on Nukuhakari station, John Austin looked out through the half-open window of the ute at the many goats on the hill faces and shook his head. There wasn't a great deal you could do about such an adaptable and versatile animal, was there? He slipped a hand inside his oilskin riding coat and found his cigarettes and matches. He struck a match inside the cupped bowl of his hands, as though to protect the flame from a stiff breeze, then he dipped his head and lit his cigarette.

'Cheryl always thought there was something to that Maori tapu on the place . . .' He blew out a cloud of smoke, 'She still does.'

'And did you change your mind, too?'

John Austin shrugged. His expression said neither yes nor no.

It was a fine, calm midmorning on Nukuhakari station. Cheryl Austin was away from the property, visiting a family friend in North Taranaki. Since it was a public holiday, all but John Austin and his son, Colin, had left the property. Father and son decided to go fishing. This

On Nukuhakari are shepherd Don Woodds and head shepherd Brian Kurigr. The highest point on the property, Mount Whareorino, dominates the background.

was a wonderful way to relax: you could turn off the pressures of work for a few blissful hours, forget all about being accountable to others who only saw the place in a superficial sense. To know the land well you had to live on it, breathe it, reach down and touch it.

In lovely conditions John and Colin Austin set off in the Toyota; John, typically, cast his eye over whatever stock they saw. They ran 10,000 Romney-Perendale ewes; a good lambing would see that swell to about 23,000. Cattle came to 1100 Hereford-Angus breeding cows.

Like the previous manager on the station, John Austin was not the type to believe in the paranormal. Fishing off the rocks where three had been killed held no secret fears for him. Why should it on this fine Waitangi Day? The sea was flat, dead calm.

Presently they reached that spine-like finger jutting out to sea, a minute peninsula with the waves, when rough, swelling up on either side of it. As they unpacked their tackle and baited fish-hooks, John Austin felt that all was right with his world. He glanced out to the millpond-like sea. They cast their lines into the water.

As they fished the sea changed a little. A tiny swell,

They run Romney-Perendales here.

creating equally small waves, began to roll in towards the rocks. If either man noticed the difference, then he didn't attach any significance to it. A snapper leaped on the end of John Austin's line. Father and son grinned at each other; this was really living, right?

It happened suddenly and unexpectedly, when John was looking away from the sea and Colin's attention was on the point where his line vanished into the deep blue of the sea. A wave was rearing up at them, breaking above them, coming down with tremendous force and slamming them both onto the rock.

Panic was a shellburst in John Austin's mind.

Then the wave began to recede. Somehow, in this particular instance, it went without the men, leaving them dazed, clinging with bleeding fingers to sharp, cutting rocks. Still holding on for dear life, John looked out to sea and saw his hat bobbing in the swell at least 40 metres out. They, he realised, sick to his stomach, could so easily have been out there, too.

There are those in the region north of Awakino who will tell you that had the tapu not been placed and later lifted, John and Colin Austin would not be alive today.

17

PLAINS COUNTRY

A different scene on Poronui

While the early history on Poronui station is somewhat vague, it does appear that during the early days of settlement east of Taupo it was once included in the original 30,500-hectare Lochinver block. Certainly, a man known as McFarlane leased the run from its Maori owners around the turn of the century and possibly still held it until after the First World War. At that time the Tuhoe Trust Board stepped in. They hired a Pakeha manager and used mostly Maori staff; that remained the case until the Lands and Survey Department took over handling the station for its Maori owners.

By the mid-1960s, Poronui had increased in size to 9000 hectares and carried 19,000 sheep and 200 head of cattle. Then, in 1967, it was taken over by a company called Anzamco (Australian, New Zealand and American Company). Really, this was as American as GI Joe. The president and managing director of the company was one W. B. Mendenhall, a self-made millionaire and prominent member of the Mormon Church. Mendenhall had fallen in love with this country during a previous visit.

Poronui now achieved its highest profile, featuring in numerous magazines and newspapers. Mendenhall was never less than good copy. Yes, those days were well remembered in the Taupo district, when no one who drove between there and Napier could fail to see the huge sign by the road proclaiming the station's new name: El Rancho Poronui.

Later, Joe Howard purchased the station from Anzamco for a reputed $5 million. Howard had no long-term interest in the station; it was really a money-making venture. He sold off 1800 hectares of Poronui's frontal country (now included in Lochinver); when he finally got out, he retained 250 hectares for himself and his family,

166 • STATION COUNTRY

PLAINS COUNTRY • 167

where the nerve centre of the property was in the old days. The new owners weren't into sheep and cattle — far from it. They were the Caxton Pulp and Paper Company and they had seen the station, about midway between their Kawerau and Whirinaki plants, as ideally located for future operations. Moreover, the valley of the Taharua, where the station was located, was well drained and, even in the wettest winters, could be logged. Things started to happen fast on Poronui: all the stock was sold off, grazing rights were leased, and a deer farm was started.

In charge of the deer farm was Paddy Clark, until that point the station's resident possum trapper. Paddy was, of course, clued up where deer were concerned. He had been involved with them at all levels, from professional shooting to running his own deer farm. Later, Paddy accepted the job of manager on the station.

In the still of the late autumn evening, Red hut, fashioned of kauri, stood as it had done for about 70 years on the bank of the Taharua River. Originally, this was a rabbiters' camp. Later, government hunters of the late 1940s and early 1950s stayed here, too; during this period it was also treated as an outstation of Poronui. The Red hut stood on a large clearing of sorts and, as Paddy and I entered the kitchen area of the two-roomed dwelling, he paused and tapped the back of a hand on the wall. It made a ringing sound.

'Made to last, I reckon.' He smiled wryly. 'When you think about it, there must've been a bloody lot of rabbits here to warrant using kauri, eh?'

Paddy was right about the long-term durability of kauri; it is a superb wood, among the most enduring of timbers. It is a thing of great beauty, too. The rabbits were here in plenty once. The dry nature of the country suited them well.

'Like this hut, y'know,' Paddy said, moving into the bunkroom.

The old Red hut on Poronui station.

I nodded; I knew what he meant. Apart from its wonderful location, the hut had the right feel about it. I said as much and Paddy's vivid blue eyes, set in a tanned face, flashed like so many diamonds hurled at the face of the sun.

'My word, yes!' His enthusiasm was contagious.

We went outside again; the sun was now hidden behind the not-so-high hills to the west. The evening was drawing in and it was becoming a little colder, but not really chilly yet.

Paddy indicated the river. 'Best trout fishing in the world here!'

The upper Mohaka River and its tributaries, of which the Taharua was perhaps the most significant, had a reputation as the best and, certainly, most prolific brown trout fisheries in the country. The first liberation of brown trout took place in the Mohaka catchment in 1878. The trout were unable to migrate from the Mohaka into the Taharua — because of a particularly steep rapid — making them the purest strain of brown trout in the country.

Turning away from the river, Paddy told me that Poronui Ranch, as it was now called, catered for overseas fishermen and, among their recent clients were the husband and wife actors Robert Wagner and Jill St John.

Pausing, hands on hips, Paddy looked at the nearby hills. They appeared to be pressing in on us; it was a trick of the light, I expect.

'Deer on your doorstep, too,' he said, grinning.

I looked up at the hills. They were turning blue, becoming less distinct. Whole hillsides were covered with manuka scrub, and, high in the gullies, V-shaped stands of beech and other forest growth emerged. This was superb deer country, all sika: a far cry from those days of 40 years ago when there were just as many red deer here. Still, like many hunters, I had a great deal of respect for the magnificent sika deer. For the record, the original liberation of this species took place on Poronui in 1905.

As Paddy clambered athletically into the cabin of his

During the period that American interests controlled Poronui station it achieved its highest profile.

four-wheel-drive, he said, 'Might see a sika the way we're going.'

Within a few minutes of gunning away from Red hut, Paddy was slamming a booted foot hard down on the brakes. Standing just off the track, on the edge of a dense belt of scrub, were two deer. They were both stags, one big, one small. The larger one drew my attention. He was dark coated and deep chested, and carried fine antlers, of good length if rather narrow spread. They were a good handful, the timber dark at the base, running up to clearly defined points, almost needle sharp, tips like polished ivory.

'Jeez!' I breathed.

'Yeah . . .'

Then they whipped about and plunged bodily into the manuka. Wonderful stuff, I thought, as thrilled as a kid seeing his first-ever deer on the hill. Paddy, I noticed, was almost as excited.

The track climbed through the tangled scrub, up and up into the beech forest, then out of it again, cutting around a hill face, way above the valley. Soon we came to a halt. The valley of the Taharua was spread out before us, so that I could look over almost all of the station.

'Never weary of this view,' Paddy said, propping himself against the side of the vehicle. 'It'll be one big forest in a few years' time.'

I couldn't work out whether or not he was pleased about that.

To date, they had planted 650 hectares of exotic trees on Poronui, and they planned to plant a further 200 hectares every year. Eventually, there would be very little open ground left on the station. They were planting radiata pine and eucalyptus here. The latter was a variety of gum tree from the high, alpine regions of eastern Australia; it was frost resistant and would do extremely well in this type of country.

I tried to imagine how the valley would look once the trees were well established. Certainly, it wouldn't have the appeal it now held and yet, to be perfectly fair, it would have its own kind of beauty. Only when the milling started, well into the next century, would things take a marked turn for the worse. Then the land would appear entirely different — ugly and totally devastated.

Suddenly —

Whump-whump-whump!

A chopper was barely skimming the tree tops, starting its descent. It was heading into Heli-Sika's base of operations, on the land that Joe Howard retained. It was

Sika deer fawn in typical manuka habitat.

the rutting season and enthusiasts from many parts of the country were taking full advantage of the excellent service this outfit had to offer, ferrying hunters into landing sites deep in top sika country.

'They've been flat out lately,' Paddy said. 'Took in more than seventy jokers one day, I hear.' He pulled a face. 'Must be like a madhouse in there.'

'More like a three-ring circus.'

Paddy smiled. 'Right.'

Later, heading out, I reflected on what I had seen on Poronui. It was the only station I had visited that had gone out of stock and into timber. Was it a foretaste of the future for other parts of the country?

Paddy Clark.

Lochinver

As with Poronui, details of the early days of Lochinver station are vague. It does appear, however, that it was first taken up in the 1870s by Lane and Carswell, and that James Carswell, rather than his partner, ran the property. The original block which, of course, included Poronui, was about 30,500 hectares. Gradually, sheep numbers were increased to around 55,000.

Things did not go well on Lochinver. Rabbits and wild pigs caused untold problems. There was a serious lack of cobalt in the soil; the stock became sick — locals called it bush sickness. Eventually, Lane and Carswell became disenchanted with their pumice-land property and invested whatever they had in more fruitful ventures. The cleared land soon reverted to scrub and bush.

Years later, a Hawke's Bay identity, Ralph Lowry, acquired the lease to Lochinver, but it remained a station in name only. In 1960 the property was purchased by W. A. Stevenson Holdings. The 5300-hectare property was virtually unfenced and only partly broken in, so they would be starting pretty much from scratch. On the credit side there was an old homestead and an aged but serviceable woolshed. Out in the scrub and forest, or on clearings amidst scrub, were wild sheep, pigs, rabbits, horses and two species of deer. There was only one way Lochinver could go. Up.

Under the new order the staff stood at just two, Ross Stevenson, son of the head of the company, and Leo Morgan. By 1963 their efforts had cleared the way for large-scale development on Lochinver.

Peter Newton visited the station in 1968 and wrote:

> The Lochinver story is the story of a development project which, as a private enterprise, has probably not been equalled in this country. In 1965, it was carrying 4000 ewes; by 1968 it was going into winter with 15,000 ewes, and in all probability there will be a similar increase in the next three years.

In closing his short piece on Lochinver, he concluded:

> All told the Lochinver story is an amazing record of achievement and the fact that the station is situated in the very heart of this harsh unlovely area must surely place it as one of the greatest private farming enterprises that we have seen. Just what the picture will be in ten years' time remains to be seen but one thing is for sure — Lochinver station will be well worth seeing.

One can only wonder at what Peter Newton would have made of Lochinver station a quarter of a century down the track.

A heavy mist overlaid the Rangitaiki Plains as I drove away from the modern homestead on Poronui station, where I was staying with Paddy and Belle Clark for the duration of my stay east of Taupo.

The mist became thicker, so that visibility was dangerously reduced, especially in the event of a huge stock truck thundering around a sudden bend in the road. It was like the river mist in and around Hamilton, which clings tenaciously to the ever-winding path of the mighty Waikato River. The same mist is common near Twizel in the Mackenzie Country, or at Cromwell and Alexandra, where the Clutha is the major river. Wherever you encounter it the story remains the same: it's real bad news.

I wasn't too concerned about the miserable state of the weather now that I was firmly on Lochinver land — all 16,500 hectares of it. The property had increased in size since Stevenson Holdings had arrived on the pumice plains. They had swallowed up some of Poronui's frontal country, all of Taharua station and Lilburn estate, and a heap of Maori land. Now, it ranked only second in size in the North Island to the sprawling Ngamatea.

The nerve-centre of Lochinver station was unlike any I had seen. It was on a tarseal road only a short distance off the main Napier–Taupo highway. Here, then, was a modern office complex, complete with receptionist and impressive boardroom. Eric Campbell, 43, was the manager of the station. A friendly, likeable type, he had previously managed a small farm at Kinloch and had played a significant part in the opening up of the Whakatau complex in the Matea area of Kaingaroa Forest.

Over a cup of coffee, Eric gave me some facts and figures about the station. They wintered around 70,000 sheep and lambing began in late September. They were featured in the *Guinness Book of Records* for their 1 January 1990 head count of 133,231 sheep. Lochinver station carried more sheep on its moderate acreage than any other sheep station in the country. In comparison, that year the largest sheep station in the world — Commonwealth Hill, in the northwest of South Australia — carried 70,000 sheep on over 1,000,000 hectares. And there were about 24,000 uninvited 'roos to take into consideration, too. Not that anyone bothered about shearing them.

Lambing, then, got underway in the first month of spring. Since horses had been phased out about seven years earlier, they mostly used four-wheel-drives for shepherding. The country was remarkably easy to get around and only about 4000 hectares remained unbroken.

Considering that I had been on Nukuhakari only a few days previously, it was a remarkable coincidence that John Grey's son, Colin, should be the stock manager here, as he had been on that fateful day when his father was drowned. He had four head shepherds and four shepherds below him.

The docking of lambs was done in the paddocks, with three gangs averaging 2000 lambs daily. For the record, the paddocks averaged 60–70 hectares in size. The lambs were also vaccinated (for tetanus and pulpy kidney, with selenium additive); earmarked; tails whipped off with a searing iron; and jetted for flystrike. Weaning began in early December. The main shearing began in early January; the station's regular shearing contractor was Paewai Mullins of Dannevirke. Three sheds were in use, with 23 stands between them. The 23 shearers handled between 6000 and 7000 sheep a day, adding up to a grand total of around 83,000. About 280,000 kilograms of wool was the result, something like 1750 bales. In 1961, in contrast, only 27 bales of wool came off Lochinver! During October and March the hoggets were shorn, while crutching was carried out in August.

A pale wintery sun was shining and the mist had mostly burned off when Eric Campbell and I left his office. Shivering, I looked across the road to a paddock where sheep were eating up large on the whiskery stubble of a barley crop.

'Stud Perendale ewes,' Eric informed me. 'We've got both a Romney and a Perendale stud, with about 1000 ewes all up. Colin Anderson's the stud manager.'

They first went into barley here in 1977. In 1991, for example, they planted 100 hectares of barley and 600 hectares of oats, for a crop yield of about four tonnes per hectare. Eight huge silos held most of the crop, with an overall capacity of about 1300 tonnes.

They also grew 400 hectares of hay, and from that got 30,000 bales, plus 250 large buns, which, along with 200 hectares of swedes, was used as supplementary winter feed, something the deer appreciated immensely. The deer farming side of things covered 80 hectares, and usually they ran about 275 mixed animals. The velvet crop (the growing antlers of stags in a pre-hard stage) was, in 1992, expected to top 150 kilograms.

They first planted trees on Lochinver 25 years ago and more than a million had been planted in stands that doubled as shelterbelts for stock; the winds that raced across the Rangitaiki Plains were often cruel. Tree pruning was an essential job on Lochinver. Some of the timber was felled for use on the station as fence posts and so on.

Beyond the paddock where the stud ewes were making short work of the tasty, nutrient-rich barley stubble, a house sat on a lowish hill. This was where Eric lived with his wife. Dianne Campbell worked for Landcorp in Taupo; she would later prove immensely helpful when I was researching the Whakatau complex.

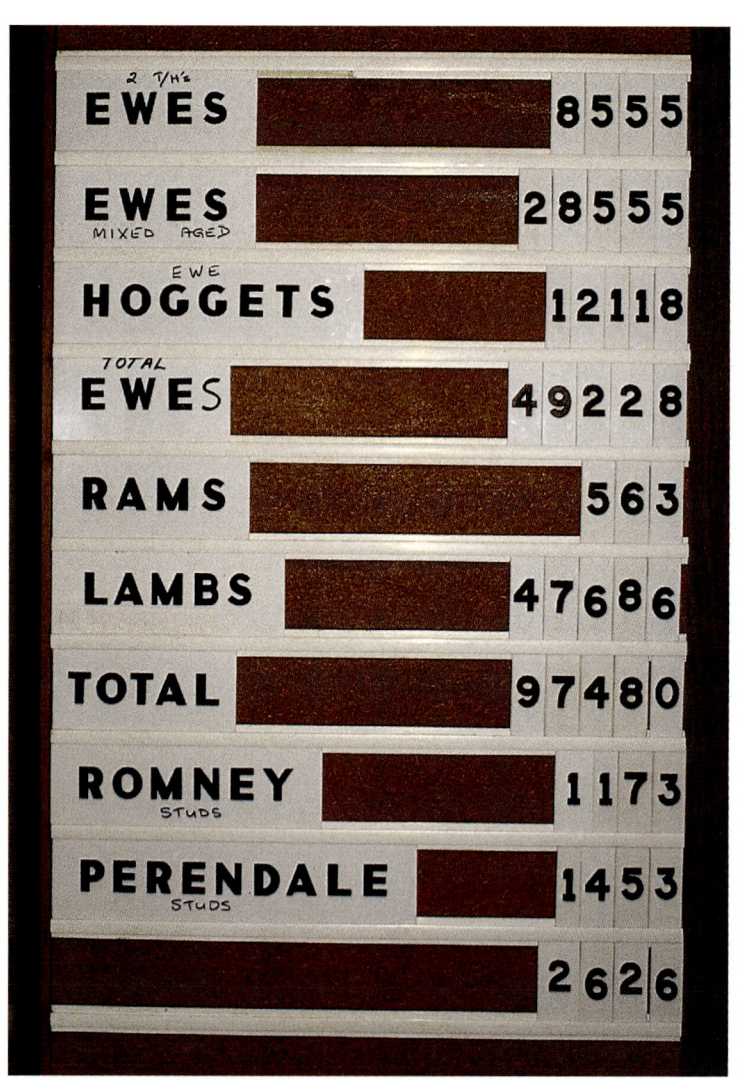

The stock count on Lochinver.

Perhaps the most unusual aspect of Lochinver was that all the staff houses were spread right around the station. Driving around the place, I'd suddenly see a house all on its own, with a signpost indicating it was Homestead such-and-such a number. Most of the homes were simply functional, the term 'homestead' didn't seem appropriate.

There was a good reason why the homes were so widespread on Lochinver. As Eric explained, the shepherds had specific areas to look after and they lived close to where they most often worked. This saved travelling time and, because they were so close to the stock, made the men all the more efficient. I could see the sense of that, all right, but it was still rather disconcerting to come across a machine operator and his family living away out back with not another dwelling in sight.

Later, I drove around some of the station's 120 kilometres of roading, all pumice. At one point I was overtaken by a school bus. Two buses transported station children to the local primary school or to a point where they could connect with commercial transport that took them to college in Taupo. While on the road, I observed some of the 2700 beef steers they ran on the place. They were bought as weaners, fattened up like grain-fed hogs, and then sold as two- to three-year-old bullocks.

Three water wheels of varying sizes pumped water to tanks on hills; a simple gravity feed system operated from there. Because of the nature of the soil on Lochinver, stringent tests were carried out each year and any essential minerals, found to be lacking, were applied by fixed-wing aircraft (there were four airstrips) or, where the country was easy, by a bulk-spreading truck.

The station employed five machine operators and a couple of builders and handymen. The workshop kept two men busy, and a plumber kept an eye on the station water supply. The gardens on Lochinver were far from unkempt; the station employed a gardener to look after them.

To say I was impressed with what was going on here is putting it mildly. Peter Newton said all those years ago that Lochinver was 'one of the greatest farming enterprises we have seen'. It still was.

Given its high profile, Lochinver has become extremely popular with groups wanting to see what is undoubtedly the most progressive station in the country. For relevant information, contact:

> The Tour Organisers
> Chris and Cathy Barker
> Lochinver Station
> RD 3
> Taupo
>
> Phone 07-384-2505

At Poronui station homestead
Once again a dense mist blanketed the Rangitaiki Plains. Snow was scattered lightly on the ground. Outside, horses, wearing covers, mooched passed the living room window.

While Paddy prepared breakfast we yarned about those days when we had both shot deer for a crust, the places we both knew, a particular mutual mate we had shared camp with. It was the Manson country — on the back of Ngamatea station — that we mostly talked about. I had shot there as a deer culler in the early to mid 1960s; Paddy's time, as a meat hunter, had come some years later. My last mate as a deer culler, in 1968, had been Dick Hart, when we'd been in the northwestern Ruahines on the Mangaohane block. Later, Dick had teamed up with Paddy and in 1972 they had shot the Manson country, using a team of packhorses to bring out the carcases.

It's funny how you remember certain little things. Take the old Manson hut, for instance. I can't say for sure when it was put up by the station folk on Ngamatea. They ran sheep then and the Manson country muster was quite an event. The hut wasn't the best place to camp in. It was a big, barn-like affair with malthoid-covered walls; when the wind blew, which was often, it rampaged into the hut through numerous gaps and the fire smoked something awful. The fireplace was huge but, even if you had half a beech tree roaring away, there was no way you could warm up the old Manson hut.

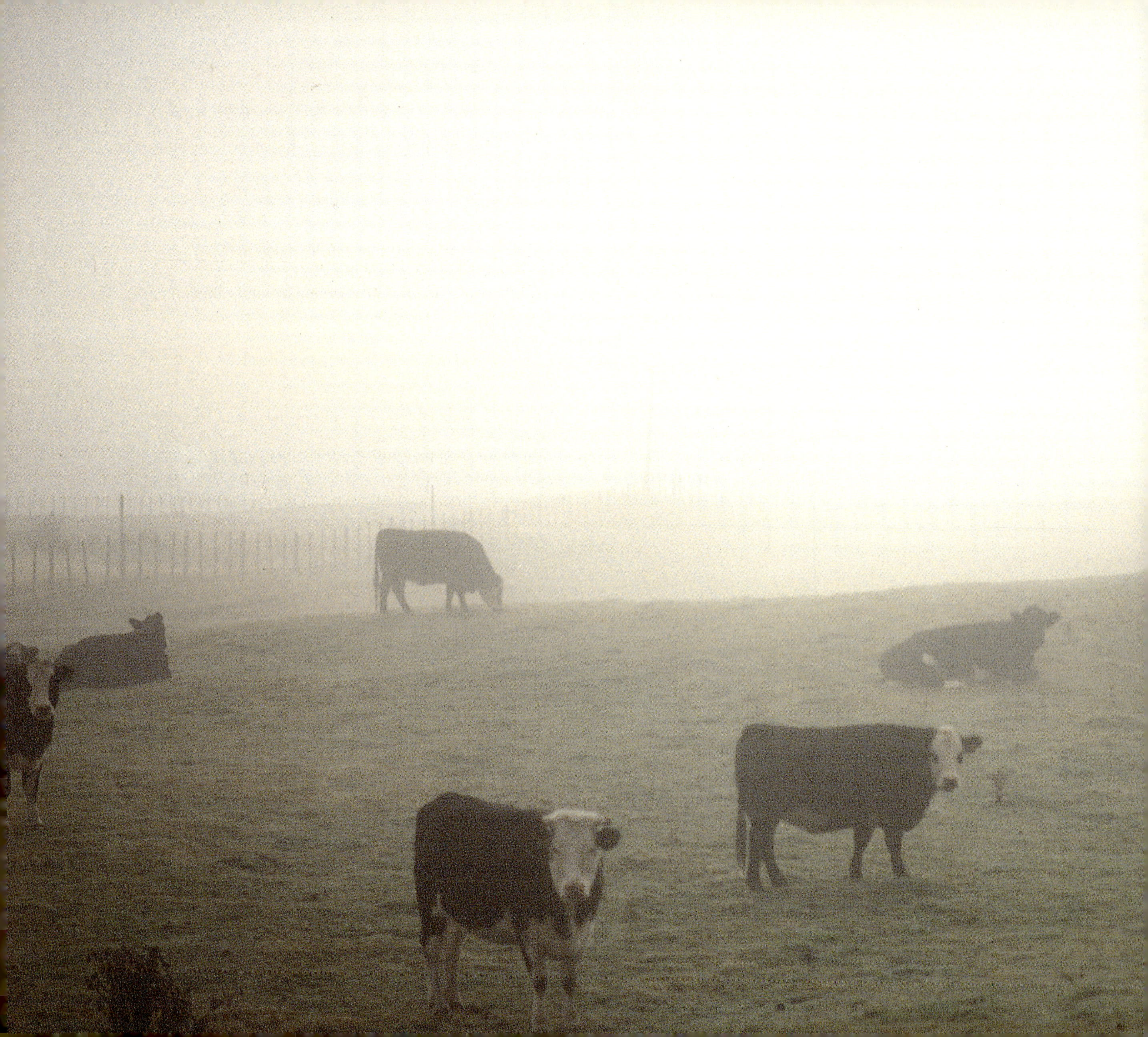

What I recall most about there, however, was what was positioned in the fireplace: a massive cast-iron camp oven. Pity the poor packhorse that had lugged that in!

'Listen, Paddy,' I said, 'was there a huge camp oven at the hut when you were there?'

Paddy, hunched over the stove, was checking on sika backsteaks sizzling in a frying pan.

'Shit, yeah!' he said, not turning around. 'Biggest camp oven I ever did see.' He chuckled.

I smiled fondly, remembering how fellow deer culler Dick Steele and I had arrived at the old Manson hut for a few days in the roar of 1965. We'd come up from Kiwi Mouth hut with a heap of foodstuffs suitable for stew; the meat, you must realise, was still on the hoof. As we'd neared the hut, knees sagging on account of the great weight we were both packing, a sheep suddenly appeared on the bush edge. I looked questioningly at Dick; he returned my look. The stew we cooked up in that monster of a camp oven was not the usual venison stew at all!

Now, facing me, smiling as though he had no intention of sharing the joke, Paddy said, 'It's here — out back in the shed.'

'What is?'

'That camp oven you're ravin' about.'

In the period that Paddy and Dick had shot the Manson country, it had been sold by its owner for a pittance to the Forest Service. Knowing there would be many more hunters coming in now, Paddy, fearing the camp oven would be removed, had decided to take it himself. He had had it flown out with a load of venison and here, 27 years later, I was once again looking at a particular camp oven that, for no good reason, had remained in my mind.

Later, a visitor called in: Eddie Hose. This was a lucky break. Eddie was the manager on Otangimoana station, one of the four properties that made up the Whakatau complex.

'Brew, Eddie?' Paddy asked.

Mid-morning mist on the Rangitaiki Plains.

'Sure, Paddy. Thanks.'

Eddie, a handsome 38-year-old, hailed from Te Awamutu. He had first come to the Rangitaiki Plains 20 years earlier and here, on Poronui, he had gotten his first station job. The Yanks were running the place then, he said. They were real good to work for, although he took his orders from the New Zealand manager, Allan Bowley. He didn't have much to do with W. B. Mendenhall, but reckoned he was a 'great guy'.

'Tell Phil about the deer that were here then,' Paddy said.

Eddie smiled reflectively and explained that a no-hunting policy was in force on the station at that time. If you shot a deer you were down the road so fast one of Mendenhall's smart quarter horses wouldn't catch you. Deer had built up in numbers on the station and Eddie, on his lambing beat in the spring, had seen sika in mobs of up to 40 animals. At night they turned their attention to the crops of swedes and grazed heavily.

The period Eddie was talking about — the early 1970s — was remarkable for the high price paid for a deer's carcase. It was up to a dollar a pound at one time, no tax, and no questions asked about where it came from, either. So Poronui, crawling with sika deer, became the hot spot for local deer poachers. It got so bad that the station took a bold step to combat it: they hired a man to ride the boundary fences, armed like a fence rider in a Western novel.

The trouble was, this didn't stop the poaching. It didn't stop the fence posts being burned. It didn't stop a damn thing. Someone, who thereafter kept a very low profile, actually took a shot at the boundary rider as he jogged along on his horse. Apparently he was rather put out by this; he couldn't for the life of him fathom why someone had mistaken him for a sika deer.

Eddie finished his story with a laugh: it was an interesting time to be working on Poronui. Now, on his second cup of tea, Eddie finally got around to the reason for his visit: how did Paddy feel abut Eddie running a possum line on the station over winter?

'Hmmm . . .' went Paddy heavily.

Eddie looked across the table expectantly, a half-formed smile on his lips. Paddy met Eddie's eyes with a calculating expression, one ex-poacher summing up another cut from the same bolt of cloth. Paddy drummed his hand on the table; it sounded unnaturally loud.

'Okay,' Paddy said.

Eddie flashed fine teeth. 'Great! You —'

'No shootin' deer!' Paddy stabbed a stiff forefinger at Eddie's chest.

'You have my word, Paddy.'

Eddie all but crossed his chest. He had the overly solemn air of a judge about to pass sentence.

Paddy suddenly smiled. 'Stick around, Eddie, and we'll pick out a good block for you.'

Prosperity from pumiceland

You've guessed it: a thick, choking mist, like smoke gushing from a heavily banked fire, covered the Rangitaiki Plains as I swung off State Highway 5 on to a secondary road that would take me to Otangimoana station.

The story of the Whakatau complex, 48 kilometres east of Taupo, dated to 1955. At that time the station consisted of about 17,000 hectares; it was owned by Robert Holt & Sons, and, to a much lesser extent, the Crown. Historically, it represented the last large tract of virgin country to be taken up by the Lands and Survey Department for development in the Rotorua district.

The timber company had made no real impact on the land; they had merely crossed it, extracting millable timber from a low range of hills to the east of what was essentially plains country, although there were many steep-sided gullies here, too. Ground cover consisted of scrub, tussock, manuka and kanuka, and lichen moss. In 1955 this huge block, not without a certain rugged charm, was in reality a kind of no man's land.

The original Whakatau complex called for eight stations to be developed; later, this was cut back to six. Early

Eddie Hose, on Otangimoana station.

proposals for development, however, were deferred until 1969, at which time they began to clear the ground for the first station on the list: Whakatau. Once fire-breaks had been created around the areas chosen for grassing, crawler tractors were brought into play: the heavy, flanged, water-filled rollers crushed the various kinds of scrub, which, when dried off, was then burnt. The Forest Service were called in to handle the burn-offs and the first fire they lit, in February 1969, cleared 800 hectares in just two hours. In 1970, Whakatau station was stocked with 2000 Merino/English Leicester sheep purchased locally. They did not fare well and were replaced in 1983 with Perendales.

Matea station, named after the country fringing the southeast regions of Kaingaroa Forest, evolved in 1970. It was stocked with fine-wooled Romney hoggets mated to Cheviot rams. A Perendale ram-breeding programme was instigated in 1984. Next in line was Kokomoka station, which was stocked in around 1974 with Cheviot ewes; in 1982 they switched to Romneys. Runanga station was broken in by 1975 and they stocked it with the little-used Drysdale sheep. The generally harsh climate of this region made second shearing of this breed extremely difficult and so eventually they switched to Perendales. Kotara station, developed in 1976, was stocked a year later with Romney ewes, and they had remained true to that breed ever since.

It was in 1989 that changes in policy relating to the Whakatau complex resulted in reducing the number of stations from six to four. Runanga and Matea ceased to exist and the others swelled in size.

If anything, the mist was even thicker now, so that it seemed more like late evening than mid morning. Suddenly, out of nowhere, a huge cattle truck hurtled at me. Frantically, I spun the steering wheel and, as the great smoke-belching beast thundered past, I all but ended up in a ditch. Fortunately, the rear wheels were still on firm ground, so I was able to reverse out.

From that point on, I drove with utmost caution, hugging the side of the road, headlights stabbing a rather obscure path through the mist. It was so bad that even though I was close to them, it was impossible to read the names on the mailboxes. My journey ended at a smart-looking house: the homestead of Otangimoana.

Eddie Hose was in residence, of course, and at his best, eager to answer my many questions. Otangimoana, he said, had been his home since day one and he had been there when the land was cleared in 1977. He, as much as any man, knew all about the back-breaking work that goes into turning scrub-ridden pumicelands into a paying proposition.

Stock were introduced onto the place a year later — 2400 Romney two-tooth ewes and 58 rams, which were transferred from Kotara. Two months later, a further 1600 Romney ewe hoggets made the same short journey. By 1980 the flock stood at 10,750. In 1979 they had purchased a number of Booroola Coopworth rams from Invermay in the South Island, to mate with the Romney ewes. The result was a Merino-type sheep with high fertility, capable of producing twins or better.

Cattle were first turned out on the station in 1980 for fattening. Later, the entire Whakatau complex was recognised as an area well suited to breeding cattle, and there had been a steady increase in the numbers of cows ranging all four stations. The cattle I saw on Otangimoana — ghostly apparitions in the mist — were Friesian-Angus cross.

The sharp ring of a telephone caused Eddie to break off, and, while he was otherwise occupied, I mulled over what he had told me about this and the other stations that made up the complex. It seemed certain that I had been on the station before — not that it was a station then. It was the winter of 1961 when I first came to Kaingaroa Forest as a brand-new Forest Service hunter. At that time the Matea was regarded as the top block for animals. No question about it. So then, six years after the Lands and Survey Department had taken it on for future farming development, it remained untouched.

In the early 1960s the Matea was a place of seemingly limitless scrub and deep washouts that, following heavy rain, turned into rampaging creeks. The Matea had a special fascination and on a clear winter's day it was for me an alluring place. A great part of its attraction was, of course, the wildlife. Red deer were thick here; they either inhabited the Matea on a semi-permanent basis or simply crossed in a regular pattern, ranging between the wild, unbroken forestlands of the Urewera country and the southern parts of Kaingaroa Forest. Wild pigs were rampant on the Matea and they did a wonderful job of cleaning up the untold carcases of red deer the cullers left in their wake. The Matea was the very last stronghold on the Rangitaiki Plains of the wild horse.

It occurred to me as I sat waiting for Eddie to return that the changes had been enormous. On Otangimoana, sheep and cattle grazed and the land was green where, 30 years earlier, all I had seen was a blue-grey carpet of scrub and wild horses. When I next went outside and saw the sheep and cattle and a land turned green by topdressing I couldn't really believe I had once seen wild horses there at full gallop.

18

INLAND PATEA COUNTRY

Of all the North Island stations I visited, none had more significance for me than those scattered along an ever-winding mountainous route in that vast tract of land between Taihape and Napier, known as the Inland Patea country.

Two brothers, Azim and William Birch, took on Erewhon in the mid-1860s; it was then about 40,000 hectares. In this same period, G. P. Donnelly acquired Mangaohane, some 22,000 hectares. Then, in 1875, a South Island runholder, Joseph Studholme, became the first man to take on what today is the largest station in the North Island, Ngamatea.

Ngamatea was initially named Owhaoko station. It was probably around 50,000 hectares, including both freehold and leasehold land, by the time the bitter and lengthy disputes about block boundaries were settled between Studholme, Donnelly and others. As with Erewhon, Owhaoko's northwestern boundaries were poorly defined. It didn't really matter: it was wild, unbroken country where, even today, red tussock predominated. Eventually the open country petered out and bushlands took over; it was in fact no real distance from Poronui's southern range. Studholme might have carried his sheep over an area twice, even three times, the area of land that was officially his to graze.

Before the turn of the century, Mangaohane was cut up into two blocks; the smaller section, about 9500 hectares of generally easy country, became Otupae station. The same thing happened on Erewhon, for the Birch brothers divided their property: William took about 23,000 hectares on the eastern side and retained the station's name; Azim's section was the homestead area, judged the better part, and he named it Oruamatua station. Later still, Azim Birch's station was subdivided again,

180 • STATION COUNTRY

the biggest part of which is today's 12,000-hectare Ohinewairua station.

When Studholme eventually sold out, Ngamatea passed through the hands of several speculative owners. In 1931 all that altered dramatically when the partnership of W. D. and W. E. Fernie, and J. F. Roberts, purchased the station. Jack Roberts was made manager of the station, a position he held until his death six years later, when his brother, Lawrence, stepped in. Lawrence Roberts would rule Ngamatea for 30 years and when he died in 1967 the station was then owned by his two children, Jack and Margaret, and their great-uncle, Walter Fernie.

By 1971, both Jack and Margaret had married. Jack and Jenny Roberts lived at Timahanga, an outstation of 12,500 hectares, mostly south of the main road. Margaret and Terry Apatu went to live in Waipukurau. Ray Birdsall was appointed station manager. A year later, brother and sister agreed to divide the station, with Jack remaining on Timahanga and Margaret retaining the main block. Walter Fernie remained a partner in both enterprises.

So Timahanga became a station in its own right. Ngamatea was significantly reduced in size to 30,500 hectares, but remained the largest station in the North Island. While it might have appeared a rather one-sided split, it must be remembered that they used most of the land on Timahanga, whereas, on Ngamatea, which is considerably higher — 22,000 hectares of magnificent red-tussock country running out towards the Golden Hills area — the land was only rarely used.

On a gloomy May morning, Jack and Jenny Roberts were showing me the first homestead built on the station. The building was derelict and surrounded by manuka scrub and reverting forest. It had been, Jack believed, the manager's home, for Joseph Studholme based himself in the South Island. It had been built soon after Owhaoko had been taken up, in around 1875. An 1890s photograph

When Ngamatea was first taken up, it was mostly covered with a sea of red tussock that turned gold in the evening sun.

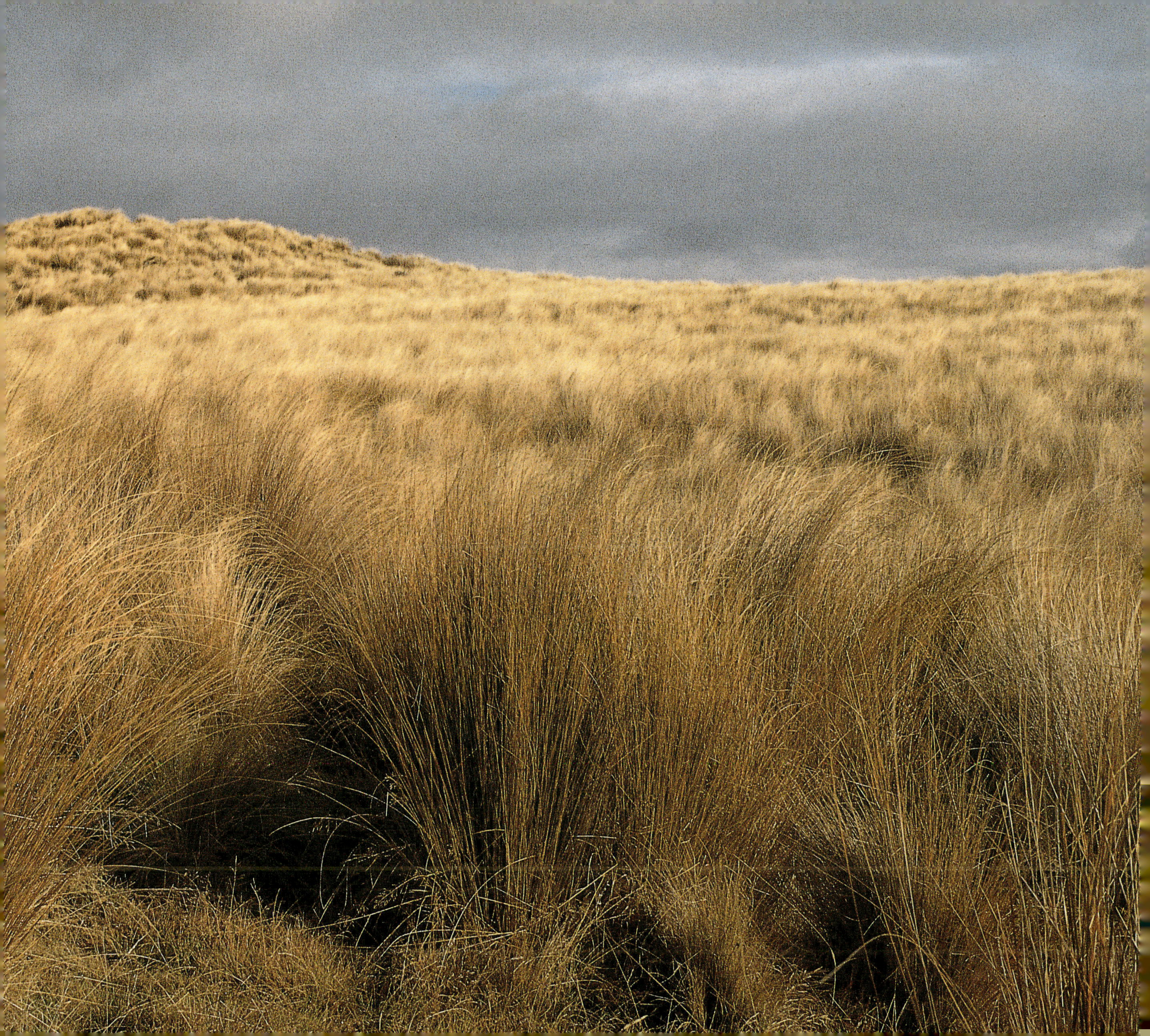

of this dwelling shows that it had a shingle roof and cob chimney. Naturally, there had been other buildings here, too. At peak times, they had shorn 65,000 sheep in the woolshed, but it was long gone. The red tussock was gone, too. Looking around me, I realised that there would have been a magnificent view from the homestead before it had been allowed to revert to scrub and forest.

The headquarters of Timahanga, nestled in a hollow below the homestead, dated to the mid-1930s. All the buildings were painted or stained a dull red. Jack, taking great delight in showing me around, pointed out the cookshop-dining area; blacksmith's shop; stables with the chaff loft perched on top of it like a pigeon coop; singlemen's quarters; two storerooms; big woolshed; and store. As on Brancepeth, the store had been well equipped and the men could purchase anything from tobacco to blankets. There was, Jack added, a similar set-up on Ngamatea.

The 30-year span when Lawrence and Winifred Roberts lived there was the station's most colourful and romantic era. They raised their two children in what, by today's standards, were very isolated conditions. The inland route was a daunting experience then — unsealed, badly rutted, often under snow, subjected to deep washouts or choking with dust. A trip to town — 80 kilometres to Napier over the Gentle Annie or the same distance to Taihape — was not to be undertaken lightly.

The station dwellings were at an altitude of 900 metres, certainly the highest set-up of any property in the North Island. Depending on the season, you might be baked by harsh, unfiltered sun or numbed to the bone by blizzards that rampaged across the high plateau. In short, you needed to have the bark on to survive out there for any length of time.

In this period they still ran stock over an area estimated at 100,000 hectares, more than half Molesworth's size and twice that of Glenary, leaving room for the odd smallholding as well. To gain the grazing rights for some of his land — Golden Hills, for instance — Lawrence

Station buildings on Timahanga date to the 1930s. The original homestead.

Roberts paid 'rabbit rates'. By North Island standards, Ngamatea was an awesome size. From the southernmost boundary, an offshoot of the main Ruahine Range to the most northerly hut, Mangamingi, it was a good 100 kilometres; you didn't cover that distance in a hurry, even on a decent station hack. The horse reigned supreme on Ngamatea then, as it did everywhere. They ran as many as 100 horses on the station, mostly musterers' hacks.

There were eight outlying huts and two tent-camps. At each one was a horse paddock or holding pen. Chaff was brought out by packhorses prior to any serious mustering. The men worked in teams of seven or eight musterers and a packer-cook. To muster the area around each camp might take four or five days, longer if bad weather set in. That was quite likely up in the Manson country or in the rolling, deer-infested hills that turned gold in the evening sun; in both places the rainfall was 3000 millimetres a year.

You could put in a big day out there in Ngamatea's back country and not see a single fence, just thousands of hectares of that glorious red tussock. The musterers didn't

The cookshop.

Timahanga station complex.

think it was so glorious: the dogs couldn't see over it and you were often pushed to see any of the half-breed sheep they were running then, even if you were within shouting range of them. There wasn't much joy in riding back to camp after a full day in the saddle and having to explain that, no, you hadn't seen a single greyback.

It was little wonder that Ngamatea became a talking point whenever high-country musterers gathered. An eight-month mustering season on Ngamatea, in the saddle seven days a week, was considered the thing to do by those mostly taciturn types who rolled their own cigarettes, and wore big oilskin coats and wide-brimmed hats. On their odd days off at headquarters, when they might have been changing hacks, they told an eager-eyed boy called Jack Roberts what it was really like out there in the sprawling land of the red tussock.

Most men who'd put in a season or two on Ngamatea agreed on one thing: Lawrence Roberts was a hard but fair man. He was the sort of tough character who never asked a man to do something he wouldn't do himself, who never backed off when push turned to shove. He was second to none in his knowledge of the area and precisely what made a big property tick. For Jack there would be no easy ride on Ngamatea, no special favours just because he happened to be the boss's son. Jack wouldn't have wanted it any other way.

Jack and Margaret Roberts had their early schooling on the station; the responsibility for that was their mother's. This eventually proved too time consuming for Winifred Roberts, and she hired a governess. As Jack recalled with a cheeky grin, one governess became two and two became

184 • STATION COUNTRY

three; each one married one of his cousins or someone on the station. In 1951 Jack entered the third form at Napier Boys High School.

When his schooling was over, he did a year of general work on the station, mostly driving a tractor. Following that there was a season with the hard-bitten mustering team, not as a musterer but as packer-cook. It was, Jack told me with a great deal of nostalgia, a full three-day ride out from the station to the Golden Hills hut. Out there, the men mustered the 6000 half-wild wethers that ranged that country for much of the year. There was also a Merino and English Leicester stud on the station; the principle was that they put a Merino ram over an English Leicester ewe.

It was the South Island next for Jack Roberts, down to the famed Mackenzie Country to work on the Grampians and Haldon station, near Lake Benmore. Back on Ngamatea, Lawrence Roberts had enough faith in his son's ability to make him head musterer. That was something to feel proud about on the largest station in the North Island.

Later, of course, Jack and Jenny Roberts took up permanent residence on Timahanga, where Jack would develop a Corriedale flock. Today, Timahanga carried 28,000 sheep at shearing time, along with nearly 900 Angus-Hereford breeding cows. The Roberts had three sons, all in their twenties. Jenny Roberts thought that John and Peter would 'come back to the land', but she was not too sure about Alan. Still, you can't do much better than two out of three.

Sleet splattered the windscreen, and the Otupae Range, away to the southeast of the road, was covered with mist to low levels when I drew level with a big sign: NGAMATEA. Significantly, I thought, they had not cleared the red tussock that flourished about it. The weather was cold out there, with an icy wind that might

Corriedale stud rams on Timahanga, with the snow-flecked Ruahine Range in the background.

This John Scott building is home to Margaret Apatu in late summer and autumn.

Right: *Typical broken country on Ngamatea.*

have been born in the Arctic wastes desperately trying to break the back of the red tussock. Still, I reasoned, it could have been worse. Just a week ago it would have been impossible to get out here because a metre of pre-winter snow blocked the road for several days. On Ngamatea they sometimes had to dig sheep out of deep drifts.

I turned off the road and headed into the station proper. A new-looking house — or rather what I could see of the roof — arrested my attention. At the end of a winding gravel drive, then, was the house Margaret Apatu had commissioned architect John Scott to build for her. They had together designed a home that won a New Zealand Institute of Architects' National Award. Margaret Apatu commented, 'because I am so small and vulnerable, the house would fold itself around me. And that is how I feel whenever I come here. Not that I am vulnerable, but that the house wraps its arms around me and protects and shelters me.' These days, Margaret Apatu spent late summer and autumn there, leaving the running of their Waipukurau farm to her husband, Terry. If that is not the best of both worlds, well, it is very close.

Presently, I arrived at the headquarters. Nothing lasts forever, but the romantic in me was hugely disappointed to discover that the old red buildings on Ngamatea had been replaced in recent years by highly functional Lockwood dwellings. Why, even the woolshed was comparatively new.

The fact that they didn't use horses all that much anymore was also hard to take. Still, the majority of land they ran stock on — 8000 hectares — was cleared of red tussock and had been planted in grass. It was such easy country that in dry weather you could have gotten around most of it in my Honda Accord. The wastelands that lay

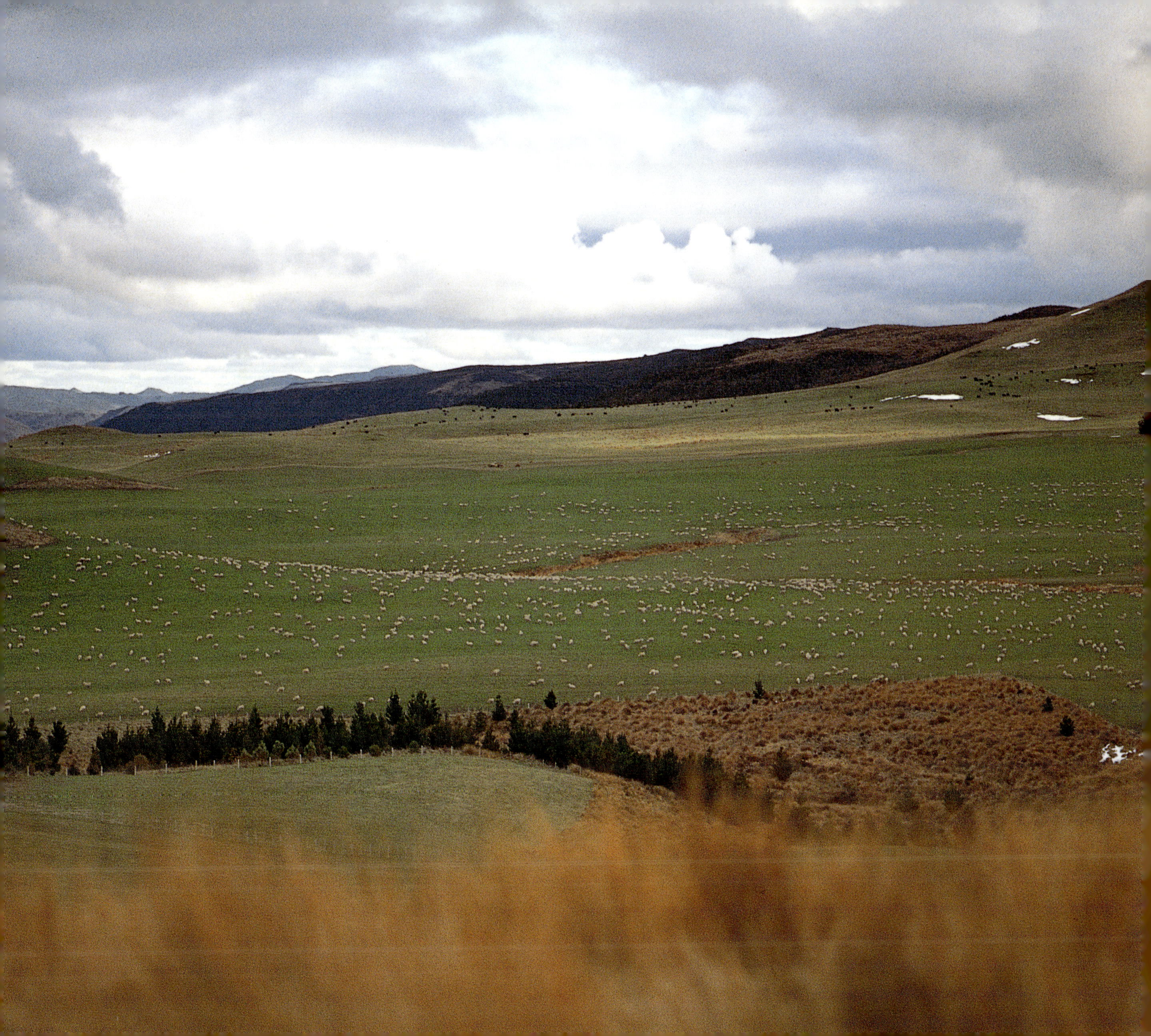

north and west of the cultivated country and ran back to Golden Hills were hardly used, except in winter, when they ran breeding cows out there; the men bringing them in with calves at foot in the spring. They used horses then, of course, and perhaps recaptured something of the romance of the past.

I was being told about all this by the manager of the station, Graham Lunt, as we stood on a lowish hill, which nevertheless offered a fine view. Graham, I discovered, had been there just over a year and, interestingly enough, had been the manager on Smedley for 20 years before that. He was no longer a robust young man seeking the great challenge, but Terry Apatu had asked him to take the job. He had read and heard about Ngamatea over the years, but really Graham Lunt had come out much too late to glimpse the very essence of Ngamatea.

I gazed over a vast area of tundra-like ground to the east — the infamous Ngamatea Swamp. According to Jack Roberts, it covered about 800 hectares and consisted of a light covering of grass over extremely boggy ground, so boggy that it had been known to swallow a cow whole. There were, Jack reckoned, two safe horse trails through it, but you had to know exactly where they were. Horses were never very happy about having to cross the Ngamatea Swamp. Sensibly, the stock gave it a wide berth.

Turning to the west, I observed sheep on a hill face so green you might have been in the Waikato. That's topdressing for you. The sheep, Graham explained, were Romneys, although now and again they would 'throw back' to the early Merino strain. There were cattle in sight, too, not far from the fringes of the swamp. They were Hereford-Angus cross; Graham ran 2000 breeding cows and 1100 heifers.

There was a deer farm here as well, in a big fenced-off area with several paddocks. The altitude there would have been more than 900 metres and it was unpleasant to be exposed to the raw wind. While the buildings on the station were lovely and warm, with underfloor heating,

John Roberts.

the deer had no such luck. To combat the elements, they huddled together in the least-exposed corner of their enclosure. There they stood as the rain came down, or bone-freezing winds blew, or snow drifted, or a merciless sun hammered on their unprotected heads. They were miserable, dejected creatures that looked out through the wire to where their ancestors had ranged free.

During the two days I spent on Ngamatea, I caught up with the head shepherd, John Roberts. The 27-year-old had been there for seven years, originally as a senior

Graham Lunt.

shepherd. An ardent hunter, he was pretty much in his element on Ngamatea — deer were plentiful, he said. There had been no helicopter activity for four years and the owners made sure the manager enforced a no-hinds policy for hunting. Sika deer, virtually unheard of on Ngamatea in Jack Roberts's time, were now spread over the entire station; they outnumbered the red deer three to one.

On a clear but chilly Sunday morning, I spent some time with the men of Ngamatea as they worked with cattle in the yards and then I started the long haul back to Queenstown. Beyond the Ngamatea signpost, I paused for a few minutes to look over some of the country I had known back in the 1960s, when I was hunting professionally. The Otupae Range was clear and, southeast of there, running back to the Ruahine Range, I could see the wonderful country of the Mangaohane Plateau. I recalled camping in station huts on the back of both Otupae and Mangaohane; I had also unpacked my gear in an old hut on the back of Timahanga station, when it was still really a part of Ngamatea. I had stayed in the old Manson hut where, in Jack Roberts's time, they ran half-breed sheep. Those experiences had enriched my life: I expect that most stationmen who had camped in these same huts would have felt that way, too.

ON THE MAINLAND

SOUTH ISLAND

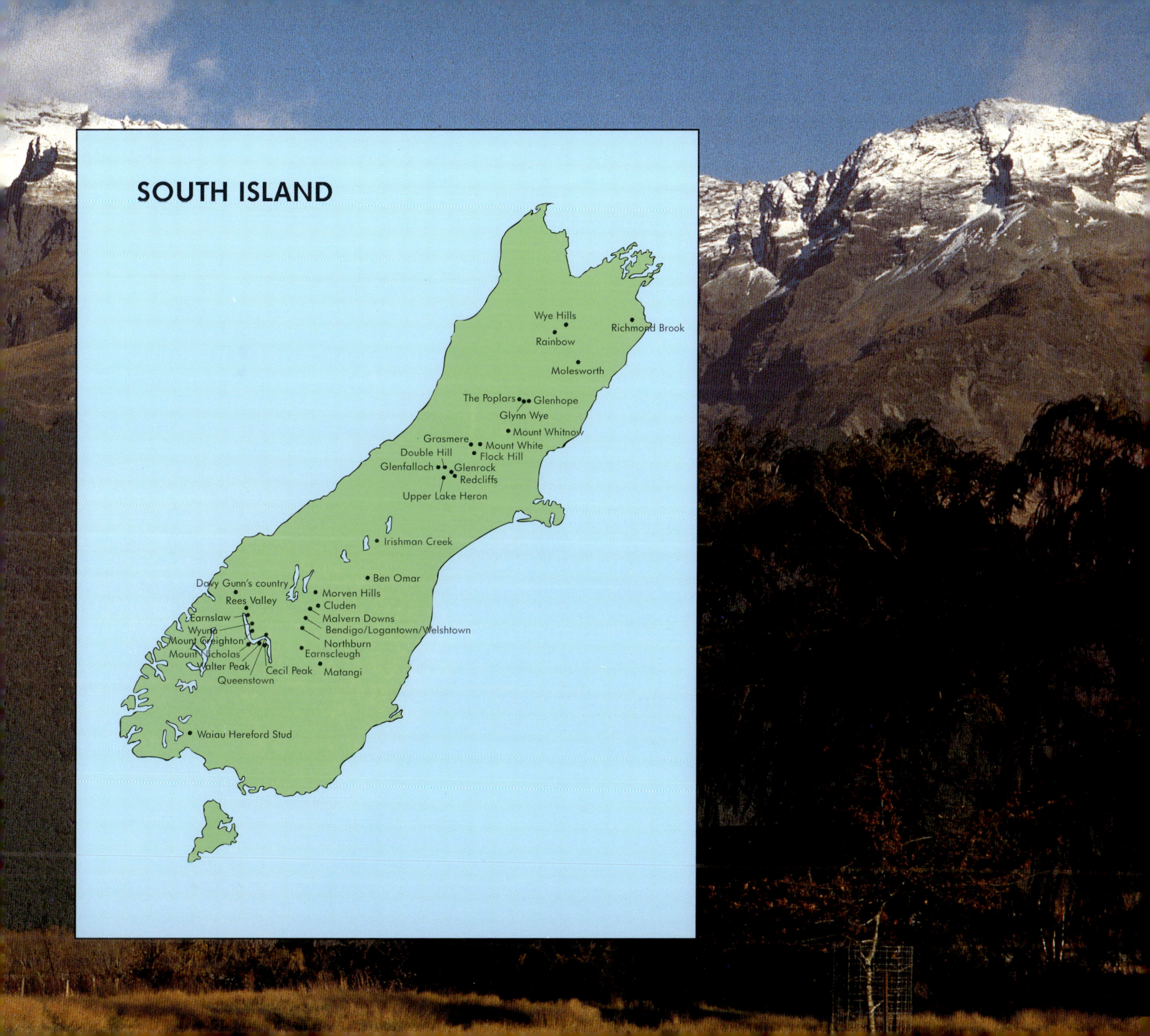

- Wye Hills
- Richmond Brook
- Rainbow
- Molesworth
- The Poplars
- Glenhope
- Glynn Wye
- Mount Whitnow
- Grasmere
- Mount White
- Double Hill
- Flock Hill
- Glenfalloch
- Glenrock
- Redcliffs
- Upper Lake Heron
- Irishman Creek
- Ben Omar
- Davy Gunn's country
- Morven Hills
- Rees Valley
- Cluden
- Earnslaw
- Malvern Downs
- Wyuna
- Bendigo/Logantown/Welshtown
- Mount Creighton
- Northburn
- Mount Nicholas
- Earnscleugh
- Walter Peak
- Cecil Peak
- Matangi
- Queenstown
- Waiau Hereford Stud

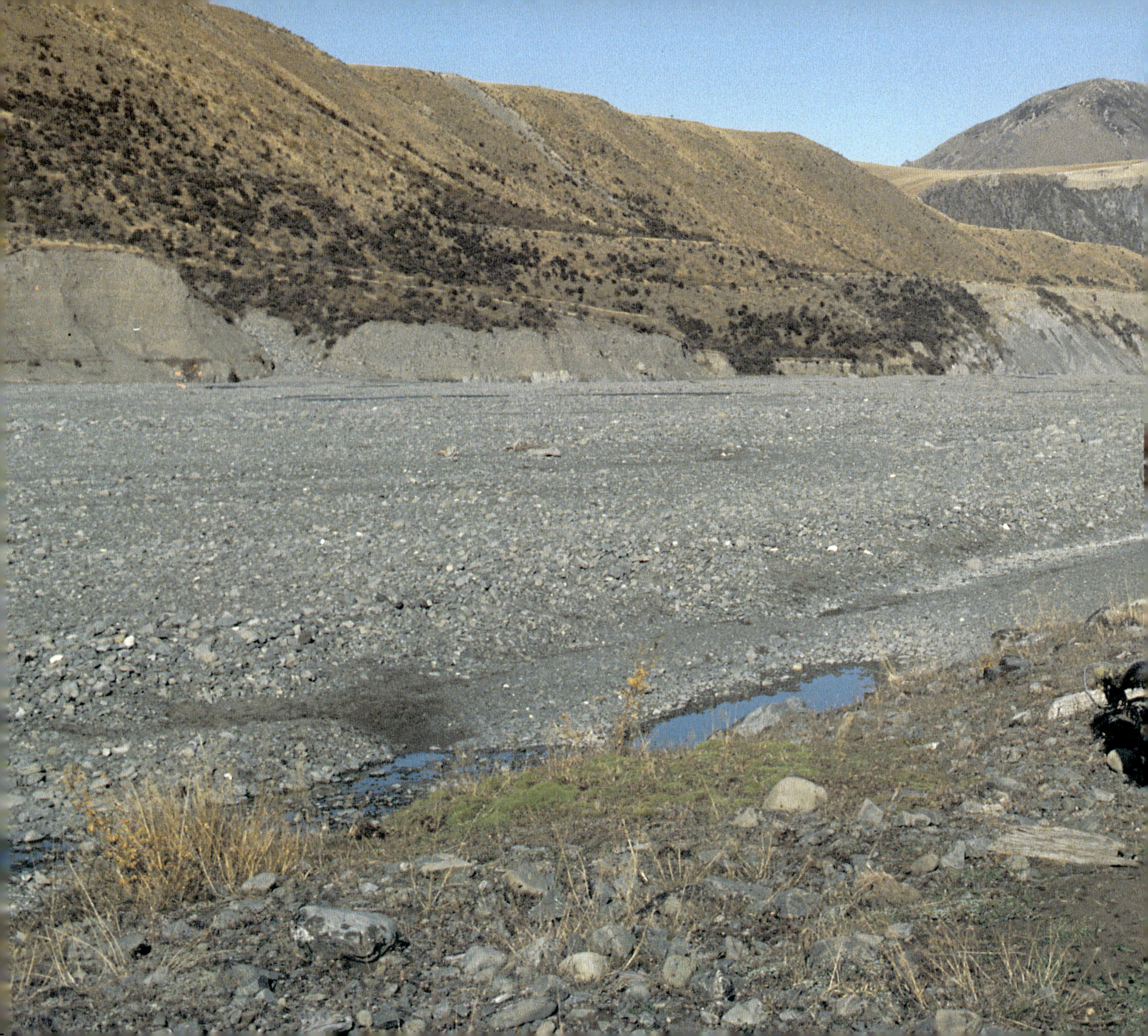

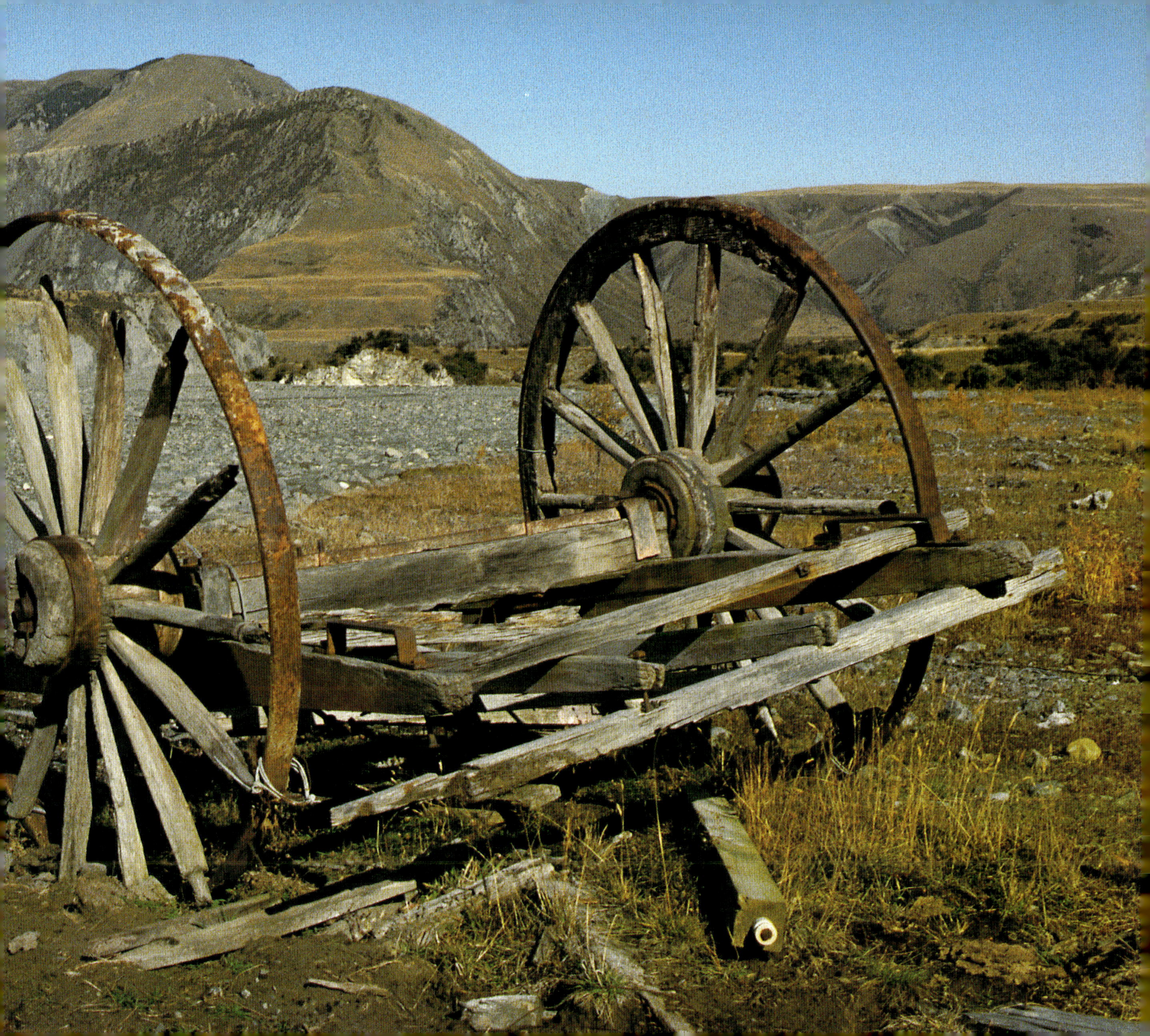

19

STATIONS OF THE LEWIS PASS

Out at the St Andrews hut, a five-roomed out-station on Glenhope, Charlotte Milne had her hands more than full, what with three young children to look after and the men at the shearing shed about to stop for midmorning smoko.

While Charlotte flitted around the kitchen preparing a big pot of tea and something to go with it, Kirsty sat quite contentedly in her high chair. She smiled at me, blue eyes flashing, and reached out a tiny hand. Little charmer! Kirsty, nearly a year old, was good-natured and as pretty as a field of wild flowers. I could imagine that her mother looked much like her at the same age.

Born in Greymouth and raised on a farm, Charlotte Milne was now in her late twenties. When she left school she had attended Telford — a farm training school at Balclutha — for a year. During that time her father took the manager's job at Cora Lynn, the last run up the Waimakariri, and Charlotte worked there on leaving Telford.

It happened that the adjoining Grasmere station was being leased by Snow Hebberd and a young lad called Rod Milne. Charlotte and Rod got together, liked what they saw, and eventually married. When the lease on Grasmere ran out, Snow decided he'd had enough of high-country runs, and Charlotte and Rod were ready to find a place of their own.

They ended up by the Inland Kaikoura road with

The Craigieburn Range rises high above Grasmere station.

STATIONS OF THE LEWIS PASS • 195

Charlotte Milne, woman for the high country.

1600 hectares, 1500 dispirited Romney sheep and 100 woebegone Hereford cattle. The drought-stricken station, called the Conway, seemed a bargain. Four years later Rod and Charlotte were proved right: the drought had been broken by consistent rain, and the land and the stock were improving. They sold up, doubling their money, and looked for a new challenge.

Glenhope station, in the Lewis Pass, lay north of the Hope River and west of the Waiau River and was dominated by the Poplars Range. The main homestead complex at Glenhope sat on a bench above the junction of the Hope and Waiau Rivers.

From what the Milnes had heard, it was a largely scrubby block of about 10,000 hectares, a real station. To the west of the Poplars Range they saw the lovely Magdalene Valley, named by Gerard Gustavus Ducarel or his brother Henri Philippe, who in the 1860s were the first to farm the area. In the Magdalene Valley the French brothers planted cypress and grapevines to remind them of home; the other exotic trees — poplars, pines and willows — were almost certainly planted by British settlers.

More than anything else, it was the beautiful Magdalene that sold Glenhope to Rod and Charlotte Milne.

As I stood on the cluttered veranda of the St Andrews out-station watching a V-shaped formation of streamlined Canada geese winging their way down-valley, Charlotte asked me to call the boys for morning tea. I started down to the shearing shed, shivering slightly on this cold and grey day.

Young Marcus and Charles Milne were amusing themselves around the shed. Five-year-old Marcus had until recently attended the Lewis Pass school, but since it closed he had had to go to Hanmer Springs. Dropping him off for the school bus and picking him up again meant that Charlotte had to ford the Hope River in a vehicle four times a day. Sometimes, when the Hope was up, they would first ride a horse across to see if it was safe. They hadn't lost a horse yet, Charlotte said

Early morning in the Magdalene Valley.

STATIONS OF THE LEWIS PASS • 197

with a smile, but in the eighteen months they had been at Glenhope Marcus had missed three weeks' school because they hadn't been able to make the crossing.

Marcus was carrying a five-week-old puppy over his shoulder like a small sack of wheat. I was pretty certain Waggy, a future heading dog, would have preferred to be snuggling up against his mother Bridie. The bitch was watching what was going on anxiously. She was chained to a poplar tree, within reach of a kennel made from a rusty petrol drum lined with hay. It was dry under the tree, but on a frosty night Bridie and Waggy would know all about 'a dog's life'.

Out on the dewy flats, Rod and his enthusiastic dogs were bringing a mob of flighty sheep up to the yards next to the shed. Inside the shed three shearers each bent over a greasy woolly-back. Weather allowing, these South Canterbury boys would be working for the best part of three days, crutching 2500 sheep.

One of the shearers, rangy Phil McCabe, had recently been working in the USA. He'd had a great time — they liked New Zealand shearers over there. It was a welcome change from the rough reception Kiwi shearers got from the average Aussie gang.

I caught Phil's attention and jerked a thumb in the general direction of the out-station. 'Smoko!'

One thing was for sure — these boys didn't need telling twice.

After smoko Charlotte found the time to tell me more about the station. They were running 5000 Merino sheep and 270 breeding cows, all Herefords. Half of the cattle ranged the Magdalene Valley and the rest were on the homestead side of the Poplars Range. Driving into the valley the day before I'd caught sight two of their dozen

Rod Milne at work in the sheepyards.

STATIONS OF THE LEWIS PASS • 199

Marcus with Waggy. Bridie is the anxious mother.

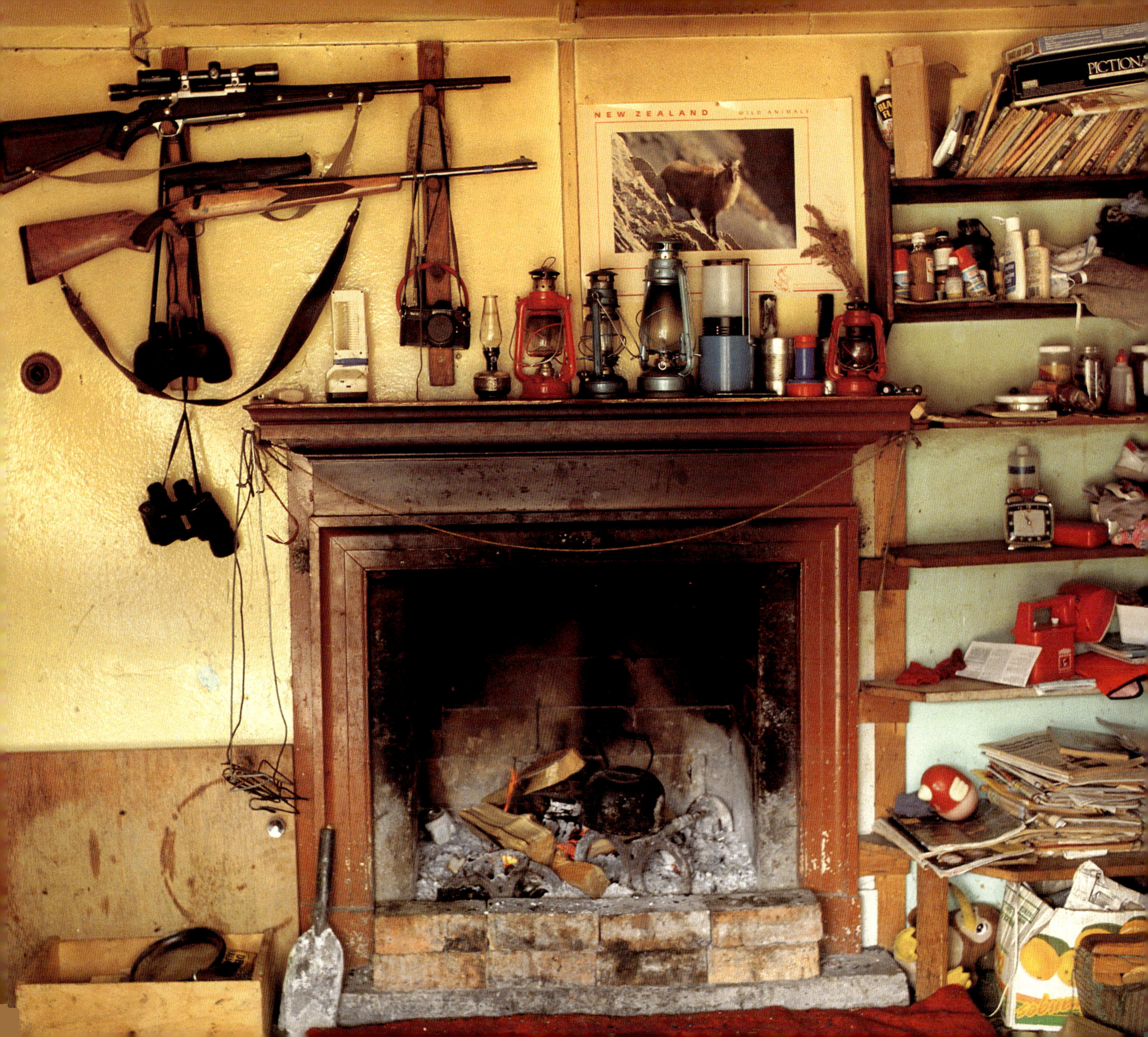
NEW ZEALAND

bulls on the Boyle River flats. Big, strapping fellows, they were.

Over winter the cattle were taken across the Waiau to the Hopefield block. It was fine country for cattle — it lay to the sun and they could forage on the ferny hillfaces or work the forested areas. When the cattle were mustered in spring, Charlotte told me, they always looked in great shape, like they'd had a holiday. The sheep were mostly taken to a winter-feed block near the main complex; it took three days to get there from the Magdalene Valley.

Later I decided to get out of Charlotte's hair and set out to look around Glenhope in a four-wheel-drive. There were birds aplenty, paradise ducks and Canada geese, feeding or in flight. There were no deer, though — they must have been hiding in the bush. I just soaked up that wonderful mountain country.

In the early afternoon I caught up with Roy Veronese. As we talked he straddled a beech log, making a big fuss of his newly acquired heading dog. Roy had called it Hope, after the river. He playfully fondled the dog's ears. Hope was uneasy, lacking in confidence, as though she had been mistreated in the past. I knew that Roy, with his winning ways and warm, friendly nature, would soon gain the dog's trust. When you've got that, well, it's for life. Dogs don't believe in half measures — they give all, and often to those who don't deserve it.

With a grin Roy said, 'We're really just getting used to each other, you know.' His smile was dazzling, a flash of white teeth even enough to advertise toothpaste.

I asked Roy what brought him to Glenhope. He told me that in 1992 he had felt a strong urge to find out

Inside the basic but comfortable St Andrews out-station.

At St Andrews they cook with a camp oven.

what station life was like, and expressed those feelings to his father. Zeff Veronese was a prominent Christchurch businessman, equally well known in hunting circles. For about thirty-five years Zeff had been coming out to Glenhope to hunt deer — the Magdalene Valley and the headwaters of the Boyle and Lewis Rivers offered ideal red deer habitat. And that was how Roy came to work at Glenhope one August school holiday.

When Roy left school he had the opportunity to take a job in the family business — making wrought-iron gates — but he hated the idea of working inside. He wanted to be where the air was clean and clear; very simply, he wanted to work on a station.

So Roy worked his way through the Christchurch telephone book. He rang station after station, but every time the conversation fizzled out after two questions.

202 • STATION COUNTRY

A home in the hills: the St Andrews out-station.

'What experience do you have? Do you have any dogs?' After he had tried thirty stations his usual optimism was beginning to fade. He made one last call, to Irishman Creek in the Mackenzie Country.

Roy Veronese could not have picked a better time to ring. Bob Peden was short-handed during a busy period: fencing, haymaking, weaning. And Bob was particularly sympathetic to Roy — a city boy, he had started out on stations in exactly the same way. Bob told Roy he could do a two-month stint. He had his start.

Eventually Roy landed a job back on Glenhope. Now he had a dog of his own, Hope, and in time he would get a huntaway. Eventually he'd become a fully fledged shepherd and then it would be up to him how far he went. For a man with Roy's initiative and sense of purpose, the sky was the limit.

As I returned to St Andrews the darkening faces of the Poplars Range seemed to lift themselves above the out-station, creating an ominous presence. Away to my right a willow-lined creek crossed the flat, but ahead of me a thin tendril of pale grey smoke rose from the chimney and a light in the window welcomed me.

The men were knocking off for the day. It was cold, but they were still lightly clad. Soon they'd sink a beer or two — no hard stuff while they were on the job — and put away a big feed. By ten o'clock they'd have turned in for the night. They would sleep as if they had been drugged until it was time for a big breakfast. And then it would start all over again.

In the early afternoon of the next day, as I drove away, the men were back at work. For Rod and Charlotte Milne the out-station was a real home away from home, where they spent as much as half their time. Looking around the lovely Magdalene Valley, I could see why.

It was about an hour's drive from St Andrews to the

Shearers three.

The young man on the land: Roy Veronese.

The Poplars homestead dates to the mid-1920s.

homestead on The Poplars, where genial John Shearer was waiting to talk with me.

There was a profusion of poplar trees fronting the homestead and, for that matter, flanking the long driveway. John explained that, no, the station hadn't been named for the trees but for the nearby Poplars Range. The trees had been planted in the 1920s, at about the same time as the present homestead was built.

John, Lois and young Andrew Shearer had come out to the station in 1983, from a 400-hectare farm at Amberley. Since high school John had held an ambition to own a big station, but it had taken twenty-five years for his dream to be realised.

John told me he was currently running 7000 halfbred Merino sheep and 700 Hereford cattle. The 8100-hectare station ran for 48 kilometres, right up to the Main Divide. During the big musters, Rod Milne from Glenhope pitched in. Good man, Rod. He'd have to be — the high-climbing sheep could get to about 2000 metres up on the range.

As the heavy clouds began to drizzle, we turned away from the homestead and headed towards the outstation and the woolshed, buildings that most likely dated back to the late nineteenth century, when W. A. Low was the owner of Glynn Wye, and The Poplars was only a part of the great run.

The woolshed was constructed of beech logs and iron, the wood cut locally and hand carved, the metal offloaded from a coastal steamer at Gore Bay. The quality of iron was far superior to that of today, and there wasn't a single trace of rust on it.

In the early days the stations in the area — Glynn Wye, Cheviot Hills, Motunau, Stonyhurst — all relied on ships to bring in supplies and take away the woolclip. The stores were brought ashore through the great surf by longboat and then carried by packhorse. Pity the poor packhorses that had to carry a load of iron up the Waiau and Hope Rivers to The Poplars.

John looked about the woolshed, almost in awe. 'You know, I estimate there's four to five tonnes of iron in this building. The quickest they could have gotten here was ten days, I reckon. Can you picture it? They would have to load up the iron on the horses in the morning and take it off again in the evening.' John shook his head and, after a long pause, added, 'What a mighty feat, eh?'

By my reckoning, the woolshed on The Poplars station was about 115 years old, and it was still in use. They built things to last back then.

Still going strong, the old woolshed on The Poplars.

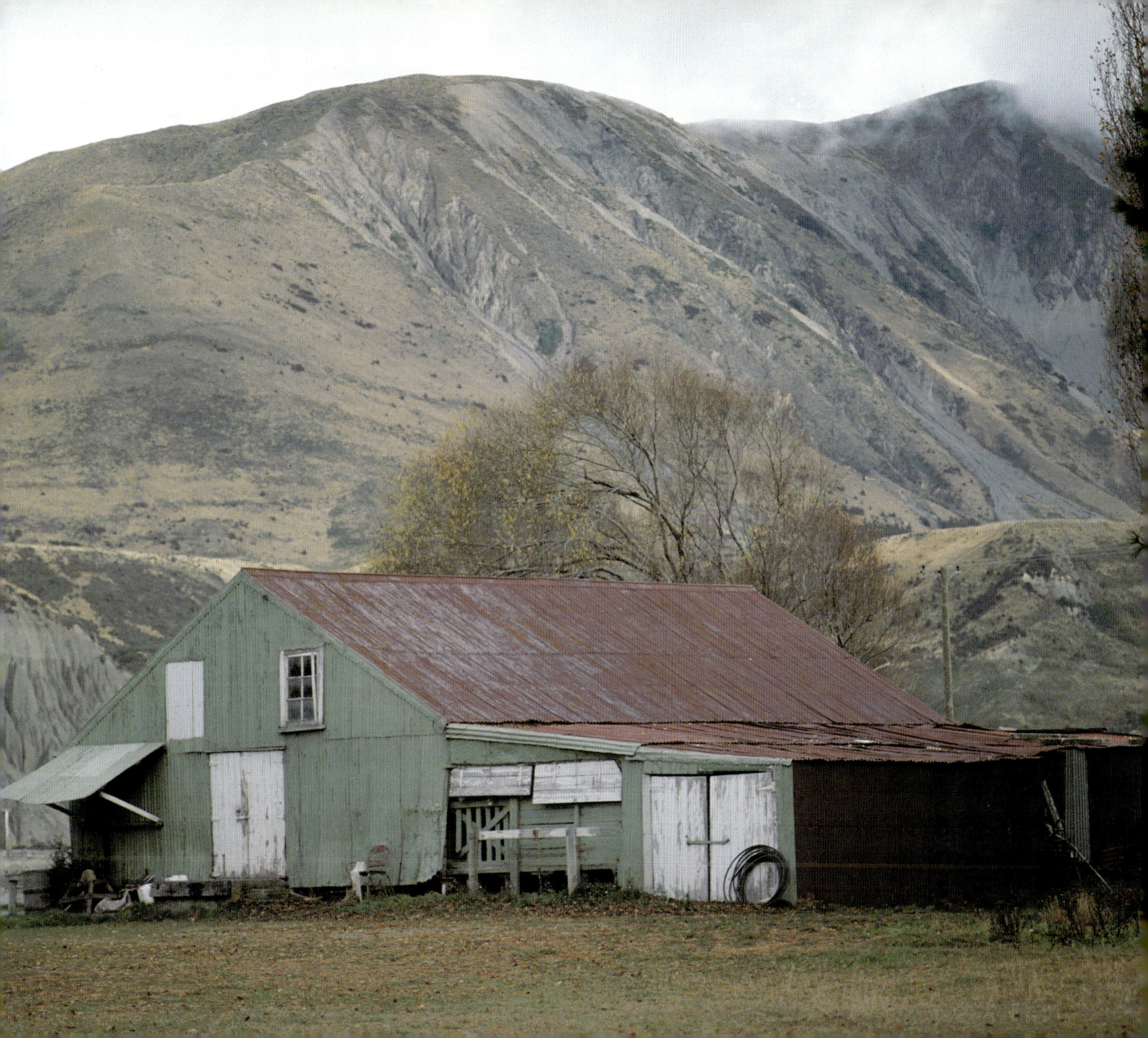

THE MOUNT WHITE TRADITION

I angled up a tussocky slope and drew rein on a windswept knoll. The view was a compelling one and I savoured it at length.

Sue, the off-white mare I was riding, seized her opportunity — a sudden hard yank on the loosely held reins — to dip her head to look for fodder. To me the vegetation, hard tack at best, didn't look too appealing. It didn't matter to Sue — she soon found something agreeable to munch on.

I stretched contentedly in the saddle. Sunlight was flooding the landscape, magically highlighting the muted autumnal tones. Truly, the Mount White station country was magnificent. Mount White, all 50,000 hectares of it, was in the vast watershed of the Waimakariri River. It was contained in the north by the Dampier Range, in the east by the Puketeraki Range, in the south by the Waimakariri and in the west by a 60-kilometre boundary with Arthur's Pass National Park.

Sue raised her head from the coarse grass and, jaws working rhythmically, stared into the distance. It seemed to me that man and horse must have been doing this for a very long time.

The Mount White country was first taken up in 1857 by Edward Minchin, who held the run until Major Thomas Woolaston White arrived on the scene in 1860. White came from a wealthy Nottinghamshire family and served with distinction in the 48th Bengal Native

The Waimakariri River from Mount White station.

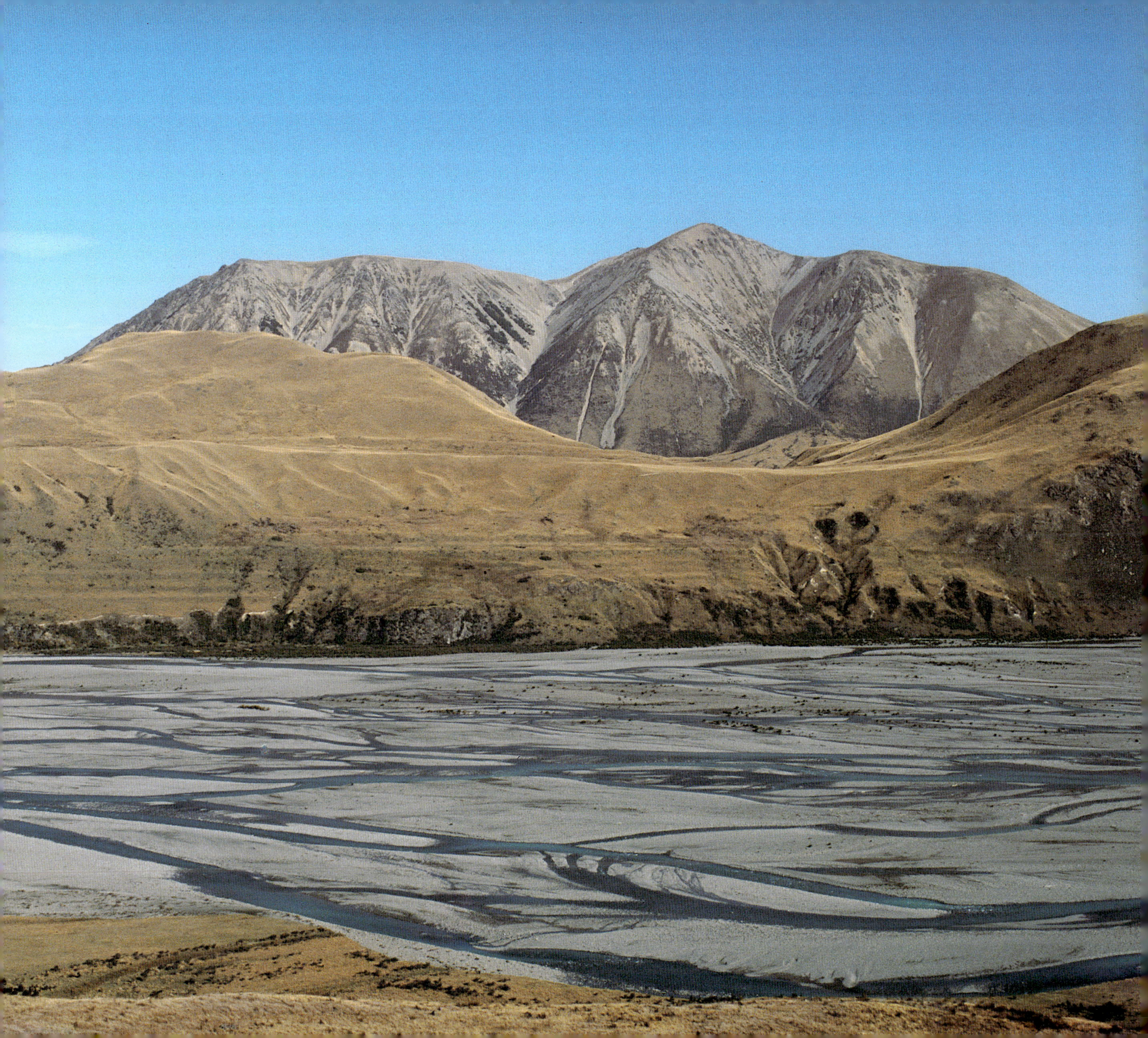

Infantry Regiment. Army service over, he emigrated first to Australia in search of gold and then to New Zealand. He gave the station its name, built a homestead and ran about 18,000 Merino sheep.

In 1869 White was forced to sell up, to an Irishman named John Cochran. All went well for Cochran and his wife Fanny until the terrible winter of 1878. Like many runholders, Cochran lost most of his sheep. The Cochrans never recovered their financial losses, and in 1884 John shot himself. His lasting legacy was an imposing new homestead that stood for over 100 years.

In 1885 Fanny Cochran made arrangements for the New Zealand Loan and Mercantile Company to take over Mount White. Over the next seventeen years horsebreeding became an important feature of Mount White life. The horses, mostly greys, were eagerly sought by musterers but many ended up pulling trams in Christchurch.

By 1902 the company was ready to sell off Mount White, together with three other Waimakariri runs: Cora Lynn, Riversdale and Lochinvar. Frederick J. Savill was the man bold enough — and wealthy enough — to buy all these stations. A few years later Savill added Craigieburn to his already substantial Waimakariri holdings. In total he controlled 80,000 hectares and up to 40,000 sheep. In 1910 Savill sold his Waimakariri runs to Walter McAlpine and Joseph Studholme.

McAlpine, a Scottish sea captain, took nonsense from no one. Invariably he settled arguments as he had at sea — with hard-hitting fists. But every fist fighter, no matter how expert, will eventually meet his match. One day, out mustering, McAlpine had taken the top beat while shepherd Bruce Pelvin took the bottom one. Something about the way Pelvin worked his beat upset the boss so much that, when they met up at the hut, McAlpine challenged him to fisticuffs. The seaman, who had given many a wayward musterer or troublesome shearer a darn good beating, was for once on the wrong end of the hiding. McAlpine, however, was a big man for a big country and was quick to shake the victor's hand. Soon after he promoted Pelvin to head shepherd.

By all accounts, McAlpine's wife Gwendoline also fitted well into high-country life. She was a fine horsewoman, a strong walker and an excellent shot.

In 1917 Craigieburn was divided into three blocks and Cochran and Studholme were granted the lease of the new Craigieburn block, which included Savill's homestead by the railway line, while James Milliken took over the other two. Milliken lived at the old Craigieburn homestead on Lake Pearson and named his station Flock Hill.

In the same year Cochran and Studholme purchased Grasmere station. In 1920, however, they sold Lochinvar to Ronald Turnbull, and in 1924 they sold him their other stations on the north bank of the Waimakariri. From this time on, Lochinvar, Mount White and Riversdale were run under one name — Mount White — by the Turnbull family.

In the seventy-odd years since the Turnbulls took over the station, there had been only six managers. The third, Peter Newton, wrote about his experiences on Mount White in *The Boss's Story*, one of his many books. For managers and musterers alike, Mount White under the Turnbull family had long been a top place to work.

If you were to ask any of the musterers who had put in a season or two on Mount White just what the appeal of the place was, they would probably have said it was

The Von River close to where the Whites built their homestead.

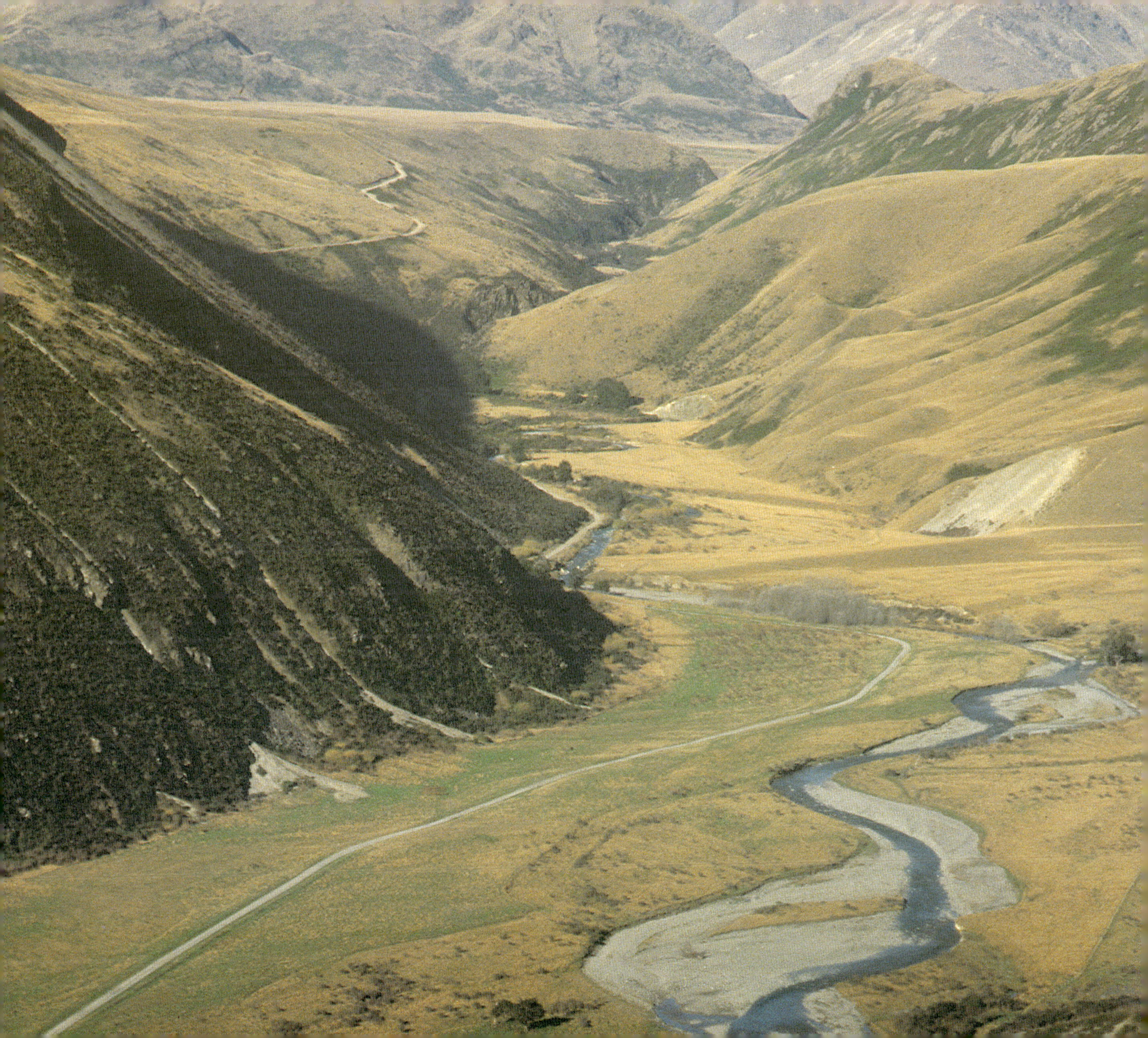

the fact that the station was run very much as it was in the early days. Rob Abbott, who mustered on Mount White in the 1950s and 1960s, certainly had many a good word.

'Dick Turnbull was a very generous employer and always produced a large cash bonus every year to all shepherds. He annoyed the other station owners by paying more than anyone else. He maintained that Mount White always got the best men, and he was right.

'We used to make our own fun. We had a golf course in the dip paddock and a cricket pitch, and we played teams from Darfield, Sheffield and Otira regularly. With these interests plus the deer shooting and excellent fishing, we were quite happy to stay put and save a bit of money.'

So there I was on Mount White on a glorious morning that gave just a hint of winter. A horseman jogged towards me and Sue. He checked his horse alongside.

'You couldn't have gotten a better day,' said Richard Smith.

The 29-year-old station manager eased himself in his

On the old Riversdale run.

saddle. His horse — Biddy, a white mare out of one the station hacks by an Arabian stallion — stamped a back hoof and blew loudly through flared nostrils. She was eager for work.

Richard hipped around in the saddle and called out to his dogs. Bounding from a matagouri-choked creek came three rangy huntaways and two heading dogs. They milled around Biddy's back legs, but she was too even-tempered to lash out.

We could hear in the distance the barking of dogs and the commanding voices of men; then came the more muted sounds of sheep on the move. Soon they came into sight over a low ridge, the sheep running every which way until the dogs got them back under control. These 2000 two-tooths were on their way to their winter range across the Esk River.

With a slight flick of the reins, Richard got Biddy moving again, in a jaunty, hip-swinging gait that ate up the miles. With winter so close her coat was starting to thicken up; soon she would look shaggy and unkempt. Sue and I tagged along behind.

Richard had come to Mount White via stints on farms

The old Mount White cookshop is still in use.

In the cookshop you'll find the shepherds' living room.

and stations in Southland and Fiordland as well as Castlehill and the mighty Molesworth. He and his wife worked as a married couple on Mount White, Sheri cooking and Richard mustering. When Ray Marshall retired as manager, the Turnbull family looked no further than Richard for his replacement.

Ahead of me, Richard and Biddy angled down-slope to link up with the other boys. I knew from the way he talked about them that Richard was proud of his shepherds. Each of them, in their musterer's gear, epitomised for me South Island high-country life. This same scene — men, horses, sheep, dogs — had been played out countless times all over the island.

The head shepherd was Kelly 'Buzz' Frame. He had grown up in North Canterbury hearing his father's colourful stories of working life on Mount White, and at seventeen had for the first time come out to the station for the summer season. Richard knew a good man when he saw one and a couple of seasons later, at the age of twenty, Kelly was promoted to head shepherd.

Kelly's sister Jackie — just seventeen years old — was the cook on the place. She recalled that her initiation to life as a station cook was a traumatic one. The previous cook had pulled out with very little notice, and Richard had been faced with the daunting prospect of a crutching team arriving and no one to cook for them. Jackie was just about to leave school and, keen to save money, agreed to help out. Two days after her last day at school she was cooking for sixteen men in a cookshop that might have stood for more than a century. After a start like that, she said with a reflective chuckle, things could only get better.

The other shepherds, Johnny Anderson and Robert Calder, were both lean 21-year-olds. Johnny's family had owned Ben Omar station near Omarama (where an annual rodeo was held) for longer than the Turnbulls had controlled Mount White, while Robert had grown up on the neighbouring Mount Whitnow. These young men lived for their horses, and each was quietly proud of the fact that he had broken in his own mount.

Presently the Esk River, cutting a broad gorge, came into sight. The mustering team dismounted; it was a steep drop to the rock-strewn riverbed and the footing was uncertain. It was much more sensible to walk the horses, zigzagging down.

Soon the dogs and sheep were well ahead of us and in seconds they were racing through the scrub by the river. I started down-slope gingerly, holding Sue on a very tight rein. She loomed up behind me, big as a house. Suddenly she skidded on the slippery black soil, wet with dew and a hint of melting frost. Thunk! She slammed into my back.

Half in fright, I yelled, 'Easy, girl. Easy!'

Snorting, Sue damn near pulled the reins from my hands as she reared back. With a powerful sense of relief that Sue was going backwards instead of forwards and over me, I allowed her more free rein.

The sheep, in no mood for an icy dip, finally forded the river under intense pressure from the dogs. Once across, they started up a long shingle fan to their sunny winter range south of Newton Creek.

Richard watched them go with a look of pure satisfaction. All of the station's 12,500 Merinos were now out for the winter. He mounted up, a good morning's work done. Back home for a hot lunch.

Soon enough we regained the wide river terraces, where the Herefords were grazing. They paid us scant attention as we rode past in single file, Richard up front on quick-stepping Biddy. The boys seemed quite happy to let the boss take the lead — that meant he had to open the gates.

Knowing she was headed home, Sue perked up. In fact she forged to the front, actually out-walking Biddy.

'Sue's showing off,' laughed one of the young hands.

'Sue's all right!' I fired back. 'She thinks I'm the head shepherd and should be leading the way.'

The real head shepherd, slumped in his stock saddle, made a rasping noise that just might have been a

Newtons Creek, named for writer Peter Newton.

chuckle. He seemed a good sort, Kelly Frame, solid and dependable as a matai fencepost. Somehow all the shepherds on Mount White gave that impression. These were men to ford a flooded river with; these were men who seemed much older than they were. That afternoon the same trio would be back in the saddle, heading off to camp out at for a couple of days at the Nigger hut. Out on the Nigger Hill block there were a number of stragglers, sheep missed in the eight-day fall muster.

Still, Sue was doing it in style. There was one problem, though — now I had to open the blasted gates.

On the river terraces there was a small paddock, about 40 isolated hectares, planted in rape for winter-feed. It would be a real pretty yellow when it flowered later on. Up on a tussocky hillside, taking full advantage of the sun, was a small band of horses, breeding stock. The station's only stallion stood on higher ground, a little apart from the main bunch.

Johnny Anderson, Robert Calder, Kelly Frame and Richard Smith.

Oregon, a Clydesdale, was keeping a watchful eye on his harem. He was a powerful brute with a decidedly spooky look.

Topping a rise, I saw the seventeen-year-old homestead. The old one, built in Cochran's time, had deteriorated and was eventually burned to the ground.

Later, in the large, cosy, kitchen and living area of the Smiths' home, I drank coffee while Sheri prepared lunch. Sheri, from South Australia, was a slim, bubbly type, younger than her husband.

'How was Sue?' she asked.

A short time ago I had unsaddled Sue and watched as, with much kicking up of heels, she joined the other horses in the paddock. On most stations the boys would have left their horses saddled during lunch, but this was Mount White. A man was only as good as his horse, they reckoned, so it paid to look after them.

Richard Smith and his dogs hunt sheep out of a gully.

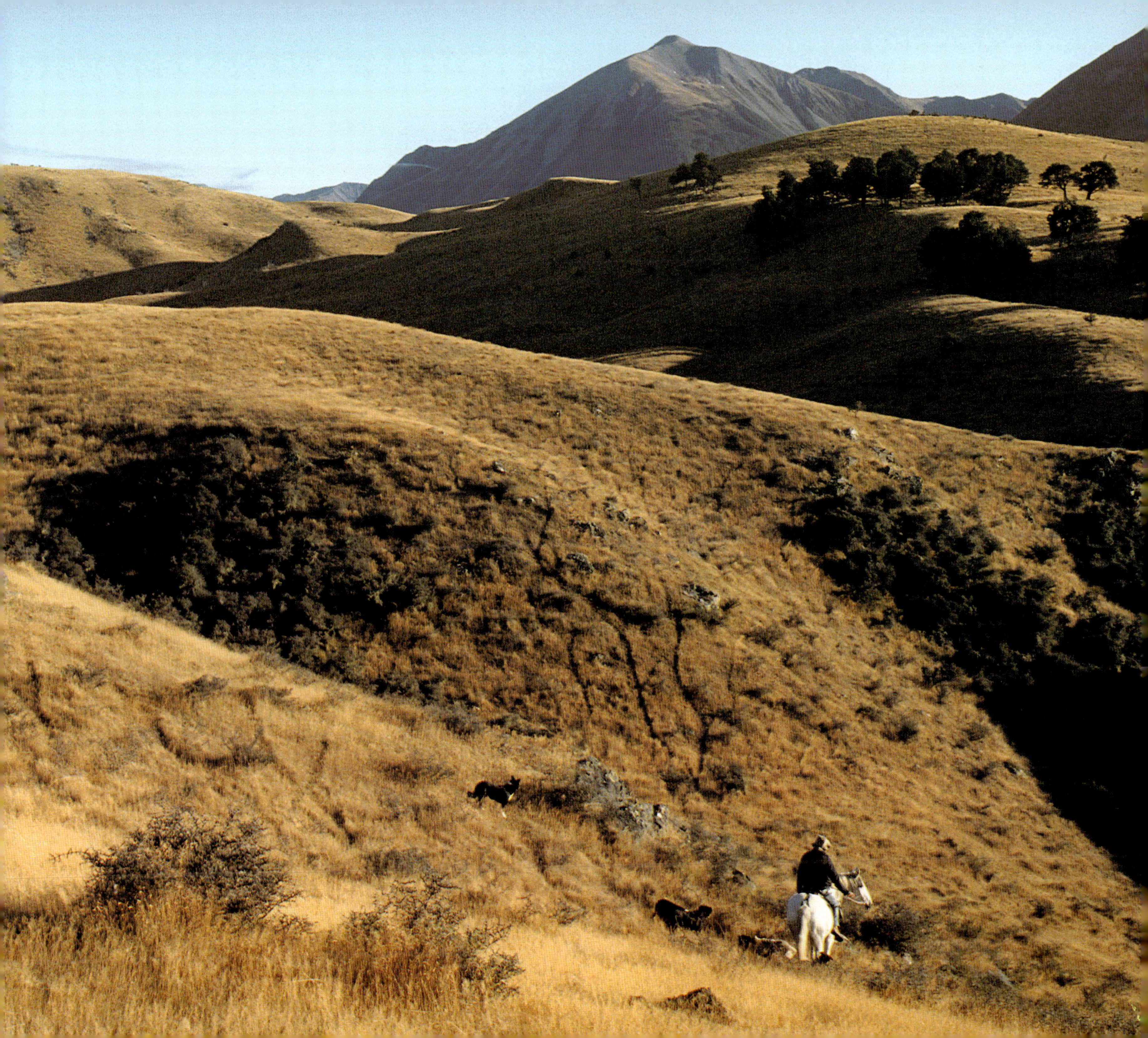

The musterers head towards the Esk River terraces.

'Sue?' I grinned. 'Couldn't have been better.'

Sue wasn't rated too highly on Mount White, but she had proven ideal for my needs. She was a good hack to ride and well enough trained that I could dismount in a hurry and drop the reins to take a photograph, and know she'd still be there when I was finished.

I wondered aloud how a young Australian woman with strong family ties coped with life out here. Sheri smiled her warm smile again. She said she had her animal friends — horses, dogs and cats — for company and had taken up gardening. She went mustering with the shepherds when she could. She had been home to Australia several times, and her parents had come over to visit.

Beyond the sheep and before the mountains runs the Esk River.

THE MOUNT WHITE TRADITION • 217

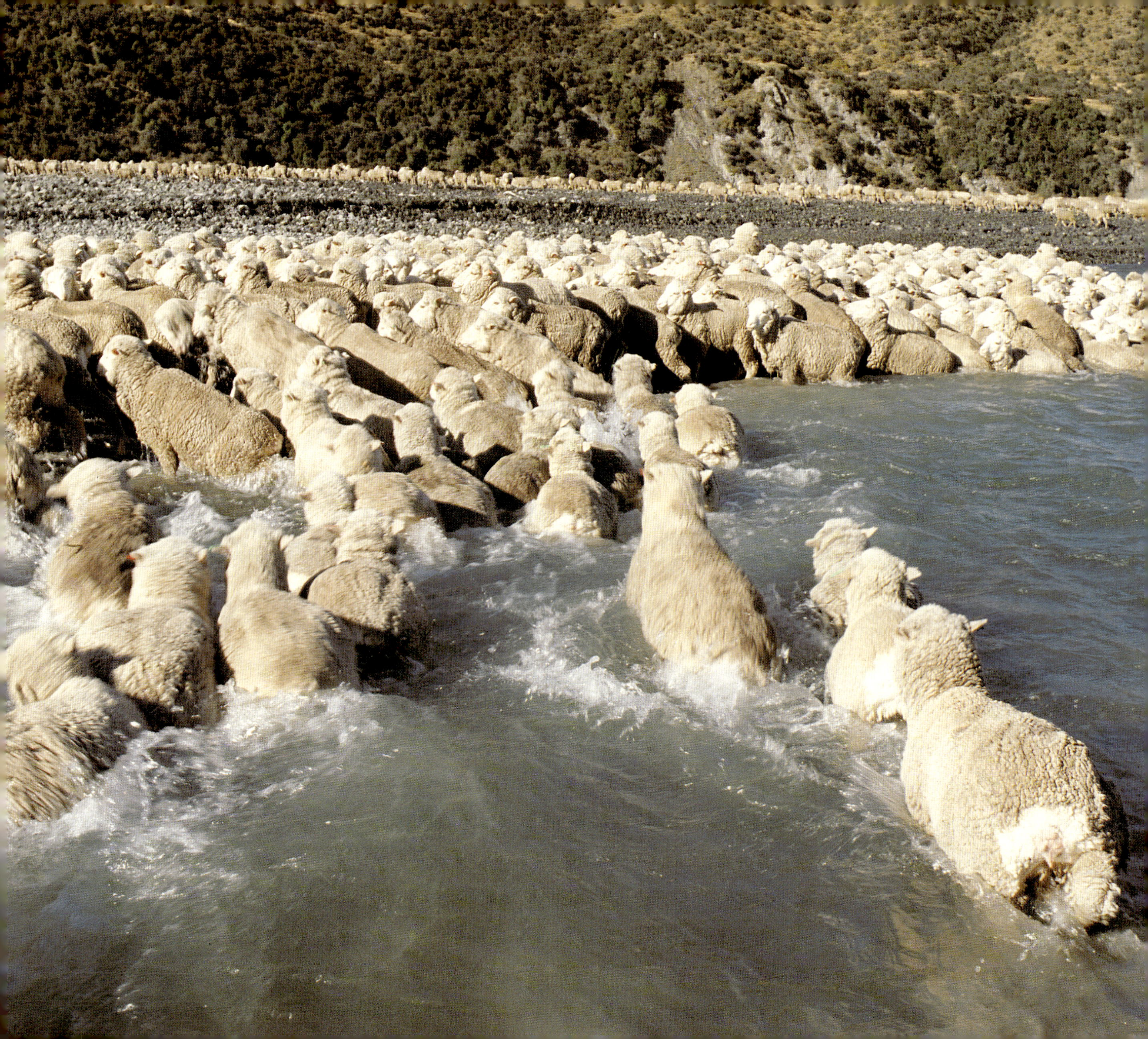

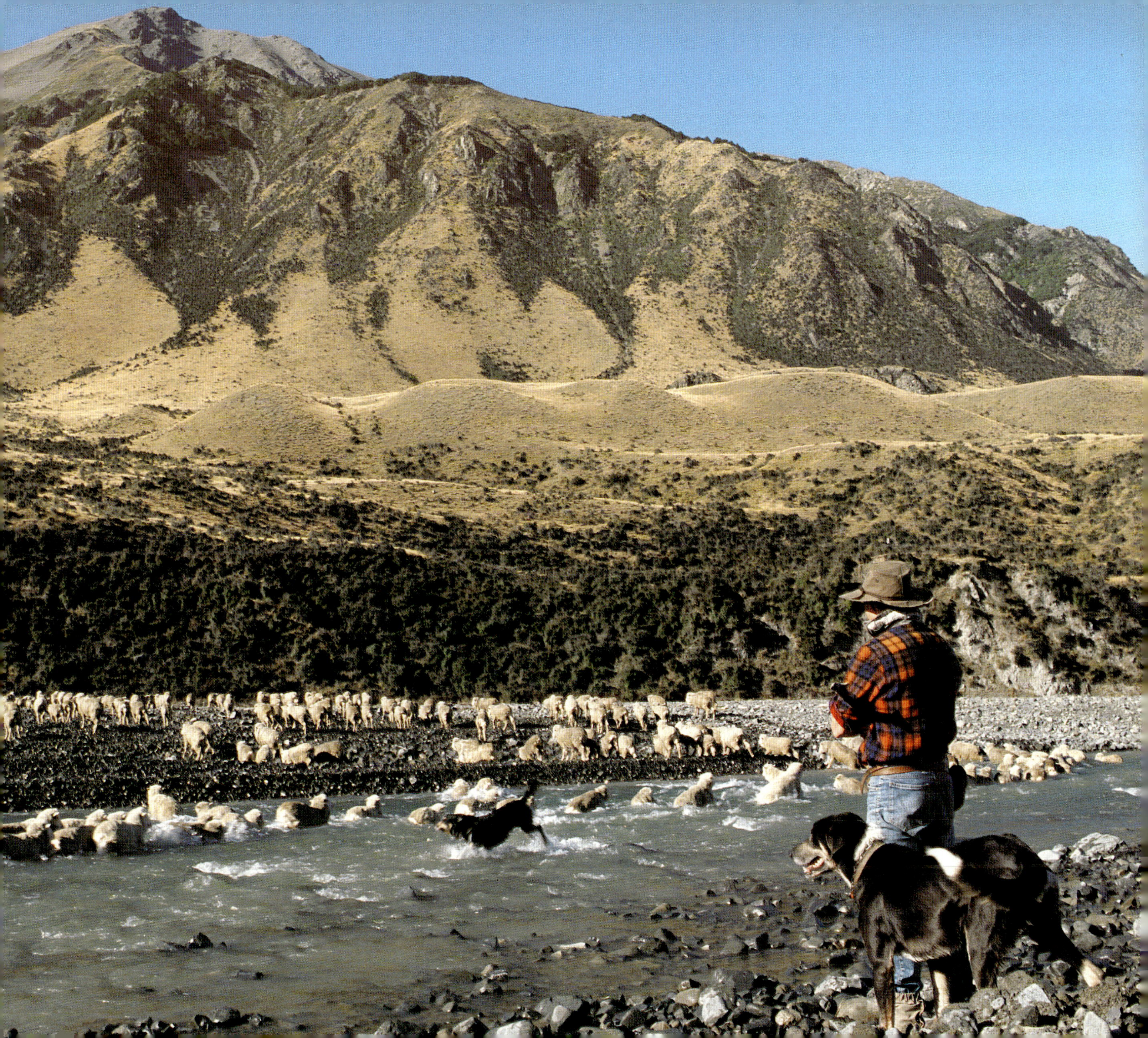

220 • STATION COUNTRY

Sheri sipped her coffee and frowned. The winters, she admitted, were tough — long and cold like she'd never known before. With the homestead at 800 metres, the frosts were like something out of the Ice Age. In the winter of 1991, when Richard had just taken the manager's job and he and Sheri were holding the fort on their own, heavy snowfalls kept them isolated for weeks.

Sometimes access could be a real bind — there was about 30 kilometres of unsealed road coming in to the station, and it was often washed out. In December 1993, when torrential rains flooded the road to town for days, Christmas presents were all too thin on the ground at Mount White station. Still, I knew the Smiths would make up for it the next year — they were that kind of people.

With the sheep safely across the water, the men mount up and head for home.

Right: The old Nigger hut.

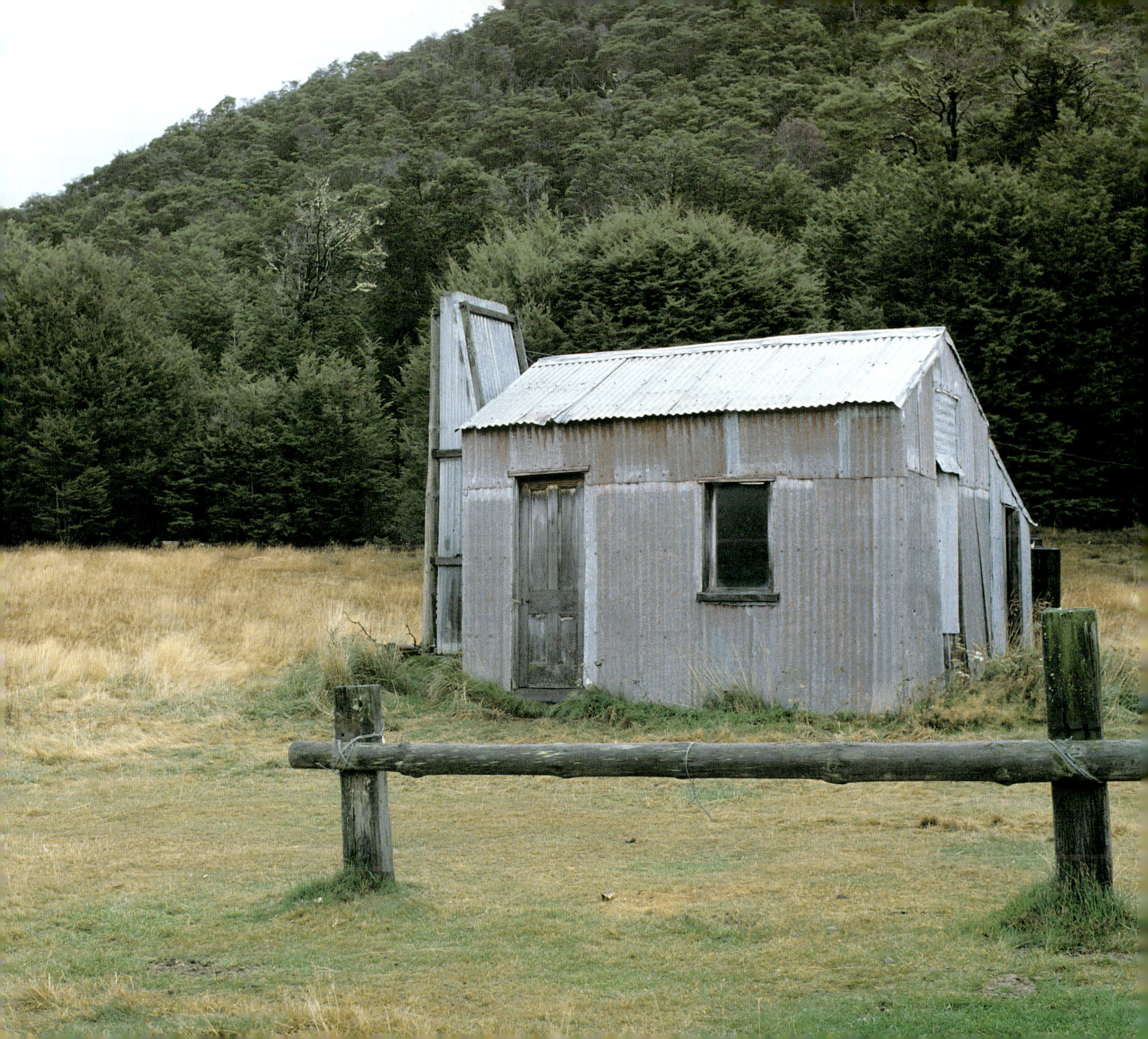

21

SOUTH OF THE RAKAIA

Set against a pleasing backdrop of towering exotic trees, the small, wooden homestead with its sloping iron roof and brick chimney looked especially inviting on an indifferent autumn afternoon.

Dave McKenzie, the 21-year-old head shepherd on Glenfalloch station, turned to me and pulled a face to show his disappointment that no one was home. 'Real pity Dave and Christine aren't here.' He looked around him as though he expected them to suddenly appear.

Wairarapa-born Dave McKenzie had headed south four years earlier and, despite his lack of experience, got a shepherd's job on Eskhead station, North Canterbury, then moved on to Walter Peak on the shores of Lake Wakatipu. To make head shepherd so quickly was testament to his adaptability and his ability to learn fast.

We had come to Upper Lake Heron station via the private track that linked it with Glenfalloch. Both properties were owned by J. A. Todhunter and Sons.

I gestured at the homestead. 'Any idea how old it is?'

He shook his head. 'Dunno . . . Must've been here a very long time.'

Tom Todhunter, the boss on Glenfalloch, was later able to fill me in on the details. The Upper Lake Heron homestead dated to around the turn of the century, the original one having burned down. The homestead had certainly been there when Tom's grandfather first arrived at the station.

Robert Charlton Todhunter was, with a man called Montgomery, a partner in the Canterbury Seed

The old homestead on Upper Lake Heron station.

Company when in 1918 it took on both Upper Lake Heron and Blackford stations. At the time Upper Lake Heron included some 14,000 hectares west and north of Double Hill. Out there you were, by local standards, in the 'back o'beyond', where the winters were harsh enough to make a Scottish shepherd shiver.

The 1600-hectare Blackford, to the east of Double Hill, was an entirely different story, being much closer to the plains. Overlooked by Mount Hutt, it was far easier to farm than Upper Lake Heron, with its lovely flatlands stretching as far as the Rakaia and laying to the sun.

Todhunter was the son of a colonist and attended Christ's College in Christchurch. The school, priding itself on its Englishness, provided a solid education that

With the Mount Hutt Range in the background, the Rakaia River enters the true Canterbury Plains.

The chapel at Christ's College dates to 1867.

included specialised training for colonial farming. Learning the theory of climate and soil could not, however, properly prepare a young man for the rigours of life on a hill-country station. It was a completely different world, one where the mountains gave birth to fast-flowing rivers, where clumps of snow tussock clung grimly to windswept slopes burnished by the setting sun.

At the time Robert Todhunter was growing up, however, on most high-country stations cadetships were available to promising young men. Of course, you had to pay a fee (anything from £30 to £100 per year) to be a cadet, which ruled out all but the wealthy. A cadet, with rosy cheeks and plum in mouth, might consider his family's money well spent as he learned the finer points of sheep mustering, but he might have questioned the wisdom of it all as he chopped wood, dug the garden, killed the dog tucker or did any of the other unpleasant tasks usually assigned to the lowest man in the pecking order.

A great deal depended on the station you ended up on. In the early 1950s a young Englishman, John Acland, was a cadet on Morven Hills. The owners of the station took him under their wing. Acland wrote to his father:

'We are in the middle of shearing, in which I take part not only in packing up fleeces, as is usual with most station masters, but I am also learning to shear myself. I hope to manage twenty a day. It is, however, hard, hot, work, but every man here ought to be able to do it, if only to know if others are doing right when he has men working under him and for the most important reason that if unable to procure shearers, a sheep farmer may not be left entirely in the lurch, but be able to do a good day's work with the assistance of the shepherd.'

It seemed safe to assume that Robert Todhunter learned the farming trade on his father's station, Westerfield — a little over 1000 hectares of good sheep country between the Ashburton and Hinds Rivers. Many years later Todhunter realised a dream when he ended a most unsatisfactory partnership, relinquishing his shares in the Canterbury Seed Company to Montgomery and becoming sole owner of both Upper Lake Heron and Blackford.

He ran Merino sheep and a Shorthorn-based herd of cattle. Like others before him, Todhunter quickly discovered that the wetlands around Lake Heron could swallow a cattle beast whole. Fortunately for him, the cattle soon learned to give the dangerous spots a wide berth.

Over winter Todhunter took his hoggets across Glenfalloch land to Blackford. It was a horseman's day

Dave McKenzie looks across Lake Stream to The Downs hut.

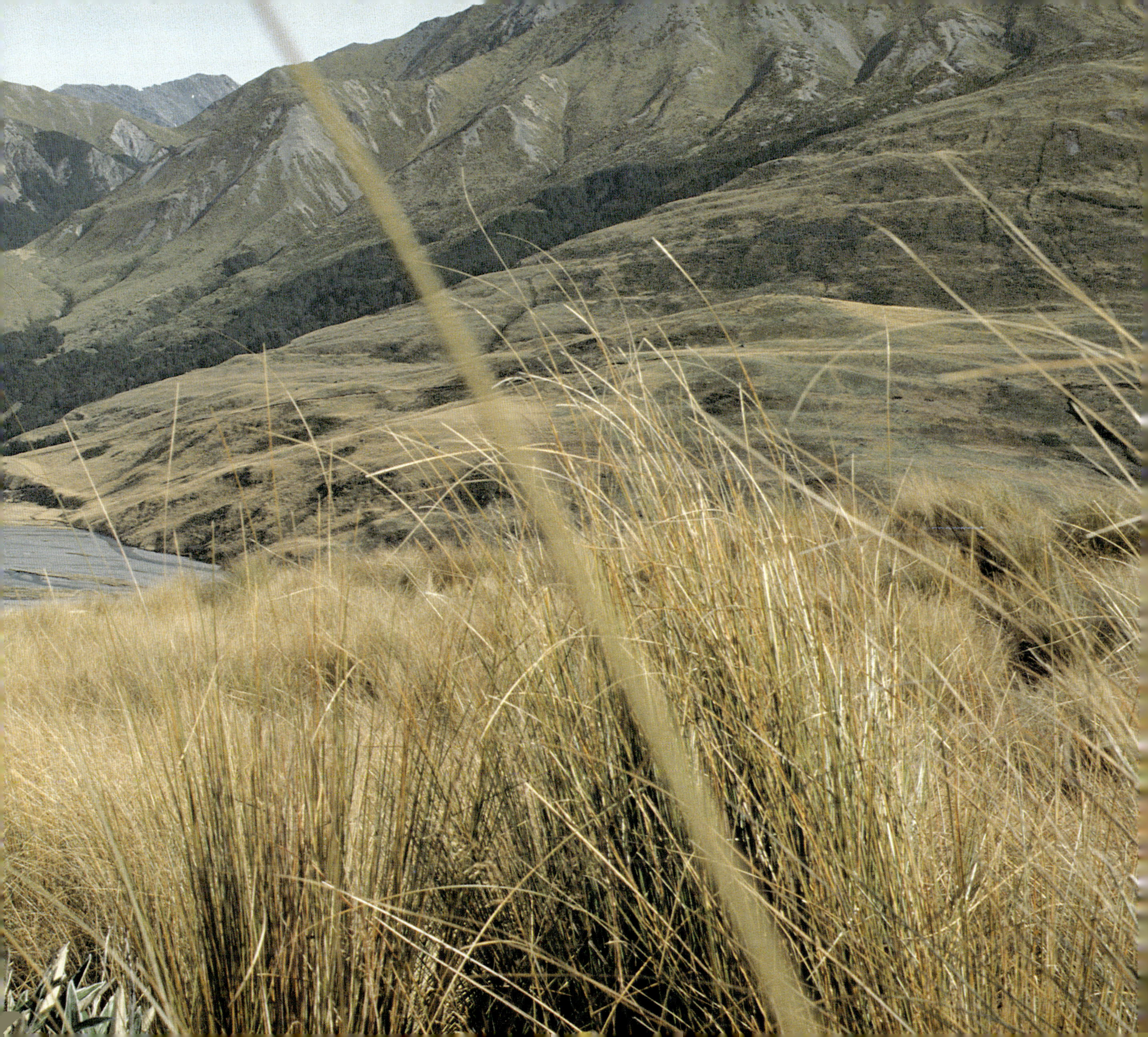

trip that took a lot longer when sheep were involved. In time Blackford became a noted Merino stud.

Like so many stations, Glenfalloch fell on hard times during the depression of the 1930s. Unlike most others, however, it didn't recover towards the end of the decade. By 1939 the station was in receivership, fences down, stock scattered all over the place. It was then that Robert Todhunter's son Joseph bought it from the Farmers' Co-operative.

Dave McKenzie and I turned away from the old homestead and clambered back into the flat-deck. The four-wheel-drive route linking Upper Lake Heron and Glenfalloch followed the course of Lake Stream most of the way. Some of the most significant wetlands in the country flanked the stream on the eastern side; Lake Heron itself was a bird sanctuary. At regular intervals Angus cattle grazed on clumps of coarse grass that would in winter be buried for months on end under deep snow. Some cattle, black as coaldust, raised their heads at the gutsy roar of the ute, considered, and resumed feeding. Above the faded landscape perhaps a dozen Canada geese speared across the sky in the direction of Lake Heron.

Dave McKenzie was keeping an eye out for Dave and Christine. No sign.

'Out mustering somewhere, I guess.' He jerked a hand in no particular direction. 'Heap of country out there — they could be anywhere . . .' His voice trailed off as though he was talking to himself.

There certainly was a lot of country out there, big country. Today Upper Lake Heron was, at 14,000 hectares, not one hectare smaller than it had been when Tom Todhunter's grandfather had first ridden in. It was top country for sheep — and deer for that matter.

Soon Dave stopped on a sharp bend where there was a commanding view. He gestured through the open window.

'See that hut? It's called The Downs.'

The red-roofed hut was situated on a flat near the wide bed of the stream. Stream? In times of heavy rain, or when the snow melted in spring, Lake Stream would turn into a rampaging giant. There was an abundance of native trees within close range of the hut. Firewood was never going to be a hassle.

'Looks a good spot to camp,' I remarked.

Dave nodded his head enthusiastically. 'We spend three nights there for spring and fall musters,' he explained as he engaged first gear. He smiled. 'Best times of year on any station, I reckon.'

Musters around here were jointly run affairs, with all hands pitching in for five days on Glenfalloch and four on Upper Lake Heron. No horses used, though, except for Shanks's pony.

'Any deer around here?' I asked.

Dave considered. 'A few . . .' He paused and licked his lips as though he was about to divulge classified information. 'Bloke stayed at the hut recently and shot two spikers.'

'They're really getting away again, aren't they,' I said, tongue in cheek.

'Dunno 'bout that! Too many choppers getting in here for them to get a decent go on, y'know.'

Dave was a keen young hunter, but he didn't get it as good as we older blokes did back in the old days. Deer poachers in choppers had stuffed it all up.

A couple of days later burly Tom Todhunter and I moved into the pleasant sitting room of the Glenfalloch homestead.

Tom had followed his grandfather Robert and father Joseph to Christ's College. Tradition was important; naturally Tom's son Charles became the fourth generation of Todhunters to attend the school. After a year at Lincoln Tom went out to Upper Lake Heron. Following his marriage to Prudence in 1967 he moved to the new homestead on Glenfalloch. The Todhunters had enlarged it several times and now wouldn't be anywhere else.

On Glenfalloch the year of 1967 was also significant for a particularly heavy snowfall in November. There was a shearing gang on the place, but this was hardly the time to lose the wool off your back.

Tom recalled, 'We put thirty-odd sheep we'd shorn in a hayshed to get them out of the weather. You know what happened? The roof caved in from the weight of the snow and we lost the lot.' More than twenty-five years down the track and that one still rankled with the man.

In just one block, he continued, they were holding about 500 ewes and their lambs. While the snow didn't bother the ewes unduly, it meant disaster for the lambs. Out of around 400 lambs they found only a dozen alive. 'That's real heartbreak stuff. That many lambs represents five years' production. And it takes another five years to get the flock back to the right ratio.'

Something I had seen — or rather hadn't seen — earlier had puzzled me. Where were the Shorthorn-based cattle Tom's grandfather had started out with? I'd spotted nothing but Aberdeen Black Angus.

Tom explained that his father had been impressed by the way the Angus breed coped with wet weather. He had seen them thrive on Mount Peel, a station that soaked up about 1150 millimetres of sou'westerly driven rain a year. In 1952 he decided it was time for a change

On Glenfalloch station.

Stormclouds gather behind the Glenfalloch woolshed.

and bought some cows from Mount Peel; they did so well that the Shorthorn-based stock were gradually replaced.

Presently on Glenfalloch they were carrying 3500 wethers, 3000 ewes, 2000 hoggets, 850 two-tooths and 350 cattle. Two Charolais bulls were used as terminal sires and all of their progeny sold off. On Upper Lake Heron they carried similar numbers of stock units. As in grandfather Robert's time, the more weather-prone hoggets were wintered well down the valley of the Rakaia on brother Bob's Cleardale.

In the afternoon I looked around the homestead area, including the woolshed and the shearers' cookshop. I admired a couple of Angus bulls in a nearby paddock, while they stared back suspiciously.

I clambered into my four-wheel-drive and crossed the

Shinty Creek.

concrete bridge over Shinty Creek. Back in the 1960s there had been a Forest Service hut on the creek, a base camp used by deercullers. Tom could remember the time the cullers passed through the Upper Lake Heron country looking for only one thing — red deer.

When I reached the broad riverbed of the Rakaia I pulled over and uncapped a flask of tea. As I looked across the river to the wide flats of Manuka Point station I thought of an earlier time. On 21 October 1897 three red deer stags and six hinds from Stoke Park, Buckinghamshire, were turned out here to fend for themselves. They were quite tame, having had a fair amount of contact with human beings, including five months of quarantine on Lyttelton Harbour's Quail Island. Once free they did not wander far, ranging between Manuka Point and Double Hill stations. In

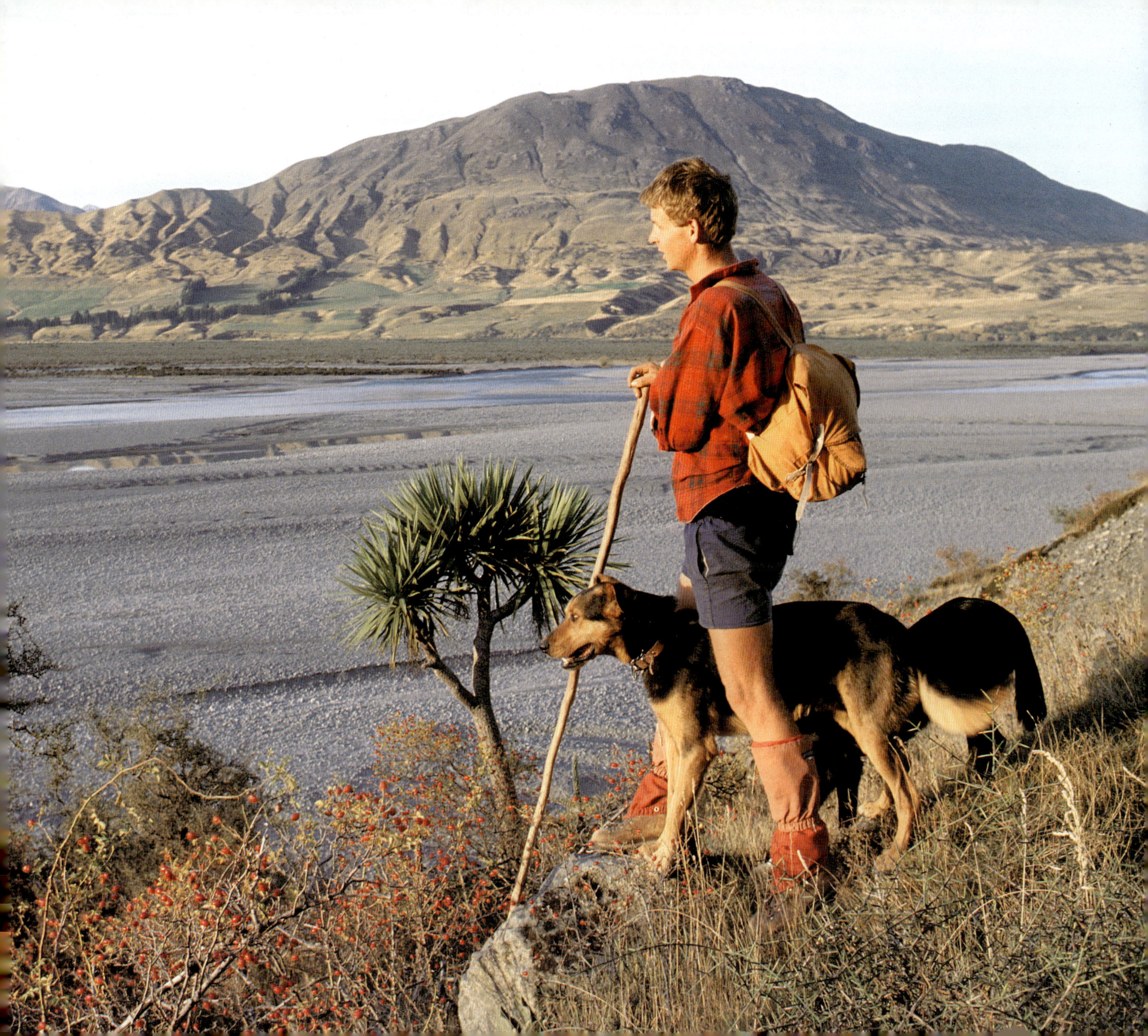

time, however, they began a slow dispersal upstream to become known as the Rakaia herd.

By the time the cloudy midafternoon gave way to a clear evening I'd gathered a good-sized load of driftwood to take home with me. There was nothing like driftwood for a good, concentrated heat.

With the sun at my back and the winding river to my left I was soon crossing Ben Hutchinson's Double Hill. They had two separate flocks — Merinos and Corriedales — on the station's 8000 hectares, something like 11,500 sheep all told.

On the metal road, with the golden sun lighting his face, was a fit-looking young shepherd who introduced himself as Ben Ensor. He'd just finished his beat in the fall muster — he waved with his hillstick at the steep mountainface plunging down to the road — and was heading home.

I asked him the names of his dogs and I wasn't too surprised to find they were Wag and Jess — I'd been running into dogs similarly named all over the country. As I drove away I glanced in the rear-vision mirror to see him striding along the road as though a brand-new day on the hill was about to begin.

I passed Glenariffe and Glenrock, both like Glenfalloch once part of Double Hill station. There was another young shepherd on the road, Andrew McKay. He explained that while he worked for Willy Ensor (no relation to Ben) on Redcliffs station, he'd been mustering on Willy's brother Charles's Glenrock.

Eleven years earlier, Redcliffs station had been a part of Glenrock and before that Double Hill. At that time Willy and Charles Ensor had decided to split up the property, which had been in the family ever since

Ben Ensor looks out over the riverbed of the Rakaia.

Andrew McKay has the scratches to prove he's had a day on the hill.

Double Hill was divided in 1912. Today Glenrock was 8000 hectares in size and Charles ran around 6500 Merino and Corriedale sheep. Glenrock was, in fact, one of the oldest established Corriedale studs in the country. For its part, Redcliffs took in 10,000 hectares including the stunning Redcliffe Saddle, and Willy ran 7000 Merinos.

Andrew McKay headed off without introducing me to his canine workmates. They might have been a bit put out at that; after all, Wag and Jess ended up with their names and photographs in this book, didn't they?

22

THE GIBSONS OF MALVERN DOWNS

On a glorious afternoon in early winter, Bill and Robert Gibson were showing me some of their Merino stud rams. The seventy-odd animals were, Bill told me with a quiet pride, the real pick of the 600 rams on Malvern Downs. About fifty of the rams cornered by the dogs in the One Hundred Acre paddock were hoggets born the previous October. They would not be put out with the ewes until the same time next year, when they would be nineteen months old.

Considering the stud rams had been out with the ewes for thirty-four days — two cycles on heat — they looked in remarkably fine fettle. Bill smiled and told me that one of the rams had had eighty ewes to look after: every time they looked the insatiable animal was hard at it.

Although it was only 850 hectares in size, Malvern Downs could, by dint of its 7500 stock units, be considered a station rather than a high-intensity farm. Bill Gibson himself described it as a farm, but to my way of thinking the Gibsons, father and son, were station people. They had the look of high-country runholders about them; they were men tempered like the finest Sheffield steel by adversity. These resilient types had lived through soul-destroying droughts, falling wool prices, devastating snowfalls.

While Bill and Robert examined more closely a two-year-old ram that displayed the strength of a young bullock, I let my eyes wander the landscape. There was much to see and much to savour. To the east were

Robert and Bill Gibson with their fine Merino stud rams.

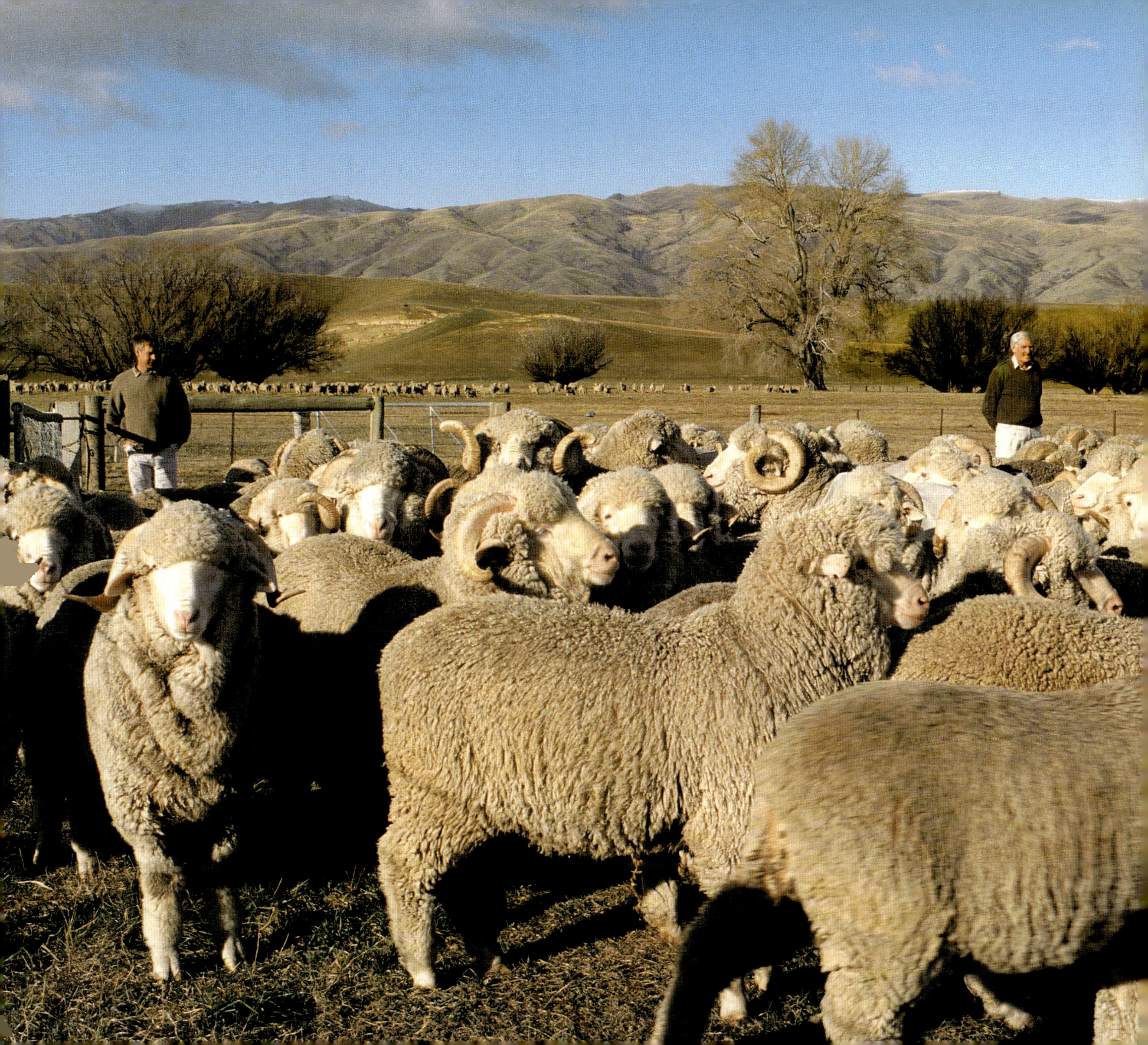

236 • STATION COUNTRY

the rolling Dunstan Mountains, to the northeast the formidable barrier of the St Bathans Range, to the west the turret-like peaks of the Pisa Range and to the southwest the tops of The Remarkables, knife edges clawing at the sky. Snow had recently fallen on all of these high places; a deep covering on The Remarkables and the St Bathans Range, a fair coating on the Pisa Range and just a light dusting on the nearby Dunstan Mountains.

Malvern Downs had been in the Gibson family since Bill's father Hector purchased it in 1924 from R. K. Smith, although originally it had been part of the giant Morven Hills station.

Hector Gibson had lived and breathed Merino sheep. His father James was a Scotsman who came to New Zealand in 1882. Hector was born about 1890 and as a young man he mustered on Morven Hills and Benmore with his good friend George Henderson. When Benmore was subdivided in about 1916 they put in for a block together, but were unsuccessful in the ballot.

By this time the 162,000-hectare Morven Hills had also been subdivided and when two of the runs went up for sale in 1916, Gibson and Henderson acquired the Old Homestead block and what was known as Black Forest Range.

In the early 1920s Gibson and Henderson decided to go their separate ways; legend has it that they tossed a coin to decide who took which block. Hector Gibson ended up with Morven Hills, and in 1924 he added the Malvern Downs block. He ran both of the stations with the help of Geoff Skinner.

In 1928 William Hector Gibson was born. Ten years later, right out the blue, Hector died of, it is said, a blood clot. He was forty-eight years old. Although ten-year-old Bill might have felt otherwise at the time, he was much too young to take over from his father, so Geoff Skinner took on responsibilities he'd never dreamed of. In 1953 a grown-up Bill Gibson took over the running of the station.

Bill Gibson's sixty-three years in the dry high country of Central Otago had been good to him. He was still trim, still tall. He had an easy way about him and a natural charm, qualities that had played a vital part in his successes away from Malvern Downs. He had been on the council of the New Zealand Sheepbreeders' Association for decades, had chaired the New Zealand Merino Breed Committee and was a highly respected shearing judge. This last role he greatly enjoyed, and it had seen him judging in Australia and South Africa as well as in New Zealand.

Perhaps the most important thing Bill Gibson would be remembered for was being in 1950 the first to introduce polled (hornless) Merino sheep into New Zealand. When he was a rangy 21-year-old he had headed to Australia, where he found work hard to come by. Eventually, however, he hit gold at a station called Boonoke. Bill Gibson found himself working in the station's ram-breeding depot, where since 1934 they had bred polled Merino rams.

Bill soon became keen on the idea of starting a polled Merino stud on Malvern Downs, and when he returned home he mated forty-five ewes from the station flock with a polled ram from Boonoke. In the years that followed, Bill Gibson's polled Merino stud gained a worldwide reputation for the quality of the wool. Today, about 70 per cent of New Zealand's polled Merinos carried the blood of Malvern Downs stock, and rams had been exported to sheep raisers in South America,

The superfine wool of a Malvern Downs Merino ram.

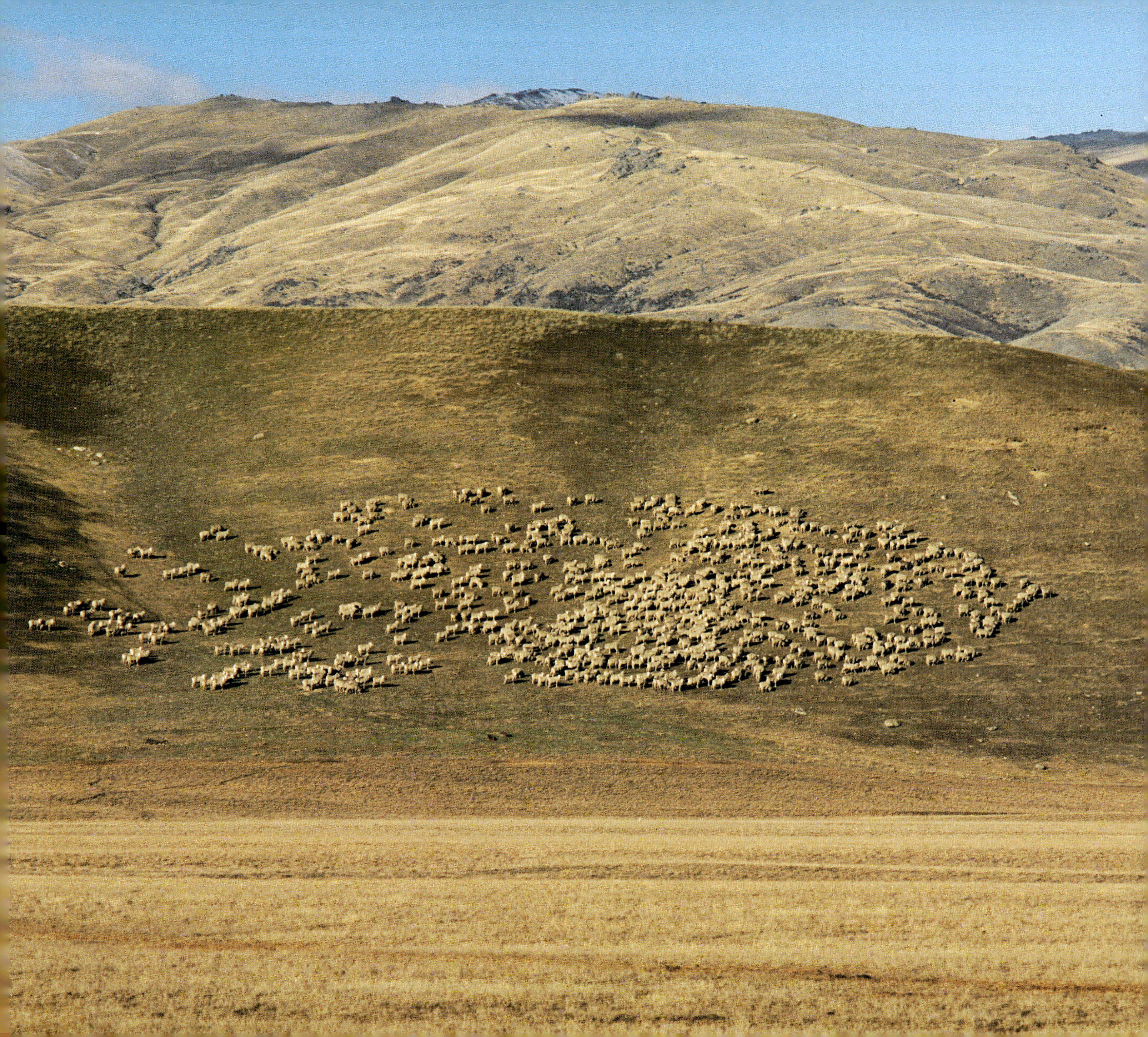

The Dunstan Mountains overlook the station.

China and Hungary. Gibson's rams had won many a Grand Championship at the Canterbury A & P Show, and fleece wool from the station had won prizes at international competitions. In 1994 William Hector Gibson was awarded an MBE for services to agriculture.

Bill Gibson and his wife Frances now lived in Wanaka, but most days Bill could still be found on the station, working shoulder to shoulder with his son. Like his father, Robert Gibson gained priceless experience by working on an Australian Merino stud. Apart from those two years away, however, he had spent all of his working life on Malvern Downs. Robert, the third generation of the Gibson family to raise stud Merinos, lived with his wife Jan and children Jessica, Charlotte and George in the old homestead, built more than a century earlier.

The current bloodlines of flockmaster Robert Gibson's stud included the strain of two other studs — Moutere

On today's Morven Hills, Richard Snow handles most of the stock work in a helicopter. Black Forest Range station can be seen on the far side of State Highway 8.

Merino country in southern New South Wales.

in Central Otago and Merryville, near Yass, in the Murrumbidgee district of New South Wales.

Moutere Merino Stud, one of the oldest in the country, was founded on Tasmanian bloodlines in 1904 by Andrew Jopp. The fourth generation of his family — Robert and Julie — today ran 11,000 sheep on 7500 hectares. They also had a stud strictly based on the famed Merryville pedigree.

Explorer Charles Sturt in his journal of 1824 recorded these prophetic words after visiting Yass: 'Sheep, I should imagine, would thrive uncommonly well on these plains.' The early British settlers were swift to follow Sturt's suggestion, grazing their flocks on the seemingly boundless flatlands. Today Yass, with a population of 4530 people, was the centre of a cattle, wheat, fruit and sheep raising area — but it was best known by far for its superb fine wool.

To discover the origins of the Merryville Stud, we must go back to 1865, when George Merryman founded Ravensworth Stud in the frontier town of Yass. Ravensworth sheep, derived from Spanish, Silesian and Saxon Merinos, would gain a reputation as heavy cutters, with fleece weights up to 7.5 kilograms.

Like his father, Walter Merryman was fascinated by the breeding of Merinos. In 1903 his father gave him 160 hectares of Ravensworth with which to start his own stud. He named it Merryville. In the years that followed there was no stopping young Walter's success; for his wool and sheep he would take out in excess of 2000 major prizes. For his services to the Australian wool industry he was knighted in 1954.

In 1994 there were at least thirty-six registered Merino studs that carried the Merryville lineage, including, of course, Malvern Downs.

Parts of the Malvern Downs homestead date to the last century.

23

ALL ON MORVEN HILLS

Leaving the Malvern Downs homestead, I pointed my four-wheel-drive in the direction of State Highway 8. As I waited at the junction for a stock truck to sweep past, my attention was caught by a large woolshed on the other side of the road.

On a whim, I switched off the engine and pondered the shed for a while. Most old woolsheds around the country had a story to tell, and this one — now over a century old — was no exception.

Sited hard against the fence, this woolshed was the focal point of a 162-hectare block of land owned by the Purvis family of Cluden station. Cluden consisted of some 12,500 hectares of such rabbit-denuded terrain that you had to wonder how they could run 17,000 sheep there. The fact that they were Merinos gave the answer.

The woolshed was now called the Cluden shed, despite the fact that it was over 4 kilometres from the southern boundary of the station. The Cluden sheep were brought there to be shorn, a tradition that dated back to 1924 when Major John Jenkins of Cluden bought the Homestead block following the subdivision of Morven Hills.

The Homestead block had first been developed by John Stronach when he was manager of Morven Hills station in the late nineteenth century. With improved access to Dunedin via a road through the Cromwell Gorge, the more central Tarras seemed a better place to have the station's centre of operations than the original site well to the north.

On a low hill Stronach built a fine dwelling with

The Tarras woolshed, now called the Cluden shed.

stunning views in all directions. Here, too, he built the then fourteen-stand Tarras woolshed (now reduced to six stands and called the Cluden shed). When the main Morven Hills activities were moved here the old station headquarters was demoted to an out-station.

Northburn was another out-station at the time.

Today's Northburn station homestead was initially a boundary keeper's stone cottage at the far, southern end of Morven Hills. Over the years, though, it had been added to considerably, and a grand stone woolshed built. The Morven Hills flock was at one stage so large that the sheep were shorn at three different sheds: the

The Northburn homestead.

massive shed on today's Morven Hills, on today's Ardgour station, and at Northburn.

John McArthur worked on Morven Hills in the 1880s and had a few things to say about shearing time: 'The menu in those days consisted of mutton, bread, sugar, tea, salt and potatoes. The cook was generally a baker and made the bread. He used to take a "cut" off the dough in the trough and add some mutton fat and brown sugar. This when baked in the oven was called "brownie" and wasn't bad when properly made. We got no butter and no spices and of course no jam. The huts and sheds were usually built alongside a running creek or river. This was our wash-basin and where we washed our clothes.

'I will now describe our sleeping accommodation. It was twenty-one feet by twelve [6.4 metres by 3.7 metres] There were eighteen men sleeping in that hut. There were three tiers of bunks right round, built in six by two for a man, usually no mattresses — at least the station didn't provide any. If there happened to be a straw stack handy some of us would use straw, but as a rule all we had on the bare boards was an empty wool bale.'

Just before the subdivision of Morven Hills in 1924, the last and perhaps the greatest muster took place. Over the course of several weeks sheep were brought from all parts of the huge run to the Homestead block. Special drafting yards were constructed next to the woolshed in preparation for the auction. The final tally was 49,849 Merino ewes, 299 Merino rams and 18,254 halfbreds.

For the auction itself Dalgety's provided transportation by coach from Cromwell. Refreshments were served by waiters in a large marquee. The sale, of sheep and bits of station paraphernalia, lasted three hours and marked the end of an era on Morven Hills.

The small stone cottage had stood there on the lower slopes of the Dunstan Mountains of Central Otago for well over a century. While its roof (almost certainly corrugated iron) had been removed many years earlier, the walls, built thick to combat the elements, appeared solid enough to see out another century. The window frames were true, too — the extremely dry atmosphere had preserved the wood well.

The building faced due north the better to catch the sun, and was placed on a gradual rise partly sheltered from the southerly wind. The view — of the Pisa Range, the St Bathans Range and Mount Aspiring in the far distance — was compelling. When the cottage was built, most likely in the early 1870s, all the land in sight was

The small stone cottage at Welshtown.

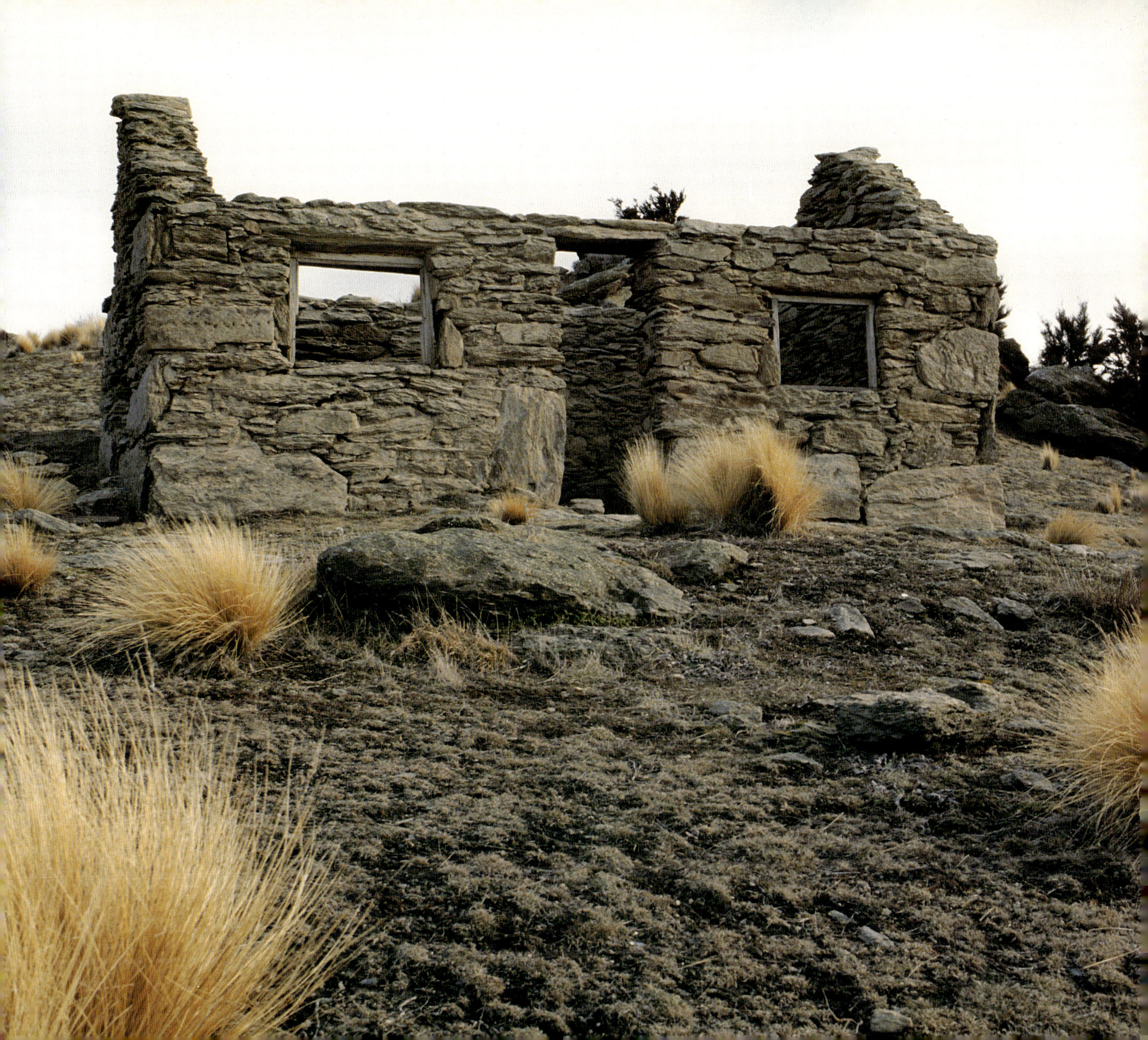

Welshtown.

part of the Morven Hills kingdom of grass; later it became part of Bendigo station.

Bendigo itself came to life in about 1862. It was named by Australian diggers after the famous gold town in Victoria. At its peak there were about 200 people living there, the men looking for gold in the alluvial lands flanking Bendigo Creek. By 1867, however, the settlement's days were numbered and only a few diehards remained. All that was left today were a few brick chimneys, the ruins of a bakehouse and a some fruit trees in dire need of pruning.

The small cottage that had attracted my attention was located in Welshtown, a gold town that grew up after a gold-bearing quartz reef was discovered in 1868 in the slopes above Bendigo. Scattered around were the remnants of other such buildings, rocks amongst rocks. A bigger construction might have been a store or a hall, but it all came down to guesswork.

With the wind in my face I cut across to a rocky outcrop. It was a July wind, cold despite the sun firing the landscape. Welshtown would have been a harsh place to live when winter's raw breath was icy and frost lurked in sheltered hollows all day. Summer wouldn't have held too many pleasures either, with the temperature reaching the searing high thirties.

Autumn and spring were a different story, the sparkling days neither too hot nor too cold, the view extended by the clarity of the air. At the onset of summer the track to Logantown would be a riot of gold and blue as the wild flowers dressed in their best.

Moving away from the outcrop, I found a more sheltered vantage point. Through field glasses I soon observed wild goats. Many of the gold miners ran semi-feral goats, leaving them behind when they packed up to follow some new dream. The four multi-coloured animals vanished into the sweet briar like a puff of smoke on a windy day.

Moments late a strung-out line of Merinos came into view, while on a nearby hillface there were a number of rabbits. They were hard to spot when they were not moving, their brownish-grey colouring blending with the muted tones of the landscape. Identification was not a problem when they scampered across the face — the undersides of their fluffy tails were like white banners.

Relatives of those bunnies were on display again as I put Welshtown and Logantown behind me. They headed for cover as I approached, into ground-hugging kanuka or sweet briar. This might now be Department of Conservation land, but these rabbits knew that vehicles also meant men with spotlights and rifles.

Suddenly a harrier hawk appeared, skimming a low ridge, some sort of small bird struggling in its hooked talons. Life and death in Central Otago.

Logantown.

ALL ON MORVEN HILLS • 247

24

RETURN TO EARNSCLEUGH

On a steamy midsummer afternoon in 1988 the rain that had been threatening for several days finally came in heavy sheets. The warm earth of Swamp paddock steamed under the watery onslaught and soaked up the moisture like a sponge. It seemed that Earnscleugh station, out of Alexandra, was getting its summer quota of precipitation in one go.

The Swamp paddock was typical of much of the station's near 25,000 hectares — it was crawling with rabbits. In fact the rabbits had taken over completely and forced Alistair Campbell to run his Merinos elsewhere. If you sat still long enough in Swamp paddock you'd get a darn good idea of how bad the problem was. There were more rabbits than you could shake a stick at in the paddock itself, and more than you could ever hope to count on the briar bush flats or up on the tawny hillfaces.

Even now, with the rain pouring down, there were rabbits in clear sight, sitting at the entrances to their burrows as though welcoming the rain. All were adults — the young rabbits, prone to killer colds and flu, would be snug and warm underground.

Naturally enough, there was a time when there were no rabbits on Earnscleugh — they were still in New South Wales. But it was a few years ago.

There was some uncertainty about the early days of Earnscleugh station. It was known that the area was

The tussock-clad lower slopes of the Old Man Range.

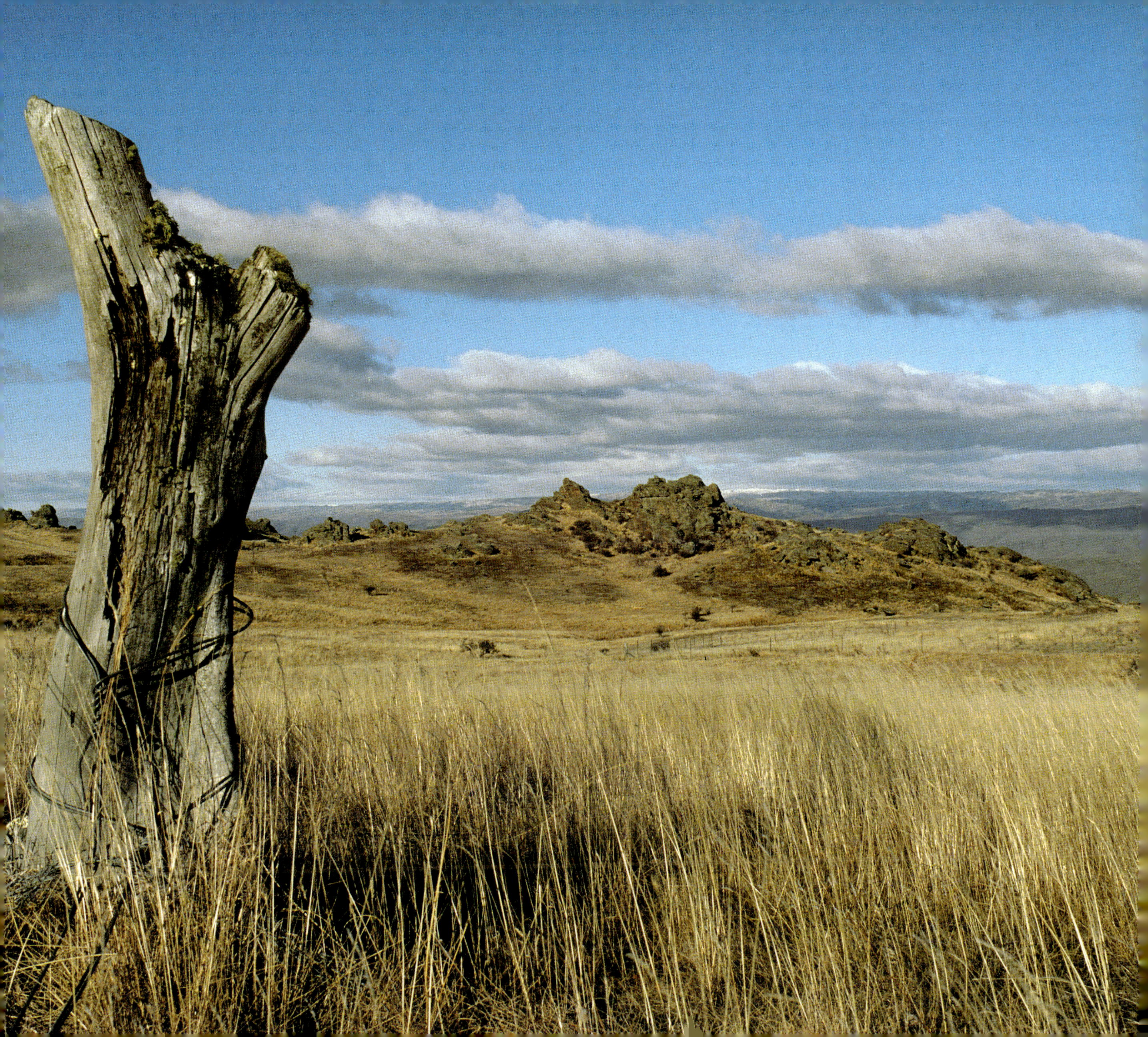

named by Otago surveyor John Turnbull Thomson after Earnscleugh Water in the southeast of Scotland; what was not clear was who first owned the station. It was possible that the Shennan brothers, early pioneers in the Dunstan and Manuherikia area, were the first on the 24,000-hectare block in the Old Man Range.

If that was the case, they did not run stock, but may have built the sod whare that William Fraser found when he arrived on the place in 1862. He would later describe it as 'a sod whare, fourteen feet long by ten feet wide with walls about five feet high, which had to serve as kitchen, dining room, store room and bedroom for the men, whilst I had to be content with a tent'.

The fit young Scotsman, of good breeding and no little ambition, had been installed on the property as manager for Alfred Cheetham Strode. Within a short time Fraser would marry Strode's daughter and become a partner in the station.

While much of the station was mountainous — rolling rather than excessively steep — there were extensive flatlands by the river at the foot of the hills. Alongside the river, named after Fraser, silver tussock flourished, in places deep enough to brush the belly of a big horse. All told, it was a fine place to run Merino sheep.

With a will — and the boundless energy that later marked his political career — Fraser set about creating the essentials of station life. First he built a stockyard, then a woolshed. The homestead was built last, of layer upon layer of local stone cemented together with mud mixed with manure and straw.

The first winter on Earnscleugh was long and hard, and it saw diggers arriving in their thousands on the recently discovered goldfields. Some were experienced men, used to roughing it, but many were not. Fraser saw an opportunity here, and supplied ill-prepared diggers with basic stores. Two of the diggers Fraser supplied, who also grazed their horses in the Homestead paddock, had come there via the Californian goldfields. Hartley and Reilly were the first to prospect in the Cromwell Gorge, and from its untouched beaches they took 39.5 kilograms of gold.

Fraser also started a ferry service, by whaleboat, across the Clutha. The northern landing, on the opposite side to the station, became the first settlement on the Dunstan field. Its name — Muttontown — clearly indicated the commodity on which it was founded.

In 1866 the Otago Acclimatisation Society took what was certainly its most ill-judged step when it introduced rabbits to the province. The liberation, of sixty rabbits, was the first successful one in the country. By the end of the year an overjoyed William Fraser reported seeing one. Fraser was delighted to have them on his land, and even liberated some there himself. When a poacher was caught shooting a couple, a furious Fraser had the blackguard prosecuted.

In this particular period, before rabbits overran the station, life was indeed good on Earnscleugh. Big wool cheques meant there was money to burn. Strode built a whole block of town houses and professional offices in Stuart Street, Dunedin, while Fraser was able to support his blossoming political career.

In 1893 William Fraser, now sole owner of Earnscleugh, was elected to Parliament and sold the rabbit-infested run to W. S. Laidlaw. Fraser later became Minister of Mines and was eventually knighted.

The winter of 1895 was amongst the worst on record in the southern part of the South Island. Before the snow melted on Earnscleugh station, half the flock had perished. With wool prices hitting rock bottom the following season and the rabbit problem seeming insurmountable, a bitter Laidlaw gave up Earnscleugh and the Homestead block reverted to the Government.

The lease was not taken up again until in 1902 an ambitious lamb-fat buyer took on the challenge of a run that boasted 240 rabbits to the hectare. Steven Spain hired thirty-two men for five months; between them they killed 250,000 rabbits. Meantime, Spain also established a Merino flock that did extremely well.

Then, surprisingly, rabbits began to pay. Both skins and meat were in demand for the export market and a rabbit-canning factory opened in Cromwell. Spain was said to have made a fortune from his rabbits.

The grandiose homestead Spain built on Earnscleugh still stood today, solid as ever. Inspired by a mansion he saw in Montevideo, Uruguay, it was a two-storey, double-bricked, castellated structure of seventeen rooms; locals soon referred to it as Spain's Folly. The

Spain's Folly?

imposing red-brick structure, its stark profile softened by exotic trees that themselves became austere in winter, was home to the Spain family until they sold out to M. F. Mulvena in 1948.

The rabbit problem showed no signs of abating. The Rabbit Destruction Council shifted into top gear, its policy to wipe the rabbit off the face of New Zealand. It was, of course, much easier said than done; for all of the thirty-three years the Mulvena family was on Earnscleugh the rabbit was a fact of life.

In 1981 the station was sold at auction to 34-year-old Alistair Campbell, a Mackenzie Country man. Thirteen years later the Campbells were still there.

The valley of the Clutha River was blanketed with river mist, the temperature was near freezing, and coming through the Cromwell Gorge I had to watch out for black ice. I couldn't see it yet, but there was a fresh snowfall on the Old Man Range. As I crossed the bridge over the Clutha my mind slipped back to a summer's evening six years earlier, when I'd watched the rain-soaked rabbits in Swamp paddock; I wondered whether Alistair Campbell was winning the battle.

Campbell was lean and wiry, a bearded type with far-ranging eyes, very much the hill-country Scotsman tending his precious flock. While we strolled around the Homestead block, watched warily by a couple of Herefords enjoying winter-feed, Alistair explained that the rabbit problem had reached a critical stage: they had stopped taking poisoned baits.

Since 1990, however, the rabbit population had been gradually whittled down, to the lowest levels Alistair could recall, as a direct result of the Rabbit and Land Management Programme (RLMP). This was a five-year project undertaken jointly by the national government,

Alistair Campbell.

the regional council and the farmers. Fifty-seven stations in Central Otago were taking part in the scheme, which was due to end in June 1995.

Over the previous four years a lot of rabbit-netting fencing had gone up, in a vivid reminder of rabbit control methods used immediately after the Second World War. The rabbits, isolated in blocks, were then poisoned, trapped, gassed, dogged or shot. In addition to these old-style methods, they used helicopters.

Helicopters! Who would have thought rabbit control would come down to that? But as Bill Johnsen, Otago Regional Council's pest management officer for the Central region, pointed out, a top pilot and two shooters working on an hour on, hour off basis could in one hour cover an area it would take four men with dogs a day to work over. The cost, at about $5 per rabbit killed, worked out higher than other shooting methods, but helicopter shooting was more effective.

In 1991 four pilots were used in the RLMP: Harvey Hutton, Doug Maxwell, Wayne Ashworth and Donald Flower. By 19 October of that year they and their shooters had accounted for 57,000 rabbits in 790 hours' flying. Harvey Hutton's best hourly kill was 230 rabbits; on his best day he accounted for 1100.

On Earnscleugh Alistair Campbell employed three full-time and four part-time rabbiters. The RLMP and local authority covered 70 per cent of the cost, but Alistair believed the five-year operation would have a personal cost of around $800,000. From June 1995 the financial assistance would be withdrawn; I didn't have the heart to ask him how he would cope then.

There were no real answers to the rabbit problem in New Zealand. With one year left to run the RLMP had been worthwhile, reducing rabbits in most places to a manageable level. What would happen after 1995 was really anyone's guess. Certainly the secondary control methods would have to be continued and the rabbit fencing would need to always be kept in perfect order if the conditions of the late 1980s were not to be revisited.

Rabbit-proof fencing on Northburn station.

25

THE PROMISED LAND

There was a faraway look in the old runholder's eyes, a strong sense about him of things forever lost. At his home in Wanaka he was recalling a very different place and time — Mount Creighton station in the spring of 1924.

His family name, Burdon, revealed his sound English stock of blacksmiths, shipwrights and farmers. Born in the home country in 1901, he was christened George. A little over a year later his father, an adventurous type, packed up his family and took them off to distant New Zealand; in South Canterbury they purchased a small sheep farm. Young George, who worked on the farm from a very early age, would never want anything but a life on the land.

Like so many other boys from well-to-do families he attended Christ's College. When he left at eighteen, he was keen to strike out on his own and, encouraged by his father, secured a shepherd's position on The Grampians station in the Mackenzie Country.

It was a fine place for a strong young man to work — burning hot in summer, bitterly cold in winter, a raw land where the air was as clear as a high-country stream. After two happy years, however, he was ready for a station of his own. He was offered a leasehold run, Mount Creighton, on the eastern shores of Lake Wakatipu. It was, he was told, an 18,000-hectare property that climbed to over 1800 metres and carried 7000 Merino sheep. At this point the land agent, Len

The TSS Earnslaw, *the lovely old lady of the lake.*

THE PROMISED LAND • 255

Barret, cleared his throat and admitted there was one drawback — there was no road access.

From around the turn of the century there had been a well-voiced dissatisfaction amongst the runholders on Lake Wakatipu who depended entirely on water transport. By 1912 something had been done about it: the TSS *Earnslaw* had been commissioned, built in Dunedin, dismantled, transported by train to Kingston, reassembled and launched.

George Burdon was intrigued enough to want to see Mount Creighton for himself. It was a lovely day in early spring when they set out on the *Earnslaw* from Kingston. Lake Wakatipu, third-largest sheet of water in the country, sparkled in the sun. Len Barret pointed out Cecil Peak, Walter Peak and Mount Nicholas, all grand old stations steeped in history.

So too, though, was Mount Creighton. Like the other stations it was closely linked with Queenstown's first resident, William Gilbert Rees. The locals referred to him as King Wakatip, and for a time he was indeed royalty.

Born in Wales in 1827, W. G. Rees was a tall man, powerfully built, and a natural leader. In 1852 he emigrated to Australia to try his luck on the goldfields, but lacking success became the manager of a sheep and cattle station. Rees liked Australia well enough but, after a series of natural disasters that almost brought the sheep industry to a standstill, he decided to move on to New Zealand. In partnership with George Gammie and Colonel Lewis Grant, he crossed the Tasman in search of what he would later describe as 'the promised land'.

Rees and his new wife ended up in Dunedin in 1859, where the handsome Welshman was soon making

Lake Wakatipu, with Mount Nicholas on the left.

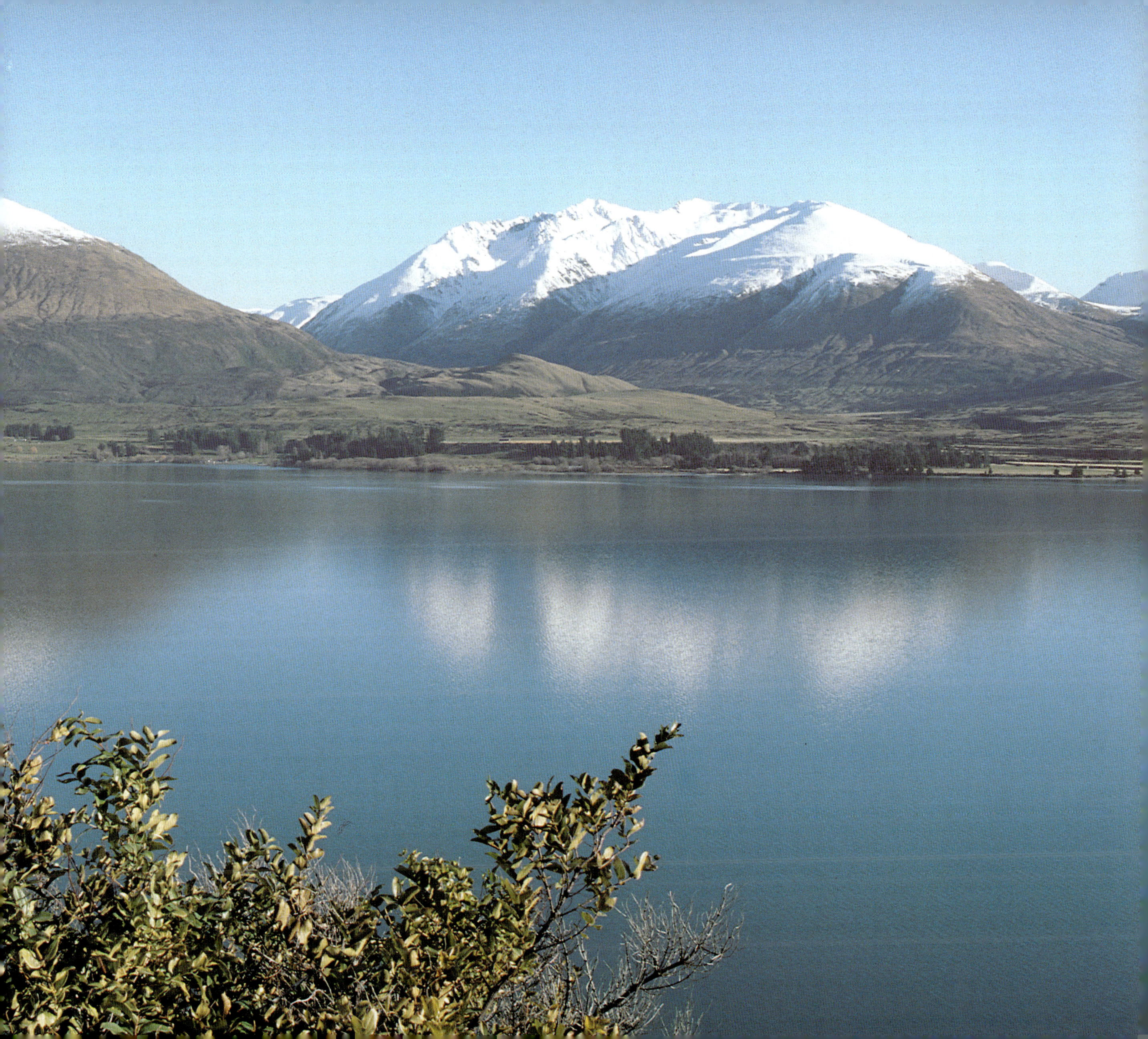

arrangements to bring 3000 Merino sheep over from Queensland. By the winter of that year he was organising a trip into the largely unknown country beyond the Clutha River.

The trip was delayed until January 1860, when a large, good-natured crowd gathered to see six men, each leading a packhorse, depart. The party made its way to Morven Hills station, from where a shepherd guided them to the lower Cardrona Valley. Only Rees and N. P. B. von Tunzelmann went on from there.

So it was that on a very hot February day the two men, carrying a month's supplies, topped a ridge on the Crown Range and before them a marvellous view unfolded. Rees would later describe it as 'an open country, not perfectly level, but broken by small hills and terraces; whilst a large lake, or arm of a lake stretched away in the distance almost as far as the eye could see'. The lake was Wakatipu; the arm was the Frankton Arm. Today motorists travelling State Highway 89 could pause on the Crown Terrace to see the vista that so captivated Rees.

For two days the men explored the Queenstown area,

The promised land: the Homestead block, with the Peninsula block beyond.

the forerunners of the untold numbers of sightseers who visited the area today. By now Rees was quite certain he'd found his 'promised land', while von Tunzelmann was more than pleased with what could be seen of the country on the other side of the lake.

Back in Dunedin, Rees and his partners were granted by the Waste Land Board four separate runs — Staircase, Peninsula, Homestead and Bucklerburn — adding up to 115,000 hectares. Von Tunzelmann, although he had lodged a claim for the land on the western shores of Wakatipu before he left Dunedin, was too late — the land south of the Von River had already been granted to John and Taylor White, who would set up the first run on Wakatipu, Mount Nicholas. Instead, von Tunzelmann took up the land north of the Von through to Elfin Bay.

Rees built his homestead and brought in his sheep, but before long his splendid isolation on what is now the Queenstown waterfront was disturbed. In late 1862 gold was found in the Arrow, Shotover and Kawarau Rivers, and soon much of Rees's best country was overrun with diggers. A small town mushroomed around the homestead, but Rees saw no reason to be bitter about it. When the station supplies arrived, it was said, Rees divided the food equally between himself and the starving diggers.

Legend had it that Rees once caught a digger red-handed in the act of skinning a sheep.

'What do you mean,' Rees roared, 'stealing my sheep — in broad daylight, too!'

The digger stood up, his manner defiant. 'Listen, Mr Rees, I'll kill any bloody sheep that tries to bite me.'

Fortunately for the digger, Rees could see the funny side and, noting how wretchedly thin the man was, asked the man when he had last eaten. When the digger admitted it wasn't recently, Rees simply nodded, gathered up the reins and rode on.

The gold rush was to be Rees's downfall. Soon the lease to the jewel in Rees's pastoral crown, the Homestead block, was cancelled and the land declared a goldfield. He had already converted his lakeside woolshed into a hotel, and at any one time there could be as many as 2000 boisterous diggers in Queenstown. Rees built a new homestead across the Kawarau on the Peninsula block, but by 1866 the seven-year partnership between Rees, Gammie and Grant was dissolved and their many holdings split up.

A year later King Wakatip and his family left the area. Not yet forty, Rees found employment as manager on a series of stations. In his mid-fifties he became a government stock inspector; he died in Marlborough aged seventy-one.

The Acacia homestead dates to 1906.

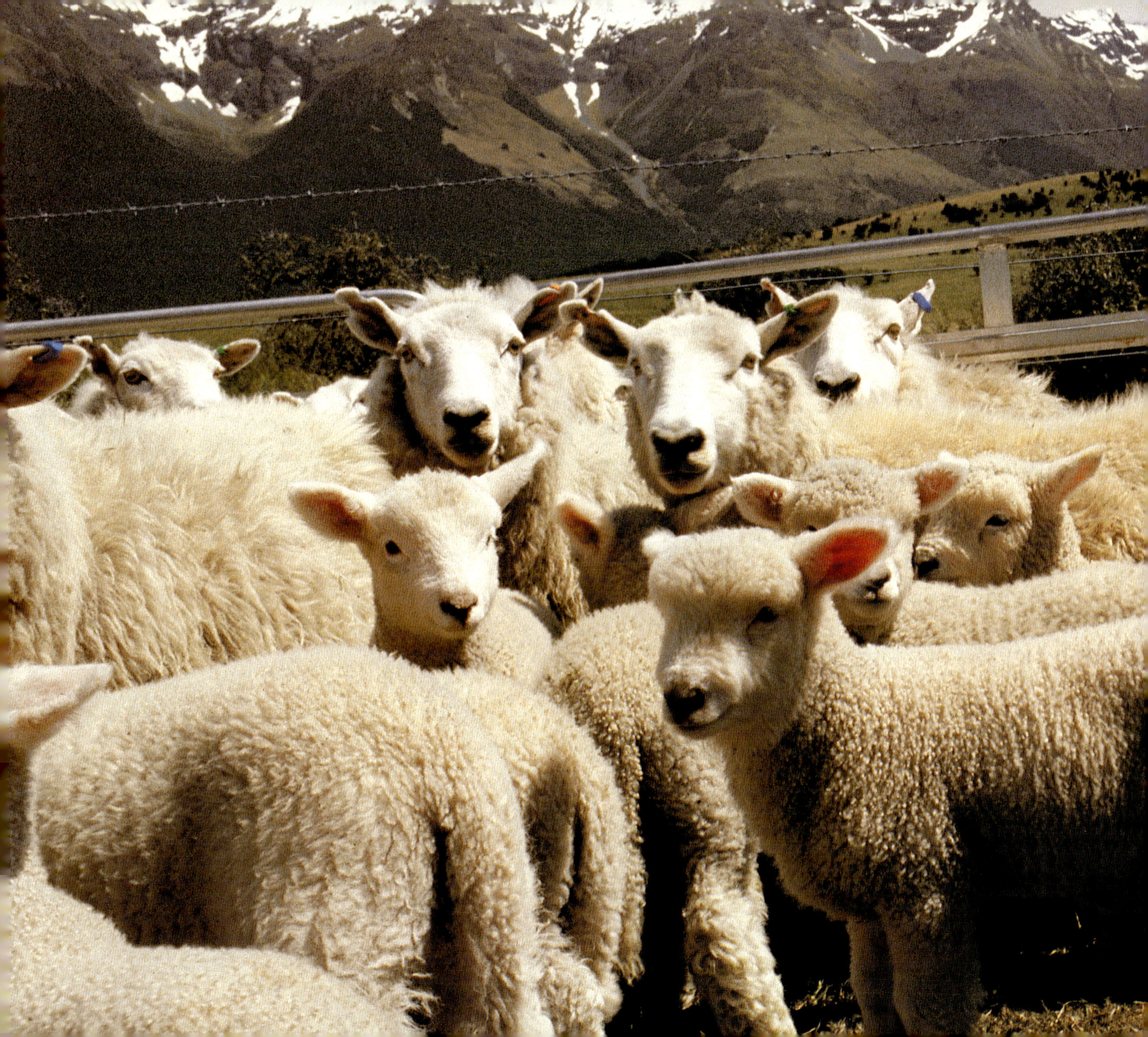

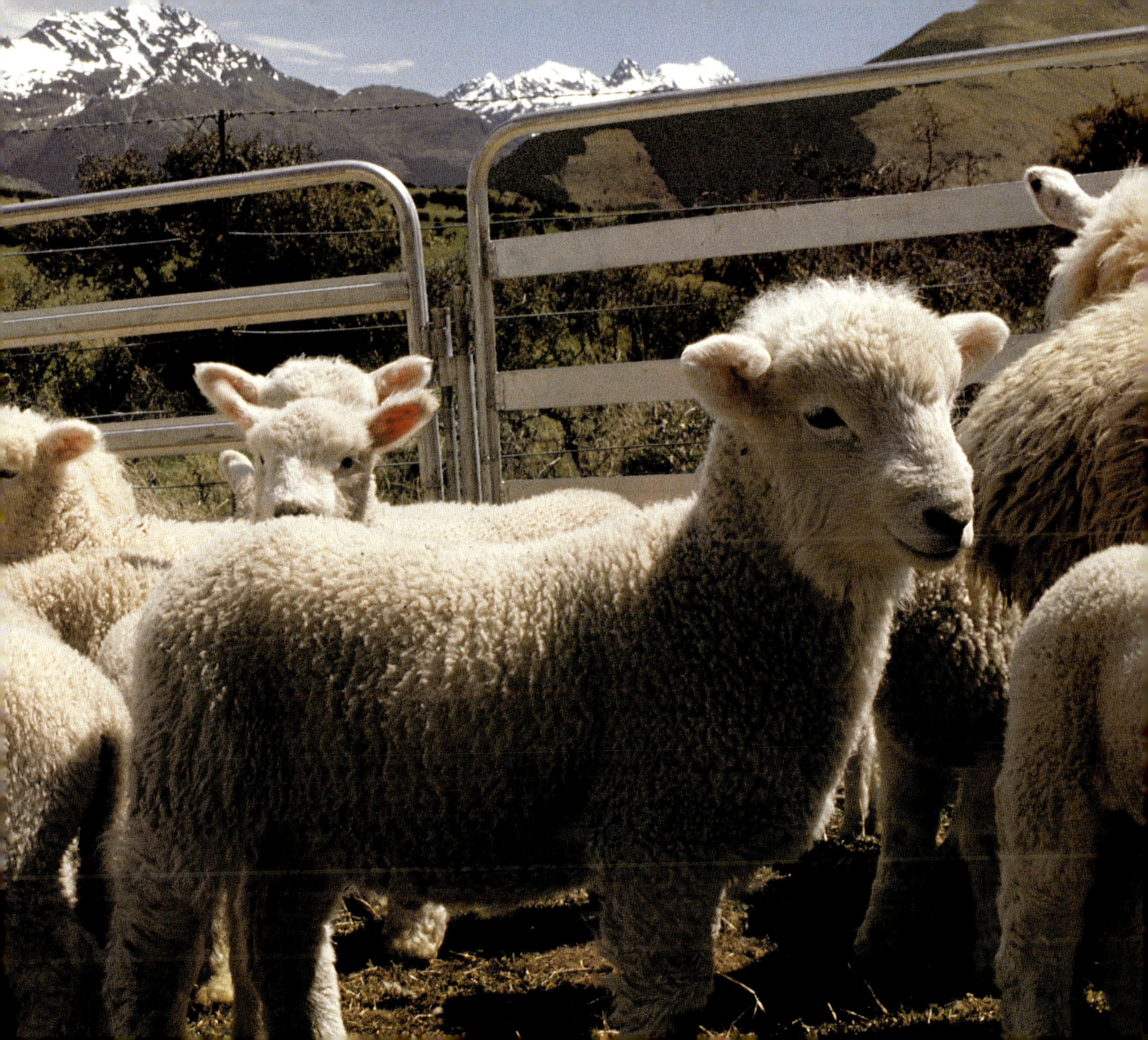

262 • STATION COUNTRY

Previous page: Perendale ewes and lambs on Wyuna station.

In 1887 North station, the northernmost of Rees's four original runs was split into six: Wyuna, Temple Creek, Rees Valley, Acacia and, of course, Mount Creighton.

At his home in Wanaka, George Burdon hesitated for a moment, collected his thoughts, and picked up the thread of his story at his arrival on Mount Creighton station seventy years earlier.

'At the homestead we were met by the owners. The house was a very old building and the dining room was paved with enormous stone slabs and this acted somewhat as a central heating system during the winter. There was an enormous fireplace about six foot wide at the far end and in winter a fire was kept burning night and day.'

The property covered George's requirements — adequate provision for tupping the ewes, sunny country to rear hoggets, somewhere to keep rams in autumn — and in 1922 he, in partnership with Jack Manson, took over the run. Later Manson would sell his share to his partner.

George Burdon would remain on Mount Creighton until 1929, when he moved on to Mount Burke, an 18,000-hectare run between Lakes Wanaka and Hawea. Sixty-five years later the station — now split into two properties, Mount Burke and Glen Dene — remained in the Burdon family.

Top left: Wyuna station.
Bottom left: Peter Lucas runs Perendales on Wyuna.
Right: The Remarkables from the crest of the Peninsula block.
Following page: Rees Valley station.

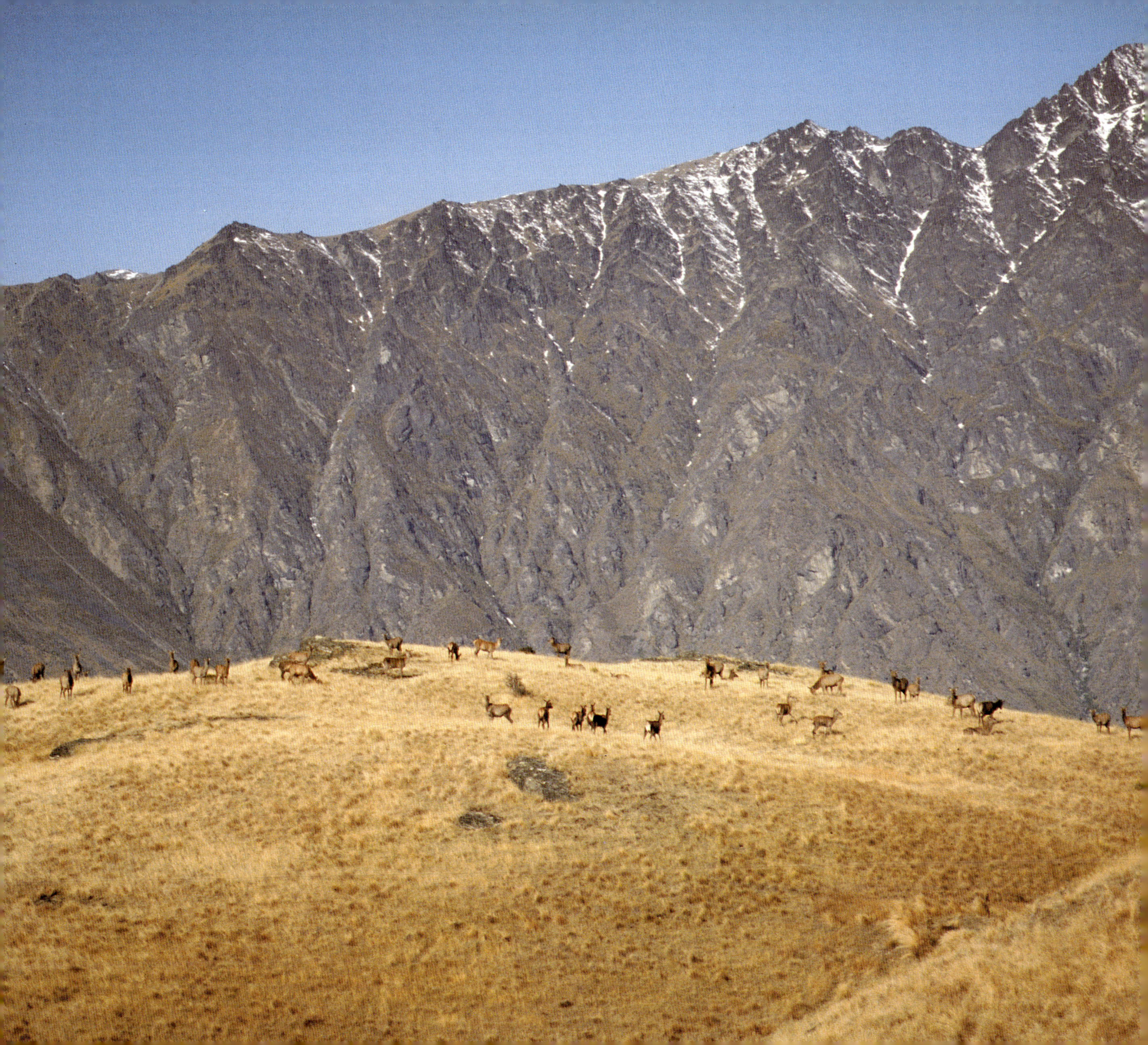

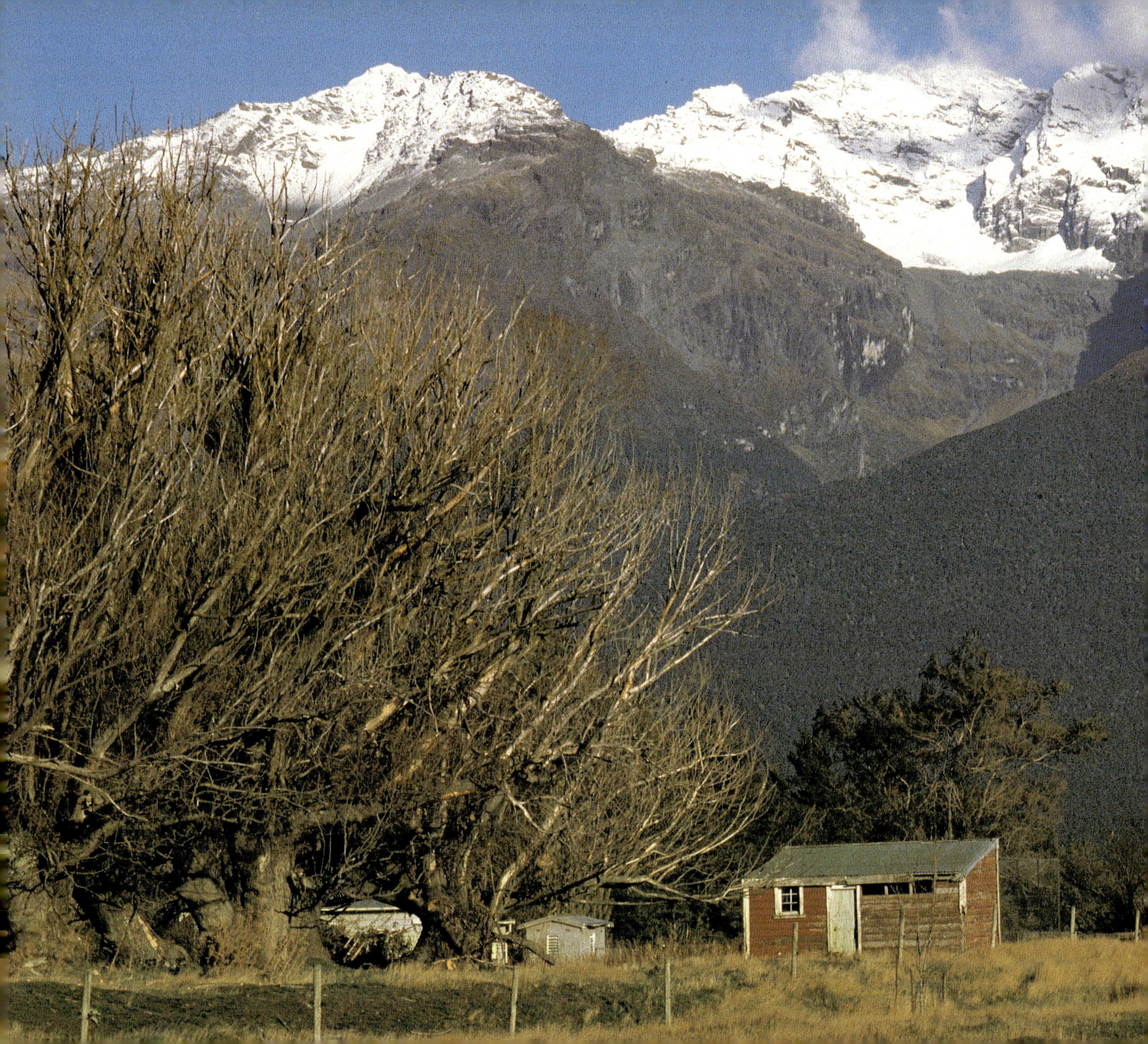

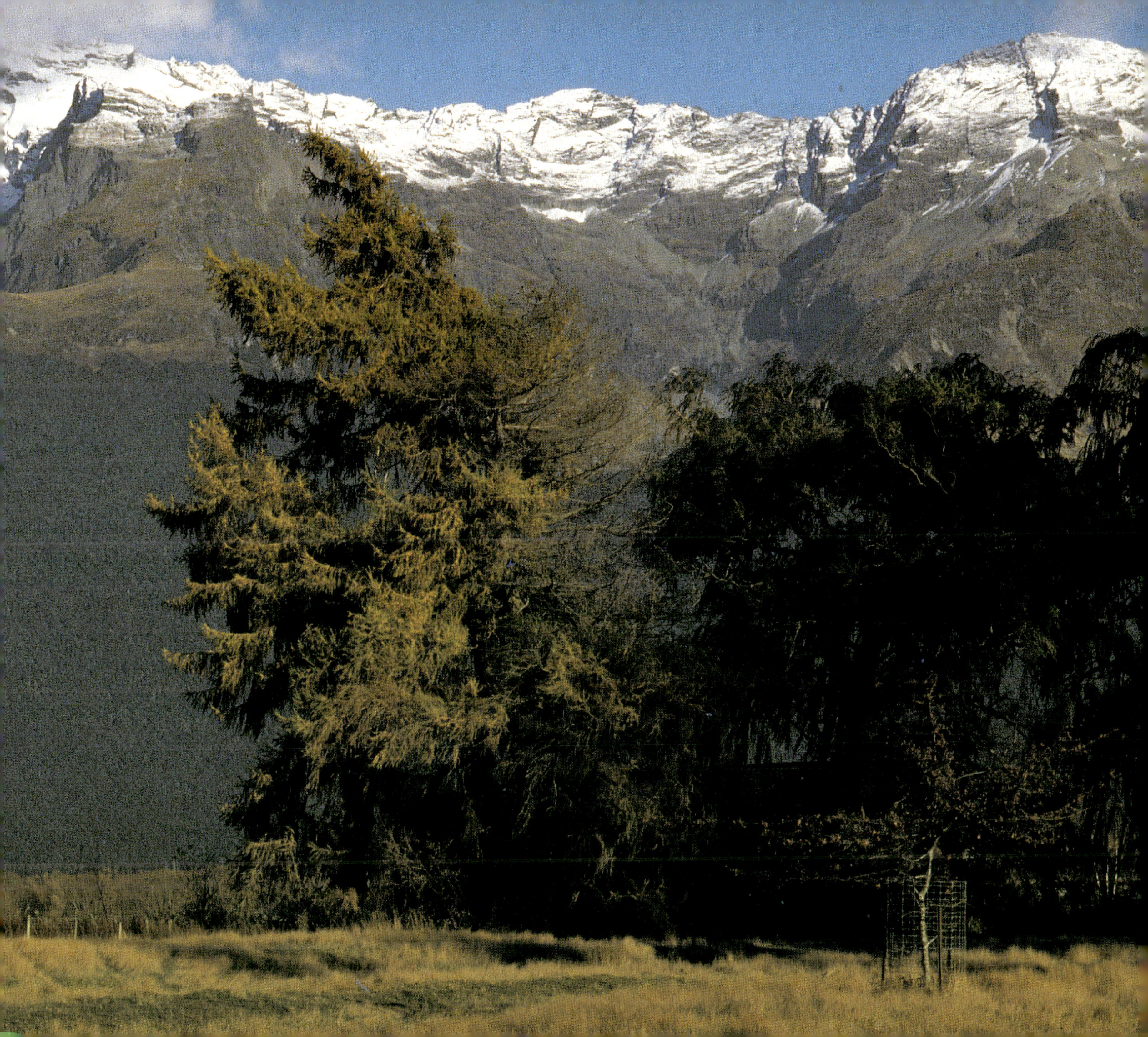

26

ON FIORDLAND'S DOORSTEP

Colin and Fay King ran Romney sheep and Hereford cattle on their 2000-hectare high-rainfall station in the Lill Burn valley of western Southland. The excessive rainfall was to be expected — their western boundary, a well-defined bushline in most places, was also part of the eastern boundary of Fiordland National Park.

Officially, winter was about done the day I arrived at the homestead in time for lunch. Mother Nature never being one to take notice of bureaucracy, however, there was fresh snow on the mountains of Fiordland and overnight near-torrential rainfall had turned many of the already waterlogged paddocks into swamps. The King family had long since learned to accept philosophically the caprices of Southland's weather.

By evening the sun had appeared, and the weather was spring-like as I clambered into the cabin of the 1958 Land-Rover. On a steepish hillside behind the homestead a budding kowhai had attracted a score of kereru. Fay, turning the ignition of a no-frills machine that might see out another thirty-five years, told me that the bird life there was wonderful — only the other day she had heard a bellbird.

We started down the tree-lined driveway towards the road. Out on the grassy flat facing the arched entrance to Waiau Hereford Stud, Romneys grazed amongst puddles, paradise ducks and oystercatchers. Much further back there was a sweep of forested land and beyond the unseen Lake Hauroko rose the snow-capped Princess Mountains. This was a particularly lovely, if little known, part of the country.

Waiau Hereford Stud.

Floundering in the glutinous mud, I jerked open a heavy wooden gate and watched the Land-Rover, slewing slightly, enter a paddock containing only cows that huddled together on the high ground.

As I got back into the Land-Rover Kay said, with a flick of the head, 'We feed the bulls before them.'

The tucker was in the back, contained in small drums — Fay laughingly referred to the Land-Rover as Meals-on-Wheels. Feeding out was a twice-daily, seven-days-a-week chore that went on regardless of the weather. We entered the next paddock, which contained the bulls.

They numbered four: BB Power and three young bulls, two of which were his offspring. BB Power had been imported as a calf from the famed BB Ranch in Washington. Now aged four, he was one of three Hereford bulls the Kings had brought in at the time. The

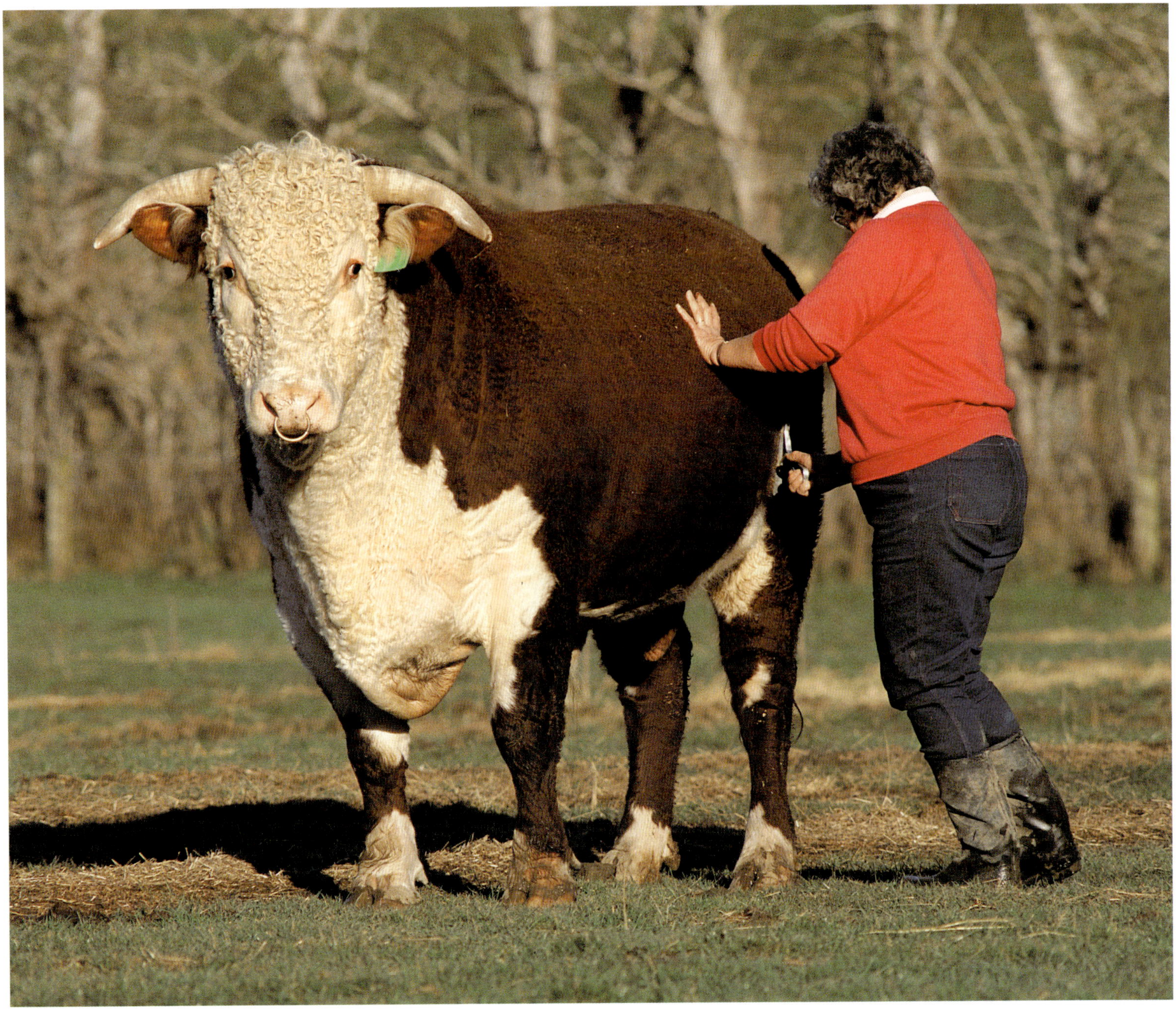

progeny of these bulls had longer bodies than those sired by local bulls, they weighed a great deal more, and they were more muscular.

While Fay groomed a placid BB Power, I asked her if she ever felt at risk working with him. After all, he was a whole lot of bull by any reckoning.

Fay smiled and shook her head as she stroked him. 'No, I don't think so. He's very affectionate, really.' She paused and ran her hand down his rump. 'But you couldn't put him with another bull of the same size — there'd be fireworks then!' She gestured at the calves. 'He's obviously the dominant one here, and that's all that matters to him.'

Back in 1862 the Lill Burn Valley was in the hands of Robert Walker Aicken, a Tasmanian farmer who had in the previous year established the vast, ill-defined Clifden station just down the road. He considered the Lill Burn Valley mostly unsuitable for sheep because of its swampy ground. He put in cattle instead, but to his dismay many were lured by wild cattle into the bush that, to the south, ran unbroken to the coast.

It was in the 1870s that Aicken and a man named Harrison hit upon the idea of using the low-lying Hump Range, to the east of Lake Hauroko, as summer range for their respective flocks of sheep. They engaged the services of Archie Cameron to organise a suitable track; in the end he became a partner in the so-called Hump Venture.

The next project for the partners was to cut a stock route to the Princess Mountains, whose untouched tussocklands promised magnificent summer range for sheep. The project involved bridging the Wairaurahiri

Fay King grooms BB Power.

River where it left Lake Hauroko, although there was no evidence of that bridge today.

By the autumn of 1877 there were sheep high on the brawny shoulders of the Princess Mountains. But winter came early that year, too early. On the Hump Range and on the Princess Mountains thousands of sheep perished in raging blizzards. When the snow melted in spring the rivers rose to unprecedented heights and even more were lost.

That was the beginning of the end for Aicken, and in 1881 he sold out. By the early 1890s Clifden was in the hands of the government, who divided the run, including the Lill Burn Valley, into about a dozen farm-sized properties.

At breakfast time the next day the mist blotted out the high country to the west and it was raining steadily. As usual — this had been the wettest winter on record. Even some of the paradise ducks had headed north to find a drier spot.

Fay's porridge was hitting the spot, all right. Colin was hunched over some less solid fare — the big man was on a diet and was remarkably good-tempered about it. Nudging sixty, Colin King stood a good 1.93 metres tall. In his prime he had been a rangy, broad-shouldered man, the type who looked just fine on the back of a horse.

For as long as he could remember, Colin had wanted to work on the land; he left home at fourteen to do something about it. For ten years he'd put in his time on stations, changing jobs often. The roving life came to an end, though, when he married Invercargill-born Kay.

They decided to lead a more settled life, and for Colin that meant leaving the land. During the years he spent

Lake Hauroko and the Princess Mountains.

as a wharfie in Bluff or a freezing worker at Ocean Beach, he never gave up his ambition to have his own farm. Nothing would have suited Kay better, either — she loved animals and had a special affinity with them.

Finally, Colin King had a gutsful of life in the works — the sickening stench of the endless killing chain, the sheer physical effort required to punch the skins off, the swollen fists it caused. The answer came in the form of a manager's job at Tara Downs, a smallholding out of Invercargill.

Before too long the Kings had saved enough money to get a small place of their own, Castlerock, 240 hectares of fine country between Mossburn and Lumsden. They would remain there for the better part of ten years.

Until, that is, Ted Edmonds offered to sell them his station in the Lill Burn Valley. Ted had had a few problems hiring staff — the place was a bit out of the way for anyone hankering for regular trips to the pub — and for years Colin had been assisting him when he was short-handed.

It would be a dream come true for Colin, to own a property that had a Hereford stud as well as a sizeable flock of Romneys. But the asking price was more than he and Fay could manage. Ted was keen to sell to such a good friend as Colin, and it was he who came up with the solution: if Colin and Fay could come up with half the money, then Ted would remain in partnership with them for five years.

This was too good an opportunity to pass up, and in 1979 Colin and Fay King sold their Castlerock farm and moved to the Lill Burn Valley.

Yet again it was feeding-out time at Waiau Hereford Stud, but this time I was to accompany Colin on his rounds.

'Ready?' Colin asked as he pushed back his chair and lumbered to his feet like Smokey the Bear.

I nodded, gulped the rest of my tea, nearly choked on a piece of toast and started for the back door.

'Say g'day to BB Power for me,' I said to Fay.

In the steady drizzle that had replaced the rain we took a truck to the main station complex — woolshed, garage, implement shed, workshop, feed bins, married quarters and a fine old homestead that could have dated as far back as the early 1890s. The homestead was home to 34-year-old Darryl King, his wife Nikki and their young ones.

Darryl, taller even than Colin, discussed the day's activities with his father. He was in good nick, with a long-limbed build reminiscent of Colin's thirty years earlier. Feeling like the runt of the litter, I moved away, hunkered down, and tried to stroke a pretty ginger kitten, one of several semi-wild cats about the place. Nothing doing.

Colin, Fay, Darryl and two staff made up the workforce on the station; theirs was the responsibility of 2000 cattle, 7000 sheep and 500 red deer. The foundation of the deer herd had been trapped on the place in the late 1970s or early 1980s; Colin was able to say proudly he had not bought a single deer.

An icy wind kept the drizzle company as we pressed on down the road. The paddock containing the cows was as green as the Waikato in winter. The Lill Burn

Darryl King and shepherd James Lowe.

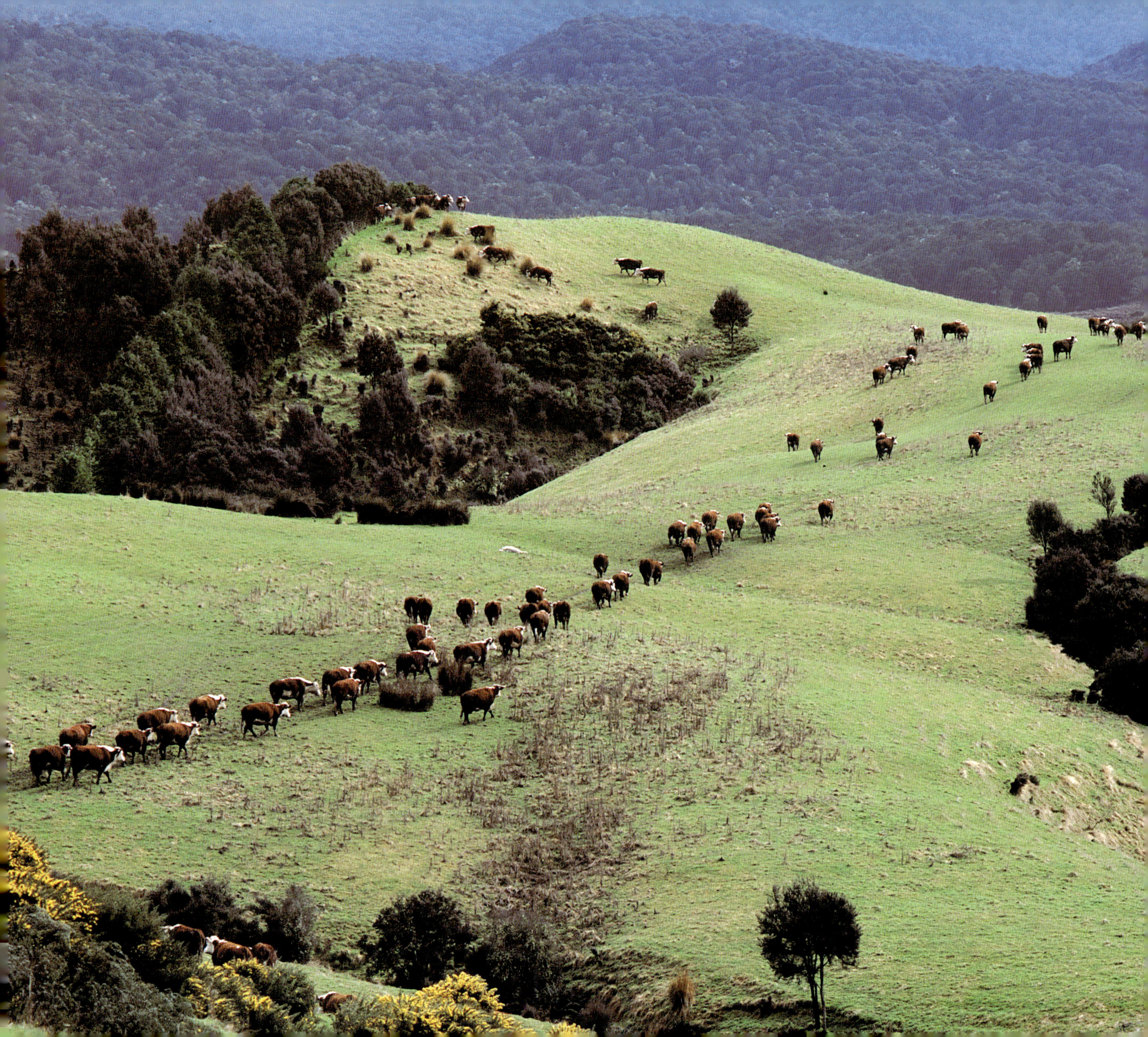

Above: Colin and Edward reunite a calf with its mother.
Left: Herefords heading out to the back paddocks, where the station's western reaches meet the heavy bush of Fiordland National Park.

meandered through it and the hunter in me recognised some good red deer country in the forest beyond.

Some of the cows had already given birth, and they were very protective of their big-eyed young. Any calf more than a day old was already eartagged and the details entered on computer.

Presently Colin, feeding out, spotted a days old calf they had overlooked — its mother must have hidden it too well in the rushes that were dotted around the pasture. With young hand Edward still sitting on the bonnet, Colin pointed the truck straight at mother and child. Not surprisingly, the cow took off, closely followed by the little one.

Colin gunned the engine while Edward clung on grimly. When we were nearly nudging the calf's backside, Colin slowed down and Edward, looking like something out of the rodeo, jumped off and hit the deck running. He launched himself at the calf in a spectacular headlong dive. And ended up face down in the mud, having missed completely.

Colin and I were still laughing as Edward regained his footing.

'You're supposed to grab its tail, y'know!' Colin pointed out.

Edward muttered to himself, looked skywards for a moment, considered his muddy overalls and shook his head. He made darn sure that at the next attempt he got hold of the calf's tail.

They did a great job on Waiau Hereford Stud. Most of the time!

27

A LEGEND CAME THIS WAY

By any reckoning the wide valley of the Greenstone River was in midsummer very lovely country, and the mobs of Hereford cows and calves only enhanced the picture. The cattle belonged to the Metherell family, who owned Elfin Bay station. The station was once part of Hugh MacKenzie's mighty Walter Peak run.

The Greenstone Valley route from Lake Wakatipu to the West Coast was first used by the Maoris while searching for precious pounamu and hunting moas. The area was rediscovered by Europeans in 1861, when David McKellar and George Gunn headed up the Mararoa River, west of Wakatipu, looking for somewhere to run sheep. They came to the Greenstone Valley and eventually to a beautiful lake, which they named Lake McKellar. Soon they were climbing and became the first Europeans to stand on top of Te Tatau-a-Raki, which they referred to as Key Summit.

In later years this same route would be used by another Gunn — the legendary Davy Gunn — who raised Herefords in the Hollyford Valley. Every year in the late spring he left his beloved West Coast run to take a sizable herd to Lorneville, out of Invercargill, for the November sales. Gunn's yearly droving trek of more than 300 kilometres, much of it through difficult terrain, took a full three weeks.

It was in 1926 that Davy Gunn, in partnership with William Fraser, purchased the run. The property took in much of the Hollyford Valley and all of the Pyke River,

In the watershed of the Mavora River.

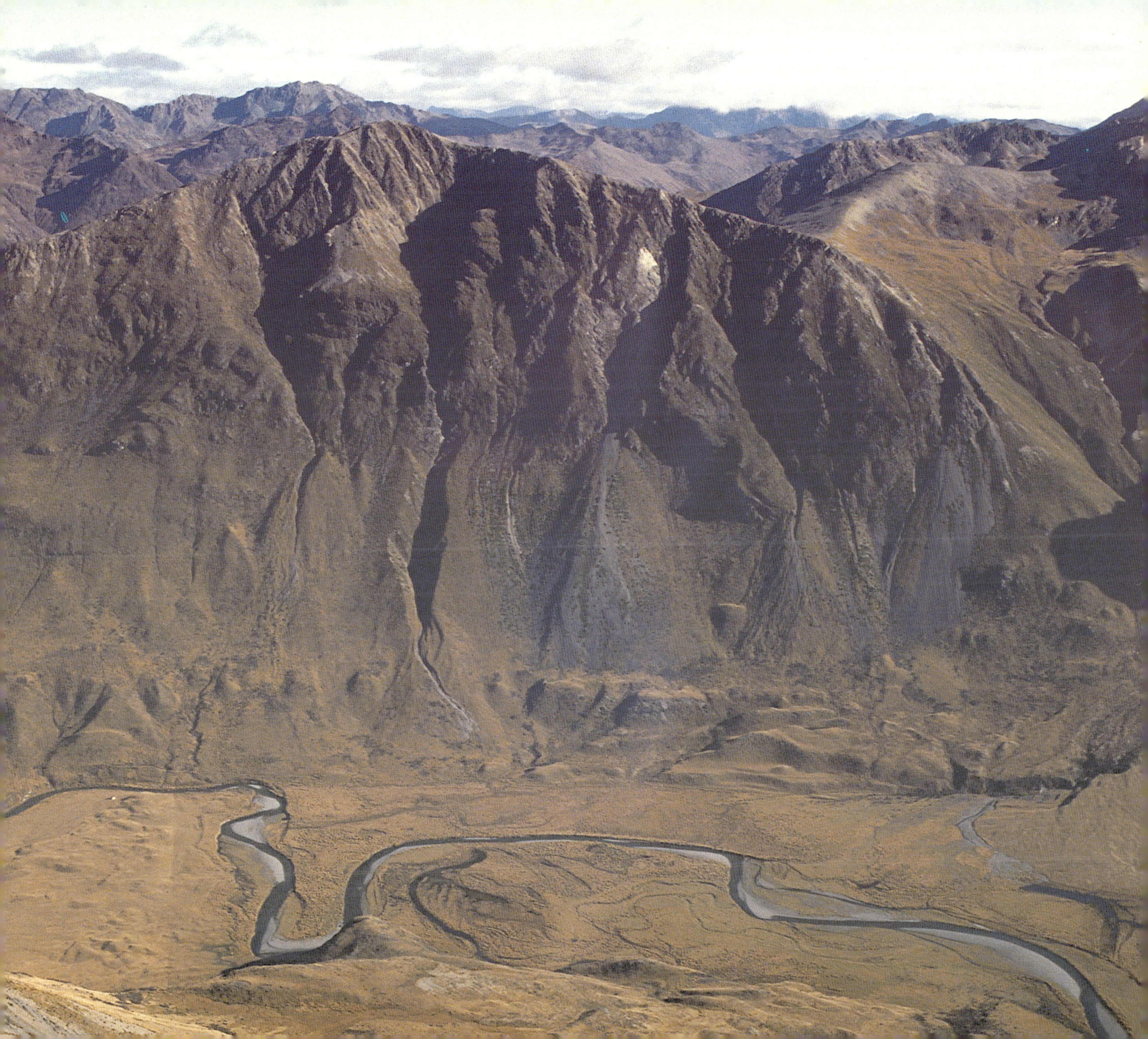

but only about one-tenth of its 60,000-hectares was open country. It was extremely isolated, and the only serious means of access was by sea.

William Fraser soon became disenchanted with the primitive conditions, but Davy Gunn revelled in it all, his keen eyes shining with enthusiasm — within a few years he had bought Fraser out. Slowly he built up his herd of cattle, taking on help when he could afford it. There was no fencing, so the cattle were run semi-wild: the bulls remained with the cows year-round, and the calves were, by and large, self-weaned. By the late 1930s Gunn was running close to 1000 head of cattle and considered the lower Pyke the best country he had.

It was Davy Gunn's droving trips that lifted him to celebrity status in the region. His cattle treks were the stuff of legend, not so much for the distance covered as for the rugged country they traversed. The trips usually involved about 100 head of cattle, the maximum that could be safely handled.

The trek began in Gunn's Lake Alabaster holding yards. Gunn and his men found their way out of the Hollyford Valley via the incredibly steep Deadmans Track, then crossed the Howden Valley, perhaps staying overnight at Lake Howden. The Greenstone Valley was next, followed by the Mararoa Valley. On past the Mavora lakes they went, down the Mararoa, until they reached Mossburn. Trail's end was Lorneville and, with enough cash in his pocket to see him through the year, Gunn wasted no time returning to his run.

Once the Milford road was opened in 1939, Davy Gunn took his cattle via the Eglinton Valley and Te Anau. He was befriended by the Chartres family of Te Anau Downs station; it was here that Colin King first met the legendary Davy Gunn.

By this time Gunn was well into his sixties, a strong man nevertheless, and Colin was not yet twenty-one. Perhaps the older man saw something of himself in the Southland musterer; in any event the two got on well.

Davy Gunn told Colin a story about one of his droving trips. He had been paid for his cattle at Mossburn, from where they would be transported by rail to Invercargill. In typical fashion, he returned home quickly, taking four days. Back at the homestead, he put his hand into his trouser pocket to get out the money. Nothing. He always put the tight wad of notes into the same pocket, and he could only deduce that somewhere along the way it must have fallen out.

Mounting up, Davy retraced his steps, eyes rarely leaving the ground. Finally he came to the main highway near Mossburn — still no sign of the money. He turned his horse's head about and started back, a year's income lost.

Nearly a year later Davy Gunn's cattle were again yarded in preparation for the yearly trip. Readying his horse for the journey, he picked up the saddle bags and gave them a good shake — and a wad of notes fell out. 'It was,' he later said, 'like getting two incomes in one year!'

By this time, the early to mid-fifties, red deer had invaded Davy Gunn's country from the north. Davy had seen it coming — 'Shoot every one of them you see!' he'd ordered his men — but it was too much for just a few men to handle. Such was the devastation that his 1000 head of cattle had to be reduced to around 400. Davy held grave fears that, lacking winter-feed, some would not make it through the winter. But cattle, like most domesticated stock, are survivors when placed in jeopardy; such were Davy Gunn's semi-wild Herefords.

Looking across Wakatipu to where the Greenstone discharges into the lake.

A LEGEND CAME THIS WAY • 277

With his cattle business in decline, Davy stepped up his tourism activities to supplement his income. Huts were built, tracks improved and horses purchased. One of Davy's favourite tourist trips was down the valley of the Hollyford, on to Martins Bay and Big Bay, then back home down the Pyke. Riding in single file below the Darran Mountains, Davy might well have looked up at the towering peaks and recalled one summer day many years earlier.

Davy was up on the tops searching for high-ranging Herefords when, right on the crest of the range, he slipped and plunged headlong into space. Were it not for a narrow ledge some 4 metres below, Davy Gunn would undoubtedly have died. Badly bruised, shocked and in increasing pain, he found himself unable to move. He remained on the ledge as night fell; if for nothing else he was thankful it was summertime.

In the morning one of Davy's men went looking for him, and found a badly shaken Davy still on the ledge. He helped him climb to safety and took him down the mountains to Deadmans hut. 'The mountains nearly got me that time,' he would later say.

Davy Gunn's tourist parties always camped at the hut at Big Bay. They were there on a day Davy would never forget — 30 December 1936.

While he and his clients were on the beach a light aircraft came into sight. It was planning to land on the hard-packed sand, but as it came in something went wrong and the plane crashed. Sutton Jones, a journalist, was killed instantly; the other three passengers were badly injured. Only the pilot escaped serious injury.

Help had to be obtained — fast — and Davy Gunn knew it was all up to him. The nearest telephone was

The Darran Mountains.

A LEGEND CAME THIS WAY • 279

85 kilometres away, at Marion Camp on the yet to be finished Milford road. Cursing the lack of horse, he set off at a run. It was a slow 25 kilometres to Lake McKerrow and it was nearly dark when he got there.

The track fringing the lake was not called the Demon Trail as a joke; it was tough enough in daylight, let alone at night. Fortunately Davy had a boat moored on the lake and, with a will, he rowed the 20 kilometres to the head of the lake almost non-stop. There was a hut there and Davy paused to make a brew.

Suddenly he heard a whinny. It was one of his free-ranging horses. The lonely animal responded to Davy's soft call and, saddling up, Davy pressed on into the night.

The following afternoon man and horse arrived at Marion Camp. Davy Gunn, nearly fifty years old, had covered 85 kilometres on foot, in a rowboat and on horseback in twenty-one hours. Stones commemorating his heroism were placed at Marion Camp and in the lower Pyke River.

After leaving Big Bay, Davy's tourist parties would spend a few nights at the huts on the outlying parts of his huge run. From time to time they would run into wild cattle. Real wild cattle, born mean. These scrub bulls would snort and stare defiantly at the intruders — as likely as not the first human beings they had ever seen. Davy would always keep his .303 at the ready, just in case.

Bill Norman, who later farmed in Southland, worked with Davy in 1939 and had several hairy encounters with wild bulls. The most serious happened during the annual muster when, quiet as a cat, a bull confronted them in the thicket-like growth. Davy was on foot.

Bill spotted it first: 'Watch out, Davy!' he warned.

Too late. In an instant the bull was upon him. Thunk!

Lake Howden.

Davy crashed to the ground. The bull could have had him then, for Davy was momentarily stunned. Instead the animal went for Davy's horse. One slashing blow of its deadly horns and the horse's throat was ripped open. Wheeling, the bull then attacked Bill's horse without causing critical injury. The beast raced off, smashing through the tangled undergrowth like a ten-tonne truck. This was tiger country, all right.

On Christmas Day 1955 Davy Gunn, giving seventy years of age a hard nudge, was guiding a three-strong party of tourists. When they came to cross the lower Pyke, Davy put Warren Shaw, at twelve the youngest amongst them, behind him on his own horse.

The Pyke was running faster and dirtier than normal. No matter — this was a regular cattle ford, as safe as houses.

'Hang on, lad,' he laughed as they went in.

Part way across the horse stumbled and fell into a newly scooped hole. Had the river not been running so strong, the horse would have regained its footing in an instant. As it was, it went down on its side, pinning Davy underneath it for a moment. With a mighty effort the horse scrambled to regain its footing, with Davy and Warren clinging to the saddle for dear life. The saddle slipped around the horse's belly and, losing their grip, Davy and the boy were swept away by the

Herefords have grazed for a very long time in the valley of the Greenstone.

current. The rest of the party could only look on in dismay.

Like many a back-country man, Davy Gunn had never learned to swim. Not so the boy, who was considered a good swimmer. In the end it didn't make any difference — the Pyke claimed both lives that Christmas Day.

The news of Davy Gunn's death stunned all who knew him; he had seemed indestructible. But fate, as fickle as the high-country weather, had its own plans for Davy, and in truth it was only right that he should die in the place he had loved for thirty years.

Following the death of his father, Murray Gunn took over the run. A few years later the government included some of the run within the boundaries of Fiordland National Park and ownership was transferred to the Public Trust. There was a muster; it rounded up 360 cattle of which 120 were taken to Lorneville. An attempt was later made to muster the rest, but after two musterers were drowned the Public Trust gave it up as a bad job.

Davy Gunn's cattle would still be there were it not for the helicopter boys. When in the 1960s the airborne hunters came in for red deer, they also accounted for the several hundred cattle that were the last of Davy's once fine herd.

28

VALLEY OF THE WAIRAU

The river was the Wairau, given life in the northeastern reaches of the Spenser Mountains on the border of North Westland and Marlborough. In a far distant time the river, quickly gathering strength on its journey north, had cut a deep and tortuous path between the Raglan Range and the St Arnaud Range. Now as it emerged from the mountains onto a great plain to enter the sea at Cloudy Bay, northeast of Blenheim, it was more powerful still. From start to finish the river ran for 170 kilometres, and most of it through station country.

It was through this valley that a stock route linking Nelson and Canterbury was opened in the 1840s. Today a road travelled much the same route as the old trail through, amongst other places, Rainbow station.

The drive down the valley of the Wairau was usually a pleasant one; the country was fine and the weather dependable. Not so today. I was on my way to Picton, bound for the North Island, and this was my first time on this particular road in many years. The area had special significance for me, however — Rainbow was the first New Zealand station I had ever seen.

I still remember clearly the scene on Rainbow. The men were shifting cattle, Herefords, as I recall, well upstream of the main station. They wore stockmen's clobber — heavy grey woollen trousers and wide-brimmed hats — and they rode strong hacks. Stockwhips cracked. Dogs barked. Cattle bellowed as though in pain; perhaps they were, because the river they were plunging into was both swift and icy-cold. That river was the first I would ford the hard way. One

River terraces on Rainbow station.

way or another, I guess you could say I've been crossing dangerous waters ever since.

On the southern side of the valley there were once three big runs: Hillersden, Lansdowne and Birch Hill. Taken up in the mid-1840s, Hillersden covered over 60,000 hectares, upon which they ran 60,000 sheep. In the early days Hillersden ranked as highly as Clifford and Weld's Flaxbourne. Lansdowne and Birch Hill dated to 1848; by 1882 Lansdowne was a Merino stud.

All three huge runs had long since been broken up into much smaller holdings, although the Merino sheep naturally remained. Of the thirty-odd stations in the valley, at least five were registered Merino studs: Bounds, Moutere North, Ramshead, Saltwater and Wye Hills. The Merryville connection was to be found in Ron and Sue Small's Moutere North, once part of Hillersden.

Perhaps the most significant station in Marlborough to include the Merryville link in its current bloodline was Richmond Brook. One of a cluster of stations in the lower Awatere Valley, the run was first taken up by Major Matthew Brook in 1848. The Major believed in Merino sheep, and the foundation of the present flock dated to about 1850, when ewes were imported from South Australia. The stud itself dated to 1923, making it one of the oldest in the country. No longer the size it once was, Yvonne Richmond's station still covered 4800 hectares and the country, running up from river flats to steep mountain terrain, carried around 7500 sheep.

With the valley of the Wairau River behind me and the hills around Picton looming ahead, my thoughts naturally turned to the station country of the North Island. What would I find there?

Following page: The Wairau runs pellmell towards station country.

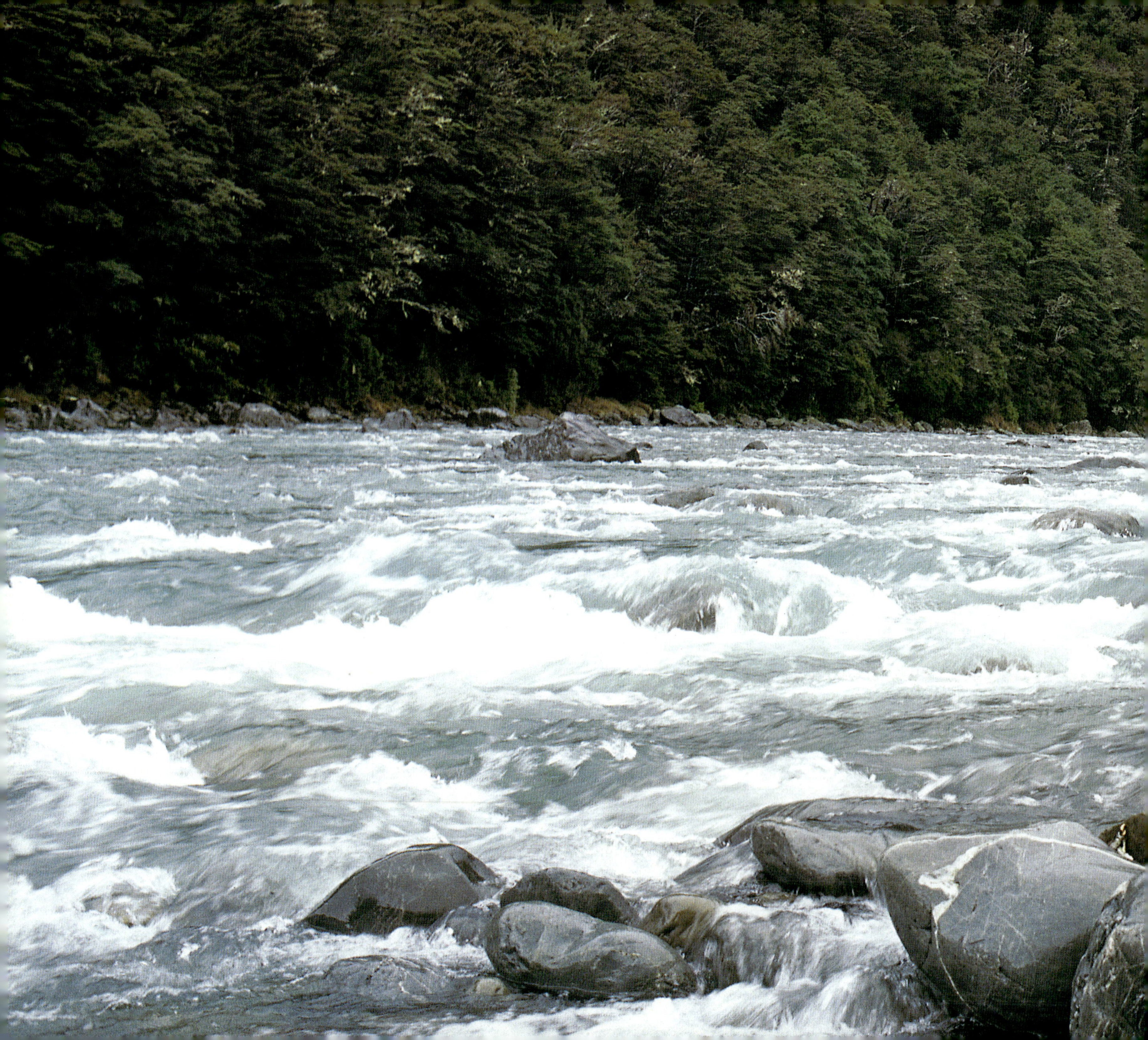

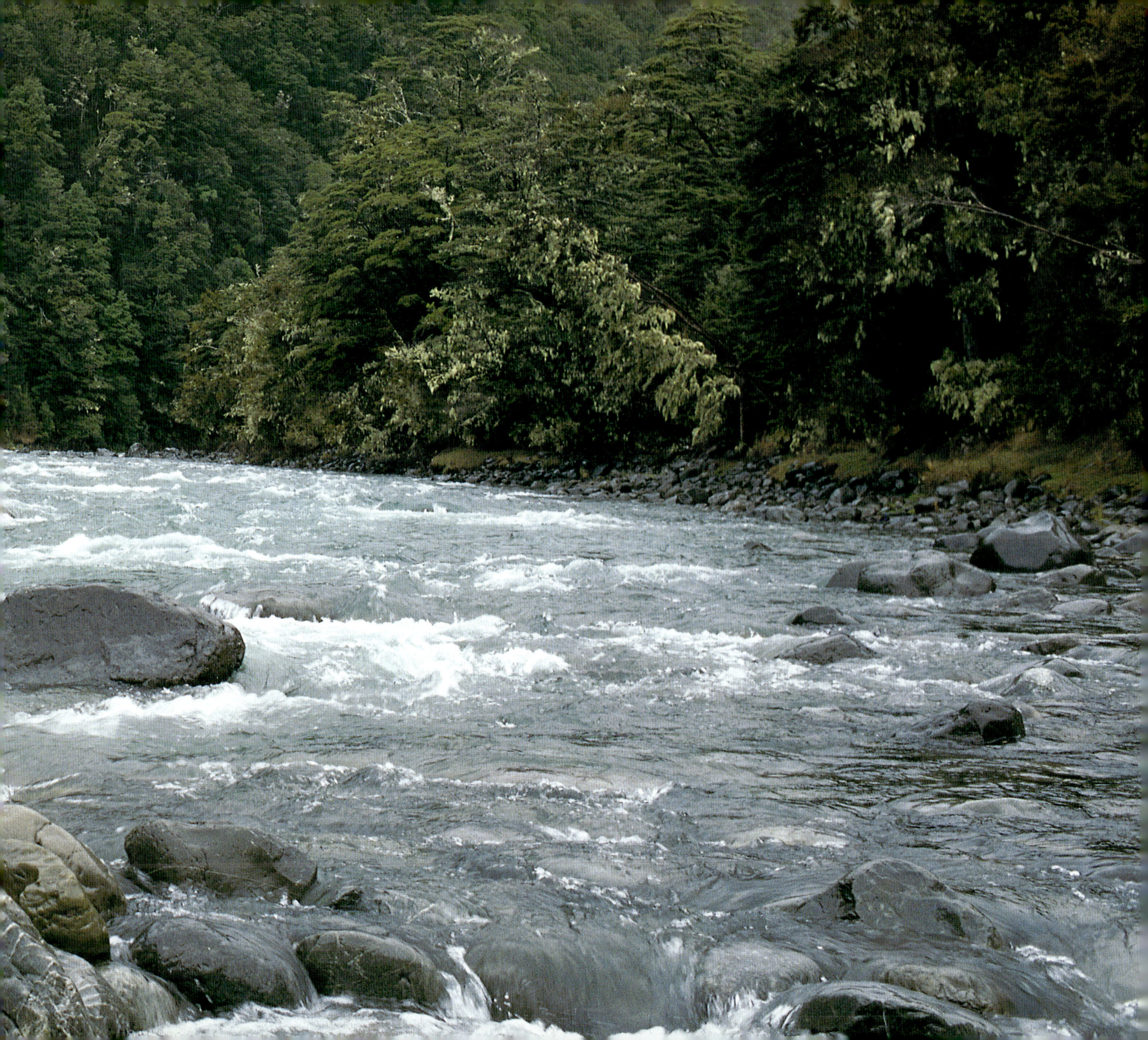

NORTH OF COOK STRAIT

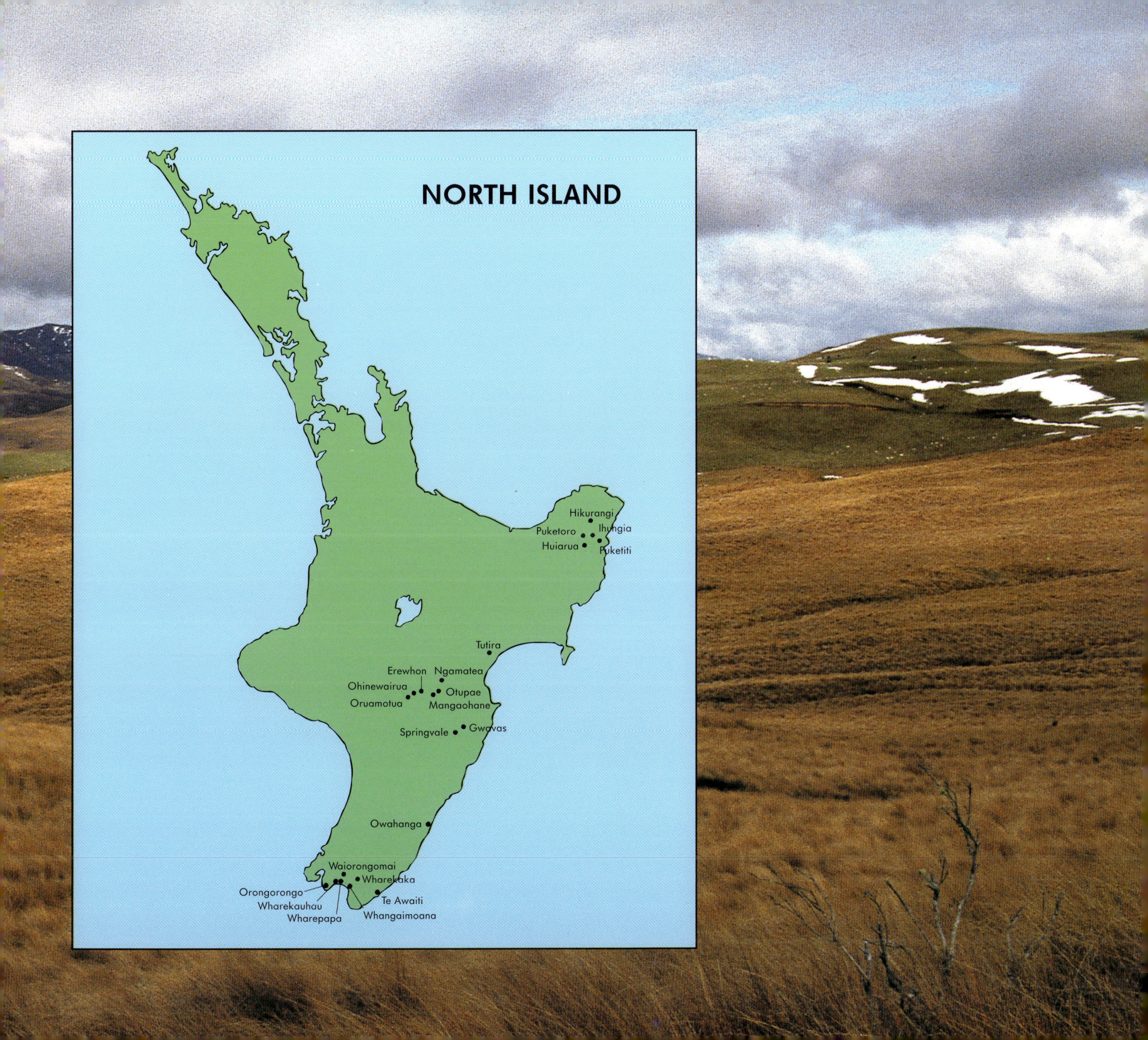

NORTH ISLAND

- Hikurangi
- Puketoro
- Ihungia
- Huiarua
- Puketiti
- Tutira
- Erewhon
- Ngamatea
- Ohinewairua
- Otupae
- Oruamotua
- Mangaohane
- Springvale
- Gwavas
- Owahanga
- Waiorongomai
- Wharekaka
- Orongorongo
- Wharekauhau
- Te Awaiti
- Wharepapa
- Whangaimoana

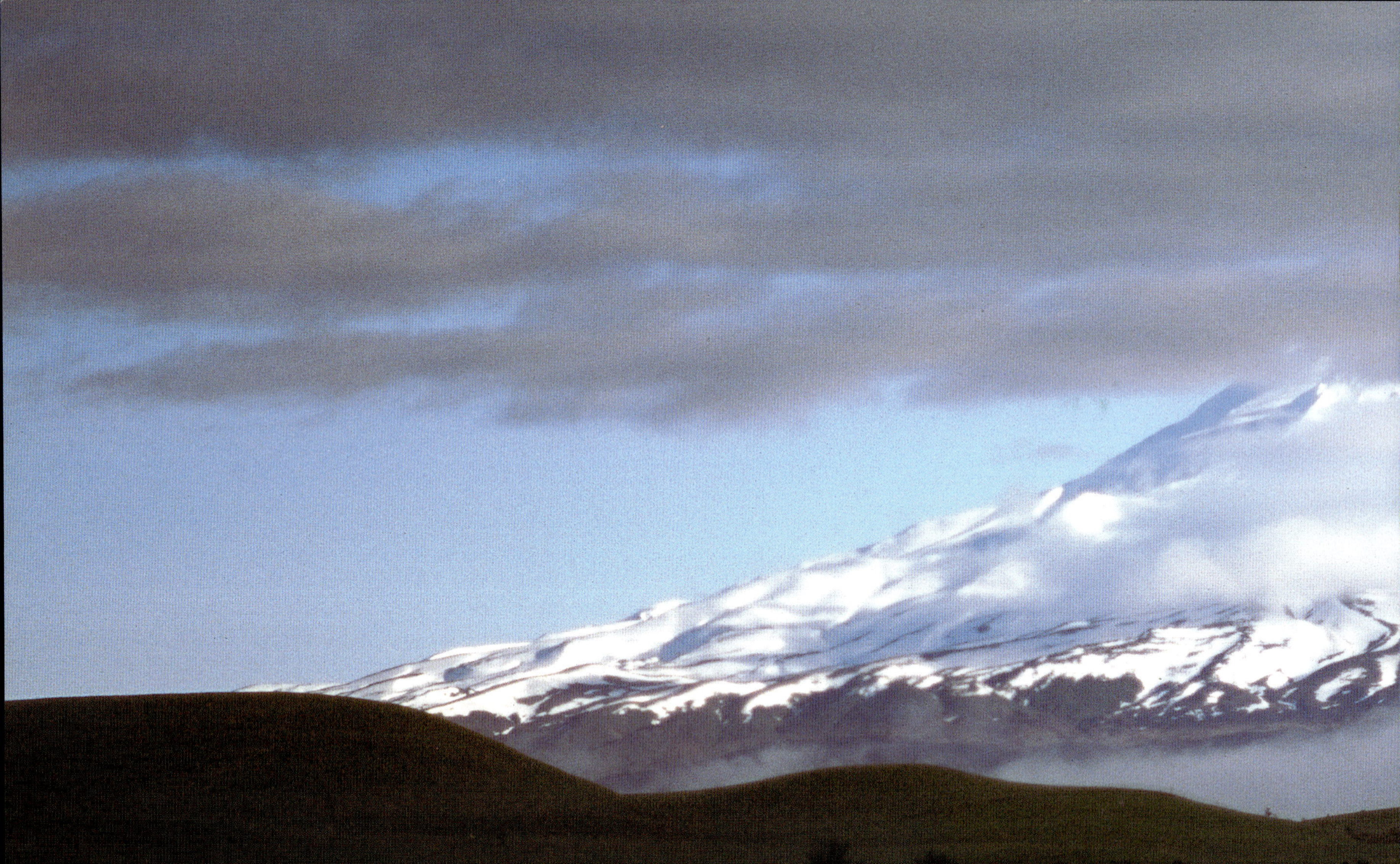

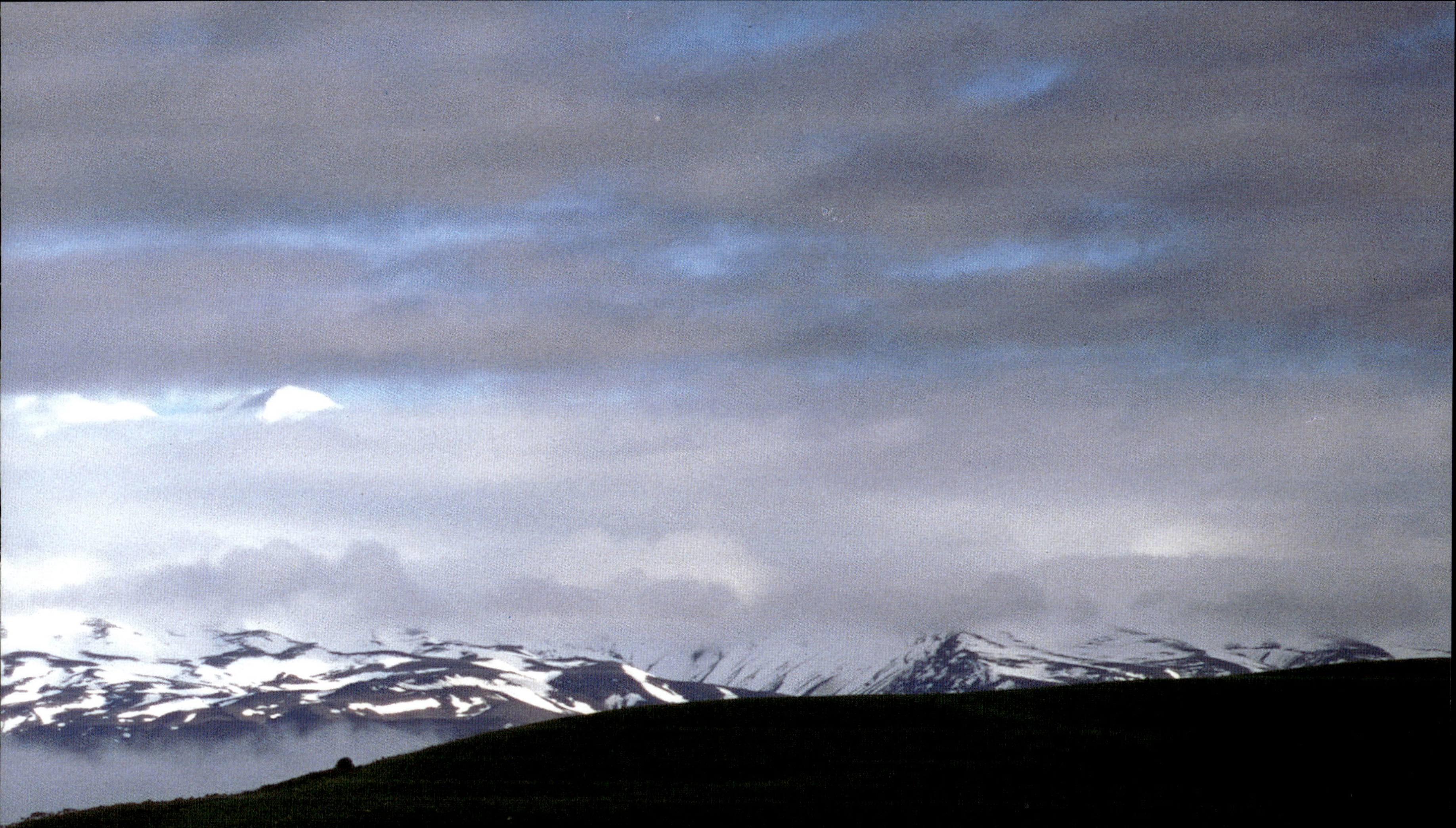

29

THE MOUNTAIN

Against the lightening sky the upper reaches of the mountain were clear, the squarish crest resembling a mesa. In the pre-dawn it seemed a massive monolith as it loomed above me.

At 1752 metres, Hikurangi was by far the highest peak in the East Cape's Raukumara Range and in winter it was often covered in snow. To the Maoris the mountain, named after a legendary peak in Hawaiki, was sacred. Tradition had it that Hikurangi was the final resting place of Maui's great canoe — the canoe from which he fished the North Island out of the sea.

I had first come to this part of the country fifteen years earlier, but despite the sunny weather, the mountain had been lost in the mist — brooding perhaps — throughout my four-day stay. Six years later I returned but again I was out of luck and the mountain remained in hiding. On this, my third visit, I could only hope that Hikurangi would be revealed.

On this lovely fine October morning I waited patiently, filled with anticipation, at a lookout point between Te Puia Springs and Ruatoria. Surely nothing could stop me from seeing the mighty mountain for the first time.

Presently the sky to the east flushed as another day awakened. The sun came quickly to the first place on the New Zealand mainland to see the sun each day, bathing the snow-dotted peak in its washed-out orange glow. I sat on the bullbar of my vehicle, sipping coffee

Our Father, Hikurangi, seen from Ihungia station.

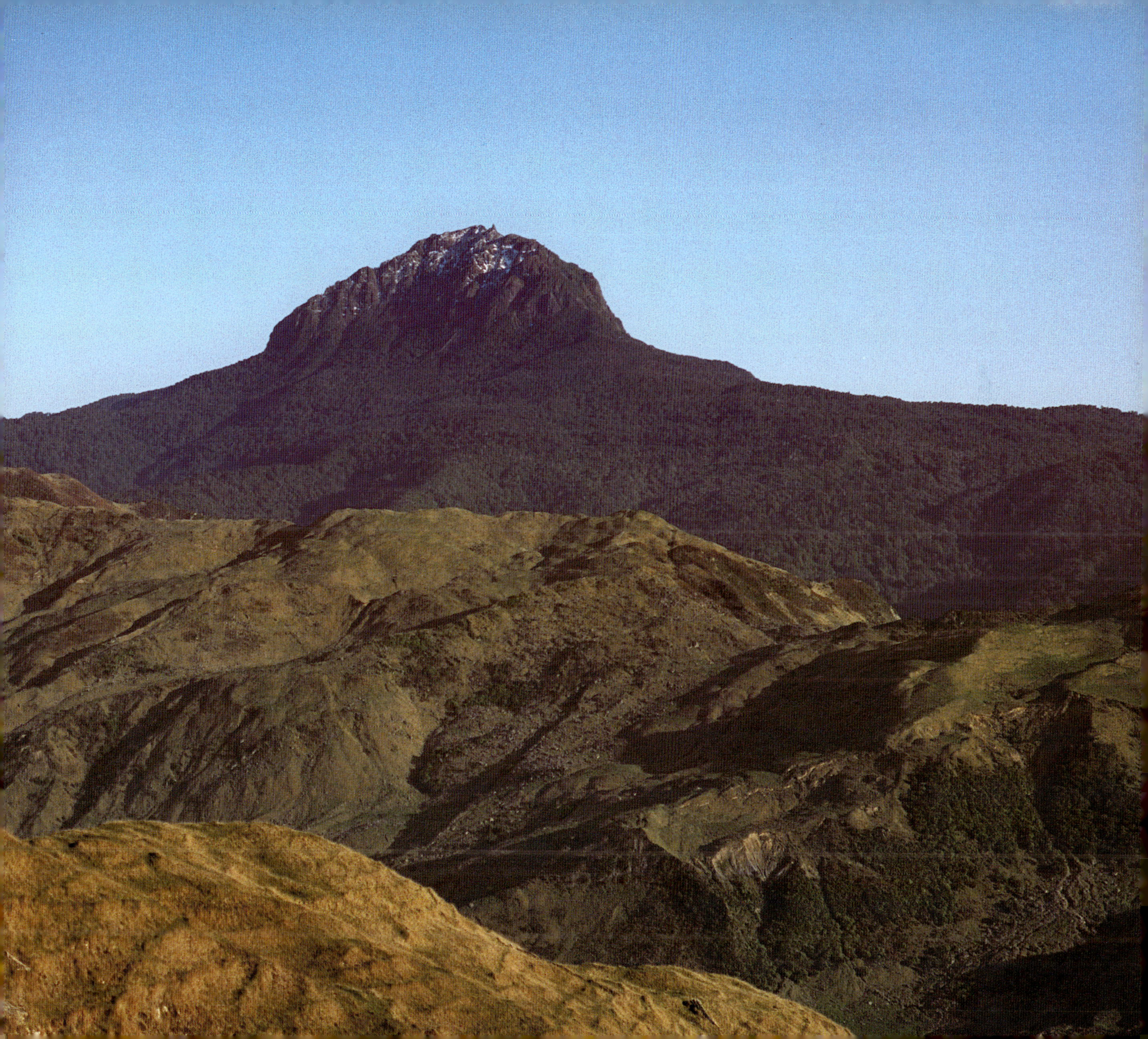

and wasting a dream-like hour as the new day gathered momentum.

Eventually I shook myself out of my trance and headed back to Te Puia Springs. By any yardstick there wasn't much to the place: hotel, hospital, primary school, store, motel and, of course, the famed hot springs. My hosts at the small motel were Sam and Noeline Awarau, who, as it happened, held the contract for the local Rural Delivery mail run.

The run, a round trip of 180 kilometres, included three outlying schools and no fewer than thirty sheep and cattle properties. I asked Noeline how they got on with the station people. Very well, came the response — in fact a few months earlier Tony Hansen, the manager on Ihungia, had given them a surplus calf.

Soon enough I was back in my four-wheel-drive, this time on the mostly unsealed road to Waipiro Bay. The first sight of the tiny settlement was a dramatic one from a high point on the road. It was easy to see why Maori settlers had chosen Waipiro: the land was fertile, the sun plentiful, the sea bountiful.

In 1883, at the age of forty-six, a Pakeha by the name of James Nelson Williams recognised the potential at Waipiro for a huge station, much larger than those found in the nearby Hawke's Bay. His idea was to combine a number of freehold blocks and a good many Maori leases.

At Waipiro, J. N. Williams talked at great length with the local Maori people. They could see he was an honourable man and agreed to lease about 15,000 hectares of Maori land. When the newly purchased freehold blocks further inland were added in, the property would extend to 40,000 hectares.

Almost all of the new Waipiro station was in virgin

Waipiro Bay.

bush. Williams knew that to develop the country would be a task of Herculean proportions, but he'd already proved he could do it in his Hawke's Bay properties. He turned to one of his Hawke's Bay employees, a slim 32-year-old Englishman named Arthur Wallis, to oversee the running of the vast station. Wallis was to be a long and faithful servant to the Williams family.

By the mid-1890s Waipiro had become a thriving settlement. The fine station homestead was at Waipiro, along with a hotel, a store and a church at which to worship the Pakehas' unseen god; Hikurangi was for the Maoris, however, a more tangible god. Based at Waipiro there were also tradesmen: baker, blacksmith, harness maker, saddler. Horses were a way of life back then, and a century later that was something that hadn't changed. The station's woolclip went out by sea from the bay, then called Open Bay.

When Arthur Wallis retired in 1902 to concentrate on his own holdings, J. N. Williams's sons Heathcote and Arnold took over the running of Waipiro station. They had had a privileged upbringing in Hawke's Bay, finishing their education at Cambridge University, but had worked at the station during the holidays. Heathcote lived in the homestead on the Turihaua block while his brother went to the Waipiro homestead. Just a few years later, however, Arnold would oversee the construction of a splendid new homestead on the Puketiti block.

On yet another wonderful early morning I headed towards Puketiti station, a little south of Te Puia Springs. Away to my right as I drove along the no-exit road, across stock-dotted pastures, stood Hikurangi. The mountain — always the mountain.

The station was a little smaller than the original Puketiti block, but at 2400 hectares it was still a substantial holding. I passed the woolshed, shearers' cookshop and living quarters and then, beyond a closed gate, followed a winding drive through the heavy shade of a stand of trees. The trees, both native and exotic, were apparently planted in anticipation of the homestead's being built. The puriris, huge, handsome

At Waipiro Bay. The horse is still an essential part of life on the East Coast.

and bearing bright-red drupes through much of the year, were a favourite of Arnold's.

Quite suddenly the trees gave way to both open ground and a dazzling burst of sunshine, and the homestead was before me. It appeared much as it had for nearly ninety years — big, double-storeyed, many-

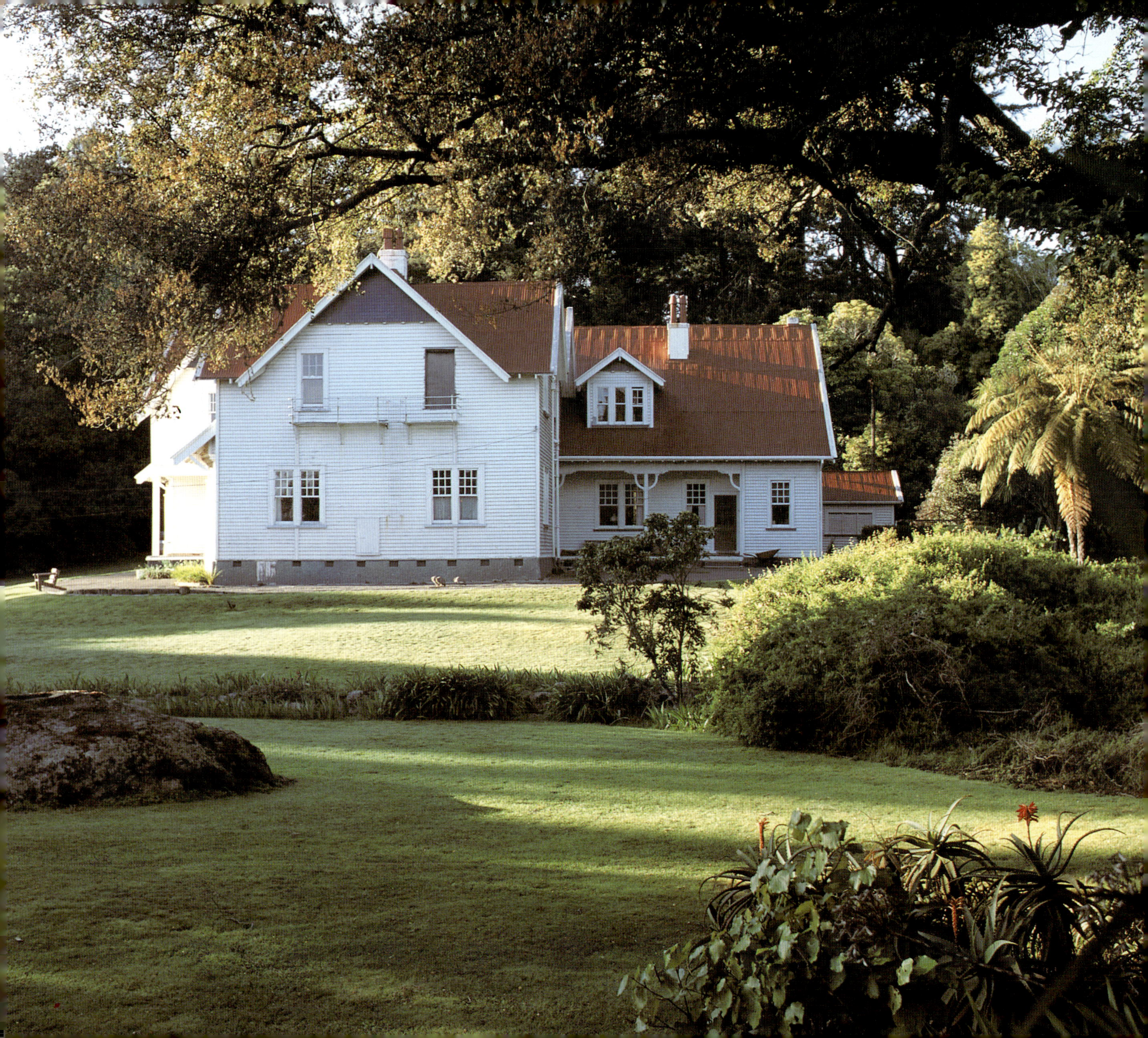

roomed. Some of its timbers had come from Oregon. Neat lawns ran up to the building while many garden shrubs were ablaze with colour. I felt as though I was stepping back in time.

The place had been home to Arnold Williams's son Des since he took over the place in 1946. Des had recently broken an ankle and was staying at Puketoro, another of the stations owned by the family trust. So for now there was no one home — except for perhaps a dozen California quail foraging on the lawn.

Almost with reluctance I turned away from the sun-dappled homestead and went looking for the property's manager, Ben Green. I found him near the woolshed. He was a fit-looking 48-year-old of Ngati Porou and he'd worked at Puketiti and Puketoro since 1963.

'Must be a good family to work for,' I volunteered.

'Been good to me,' said Ben matter-of-factly.

Ben and Dave Walsh, a fencer and general hand, were going to be working with cattle this morning. As we spoke Dave was out rounding up the nags who would help them do the job.

'Gotta be back by eleven-thirty,' Ben said. 'A load of wool's going out.' He jerked a thumb at the woolshed. 'We're in no real hurry. Come and take a look inside if you like.'

I'd already cast an appreciative eye over the woolshed, which was probably built before the turn of the century, when Puketiti was an important out-station. Inside the eight-stand shed it was bone dry, the construction still sound. Thirty-three big bales, containing the wool of 1200 hoggets and dry ewes and destined for the Gisborne Wool Company, were scattered about the solid wooden floor.

The Puketiti homestead.

Written at the top of the wooden frame of the huge woolpress were the words:

BALES
RECORD   81   4/12/06

Ben reminded me that back in 1906 the bales would have been handpressed, which certainly made the work a whole lot harder.

In the woolshed.

We moved on to the large cookshop with its immense fireplace, 1.8 metres high at least. It looked to me as if in it you could have roasted a cattle beast whole, and maybe a couple of good-sized porkers as well. The men would sit on uncomfortable trestle-like planking at the two long tables. Still and all, who worried about that sort of thing after a hard day's toil. Not a tough bunch of shearers, that's for real.

'You can smell the history in here, can't you?' Ben said. I had to agree — the place fair reeked of the past.

Ben Green, Mr Ed, Matilda and Dave Walsh.

By the time we got back outside, Dave Walsh had arrived with the horses. While Dave saddled an impatient Matilda, Ben took his time grooming a more relaxed Mr Ed. He explained that they'd just taken off the horses' winter covers and Mr Ed, like the rest of them was starting to shed his natural winter coat too.

'You seeing Des later today?' Ben asked.

'Expect to.' I paused. 'How old is he?'

'Well over seventy, I think. You wouldn't think so, though. Pretty fit for a bloke his age.'

'Must be all the clean air and sunshine.'

Ben nodded his head seriously. 'I expect it is.'

I left Ben and Dave to their work. Out on the hill, a good hack to ride, a warm spring day, Hikurangi on the skyline. Where else would you want to be?

As I put the main station complex behind me I watched the freshly shorn sheep making their way up to the sunny spots in an effort to keep warm. It occurred to me that it would be a pretty traumatic experience to be so suddenly stripped of your warm coat.

The Williams family had originally brought with them from Hawke's Bay their Lincoln sheep, but the animals struggled with the much heavier rainfall. On Puketiti annual rainfall might reach 2200 millimetres, about twice that of Gisborne. Eventually they turned to the more versatile Romney; today they ran 4000 of the breed. They also operated three separate studs — Romney, Cheviot and Perendale — to breed rams for use on this and other Williams properties.

As I continued towards the main road I spotted an old Land-Rover parked on the side of the road. A young bloke was standing up against the fence yelling instructions to a big huntaway tearing across a hillface after a mob of flighty sheep. Several dogs were avidly watching the action from the back of the Land-Rover.

The 440 hectares north of the road into Puketiti, once part of Puketiti station, was now called the Potae Estate, and the good-looking bloke making all the noise was its manager John Pardoe. The 25-year-old had come up from Gisborne — considered the big smoke round here — five years earlier. He explained that they were running 900 Romney-based sheep on the Potae Estate.

John Pardoe and his dogs.

'This your first manager's job?' I asked him.
He pulled a face. 'Yeah.'
'Not what you expected?'
He merely shook his head.
'Too small?' I wondered.
'Yeah, that's it. Too small.' He hollered at his dog, then continued, 'It's much better on a big place, where there's a lot of horse work and you don't work sheep by standing on the side of the road.' Again he shouted instructions to the dog, this time questioning its parentage. I left him to it.

In 1915, at the age of seventy-eight, J. N. Williams died. The great respect the Williams family were accorded in the region shone through in the impassioned speech made by Sir Apirana Ngata following the great runholder's death. He commented on the envy displayed by some who arrived on the East Coast to find the Williams family already settled on well-established stations:

'They forget the amount of work these men put in during the thirty years they held the land, the good management they showed, and the excellent results they obtained. They have become rich, undoubtedly, and this they deserve. But let it be understood by members of this House that in acquiring those lands and occupying them they injured not a single native of the district of Waiapu.

'No family in this country — I doubt whether any family in any country in the world has done so much for any group of people as the Williams family has done for the Maoris of Waiapu County — the assistance they have rendered to the Maoris has been far more than any businessman would have dared to give.

'No bank dare make the advances they have made to the natives — security was so inadequate. In many cases the security was that which the old chiefs gave to their fathers and grandfathers — just the bare word.'

J. N. Williams's huge holdings on the East Coast — known collectively if inaccurately as Waipiro station — were dispersed as the leasehold land reverted to its Maori owners. The freehold blocks were divided between Arnold and Heathcote Williams, with Puketiti, Ihungia, Tuakau and Puketoro going to Arnold and Heathcote settling for Turihaua and Huiarua. A golden era had ended.

At the entrance to Puketoro station I paused to take it all in: stock horses grazing on lush spring growth, an old woolshed, stands of immature pines on the erosion-prone hillfaces.

As I headed on down the gravel driveway a large-antlered stag, the biggest of a bunch of velvet-topped redskins, eyed me warily from behind the high wire. The deer paddock looked just fine: plenty of natural cover, mature trees and places where the deer could escape the prevailing winds. There's nothing worse than seeing deer in a perfectly flat paddock with no cover, left to take whatever the elements hurl at them in the form of stinking heat or freezing cold.

I came across Rodger Lougher, the manager on the place, before I reached the homestead. The 57-year-old was an East Coaster through and through. Round here, it didn't matter how long you'd been in the area or how well you were regarded — if you weren't born here you weren't an East Coaster.

'How big's the place?' I asked Rodger.

'Oh, about thirteen thousand acres these days.' That was around about 5300 hectares. 'Not quite as big as Ihungia — that's about fourteen thousand acres, I think.'

'Still a big place.'

'Big enough when you have to get round it.'

'What about stock?'

'What about it?'

'What are you running?'

'Sheep, cattle, deer,' Bob replied a little too tersely. Then he grinned. 'We've got five-and-a-half thousand Perendales. This is the oldest Perendale stud in the Poverty Bay and East Coast region. It started in about 1953. The cattle are all Angus — over a thousand head.'

Rodger had better things to do than stand around talking to a curious writer, so he soon sent me off to see Des Williams for a history lesson.

At the entrance to Puketoro station.

Despite his broken ankle, Des looked at ease on the settee. He seemed pleased to see me and was talkative — something Rodger had warned me might not be the case. A bachelor, Des was trim and fit, the result of a lot of hill-country walking. He'd pretty much given up horseriding twenty years earlier, after a nasty fall. He was as keen-eyed as he was hawk-faced and, with his fine sense of humour, he was easy to warm to.

We talked about many things — the history of the place, sheep, and the inroads forestry was making into good pastoral country. Of course, we talked about Hikurangi too. Des loved the mountain and had climbed it no fewer than ten times. He had even slept up there to see in the decade of the 1990s.

'It means so much to the Maori people,' he told me. 'They call it Our Father. Did you know that?' He lapsed into silence.

Hikurangi, Our Father, standing tall. The mountain — always the mountain.

30

THE MIGHTY IHUNGIA

The road to Ihungia was a twisting one that ran through a valley. To the north of the road was Ihungia and to the south Ruangarehu; both were owned by the Williams family.

I pulled off the road and paused to look at the arresting view. There was movement on Ruangarehu station. Down on the flats men were working at the woolshed complex: floating towards me on the breeze came the sounds of men's raised voices, the shrill barking of dogs and the distressed bleating of sheep. Well above the flats stood a lovely old homestead on two levels, home to Mark Williams and his family.

I looked across the road to Ihungia's station headquarters — woolshed, yards, shearers' cookshop, schoolgrounds. It was an impressive set-up and it looked neat and orderly. The dairy cattle just below me looked happy with their lot.

I met Tony Hansen at the bottom of the driveway to the manager's residence. It was early evening and he'd just knocked off for the day. He was in his mid-forties, of compact build, lean and tanned. He hadn't been last in the queue when they were handing out good looks. With his dusty hat, brim pulled low, he wouldn't have looked out of place on a cattle station in the Northern Territory of Australia.

'How'd you find Des?' he asked as we moved towards the house.

'Laid up.'

He smiled. 'Yeah, I know *that*. What I—'

'Couldn't have been better.'

Headquarters at Ihungia station.

'Top man, all right,' said Tony, pleased. 'Come and meet Gay.'

The Hansen family had just returned from a gymkhana, and for Tony's Western Australian wife there was a heap of work to catch up on. Piles of washing, for instance. There was also an evening meal to prepare and three boys — Christopher, Jeremy and Matthew — to be supervised. The oldest boy was away at school in Hawke's Bay.

With Gay busy in laundry and kitchen, twelve-year-old Christopher mowing the lawn and the younger boys under duress to take their showers, Tony said to me ruefully, 'You'll have to take us as you find us.'

We busted open a can of beer apiece and Tony explained that his five-strong mustering crew were spending the night at Pukeremu out-station. Tony and the boys had put in a big effort today, but there were still a fair few of the 500 head of Angus out there.

'We'll get away early,' Tony said. 'Before daybreak. Not too early for you, is it?'

'Hell no!' I replied, but my heart sank just a little. We were back in station country, all right.

Next day I was awake and raring to go well before daybreak. As I lay in bed waiting for the day to begin, a cool breeze brushing my face, I mulled things over.

There were hundreds of stations all over the country, each different in its way, but there was one thing almost all had in common — horses. It was the traditional use of horses that for me kept the romance of station life alive.

There wasn't a more horse-oriented place in the land than Ihungia. They ran 120 horses — brood mares, hacks and two stallions. Farm bikes were a non-event on this station, so if you didn't like horses there wasn't much point working here. The men often rode out before daybreak, perhaps as early as 2.30 am in summer, and might not be back before dark.

The night before, I'd listened to Tony talking on the telephone with a young man from down-country. The bloke had heard that there was a job going. 'Can you ride?' Tony asked. 'Good. You'll need dogs — three of them . . . You have? Great! You'll need a saddle, bridle and bedroll . . . No worries, then, is there? . . . Transport? . . . Fine. It's about two hours from Gisborne if you step on it . . . Sunday's fine. See you then.'

Many years ago, I thought to myself, that could have been me on the other end of the line.

Putting down the telephone, Tony had said, 'Sounds a promising type.'

'What's a single shepherd worth these days?' I had asked.

They go in for horses in a big way on Ihungia.

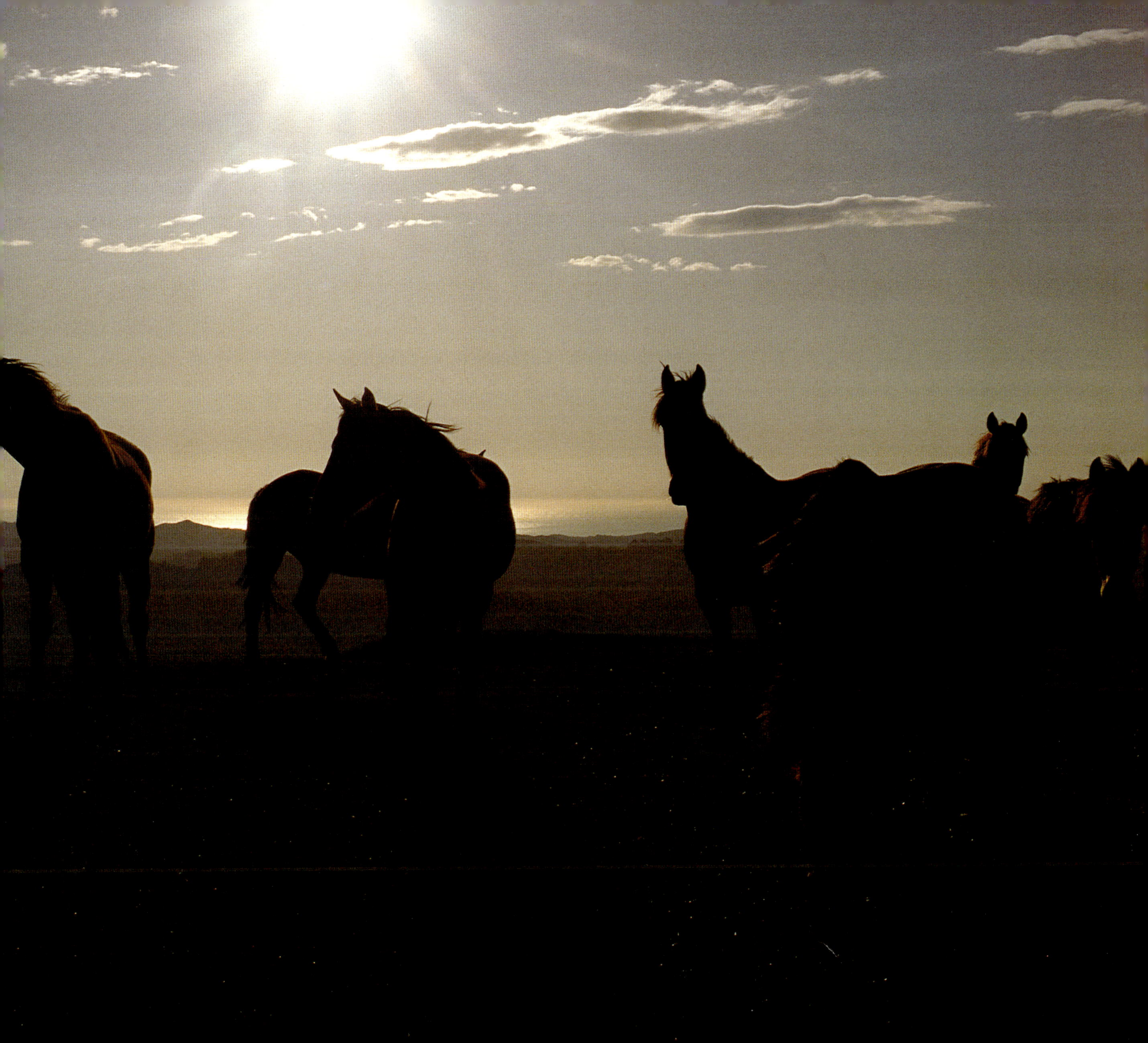

The man himself: Tony Hansen.

'They make about three hundred bucks a week and all found. Less tax, of course. It's still a bloody good way of life.'

Remembering those two-thirty starts, I reckoned they earned every penny of their pay.

The way things worked out, the sun was up by the time we left. Tony picked up the dogs, and they were overjoyed. His arrival meant they were going to spend a day away from the utter boredom of the kennels. A day on the hill, smelling strange smells and chasing stock.

With the dogs on the back of the flat-deck, it was off to the cookshop. Tony paused to let some heavy-uddered cows lumber across the road. Behind them, in no hurry, was a white-bearded old-timer by the name of Jack Cahill. You couldn't hurry milking cows — it upset them too much.

At the cookshop we picked up the tucker box for the boys out at Pukeremu, and headed on past the school. There were nine pupils there, presided over by teacher Margaret Howard. Not too long ago, at the time Mata School on Huiarua station had closed temporarily, the roll had stood at twenty-four.

With the sun spearing across the valley we climbed, constantly turning. Angus cattle ranged the eroded hills. Tony told me they wintered 30,000 stock units on Ihungia, mostly Perendale sheep. They found the Perendales free-moving, easy to handle and very productive.

Suddenly a rank smell invaded the cabin.

'Jeez — what's that, mate?'

'That's one of the dogs,' Tony said heavily. 'I know just which one of them it is, too.'

'Maybe he should be walking.' The smell seemed to intensify. 'What are you feeding them? Dead possums?'

'You'd think so, wouldn't you? Sorry, mate.'

'What's to be sorry about, Tony? You're not doing all the farting!'

Tony laughed. 'Just as well, eh?'

Presently we left the road and took a track. When we came to a closed gate, Tony, hat tipped low over his eyes, gave me the hint. 'Glad you're along, mate.'

The gate was not only latched, but secured with number-eight wire. To my surprise each of the many gates I jumped out to open was fastened in this way, and each time it took a while to wrestle the gate open.

Margaret Howard with pupils of the school.

Eventually I came to a gate that was simply latched. I couldn't resist it: 'Run out of wire by the time you got here, Tony?'

The manager explained that the wire was double security to avoid leaving the gates open accidentally. It was a small price to pay, he reckoned, if it meant you didn't have to remuster a paddock because the stock had got mixed up because of an open gate. Of course, the boss usually had some poor bugger in the passenger seat to do the work for him anyway.

The whare at Pukeremu might have dated to some time at the turn of the century, but it was sound enough. Its deep veranda looked as though it would have been wonderfully inviting when the summer heat proved too much. There were cattleyards and a small woolshed nearby. Of the stockmen there was nothing to be seen. Tony told me they would have been away before dawn to bring in the last of the cattle from their winter range.

Tony lifted a saddle of the back off the flat-deck and went across to saddle his big brown gelding. As he mounted up I asked him what the horse's name was.

'Hitler,' came the bland reply.

'Hitler?'

'Yeah, Hitler.' He turned the gelding about. 'Think about it,' he yelled over his shoulder.

'Tony!' I yelled after him. 'He must be a real bastard of a horse.'

'You nailed it in one!'

By the time Tony had yarded one small mob of cattle, another bunch trotted into sight. Two stockmen and their dogs were giving them the hurry-up. Head shepherd Neville 'Cooch' Higgins and senior shepherd Will 'Tank' Banks dismounted at the yards, while their dogs stretched out in the sun. The rest of the boys rode up soon after: Dan James, Tim Rhodes and Bruce 'Chip' Connolly.

Each of the men, I soon discovered, had a powerful handshake. When I commented on this to Tony, he replied perfectly seriously, 'If they haven't got a hard handshake they don't get a job on the station.'

It was time to start work. With raised voices and waving arms Dan, Tim and Bruce encouraged the cattle to move from the big yard down a narrow race. Midway along the chute Cooch leaned over with the pour-on drench to treat them for parasites.

From time to time there was a lull in the work for Cooch while the boys brought up more cattle, and I took the opportunity for a snatched conversation. I asked him, of course, how he got his nickname. He told me that, according to the boys, he was a dead ringer for the character in Murray Ball's Footrot Flats cartoon.

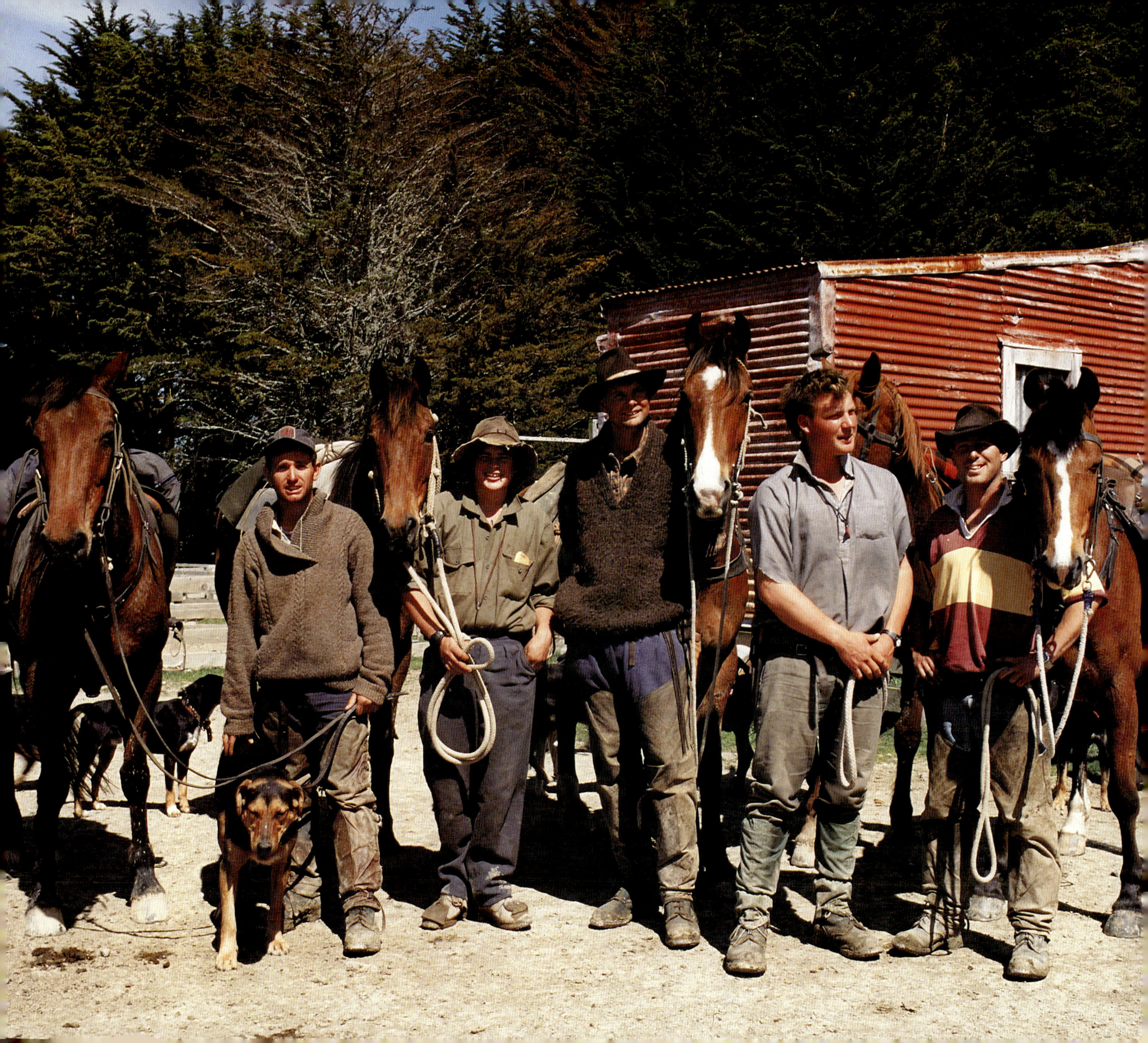

As he pushed his wide-brimmed hat well back, he informed me they'd gotten up at three o'clock that morning.

Bruce, just within earshot, called out in mock indignation, 'You mean I did!'

Cooch nodded in Bruce's direction. 'He was the bitch this morning.'

'Bitch?' I asked.

'That's what we call the cook of the day around here.'

Back in my Forest Service hunting days we'd had a different name for the cook of the day — the greasy. I'd never much liked that name and, truth be told, I liked the Ihungia version even less. Still, that was the way they did things around here.

By late morning the drenching was done. Tony was well pleased and told the boys to knock off for the day once they got home. But before heading back, it was smoko time.

While Cooch chopped firewood, Tony lit the fire. I took the opportunity to look around the whare. It had two rooms, a kitchen-cum-living room and a bunkroom. On the walls were written the names of the men who'd stayed there. Some of those stockmen would be dead now, ghost riders in the sky.

Tony looked sourly at the dirty dishes and the fat-coated frying pan. 'Boys must've left in a hurry.'

With the billies boiled and the tucker box open, it was every man for himself. Glad to be out of the sun, the boys sat on beer crates and enjoyed a good feed.

Tony, munching on a meat sandwich, said, 'So who's gonna lead my horse for me?'

Left: The mustering gang — Bruce Connolly, Tim Rhodes, Neville Higgins, Will Banks and Dan James.
Right: A horse called Hitler.

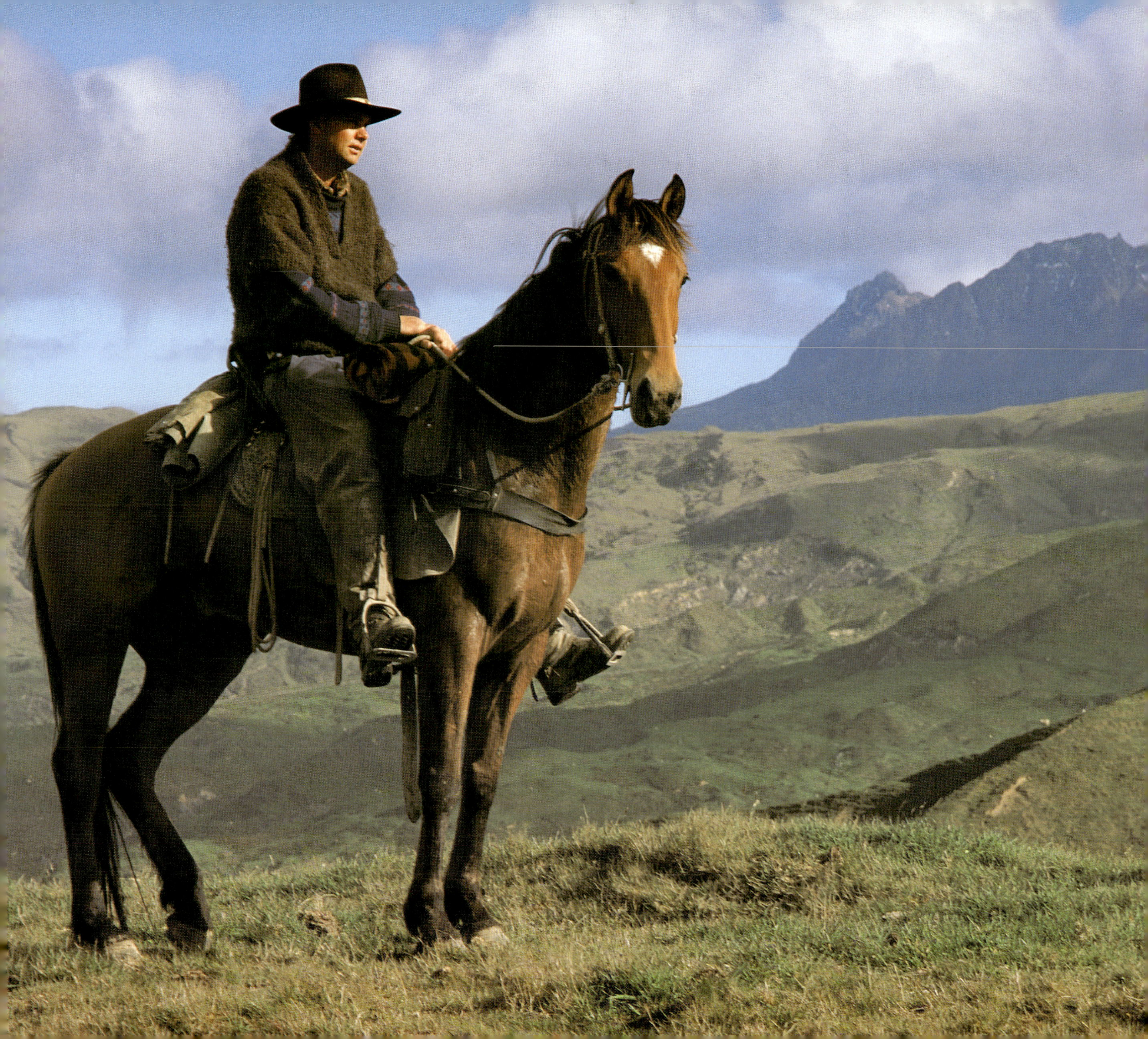

There was a rumble of dissent through the ranks, and it was Dan James who rose to the bait: 'That Hitler's a prick of a horse!'

'Should be put down,' someone else chimed in.

Tony raised a sandwich-filled hand in the air. 'He's not that bad.'

I caught Tony's eye and winked. 'Not many volunteers, are there?'

'Bit light on the ground.'

The drift of the conversation turned towards the following day's work. The team would run in some brood mares and foals from one of the back paddocks where they wintered to the yards at Pukeremu. Of course, that would mean another early start, setting out from headquarters before daybreak. It sounded like an interesting day's work, and when Tony invited me to join them I was quick to take him up on the offer.

Tony tossed the dregs of his tea into the long grass and stood up. 'Now who' — he raked his eyes over the upturned faces of the men — 'is gonna lead my horse home?'

For the third morning in a row I watched the sun rise and light a welcoming Hikurangi while the rest of the country was in darkness. And the mountain formed the backdrop when fifteen brood mares and their high-spirited foals came into sight and cantered down towards the yards at Pukeremu. Behind them came big Cooch Higgins.

For several hours, as the day warmed up, the men were hard at it. They clipped the mares' hooves and filed them neatly, then groomed their knotted manes

Cooch on Quake, with Hikurangi on the skyline.

Time for the horses to receive their beauty treatment.

and tangled tails. For the most part the mares were pretty stoical about it all, but the odd horse proved hard to handle.

Flint in particular gave Dan James a hard time. Twice as Dan worked on her feet Flint exploded into life, barrelling the stockman to the ground. Each time Dan rolled himself into a ball to protect himself, and he emerged with only a few bruises and badly skinned knuckles. And each time he bounced up hurling abuse at the animal.

After the second time, Tony pointed out that Dan was lucky not to be badly hurt and decided to take over. When he spoke to Flint in a soft voice and took his time, the mare quietened down and Tony was able to finish the job. But then the long-time manager on the mighty Ihungia never seemed to raise his voice, and never seemed to be in a hurry.

31

ONCE WERE TUSSOCKLANDS

Valerie Cottrell, as animated as she was English, proved to be a charming hostess on Oruamotua station.

We walked together in the early morning sun from her modern home to view a slice of history: the original homestead on Erewhon station. The single-storey building was in very poor condition, a real shame I thought. I said as much to Valerie.

'I agree, but the cost of keeping it up would be just too great,' she said. 'It was a very gracious house in its time. A lovely veranda, as you can see. The old Napier–Taihape road went right past it.'

She was referring to the old Maori trail that became known as the Inland Patea road. For years it was no more than a bullock track, and a trip from Napier to Taihape was a major undertaking.

'They had to pack everything in to build it,' Valerie Cottrell continued. 'It was all tussock country, you see.'

That was certainly true when Azim and William Birch took the run up in the 1860s. The snow tussock ran like an uncharted sea north to the Kaimanawa Mountains; the entire block of 50,000 hectares, contained by the Moawhango and Rangitikei Rivers, was truly a kingdom of grass.

Very little was known about the station's early days, beyond that the Birches ran sheep and had a good relationship with the Maoris of Moawhango. In any event, both Moawhango and the Birch brothers would

Oruamotua station, on the Inland Patea road.

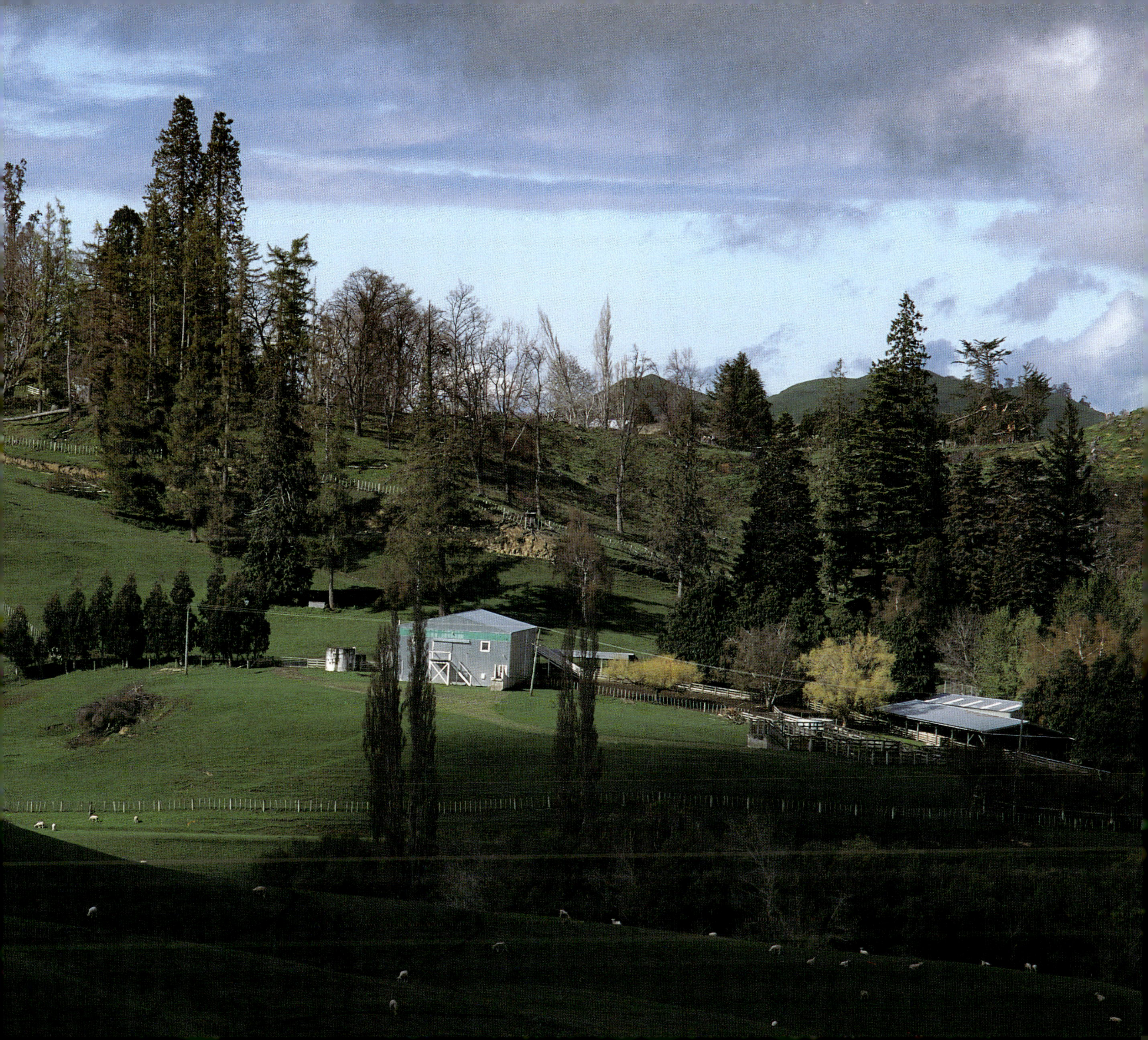

one way or another play a significant role in the life of one R. T. Batley.

Batley was a young lad when in 1863 he ran away from home in England and signed on as a cabin boy on a brig bound for New Zealand. When the *Royal Bride* was anchored off Napier a ferocious gale sprang up, the anchor was dislodged and in mountainous seas the ship corkscrewed towards the shore. Meantime, scores of Maoris gathered on the beach to watch the drama unfold.

When the order was given to abandon ship young Batley was terrorstruck — he could not swim. Within minutes he was the only man left on board. Recognising the man's plight, several of the Maoris on the beach locked arms and plunged into the sea in a human chain. Before long there was a line of two dozen men, those farthest out swimming, that extended about a third of the way to the ship.

They yelled out to the boy to jump for it, but for a lad fresh from the home country the prospect of the Maoris getting hold of him was almost as daunting as the pounding surf. 'Them fellas'll eat yer as soon as look at yer!' was the way most of the crew summed up the Maoris. Steeling himself, Batley plunged into the sea, which gobbled him up and spat him out like a piece of driftwood. The eager arms of the chain of men caught him and relayed him back to the beach.

The young cabin boy stood on the beach, frozen to the bone in all the clothes he owned — shirt, trousers, shoes — and without a penny to his name. R. T. Batley, all of thirteen years old, had finally arrived on the East Coast.

Batley stayed with his rescuers for several days — he would never forget their kindness — before setting off in search of a job. He found work on Maraekakaho, west of Hastings, and after two years' hard slog on the station considered himself a fully fledged shepherd.

For three more years Batley worked on the Hawke's Bay land, until in 1867, when he was eighteen, he heard talk of gold in the Inland Patea. He headed towards the centre of the island with his bedroll, his rifle and a few provisions. He was wary as he travelled — Maoris were still waging guerilla war with the British militia and could turn up just about anywhere.

Out on Erewhon station our hardy young adventurer met up with the Birch brothers. Gold? The only gold around here, they told him with some amusement, was still on the sheep's back. William Birch, however, admired the lad's courage in coming out to New Zealand alone, and offered him a job. R. T. Batley gladly accepted; already he had fallen under the spell of the Inland Patea.

Two years after Batley found work on Erewhon word spread through the Inland Patea, like fire in the tinder-dry tussock of high summer, that Te Kooti was heading south. The rebellious Maori leader was being hotly pursued by Colonel Thomas McDonnell and his troops, among them the feared Forest Rangers.

As it happened, Te Kooti and his followers were travelling more to the west than to the south, to the wilderness beyond Ruapehu. It was in this barren country that Te Kooti and McDonnell played a desperate game of hide-and-seek that went on just too long for the government forces — they ran out of food. When the Birch brothers heard of the situation, they decided to come to the rescue with food on the hoof — a big mob of sheep.

R. T. Batley and a handful of shepherds were assigned the responsibility of delivering the sheep safely to the

The old Maori trail came through this valley east of Moawhango.

Pakeha encampment. It was a dangerous job — there was always the possibility of ambush — but Batley was the man to take it on. In the end it was not the Maoris that gave them their biggest scare, it was the land itself. As they crossed the southern Kaimanawa Mountains Ruapehu, which had long been considered dormant, suddenly and violently erupted. With the mountain belching steam, ash and mud into the sky the sheepmen pressed on resolutely. There was no thought of turning back — not with the likes of R. T. Batley in charge, at any rate.

By the time he was twenty-four Batley had been made manager of Erewhon. In 1876 he made plans to return to England for a visit and his days on Erewhon came to an end. In his diary he recorded his last days on the station like this:

'December 30, 1876. Fine day, very warm. McI. and I rode out to Korokonui and counted and took delivery of over 5000 pieces of timber. Measured 48 chains of bush road. Rode back to Erewhon. Reached there 8.30 pm. Caught fresh horses and rode right down to Hastings without a spell, reaching there a little before 12 noon on Sunday. I had ridden nearly 100 miles, and 85 without rest or food of any sort, and no sleep since a little after 4 o'clock on Saturday morning.'

And so the young man, already with a lifetime of adventures behind him, returned home. While he was in England he met, courted and married Emily Snelling, and a year later he returned with her to the land he now regarded as his real home.

He found employment at a Hawke's Bay station before himself taking up land in the headwaters of the Waikato. There, with the blessing of the local tribe, he grazed his sheep on Tongariro's sacred slopes. But the lure of the Inland Patea was too strong and in 1882 he took up a small block at Moawhango and opened a store there. Later, in partnership with the Maoris, he developed a sheep station that eventually ran as many as 70,000 sheep.

R. T. Batley died in 1917. They said that out at Moawhango the sun went down early that day.

From what Valerie Cottrell was able to tell me, it seemed pretty certain that Azim and William Birch — a volatile

At Moawhango.

partnership at times — had an irreconcilable disagreement in the late 1890s and decided to divide the station. They both declared that they wanted the part that included the old homestead, but it was Azim who ended up with it. A disgruntled William took on the less desirable part of the station but insisted on retaining the station name of Erewhon. Azim named his station Oruamotua, after the survey district and the meeting house in Moawhango. The stations both stayed in the Birch family until 1920, when they were further subdivided.

Today Oruamotua station was run by Mark Cottrell, Valerie's stepson. They ran Romney sheep on 525 hectares on which, as far as I could see, not a clump of tussock grew.

Presently Valerie and I left the old homestead and

came to the track that had once been the Inland Patea road, and before that an ancient Maori trail. And then I was on my way, driving out past the cherry trees that Valerie's late husband had planted.

As I left the station, Valerie's parting words were still with me. 'Part of me is entirely here,' she had said with deep feeling. 'It is a magic spot for me. I love it.'

She wasn't alone in feeling that way.

They were flat out at the sheepyards when I arrived at Ohinewairua station, once part of Azim Birch's block. Richard Hayes, owner of the station since 1974, was working hard, alongside his son and stock manager Mark, and three shepherds.

When things had quietened down a little, Richard took me for a run out back, to the highest point on the station. From 1020 metres we overlooked the valley of the Aorangi Stream. In the valley was a cluster of buildings near the stream — homestead, woolshed, sheepyards, cattleyards, shearers' quarters. Richard told me this was the Aorangi out-station, an easy thirty-minute drive from the main station complex.

Directly below us sheep grazed beneath the rimrock bluffs. Back in the time of the Birches the Ohinewairua flock were Merinos; later Romneys were tried and, since Richard's arrival, Corriedales. The flock now had a very strong Corriedale influence — according to Richard, they were a great sheep for the high country. They wintered over 50,000 stock units, including over 1000 cattle — these were mainly Angus — and 900 red deer.

We turned away from the lookout point and made our way back to the vehicle, passing the occasional lonely clump of snow tussock. The valley of the Aorangi looked real fine now, I thought, but how grand it must

The sheepyards at Ohinewairua.

have looked 500 or 600 years ago, when moas ranged the tussocklands.

We returned to the homestead by a different route; on the way Richard remarked on how lucky we'd been with the weather that day. They'd just had more than a week of rain, sleet and snow and that, as Richard put it, rather took the edge off things.

I couldn't disagree with him there.

There wasn't much sign of life when I arrived at Erewhon station; apparently the men, under manager Larry Walker, were off docking. Around here docking took eighteen days.

I spent some time with cook Vickie Bryan, who'd had seventeen years on stations at Hunterville and on the East Coast before coming to Erewhon. Her husband David was a general hand on the place.

That morning Vickie had cooked a six o'clock breakfast for the four regular men as well as several casuals, and she would serve up another feed for them all in the evening. She reckoned life was pretty busy on Erewhon.

The station was owned by Auckland businessman Peter Spencer. He didn't visit too often, but planned to renovate the old homestead. The building looked to me to date from the time the Birches owned the place.

Spencer had recently bought the adjacent Springvale station, which brought the property up to 6900 hectares. They had wintered about 70,000 stock units.

Close to the Napier–Taihape road, east of the bridge spanning the Rangitikei, stood an isolated cottage. The last time I had passed this way Otupae out-station had been empty, but this time it was a different story.

A big black dog came bounding up to the closed gate when I went to open it. I hesitated — it paid to be wary of big black dogs on the other side of closed gates. There was no need for concern, though, because this particular big black dog was grinning like a high-country idiot.

'Hey, fella,' I said in greeting, matching his smile with an equally loony one of my own.

Big black dog stood with his paws on the top of the gate, swatting at invisible flies with his long tail and slobbering quietly. Behind him a slim, smiling woman strolled up to meet me. She introduced herself as Jane Dick.

'Great guard dog,' I remarked.

Vickie Bryan, station cook at Erewhon.

A snack for some of Jane Dick's friends.

ONCE WERE TUSSOCKLANDS • 317

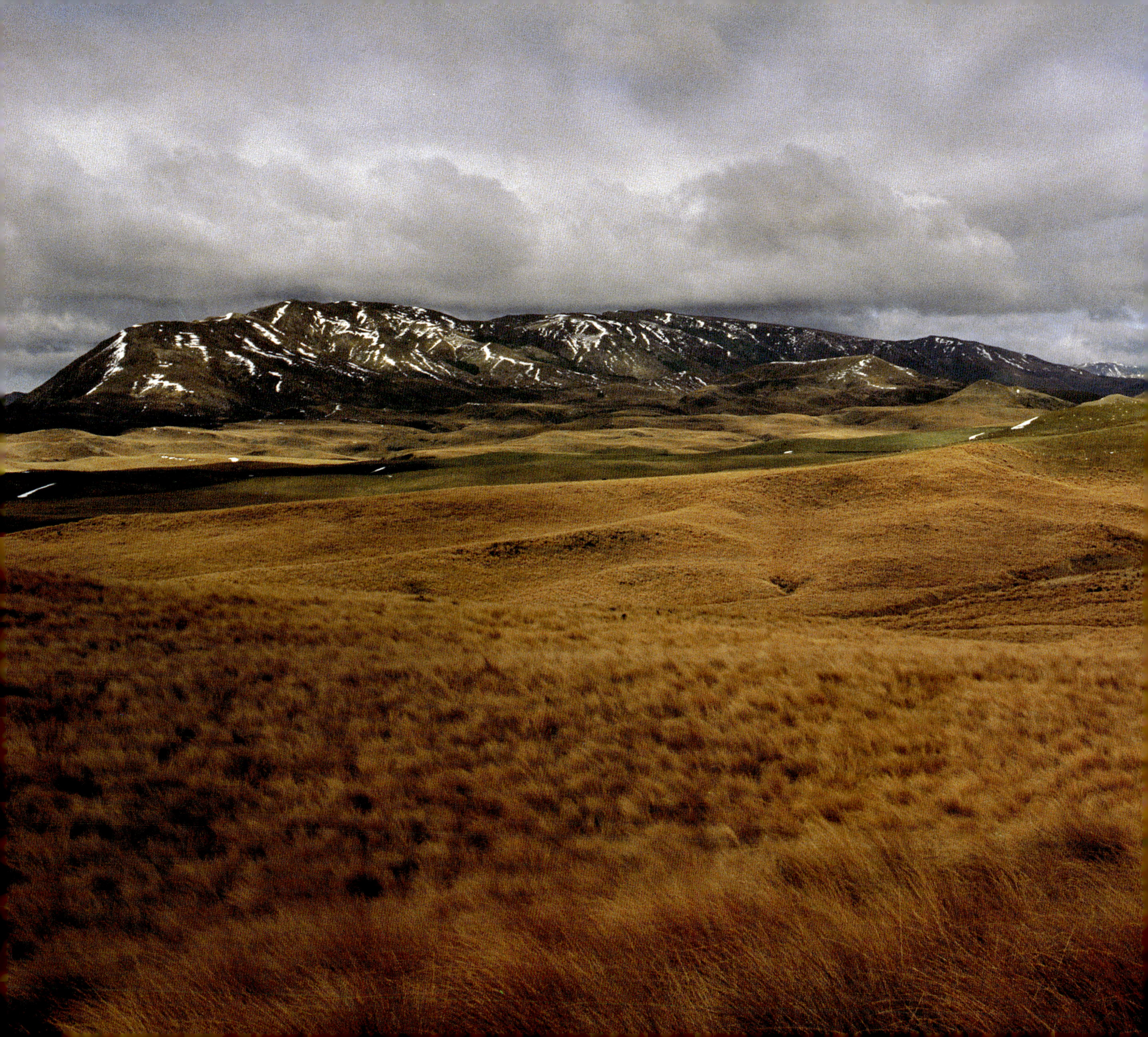

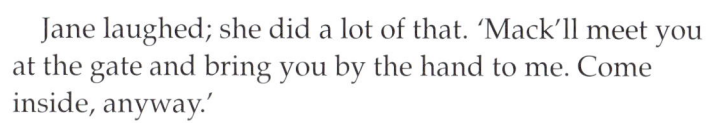

Jane laughed; she did a lot of that. 'Mack'll meet you at the gate and bring you by the hand to me. Come inside, anyway.'

I followed Jane to a warm, pleasant kitchen, basic but comfortable. I turned down a kind offer of lunch, settling for a cup of tea. While Jane made the tea, she told me that she and her husband Bruce, a fencer and general hand, had been out there for about twenty months. Way back, perhaps twenty years earlier, they both worked down the road on Ohinewairua.

At present Bruce was feeding out on a daily basis. On Otupae's 8600 hectares, where they wintered in excess of 50,000 stock units, this was a demanding chore. Especially in bad weather.

I wondered how Jane spent her days at the remote out-station, with the kids long gone.

'I spin,' she replied. 'I grow my own wool.'

Jane had her own small flock of sheep, including Cecil, a Merino ram. His wool, she told me, was lovely and fine: much finer than that of the other breeds she had raised. Jane used the wool in knitted garments.

Out in a grassy paddock adjacent to the house we took a look at Jane's flock. All but Cecil, who was uneasy with a stranger around, came to her quickly.

'This is Jacko,' she said, picking up one of Cecil's offspring. Mack jumped up and licked the lamb, but Jacko didn't seem to mind.

'You know,' Jane said, 'I never get bored out here. How could I? There isn't enough time in the day for me.'

I left Jane Dick to her flock, her spinning, her knitting and her home. Rural neurosis? No, not for the likes of her.

Once this land was all tussock.

32

GUTHRIE-SMITH'S WONDERFUL LEGACY

On Tutira station in Hawke's Bay manager Steve Reiri grinned broadly as he recalled meeting Peter Newton, the author of, among others, a series of books about station life in the late 1960s and early 1970s.

It was about 1968, Steve told me, and he was then working on the Maori-owned Owahanga. The station took up just about 7000 hectares of northern Wairarapa coastal country between the Owahanga River to the north and the Mataikona River to the south. They carried 19,000 sheep over winter, and nearly 30,000 after lambing. The Owahanga shed, dating to 1938 and capable of holding 4000 sheep overnight in an enclosed area of 830 square metres, was the biggest in the country.

On Tutira a good quarter of a century later, Steve said reflectively, 'Yeah, Owahanga was a big operation, all right. Still is too, I hear.' He seemed vastly amused — in fact he had been smiling ever since Peter Newton's name came up in the conversation.

I asked Steve why that was.

Steve's grin was joined by a throaty chuckle; the powerful man's laughter lines became more deeply etched. 'Well,' he explained, 'Peter Newton was a South Islander and worked on many of the big stations down there. Never came up here. He was pretty hacked off because in all of his travels in the North Island he hadn't seen a decent-sized mob of sheep to photograph for his book.' Steve started laughing. 'He said that down south

The Tutira woolshed with the lake beyond.

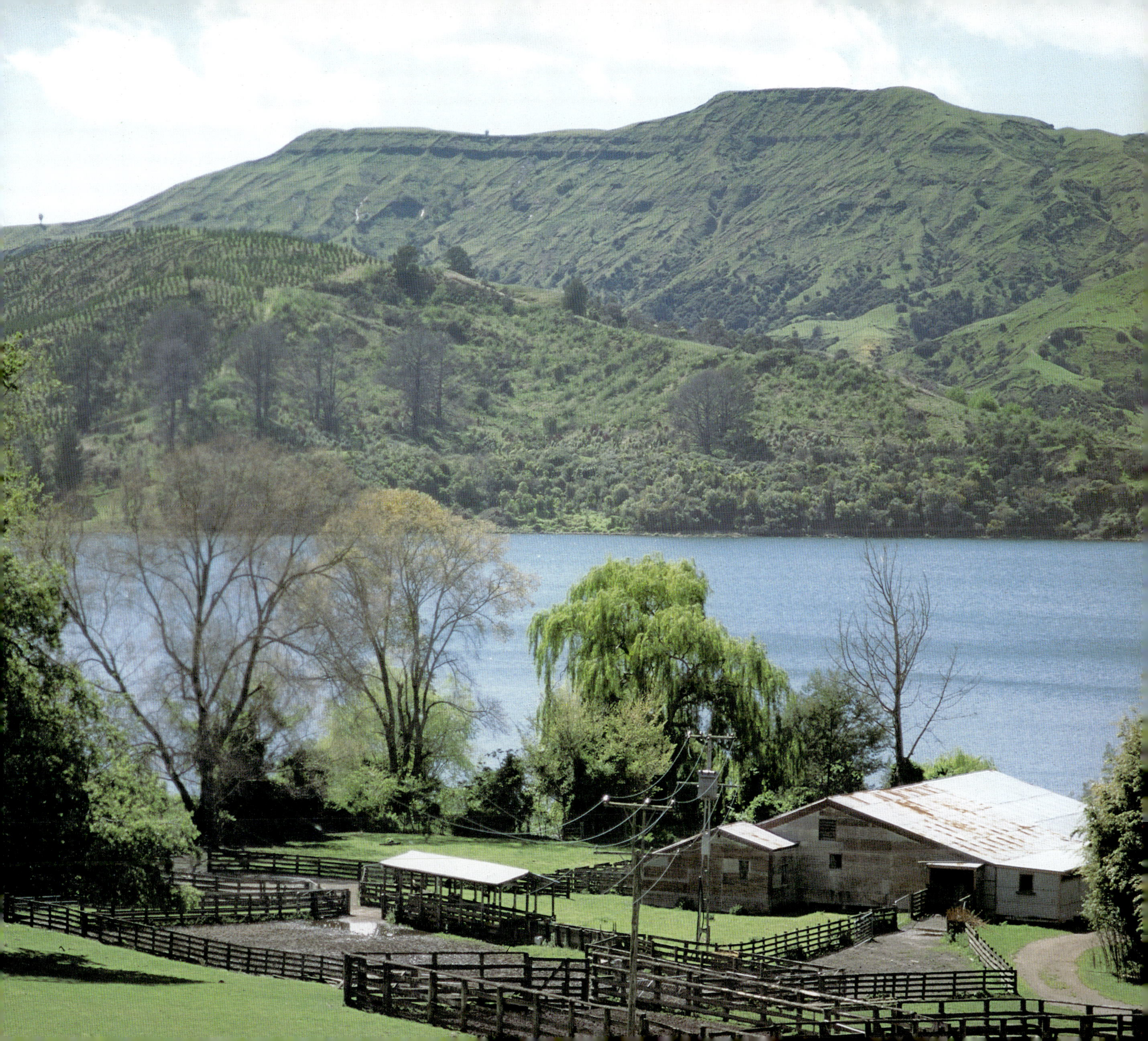

that was never a worry — big mobs were everywhere.' He laughed even harder.

I guess you had to be a sheepman to appreciate the humour.

Now, on a gorgeous Sunday morning, a relaxed Steve Reiri and I walked out of the homestead, which dated to about 1913, and strolled up a gentle incline to the place William Herbert Guthrie-Smith was buried.

It was a lovely spot in the spring. A warm breeze fanned gently across the hillside, ruffling the ferns that framed the headstone. Sunshine filtered through the branches of the tall shade trees to lie in dappled patches, light upon dark, on the ground. The air was clear and good to breathe.

From the graveside you could look down to the old woolshed on the flat, and beyond to Lake Tutira. This was, I thought, a fitting place for the great man to be buried, for the lake and the station were both a part of one man's wonderful legacy to the young people of New Zealand.

Never inclined to call himself by his first name, Herbert Guthrie-Smith was born in Scotland in 1861. In 1880 he and Arthur Cunningham, a friend from his schooldays, sailed for New Zealand, intent on becoming sheepmen in the distant colony.

For two years Guthrie-Smith learned the ropes as a cadet on the estate of his uncle, George Dennistoun of Peel Forest, South Canterbury. Then in 1882 Guthrie-Smith and Cunningham formed a partnership and took up the lease of Tutira, a 8000-hectare riot of scrub and bracken.

Good friends do not necessarily make good business partners, and so it proved with the two young Scots. Within a few years a disgruntled Cunningham wanted out and Guthrie-Smith instead joined forces on Tutira with T. J. Stuart.

The two new partners worked well together and by the mid-1890s they had taken on the leases on two more blocks of Maori land adjoining Tutira. The station was now about 25,000 hectares and upon it they ran at peak times as many as 38,000 sheep. By 1903 the station was a paying proposition and free of debt, and Guthrie-Smith was able to buy Stuart out.

The run gradually decreased in size as, first, the leases on the two blocks of Maori land expired and, second, Guthrie-Smith sublet eight farms to returned soldiers and those who had previously worked on the station. He was a rare man, Herbert Guthrie-Smith.

The lease on Tutira finally ran out in 1936. In the meantime the Maori owners had sold off some of their Tutira land to the government, including the Homestead block. Guthrie-Smith acquired freehold title to the 800-hectare block, which included Lake Tutira, and lived there until he died in 1940.

Two years later, in accordance with Herbert Guthrie-

The Reiri family: Margaret, Matthew, Megan and Steve.

The lovely Lake Tutira is serenity itself.

Smith's wishes, the Homestead block was taken over by a trust set up to help young people. A farm cadet scheme was established to assist underprivileged young men with ambitions to work on the land.

Today the Guthrie-Smith Trust was as active as ever on Tutira and an educational youth centre, looked after by manager Paul Jennings, catered for between 2500 and 3000 youngsters a year.

The day-to-day running of the station was left to Steve Reiri, who had held the manager's job for three years. They ran more than 4000 Romneys and 430 Angus/Hereford cattle. Steve handled the workload with the help of a married shepherd, Blue Macmillan.

A little later I drove down to the lake. Tutira looked very lovely as the light wind disturbed the water, making the black swans bob gently on the surface. The lake was a designated wildlife sanctuary, largely as a result of Herbert Guthrie-Smith's work in developing it.

More than just a station holder, Herbert Guthrie-Smith was an expert on natural history, author of several books — including *Tutira*, the classic account of life on a sheep station — ornithologist, conservationist and philanthropist. He was truly a remarkable man.

33

IN THE GRAND STYLE

A blood-red sun edged slowly out of sight behind the clear-cut ranges to the west and the broad plains of Hastings and its suburbs were bathed momentarily in a wondrous light. A red-painted woolshed, to the left of the road, was brilliantly accented; as I stopped to admire it the light was already fading.

To judge by the shape of its roofing, the turret and the design of a high window, this was an old building. It surely dated to before the turn of the century, back when this was station land. It would have been easy enough to find out the building's history, but for once I refrained from doing so.

Instead I was content to allow the woolshed to be for me a symbol of a different time, when the early settlers built their homes with a grandeur they saw as befitting their status. When things were done in the grand style.

My feelings for Hawke's Bay were warm — what had happened to me here was good. I felt comfortable there, for very little had changed since I first came to the Bay in the early 1960s. I was a professional hunter then, based out at Kuripapango. I was hunting in the Kaweka Range then and I often spent my time off in Napier or Hastings. Later I worked in the Ruahine Range and out beyond Rissington.

The name of one station, Gwavas, had stayed in my mind ever since those days. It was a famous old station; the Gwavas State Forest was established on land that

The red barn on the outskirts of Hastings.

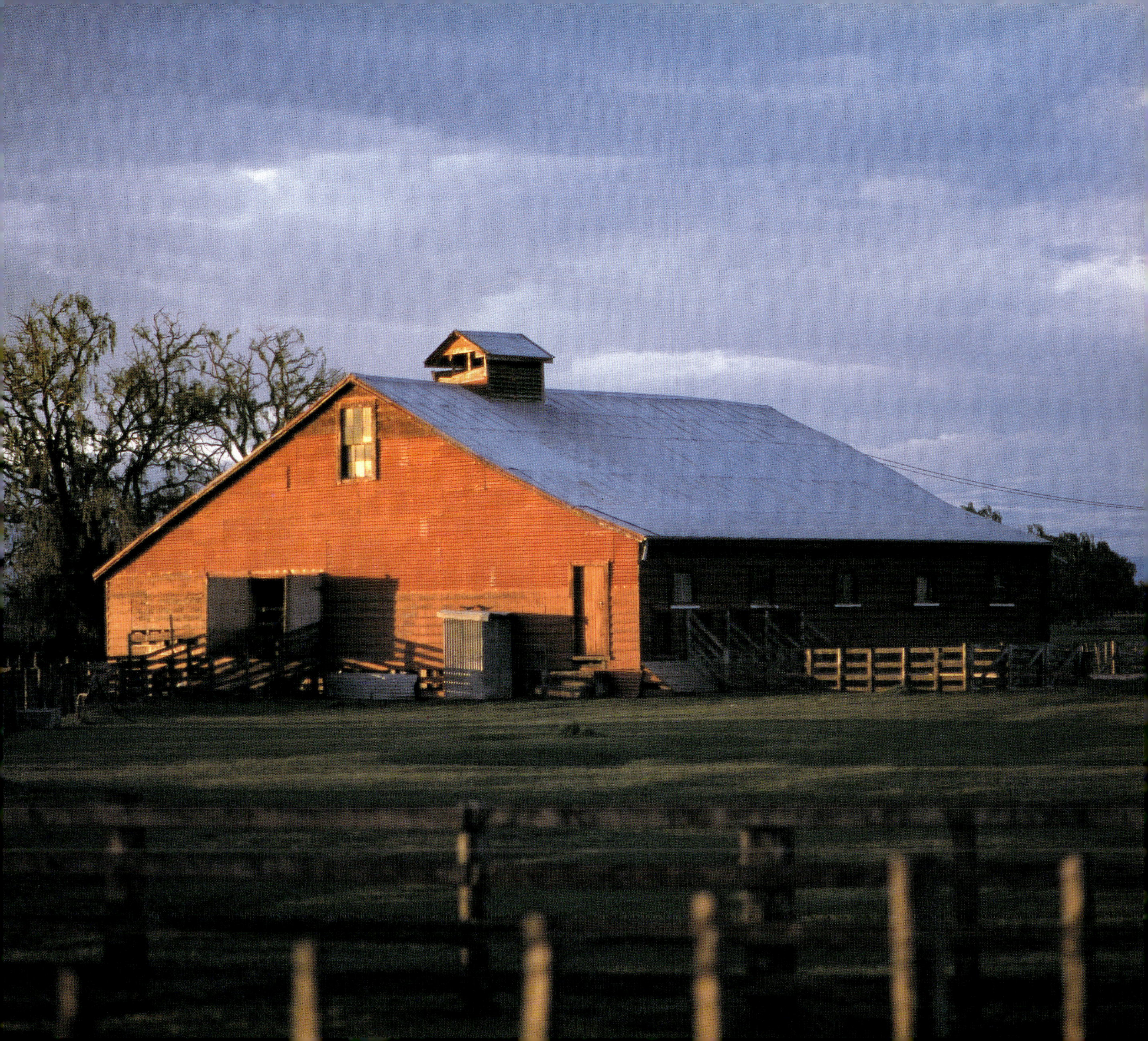

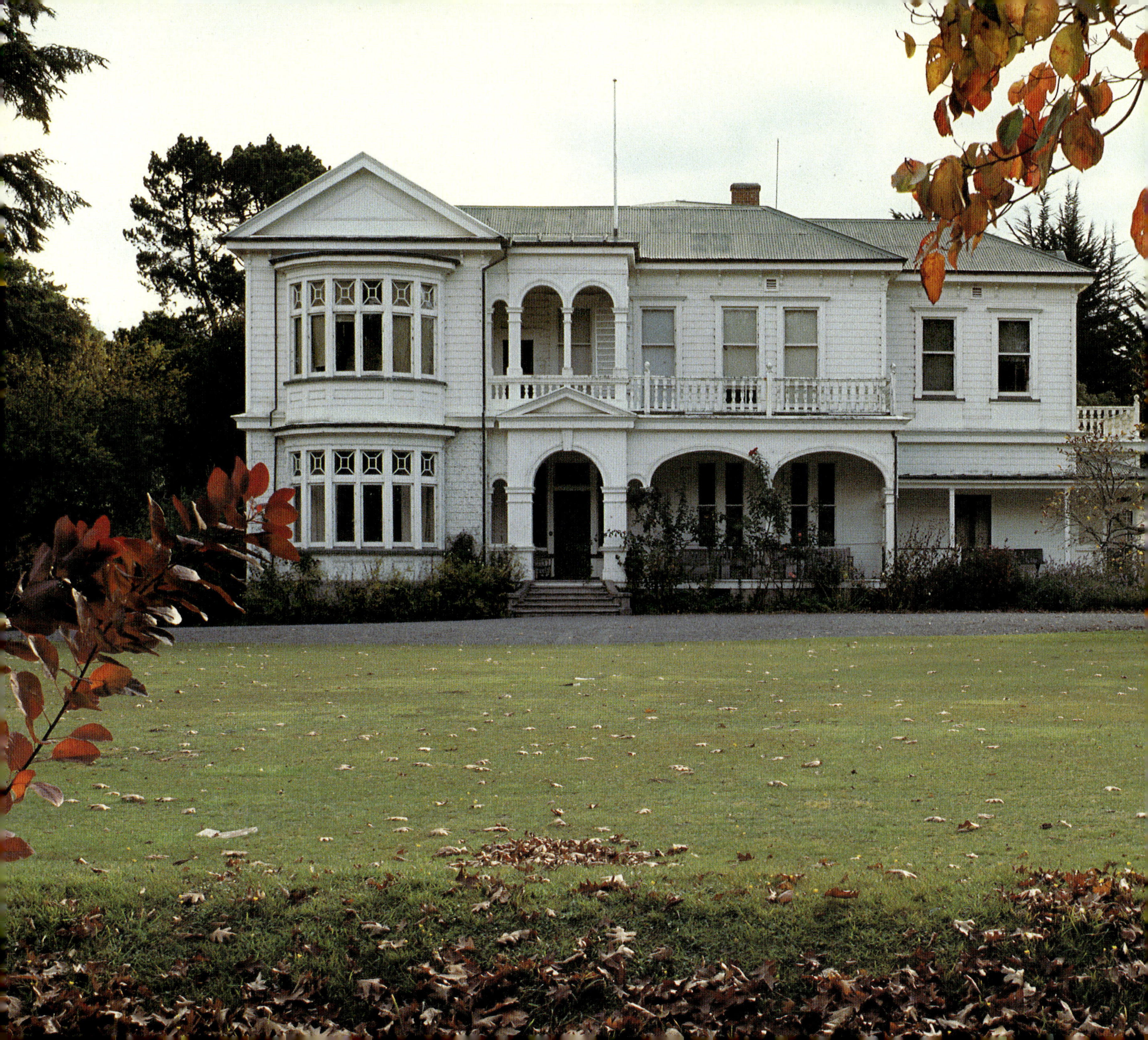

was once part of the station. Now, many years later, I came to the entrance to Gwavas station, a long winding driveway leading through a magnificent stand of trees to the unseen homestead. Today I drove on past, but two years earlier I had turned off the road and up the drive, to find myself alone in a place where time really did stand still.

It was a cool and overcast afternoon as I drove through the towering pines, planted over ninety years earlier. The gravel driveway, climbing so gradually that you were hardly aware of it, brought me to a flat area of lawns and shrubbery, and the century-old homestead.

I parked my vehicle and walked across the lawns towards the homestead in all its elegant splendour. There was a chill in the air; the brittle red and gold leaves of autumn drifted down from garden trees that would soon be bare. I might have been half way around the world in the garden of an English stately home.

I was alone. Quite alone. The homestead had not been used since 1960. I shook my head and wondered to myself why this should be. It appeared sound enough — its condition was just as good as, say, the still-used homestead on Brancepeth. Strange.

I had recently visited another fine old Hawke's Bay homestead, another that had been built in the grand style. The Springvale homestead dated to 1903, although the property had first been taken up in 1857 by Lancastrian Jonathan Holden. At the time I visited, the descendants of Holden still owned the station and lived in the homestead. This was as it should be.

Gwavas station originally comprised 10,000 hectares of freehold land and about 2000 hectares of leasehold

The Gwavas homestead, empty since 1960.

Maori land. A 33-year-old Cornishman, Major George Gwavas Carlyon, had purchased the land in 1858. By 1860 the Major was running more than 4000 sheep.

During the 1860s the Major, fresh from the Crimean War and fearing attack by the Maoris, regularly drilled his station hands and, under his skilled guidance, they all became proficient rifle shots. All the preparation was wasted — the station was never under threat.

When the Major died in 1875 he left part of the station to his son Arthur, who later gained title to the whole property. In 1888 Arthur Carlyon established on Gwavas the first Angus stud in the North Island. In time his cattle became famous and won prizes around the country.

It was in Arthur Carlyon's time that the grand old homestead was built. The staircase was panelled in locally sawn totara; the large windows were leaded and there were many shady verandas. During this period more than 20,000 trees were planted on the station, mostly as shelter belts.

Life on Gwavas was pretty good in the early part of this century. There were twenty-five permanent hands on the payroll, 21,000 Romney sheep on the hill and fifty horses in the paddock.

With the death in 1928 of Arthur Carlyon began a new era on Gwavas. The property, reduced by this time to about 7500 hectares, was inherited by Arthur's children.

Today Gwavas was owned by John Hudson and his family. John looked after the place with occasional help. The station stood at 1200 hectares and carried a flock of Romney/Lincoln sheep. When I asked John why no one lived in the old homestead, he just shrugged and said they didn't, and that was all.

The Holdens' Springvale homestead.

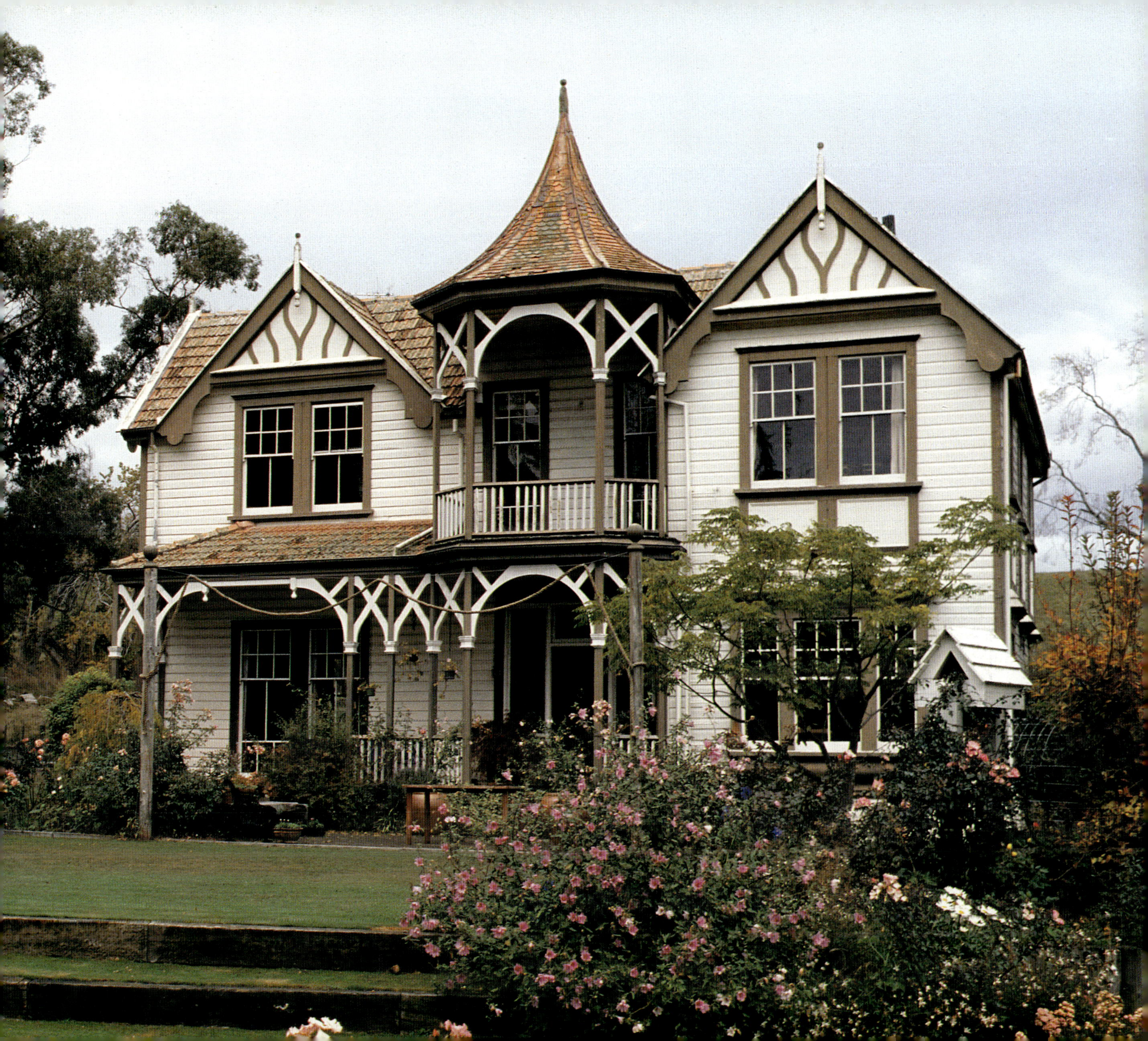

MEETING PLACE OF THE GODS

Fronting the broad sweep of Palliser Bay, the A-framed whare was sited on the boundary between Wharekauhau and Orongorongo stations. Behind the whare rose the steep slopes, heavily forested higher up, of the southern extremity of the Rimutaka Range. Over the years the whare, often battered by gales rampaging from the south, had provided shelter for many: musterers, fishermen, hunters, trampers and horseriders.

On this wet spring dawn the whare was a welcome haven for a three-strong mustering team from Wharekauhau station. Soon they would begin to muster the Mukamuka country, taking the sheep along the coast to the station headquarters.

There was time for a brew before work. Driftwood was quickly collected and a fire started in the rock fireplace in front of the whare. A Swanndri-clad Joe Houghton made the tea, while his huntaway, Sally, watched him keenly.

The men crouched near the fire to drink their tea. Why did billy tea, particularly when made outdoors, taste so much better? The rain fell lightly, running easily off the heavy oilskin riding coats worn by Bill and John Shaw. Mist lurked about the tops.

The rain increased, the wind swirled and the sea became rougher and rougher, the waves breaking over jagged rocks like so many white horses tumbling to their knees. The men moved away from the fire, eyes

Nothing quite like billy tea. From left: John Shaw, Joe Houghton and Bill Shaw.

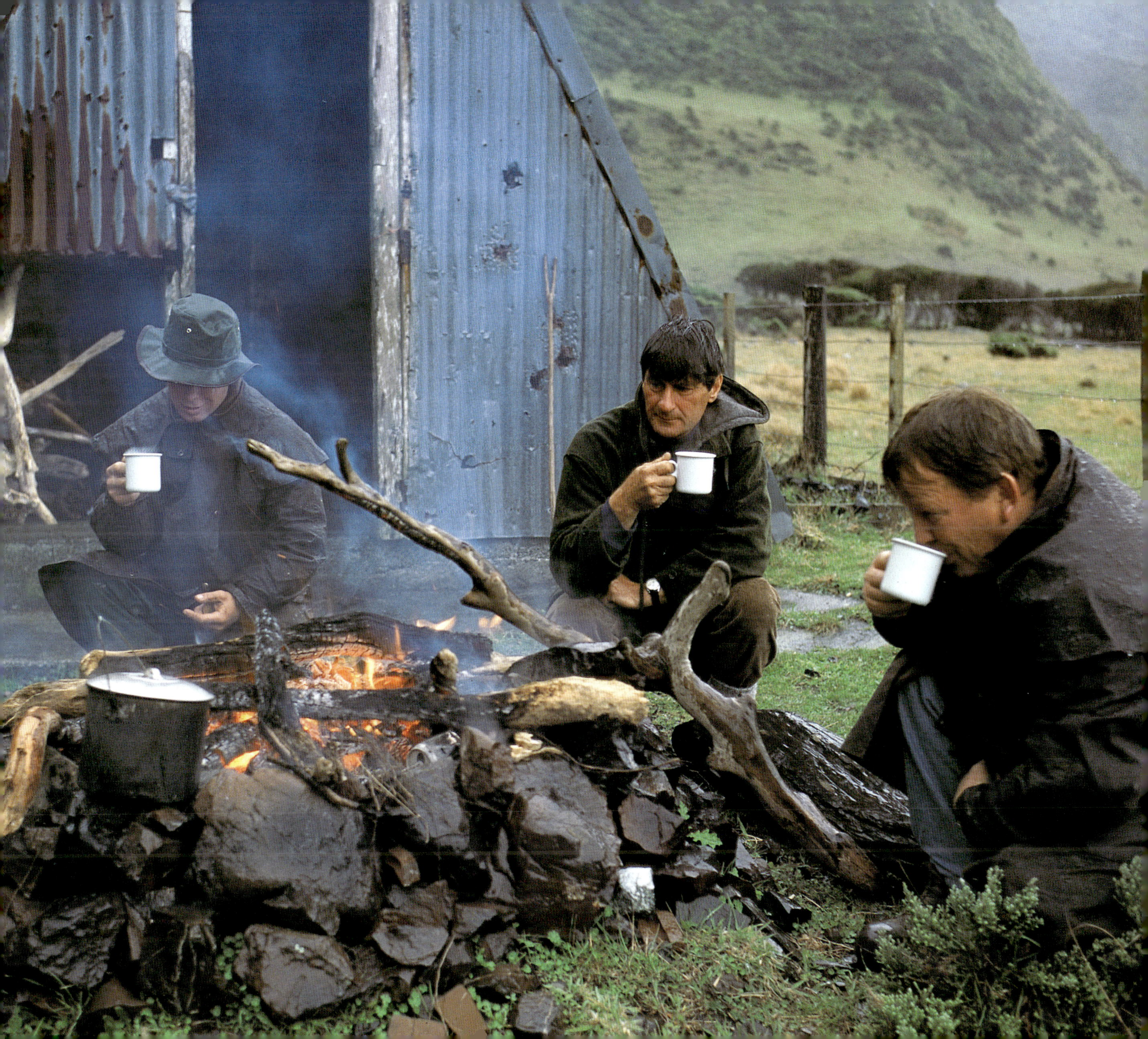

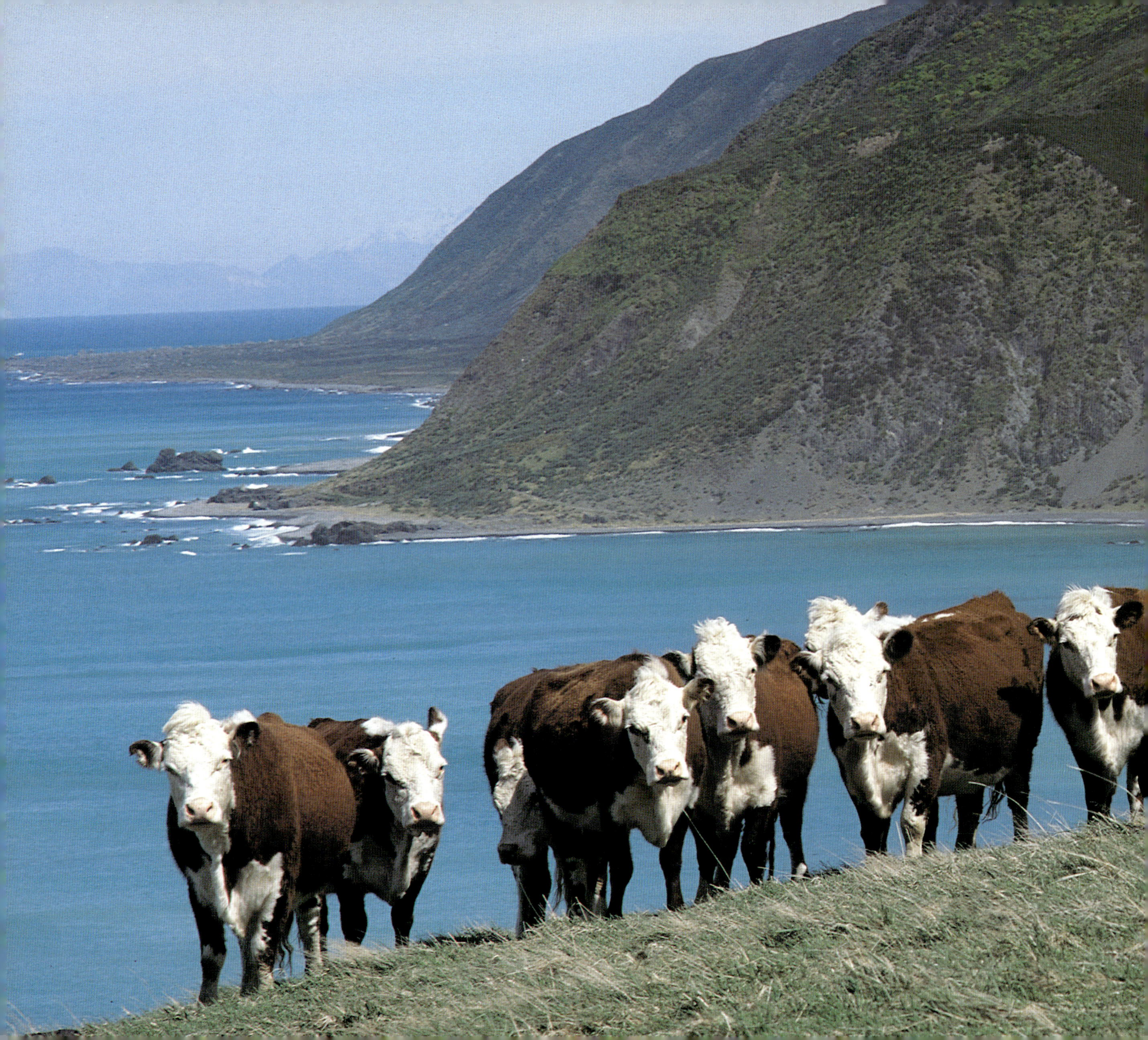

MEETING PLACE OF THE GODS • 333

stinging from smoke, and retreated to the tomb-like interior of the whare.

'It's gotta get better, Bill,' said Joe easily.

In his mid-fifties, Joe was trim and very fit, and not a grey hair on his head. He'd lived all his life on this particular piece of coastline.

Bill, too, was unperturbed about the weather. He was in his late forties, getting a bit heavier with the years, but still as whimsical as ever. Finally he said, 'Yeah, Joe, it has got to get better . . . sooner or later.' He smiled a mischievous little smile. 'Whaddaya reckon, Johnny?'

'About what?' said Johnny, straight-faced. He caught my eye and winked. Like father, like son.

John Shaw, at twenty-three years old, was in charge of stock management, which meant looking after as many as 10,000 sheep and 200 head of Hereford cattle. I doubted he was losing sleep over the responsibility — he was a very capable sort.

Five dogs peered enquiringly into the gloomy room while we had our second cup of bushman's brew and waited for the weather to lift. A powerful gust of wind slammed into the whare.

'It isn't getting any better,' Joe remarked.

'Better leave it till the morning, Johnny?' Bill asked, and Johnny nodded in the agreement. What the hell were they hanging round here for?

The next morning, by contrast, was truly delightful: a picture-postcard scene on Palliser Bay with the cattle grazing on the grassy hills above the remains of Maori gardens perhaps 700 years old. The sea was a make-believe blue; beyond it the South Island's snow-capped Kaikoura Range stood out distinctly. The Maoris had

Herefords graze on the sunny, windswept hills above Palliser Bay.

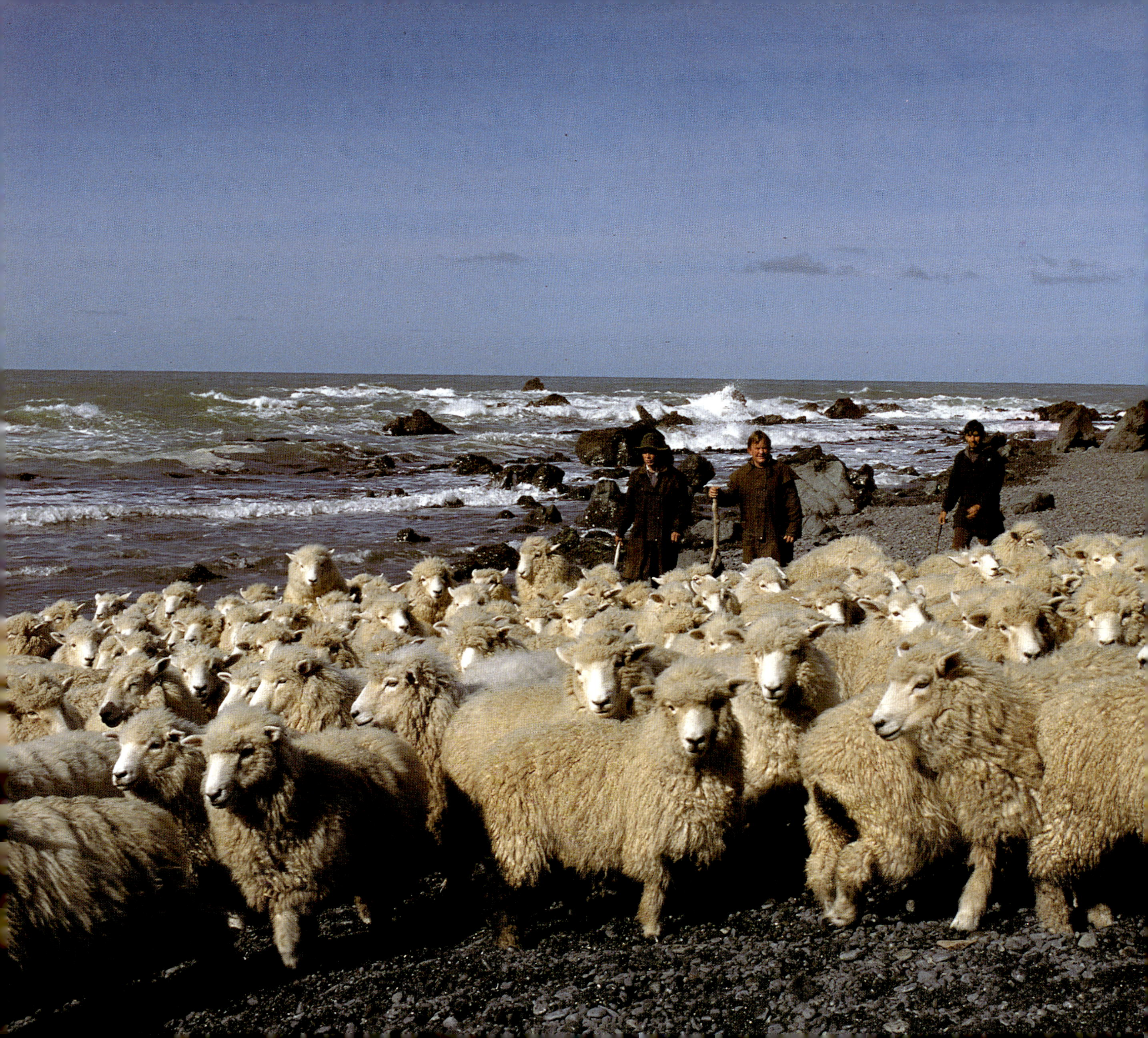

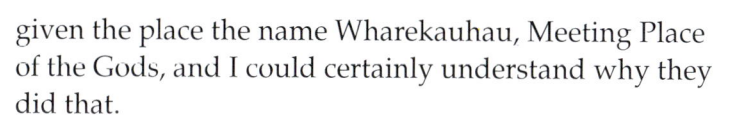

given the place the name Wharekauhau, Meeting Place of the Gods, and I could certainly understand why they did that.

Joe Houghton and his dogs Sally and Prince were working the tumbledown true left of Mukamuka Stream. Sam the labrador was also tagging along. Sam wasn't as quick as he had once been, but he wasn't past nailing possums good and hard.

The dog sniffed excitedly at the foot of a hollow tree. Joe moved quickly to it.

'Possum, for sure,' Joe said.

He craned his neck to peer into the dark recess. Lightning-fast, he reached inside, dragged out a possum and hurled it towards a small bush. Sam, growling, was on it in a flash. He took it by the neck and shook it so hard the fur literally flew, just the way a Jack Russell would kill a rat.

'Good boy,' said Joe.

Sam, standing over his kill, puffed out his considerable chest.

'Maybe DoC ought to give him a job?' I suggested. 'How does Ranger Sam sound?'

Huntaway Sally was on the job soon after, eagerly pursuing a fair-sized mob of woolly-backed speedsters as they rock-hopped the Mukamuka Stream. Joe, hands on hips, just watched her work.

Presently we came to an area of level ground where, Joe told me, the Red whare had once stood. Like so many farm buildings all over the country, it had burned down.

'Used to camp here many times in the old days,' Joe said rather wistfully.

Joe had first come out to Wharekauhau as a baby

The Romneys head for home.

when his father worked here as a shepherd. Joe himself started work on the place in 1956, and he'd stayed ever since.

'All horses back then, I suppose?' I asked.

'Huh?' I had disturbed Joe's daydream. 'Oh, yeah, all horses. Never had any time for them myself.'

Surprisingly, Joe Houghton was in fact an accomplished horseman — generally speaking, you don't reach that level unless you have a genuine liking for them. But Joe had shed no tears when horses were phased out on Wharekauhau in the early 1970s.

Within the hour the stationmen had met up on the beach, Johnny astride his four-wheel farm bike and Bill on foot. The sheep were herded together in one big bunch. They hadn't got them all but, as Joe explained, you didn't expect to in the Mukamuka. Given the rough nature of the country, even after two or three sweeps you were likely to miss some.

'Get in behind, Sally!' Joe called. 'Get in behind.'

At once the huntaway ducked in behind the sheep.

'Come in, Sally.'

Sally came rushing to her master, leaping up with dirty paws. Joe shook his head at her in mock anger.

'She's the tourists' favourite, you know,' Joe said. 'They've buggered her up, you know. Never used to jump at me — can't stop her now.' He ruffled her ears with affection. 'Still, it hasn't affected her working ability — she still does as much as ever. Eh, Sally?'

Joe later told me that, when one of his dogs was too old to work, he would never sell it or give it away. Instead it would be pensioned off to become a family pet. When his dogs died, they had a special place where they were buried, on a headland overlooking the sea.

'You know,' said Joe, 'all of our dogs on the station are our best mates.'

Joe's love for his dogs was as naked as a candle flame in an old musterers' hut.

The sheep were spilling through the layered outcrops of salt-encrusted rocks now, and the men, all on foot, crowded hard behind them.

Johnny directed his huntaways Brin and Sharp, while Joe waved his arms in the air to further encourage the sheep to keep moving. Crooked hillstick in hand, Bill was happy to mooch along behind.

The sure-footed Romneys, soon to be shorn, angled briskly through a rock-studded landscape that had been formed by a major earthquake nearly 140 years earlier. The earthquake struck just nine years after the very first sheep were brought around the coast.

The first European to bring sheep from Wellington to the natural pastures of the Wairarapa, and so the man who in effect invented sheepfarming in this country, was Charles Bidwill.

In 1844 the 24-year-old Englishman, his head shepherd William Swainson and a boy travelled with two packhorses and two dogs; the flock numbered 350 Australian Merinos. The party reached the Mukamuka Rocks some time in late April. Even at low tide each and every struggling Merino had to be manhandled down from the rocks and into the surf, and then carried piggyback to safety on the far side. Not one sheep was lost.

The earthquake of 1855 was to have a dramatic impact on the Mukamuka Rocks. The land rose by 2 metres and the sea pulled back about 40 metres, and the Mukamuka Rocks were left standing high and dry. Who said miracles didn't happen?

Johnny, Bill and Joe.

MEETING PLACE OF THE GODS • 337

Bidwill continued on around the bay with the sheep, eventually reaching the 3-kilometre long spit that separated Lake Onoke from the sea. He knew that the crossing of the bar at the end of the spit was a simple enough matter — a number of return trips in a Maori canoe. But to the young Englishman's disappointment he had come at just the wrong time. After heavy rain floodwaters had spewed out of Lake Wairarapa and were now surging over the Onoke Bar. There was no way the bar could be crossed; Bidwill had no option but to wait until the floodwaters receded.

Men and sheep wheeled about and retraced their steps in search of shelter and feed for the stock, which they found at Wharepapa. Bidwill decided it was an opportune moment to return to the Hutt Valley, and left Swainson in charge.

Meanwhile, a second party of Wairarapa-bound sheepmen had set out from the Hutt Valley. William Vavasour, Frederick Weld and Henry Petre, all of English stock, were bringing with them close to 600 sheep, mostly Merinos, belonging to Charles Clifford. The sheep were going to a block called Wharekaka, next to Charles Bidwill's block, Kopungarara, southeast of today's Carterton.

When Clifford's party reached the Mukamuka Rocks, they faced a much tougher task than Bidwill had — this time a fierce southerly airflow was whipping up the surf. There were some stock losses; only 400 out of the 600 sheep landed at Wellington reached the Wairarapa, so the losses at Mukamuka were quite likely considerable.

On 8 May 1844 Clifford's party caught up with Swainson, who was still camped at Wharepapa. Next morning they crossed the Onoke Bar by canoe, leaving Swainson and his charges behind them.

And so Clifford's party reached Wharekaka a full week before Bidwell. But any claims that Vavasour, Weld and Petre were the first Europeans to bring sheep to the Wairarapa were quite unfounded. It was Charles Bidwell, with his 350 Merinos out of New South Wales, who actually entered the area first.

Interestingly enough, in the *New Zealand Gazette and Wellington Spectator* of 24 April 1844, editor William Fox wrote:

'Mr Duke entered the Wairarapa last week with about 40 head of cattle. Mr Duke is the first settler in that fine district. Mr Bidwell has started with sheep and cattle, Messrs Clifford and Vavasour are about to send sheep there immediately. Squatting is evidently the order of the day.'

To the best of my knowledge there were no other published claims that Captain Henry Duke was the first to take stock into the Wairarapa. Was this simply irresponsible and inaccurate journalism, or was it possible that in fact it was neither Clifford nor Bidwill but Duke that was the real pioneer?

It was the birds that woke me with their dawn singsong. I wondered if there were any birds who, like people, were natural late risers.

The birdsong drifted in to me through an open window of one of the well-appointed guest rooms in the 59-year-old Wharekauhau homestead. No, well-appointed wasn't the way to describe it — this was downright luxury compared to some of the places I found myself bunking down in.

The original homestead dated to the late 1860s, a few years after the land was first taken up. It was built on the same site as the current homestead, from pitsawn rimu and totara and locally made bricks. The grand,

The Wharekauhau homestead.

two-storeyed dwelling had stood for sixty-seven years before it was dismantled and some of its timbers used in the new homestead.

Today Wharekauhau was run as both station and upmarket lodge. The Shaws catered mainly to the lucrative North American market; it was not unusual for their guests to arrive from Wellington by helicopter. Johnny and his brother James were available to take the visitors around the station to observe the birds and seals, while Bill took them on wine tours and fishing trips — or wherever else they wanted to go.

It was left to Annette Shaw to supervise the running of the homestead, and she did this with a brisk, no-nonsense efficiency. Bill and Annette's daughter Victoria assisted in the kitchen. Joe Houghton — still Mr Joe to Johnny, James and Victoria — might be called upon to do just about anything. That was because he could do just about anything.

Annette Shaw.

Still the birds greeted the new day. I slipped out of bed and opened the partly drawn curtains. It looked like it would be a top morning. Over a slow brandy and cigar, Bill and I had the night before decided to make an early start, to head off to Wharepapa station just after sunrise. Bill was generously putting himself at my disposal: the way things were organised round here, he reckoned, he could take time out when he wanted to.

I was glad to take Bill up on his offer. He was not only a great bloke, but very good company.

35

A TRIO OF STATIONS

Bill Shaw and I might have been kings of the Wairarapa castle as we stood shoulder to shoulder on a high point and cast our eyes over Wharepapa station. On this invigorating spring morning Bruce Eglinton's compact property looked mighty good to us.

Every square metre of the station — good, clean country running away to the coast — appeared to be in use. The sheep looked fine and healthy; I had seen none better. Bill told me they were Border Leicester/Romney crosses. He also told me that Bruce Eglinton was considered among the ten best farmers in the country.

Wharepapa was first taken up in the late 1840s by Charles Cameron, who stocked the rough block with Merinos. In 1850 he sold the largely unimproved station to Charles Matthews, and so began a long association between the Matthews family and the southern Wairarapa. Within five years Wharepapa's history would merge with Waiorongomai's, when it became an out-station of the larger property.

'You should make a point of seeing old Jack while you're here,' said Bill, referring to 84-year-old Jack Matthews of Waiorongomai, a direct descendant of Charles Matthews. 'He'll be able to tell you more about Wharepapa.'

'I plan to — tomorrow,' I replied.

With a nod, Bill started towards his vehicle and the lovely-looking stock, bred from two types of sheep, ran before us in the sun.

The fertile Wharepapa station.

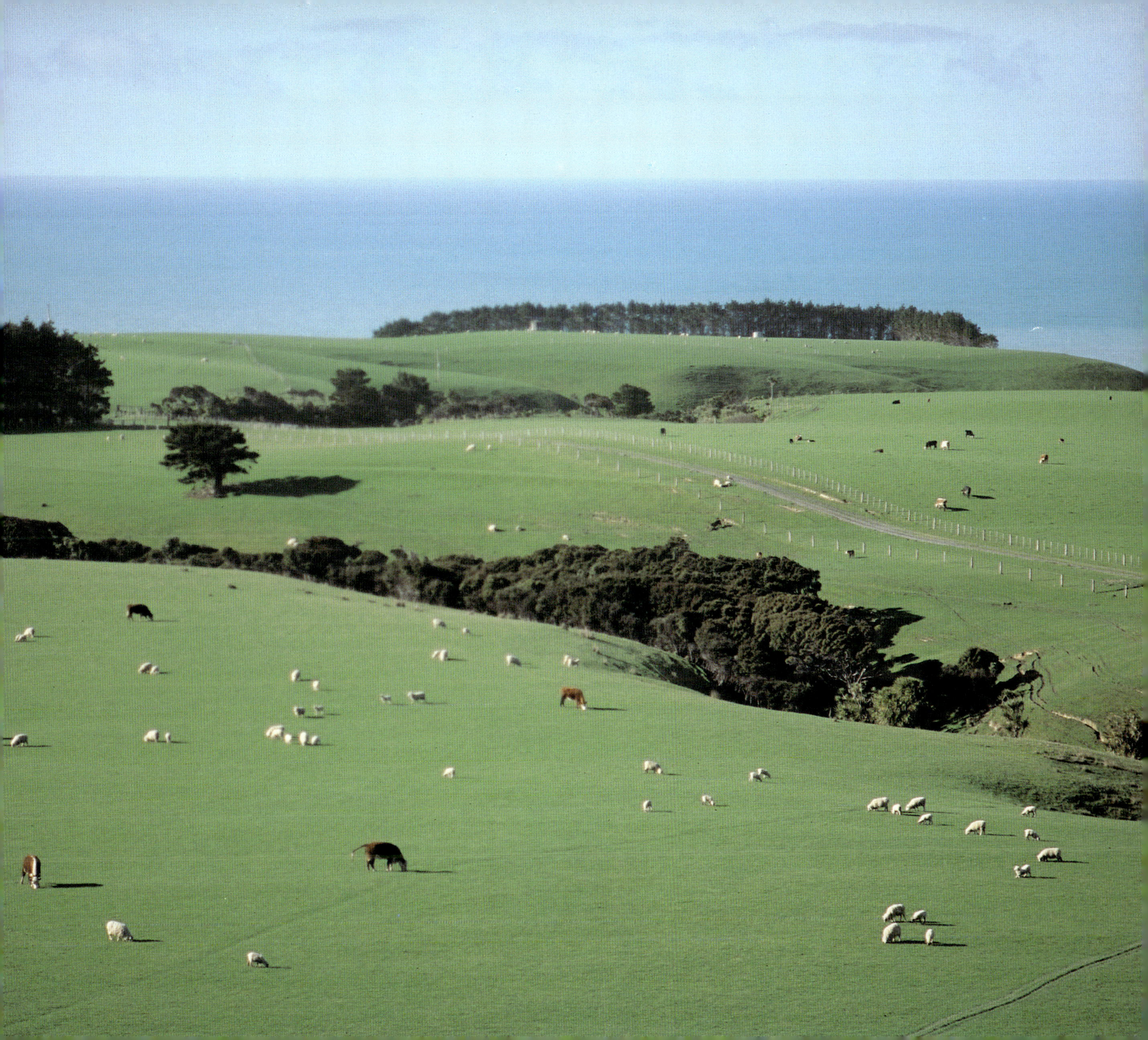

Soon we were heading along a rough track, constrained by steep cliffs on one side and the black sands of Ocean Beach on the other, towards Orongorongo station.

My attention was drawn by what appeared to be a concrete hulk out on the beach. It was the shell of a 45-foot yacht that had ten years earlier been driven ashore through the pounding surf. Joe Houghton had been amongst those to rescue the family on board.

To mariners Palliser Bay had long been a place to be wary of. It was under the influence of the Antarctic Ocean and was often subject to atrocious weather conditions. At least thirty-four vessels had been lost in the waters around Cape Palliser. The worst wreck of all was the *Saint Vincent*, a fully rigged ship of 834 tonnes, which was smashed onto the Mukamuka Rocks in the 1880s. Twenty lives were lost; only nine bodies were found.

As we approached Orongorongo I recalled the first time I had visited the station, almost ten years earlier.

It was a bleak day. The sky was a dull gun-metal grey and the wind, laden with salt and grit, whipped in from the sea with enough power to lift a ewe off her feet. A few woebegone sheep of Romney ancestry huddled wherever they could find cover.

The homestead was concealed by a shelter belt of exotic trees, as misplaced as a pohutukawa in London. The winding driveway took me to the big, open area of the homestead itself. A mountainface, stark and wind-blasted, glowered over the homestead ominously. It was easy to forget you were less than an hour's drive from New Zealand's cosmopolitan capital city.

Earle Riddiford greeted me affably enough. In his seventies, he was retired now and not, unfortunately, in good health. He split his time between Orongorongo and the family home in Wellington.

Apart from a raised circular conservatory, the homestead was on one level — all 1000 square metres of it! I wasn't surprised to be shown servants' quarters; you'd need staff to look after a place this size.

'Come with me,' Earle Riddiford said rather mysteriously, and ushered me into a huge room. 'This was the ballroom.' His expression was a little sad, as though he knew that the room had seen its last waltz.

But it wasn't the size of the ballroom — which at 130 square metres was impressive enough — that astounded me. Rather it was the dozens of shoulder-mounted stags' heads on display. They were arranged in neat rows on every wall; a conservative estimate would put the number at fifty.

A closer look revealed that the heads were all similar in shape, with the timber fairly heavy and not reaching any great length or, for that matter, a significant number of points. They had the look of Rimutaka red stag about them, quite different from a Highland stag of Otago, for example.

While the heads were not outstanding individually, they certainly were collectively. Like the grand old homestead itself, they represented a different age, a time when deerstalking was as socially acceptable as a day at the races or a lazy afternoon watching cricket.

I took a last, lingering look around the ballroom. What splendid times they must have had here, back when Orongorongo was in its heyday.

As we continued on the coastal track, Bill told me that by the late 1980s the great days on Orongorongo were

The Orongorongo homestead in 1985.

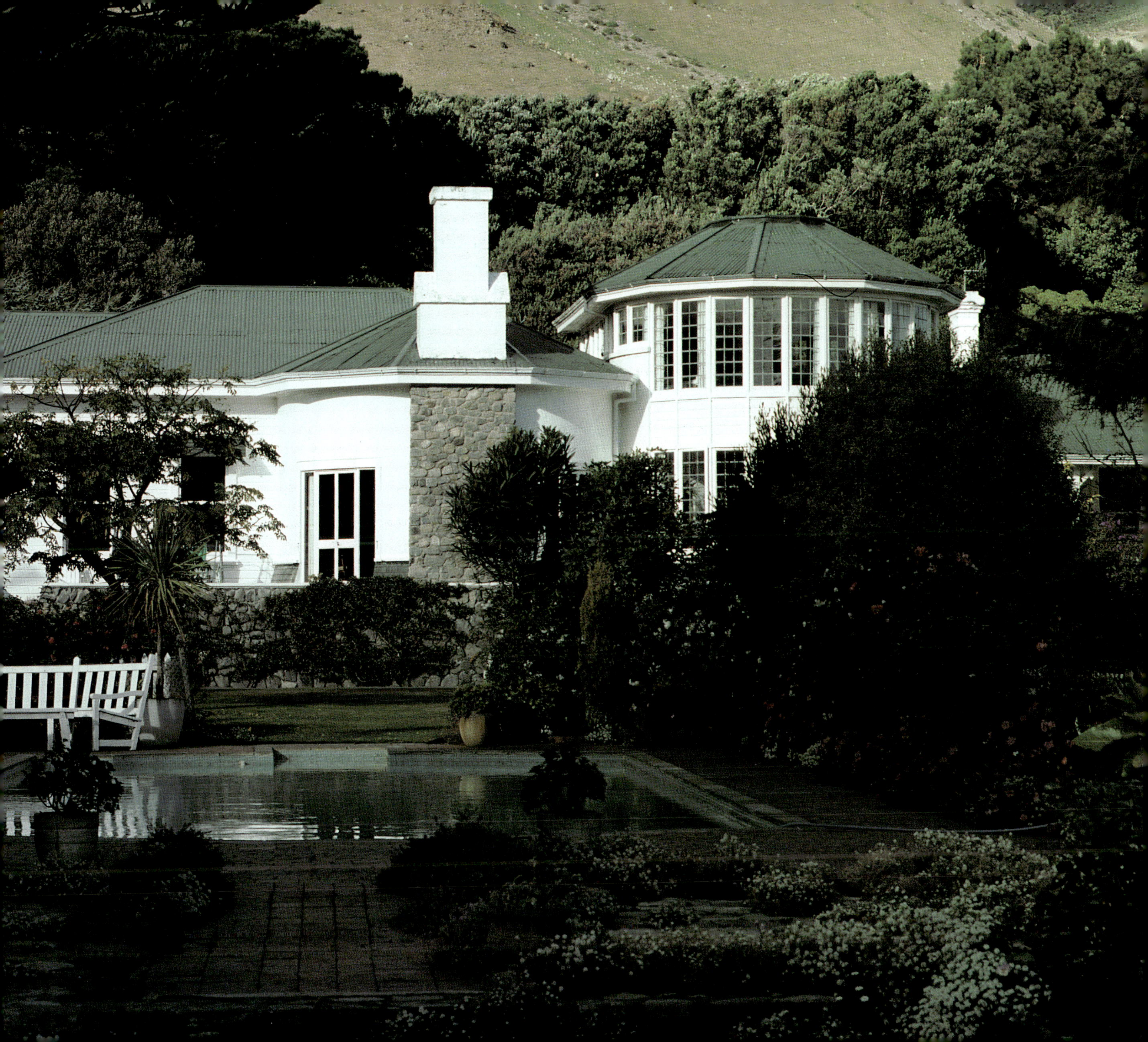

well and truly over. The station was sold to a group of Auckland businessmen who saw potential in it as a tourist destination. The homestead underwent major renovations, but later a fire destroyed it completely. If the project was not a lame duck before the fire, it most certainly was afterwards.

The station was divided into three blocks. These days they were not running many stock units and much of the country was reverting to scrub.

Presently Bill and I arrived at Barneys whare on Orongorongo station. It was a nice spot by the sea, flanked as it was by karaka trees. In front of the whare there was a grave; a simple wooden cross, deeply weathered, carried this inscription:

BILL WATSON
1788–1852

Bill Shaw couldn't tell me who Watson was. He might have been a seafarer; although there were no recorded wrecks in Palliser Bay before 1861, that didn't mean they didn't happen. Some locals believed that the grave was the final resting place of seven or eight seamen whose ship went down in the 1880s or 1890s.

By 1852 Orongorongo had been in the hands of one Daniel Riddiford for seven years. Riddiford? Yes, this was an illustrious name in New Zealand's early history.

On 10 September 1839, Daniel Riddiford and his pregnant wife boarded the *Adelaide* in London, bound for the antipodes. At sea Harriet Riddiford gave birth to a daughter. As a matter of interest, the Riddifords' second child, Edward, was to become the first child baptised by Bishop Selwyn in New Zealand.

Daniel Riddiford worked for the New Zealand Company as an agent. In due course he searched for a suitable block to lease from the Maoris, finding it at Pencarrow Head. And so in 1845 Orongorongo station was founded.

It was a lonely place to bring a young Englishwoman and three children under six. Moreover, during the next ten years Harriet Riddiford would give birth seven more times. Each time as her time to give birth became imminent, she would be taken to Wellington by Maori canoe. This must have been a terrifying journey, for the sea was most likely rough on some, if not all, occasions.

In its early days Orongorongo was linked with Te Awaiti station, which Daniel Riddiford took up in about 1849. Te Awaiti was quite a distance away around Cape Palliser. Orongorongo was used mostly as a holding block for wethers, and there were sometimes upwards of 10,000 sheep on the place. Droving time between the stations was about twelve days along the coastal route, which included the feared Mukamuka Rocks.

Seven years after the 1855 earthquake that took the sting out of the Rocks, Edward Riddiford properly entered the saga of Orongorongo for the first time. Educated at Christ's College, Christchurch, and Scot's College, Melbourne, he had been prospecting for gold in Otago when he received the following letter from his mother:

'My dearest Edward

'We regret to find that you are as yet making no movement towards your return home. In my last I begged you to return immediately, and I hope, my dearest boy, that you will no longer hesitate. You are wasting valuable time and living in a manner and at an

Barneys whare.

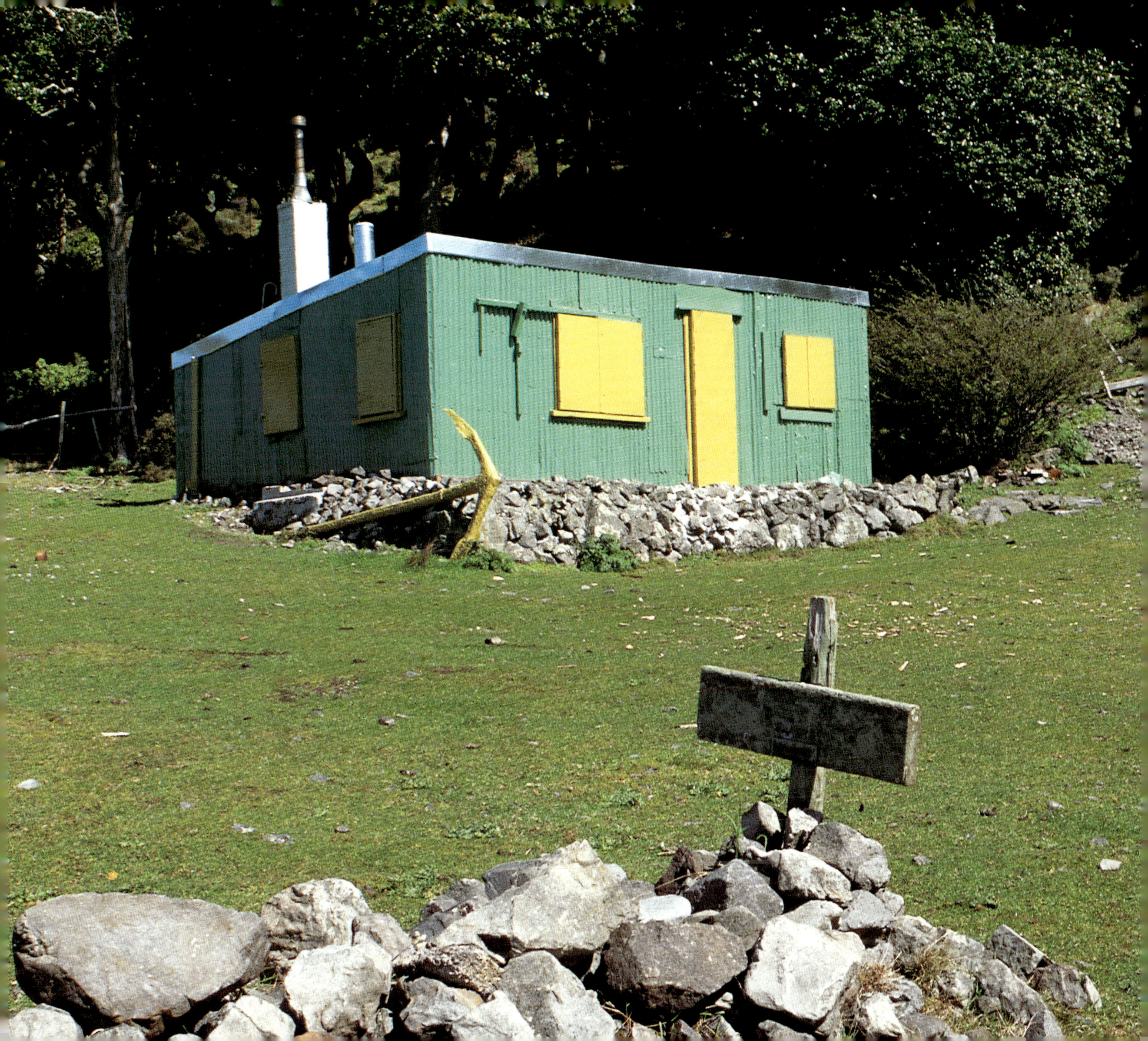

expense quite unnecessary. The unhealthy time is coming on, when in all probability there will be much sickness and great privation.

'But this alone is not the reason I desire your immediate return, and if you regard the wishes of your mother you will no longer delay. I am not satisfied with Te Awaiti. There is much to be done to put it in proper training, and I consider, dear Edward, you are the person who ought to do it. What I am now going to propose to you I have not mentioned to your papa, although I feel sure he will readily agree to it. It is, that you should undertake the management of Te Awaiti.

'From everyone we hear how expensively everything is managed. You know how little your papa looks into things when he goes there, and I will begin to feel seriously uneasy if something is not done soon. The back country must be worked and made available for more sheep. I look to you for assistance in carrying out better arrangements there, and it will be an admirable beginning for you — a start few young men of your age can get.

'Do come home at once and waste no more time in vain speculations — a perfect lottery. It is not a right spirit to begin life with and everyone here condemns you.'

Reading this letter I was reminded yet again how undervalued women were in the recorded history of this country, reminded that behind most successful men there was a strong woman. It was little wonder that, receiving so forceful a letter, twenty-year-old Edward Riddiford returned home to manage Te Awaiti.

The success that Edward Riddiford made of Te Awaiti was an often-told story. Riddiford was, at 1.83 metres, tall for the standards of the day, with broad shoulders and a dark complexion. His looks were striking and his personality powerful. He could speak Maori fluently, and it was the Maoris who gave him the name King. King Riddiford of Te Awaiti and, when his father died, Orongorongo too.

I heard a charming story about King Riddiford and a Maori called Harry Parata. One day the two men met near the Orongorongo headquarters, Riddiford in his gig — drawn by a classy thoroughbred — and Parata on his stockhorse.

They talked about general things for a while, then Harry Parata said, 'I had a dream the other night, King, and you know Maori dreams always come true.'

'So I've heard.'

'I dreamed you gave me this horse, King.' Harry Parata put a hand on the thoroughbred's rump.

'Did you now? In that case you'd better have him.'

Several days later they met again.

'I had another Maori dream the other night, King,' said Harry. 'I dreamed you gave me the harness and gig that goes with this horse.'

'Then you'd better come and get them, hadn't you?'

A couple of months went by before Riddiford and Parata bumped into each other again.

This time Riddiford got in before Parata had time to draw breath. 'I had a Maori dream the other night, Harry, and as you know they always come true. You know what, Harry? I dreamed you gave me that one hundred acres of yours.'

Harry Parata smiled an easy smile. 'I think you'd better have it, King.'

Who knows, there might even have been some truth in the tale.

At its peak Waiorongomai station, to the north-east of Orongorongo, dominated the western side of Lake

Wairarapa. It ran unbroken as far as the foothills of the Rimutaka Range, and from Wharepapa in the south nearly to Featherston in the north. After Charles Matthews had combined Waiorongomai and Wharepapa stations, the extent of the property was 9300 hectares.

The single most important thing about Waiorongomai was its place as the first registered Romney stud in New Zealand. The stud was established by Alfred Matthews, the only son of Charles and Elizabeth to reach adulthood, in the 1870s, and when in 1904 the New Zealand Romney Sheep Breeders' Association was formed, Alfred was its first president.

In his eighty-fourth year, Alfred Matthews's grandson Jack now sat opposite me in the homestead on Waiorongomai. For a second time he admitted that his

Lake Wairarapa.

memory wasn't all that it once was; I wondered whose was at his age.

The station, he recalled, was divided three ways on the death of Alfred in 1925. Raymond, Jack's father, got the Homestead block and retained the Romney stud: he was as expert with sheep as his father. Harold Matthews took the Papataki block, while Wharepapa went to Norman.

Jack Matthews had lived all of his life on Waiorongomai and had a clear recollection of the time before the subdivision. 'There were always about twenty on the payroll in those days — about ten married men as a rule, some single men and a few cadets that came here to learn all about station life.'

'Did you have any problems with wild pigs?' I asked him.

Jack chuckled ruefully. 'We couldn't lamb ewes anywhere close to the bush — the pigs'd just scoff 'em up. We lost twenty one night! Always had troubles with pigs on the place.'

Jack's recollection was confirmed by the unpublished memoirs of Alfred Matthews:

'In my younger days I must have killed thousands [of pigs] but because of the bush-covered Rimutaka Ranges, it was almost impossible to stamp them out.

'We relied a lot on our pig dogs in those days and some of them were extremely intelligent, but it was risky work and I've lost up to four a year.'

Jack continued, 'Deer were bad at times too, but nothing like pigs. They'd cause a bit of trouble in the crops — swedes, mostly. They were always hard to get because they did that at night.' He paused and, as he looked at me keenly, the years seemed to slip away. 'Would you like to see my wapiti trophy?'

I nodded. 'Like nothing better.'

Jack Matthews with his wapiti trophy.

Jack rose with some difficulty from his chair and, with the aid of a walking stick, hobbled out of the room. 'Don't get around so good anymore.'

In the hallway he nodded at a shoulder-mounted bull wapiti head. I just shook my head and wished that I too had seen the great days of wapiti hunting in Fiordland.

Jack's son Raymond carries on the Matthews story in the Southern Wairarapa.

In 1950 Jack Matthews and another Wairarapa identity, Jack Luttrell, had come across the mighty bull in Cow Valley or, as it's sometimes known, Narrows Burn. Jack had used an open-sighted .303 rifle to down the bull.

'Must rank pretty highly,' I said.

Jack shrugged as if that were of no account. He started back to the living room, a shadow of the man who forty-four years earlier had carried out of Cow Valley a nineteen-pointer measuring 59 inches by 47½ inches and achieving a Douglas Score of 431¼ points. This was the eleventh-highest scoring wapiti bull to ever come out of Fiordland.

As the old deerstalker sat down in his chair, sighing heavily, his son Raymond came into the room.

Like his father, Raymond Matthews was born on the station. The only boy of five children, he had run the station for quite some time.

Soon I was saying goodbye to Jack Matthews, and Raymond was taking me to look at some ewes near the homestead where he and his wife lived. Ray explained that at peak times they might have nearly 9000 sheep on the place; the stud boasted 1300 breeding ewes. The staff comprised five married men and two boys, and they went fifty-fifty with a sharemilker who milked 330 cows and employed a married man.

'Dad was a hard man to work for,' Raymond said, right out of the blue. 'He took no bullshit . . . Wasn't that easy.' He paused. 'But he was fair.'

I guess you couldn't ask for more than that.

SHOWPIECE OF THE SOUTHERN WAIRARAPA

To round off my trip to the southern Wairarapa, I decided to visit Alastair and Jacqui Sutherland's Whangaimoana station. On a fine Saturday I left the Shaws' Wharekauhau, crossed the Ruamahanga River below the main lake and soon found myself north of Pirinoa on the Lake Ferry–Martinborough road. The country south of Martinborough was packed with stations and Whangaimoana, although now greatly reduced in size, was one of the oldest established of them.

The story of Whangaimoana began as early as 1843, when Thomas Purvis Russell — known as Purvis — visited the Wairarapa in search of land to lease. After discussions with local Maoris he laid the groundwork for a lease of some of the dry, hilly country of the southern Wairarapa.

Purvis Russell, in his thirties and from a wealthy and influential Scottish family, had arrived in New Zealand in 1842 to take up the one-acre (0.4-hectare) Wellington section he had been granted. Within a couple of years he had been joined by his brothers Robert, Henry and John.

By 1846 the Russell brothers had finalised with chiefs Hemi Te Miha, Raniera Te Iho and Hamiona the lease of the land that would eventually become Whangaimoana. The land was not developed immediately. Robert and John Russell concentrated their efforts on 7300 hectares of leased Maori land further around the coast towards

The Whangaimoana homestead.

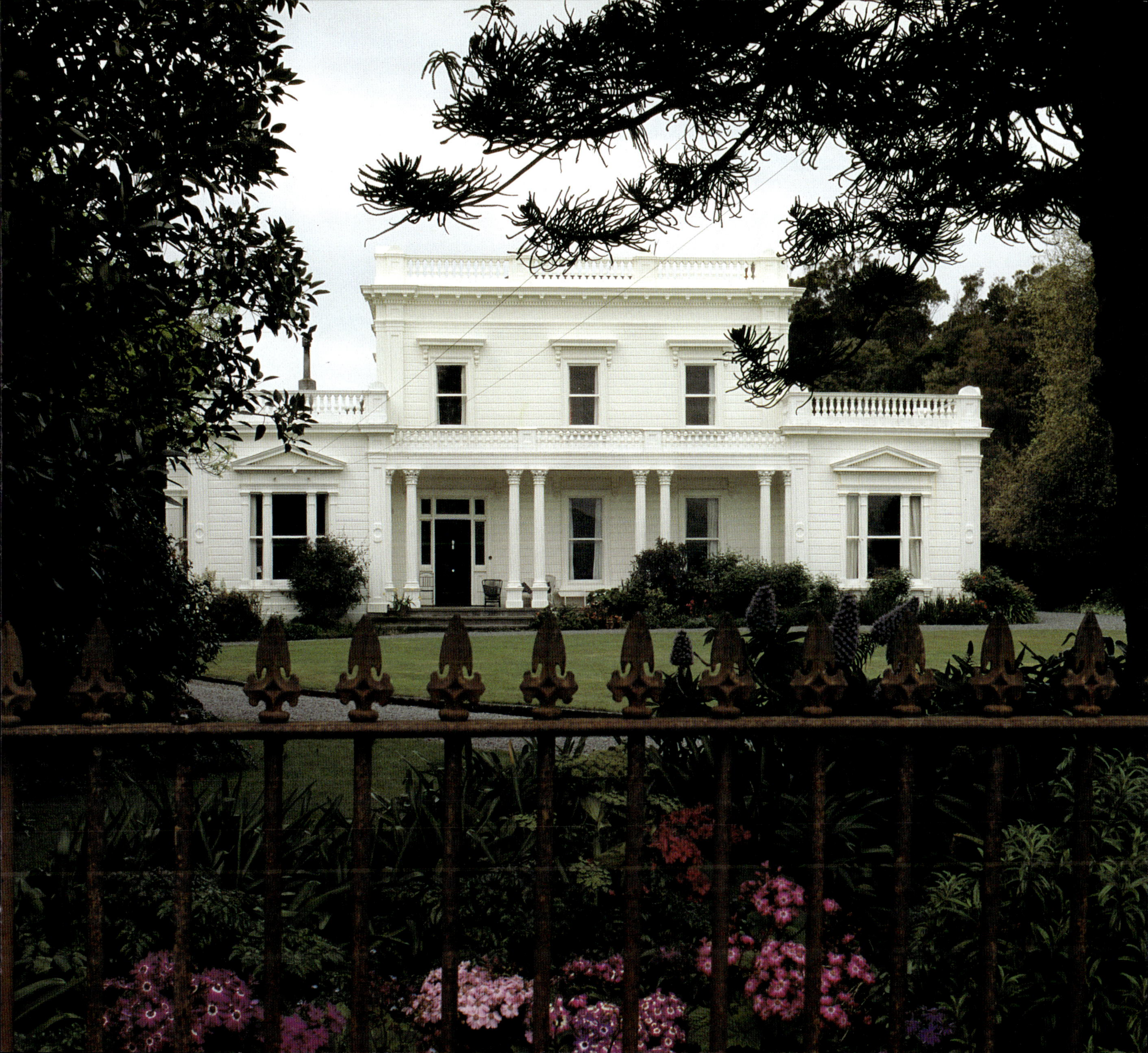

White Rock station. They called the station Kawa Kawa. Meanwhile the adventurous Purvis was with chief Hapuku in search of grazing land in Hawke's Bay.

In 1851 Purvis and Henry moved more-or-less permanently to Hawke's Bay, where Henry settled on 3200 hectares of fern-clad hills east of today's Waipukurau and Purvis went into partnership with land baron Daniel Riddiford on 5300 hectares of land southeast of Waipukurau.

In the mid-1860s John and Robert Russell transferred the lease of Kawa Kawa to Charles Pharazyn, who ran it with his Whatarangi station, and they took on Whangaimoana in earnest. With powerful friends acting on their behalf, the four brothers were in 1866 granted 720 hectares Crown land at Whangaimoana to add to the land they had leased from the Maoris.

Although the land was in the names of all four brothers, Purvis and Henry were absentee owners and in 1870 they turned their shares in the station over to John; Robert did the same with his share soon after. J. P. Russell increased his holdings by acquiring more Maori leasehold land. He ended up with more than 2800 hectares, which he ran with three permanent men.

With money not an issue, J. P. Russell, who never married, decided to build a home worthy of the property. He chose to build it in the Italianate style rather than the fashionable Gothic Revival. The totara timber used in its construction was milled locally and carried by bullock teams to the site; a tongue-and-groove machine was used to make the flooring. Most of the joinery and all of the furniture was made in England, shipped to Wellington and transferred to coastal steamer. An avenue of cedar and eucalyptus was planted and a 2.5-hectare garden, which kept as many as five gardeners busy, was created.

The gracious entrance hall and rimu staircase.

The building was finished in the mid-1870s and soon became known as The Castle. Why not? J. P. Russell, related to the Duke of Bedford, might have been the closest thing to royalty they had in the southern Wairarapa.

Jacqui Sutherland tends the garden.

Following the death of J. P. Russell in 1906 the station, then 4000 hectares, was divided into twenty-six blocks. The 500-hectare Homestead block passed through a number of owners until in 1979 Alastair and Jacqui Sutherland took it on.

As I headed south to Lake Ferry I paused at Burnside church, which dated to 1874. The church was built on land donated by Donald Sinclair of Burnside station. Funds for construction were raised from local runholders and J. P. Russell's £20 donation was much greater than anyone else's. While the church was once Presbyterian — unsurprising in a Scottish community — all denominations could worship there today.

On to Whangaimoana.

While I had seen enough photographs of Russell's homestead to know what to expect, to actually see it there before me amidst the lovely grounds and majestic trees was still a delightful surprise. The gardens, I knew, were open to the public from late August to December.

Alastair Sutherland typifies the New Zealand sheepman.

Jacqui Sutherland, showing me around the homestead, explained that when she and Alastair arrived at Whangaimoana the building had been badly in need of restoration. Now, however, the house, with its gleaming totara floors, solid rimu doors, fancy plaster cornices and ceiling roses, had been returned to something like its former glory. Whangaimoana was once again the showpiece of the southern Wairarapa.

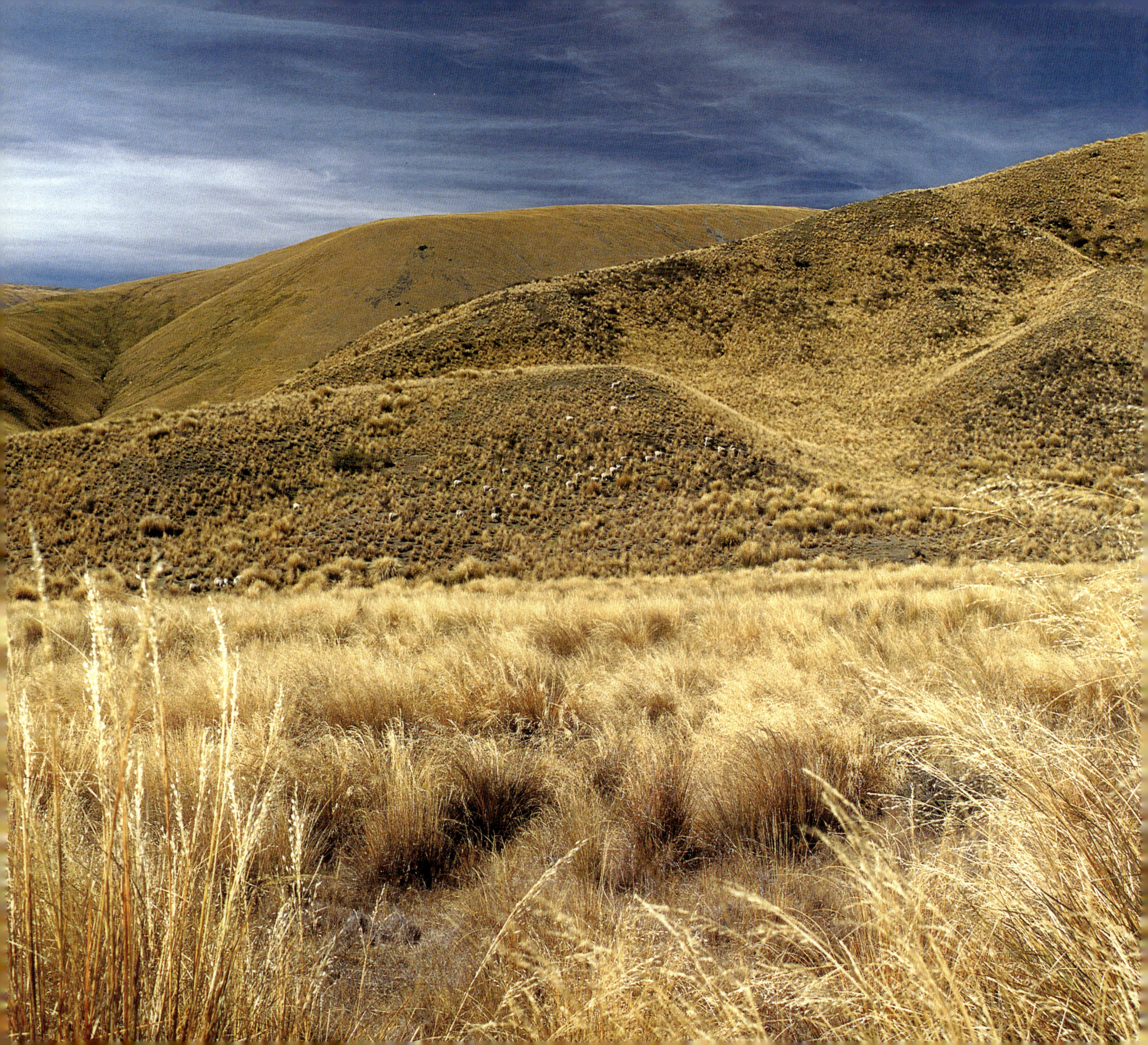

GOING HOME

It would be fair to say I was all at sea — out in Cook Strait on the Interislander. On a glorious spring day, the sea dead calm, I was heading back to the South Island.

I leaned on the rail and gazed at the spectacular southern Wairarapa coastline, at Wharekauhau and Orongorongo stations. My thoughts returned to a time in the distant past when the coast had provided the route for four Englishmen — Clifford, Vavasour, Petre and Weld — to bring Merinos into the Wairarapa.

By early 1845 the partnership in the Wharekaka venture had hired Tom Caverhill, a canny Highland shepherd, as manager. In the same year they imported more sheep, including stud rams, from across the Tasman; these too were manhandled around the Mukamuka Rocks.

But not all was rosy on Wharekaka: the mosquito-ridden swamps, later destroyed in the 1855 earthquake, were not the place to run Merinos; the breed was much too prone to footrot. The sheep were given a hard time by wild dogs and rampant pigs, and they had to be guarded by armed men during the day and yarded at night. To make matters worse, the Maoris were upping the ante on the leases.

Of all the partners, Frederick Weld disliked Wharekaka the most. It was the mosquitos that really got to him: 'No pen can describe, or mind conceive, the horror of them. They put out the wick in a tin of fat, our only lamp. They got into our mouths while eating; they filled the air with their hateful humming.'

Even so, Weld stuck it out at Wharekaka with Clifford when William Vavasour returned to England and Henry Petre moved to Wellington. In the end, though, Weld and Clifford began to wonder if Marlborough might provide better country for sheep. Weld, always the more active partner, set out in a whaleboat to investigate the Marlborough coastline. In 1847 the partners acquired a lease of 29,000 hectares of land at Ward.

Clifford and Weld named their station Flaxbourne, after the river that ran through the property. They brought in 3000 Merinos from Australia and selected 1400 sheep from their Wharekaka flock.

Late in 1848 the partners heard terrible news from Wharekaka: Tom Caverhill had been drowned in the Ruamahanga River. Clifford and Weld decided to close their Wairarapa operation and bring the rest of the sheep down to Flaxbourne. By 1851 Wharekaka was no more, its southern parts run in with Dry River and its northern area absorbed by Huangarua.

I turned away from the North Island and looked to the south, to the mainland. This was more like it. This was true Merino country.

The eastern side of the Lindis Pass is true Merino country.

REFERENCES

Acland, L.G.D., *Early Canterbury Runs*,
 Whitcombe & Tombs, Christchurch, 1930.

'Aerial Warfare', *Otago Daily Times*, 19 October 1991.

Bland, M., 'Station is run with true grit', *New Zealand Farmer*, 28 September 1994.

Bowen, G., 'New Zealand and its sheep', New Zealand Wool Board, Wellington.

Burden, G.L., *Tall Hills and Tight Lines*, self-published, 1985.

'Central Otago Merino Tour', Central Otago Merino Breeders, 1994.

Chandler, P. *Glenary*, Craig Printing, Invercargill, in conjuction with Glenary, Waikaia, 1984.

Christ's College School List 1850–1935,
 Whitcombe & Tombs, Christchurch, 1935.

Crawford, S.C., *Sheep and Sheepmen of Canterbury*,
 Simpson & Williams, Christchurch, 1949.

Creswell, D., *Early New Zealand Families*,
 Whitcombe & Tombs, Christchurch, 1956.

Cumberland, K.B., *Landmarks*,
 Readers Digest, Sydney, 1981.

Donne, T.E., *Red Deer Stalking in New Zealand*,
 Constable, London, 1924.

Duff, G.P., *Sheep May Safely Graze*, self-published, Tarras, 1978.

Duncan, A.H., *The Wakatipians*, Lakes District Centennial Museum, Arrowtown, 1964.

Fyfe, F., *The Great Drive*, GP Books, 1990.

Griffiths, G.J., *Queenstown's King Wakatip*,
 John McIndoe, Dunedin, 1971.

Harper, B., *Eight Daughters, Three Sons*,
 A.H & A.W Reed, Wellington, 1983.

History of the Australian Merino, The,
 Heinemann, Richmond, 1984.

Logan, R., *Waimakariri*, Logan Publishing, Christchurch, 1987.

McCaskill, L.W., *Molesworth*,
 A.H. & A.W. Reed, Wellington, 1969.

McClenaghan, J., *Fiordland*,
 A.H. & A.W. Reed, Wellington, 1966.

MacGregor, M., *Early Stations of Hawke's Bay*,
 A.H. & A.W. Reed, Wellington, 1970.

MacGregor Redwood, M., *A Dog's Life*,
 A.H & A.W. Reed, Wellington, 1980.

'Mount White Station', *New Zealand Herefords*, 1991.

Mitchell, J.H., *Takitimu*.
 A.H. & A.W. Reed, Wellington, 1944.

Newton, P., *Big Country of the North Island*,
 A.H. & A.W. Reed, Wellington, 1969.

Newton, P., *Big Country of the South Island*,
   A.H. & A.W. Reed, Wellington 1973.
Newton, P., *In the Wake of the Axe*,
   A.H. & A.W. Reed, Wellington, 1972.
Newton, P., *Sixty Thousand on the Hoof*,
   A.H. & A.W. Reed, Wellington, 1972.
New Zealand Birds. Readers Digest,
   Sydney, 1985.
New Zealand Merino Review 1994,
   New Zealand Stud Merino Breeders Society.
New Zealand Romney Flock Book, The, Council of New
   Zealand Romney Stud Breeders Association, 1992.
Newton, P., *Big Country of the North Island*,
   A.H. & A.W. Reed, Wellington, 1971.
Newton, P., *Big Country of the South Island*,
   A.H. & A.W. Reed, Wellington, 1973.
Newton, P., *In the Wake of the Axe*,
   A.H. & A.W. Reed, Wellington, 1972.
Newton, P., *Sixty Thousand on the Hoof*,
   A.H. & A.W. Reed, Wellington, 1972
Pinney, R., *Early Canterbury Runs*,
   A.H. & A.W. Reed, Wellington, 1971.
Rau, C., *100 years of Waiapu*,
   Gisborne District Council, Gisborne, 1993.

Salmon, J.T., *The Native Trees of New Zealand*,
   Reed Methuen, Auckland, 1980.
Scott, I. (ed.), *The Head of the Lake*, undated.
Sharpe, R., *Fiordland Muster*,
   Hodder & Stoughton, London, 1966.
Thornton, G.C., *The New Zealand Heritage of Farm
   Buildings*, Reed Methuen, Auckland, 1986.
Ward, L.E., *Early Wellington*,
   Whitcombe & Tombs, Christchurch, 1928.
Wheeler, C., *Historical Sheep Stations of the North Island*,
   A.H. & A.W. Reed, Wellington, 1973.
Wheeler, C., *Historical Sheep Stations of the South Island*,
   A.H. & A.W. Reed, Wellington, 1968.
Wild New Zealand, Readers Digest, Sydney, 1981.
Wises New Zealand Guide, Wises, Auckland, 1989.
World Book Encyclopedia. World Books, USA, 1990.
Yerex, D. *They Came to Wydrop*.
   Published on behalf of H. Beetham and T. Williams.